Talking Heads

The origin, development, and nature of language have been the focus of theoretical debate among philosophers for many centuries. Following the pioneering clinical observations 150 years ago of loss of language following a cerebral lesion, language started to be considered a biological system that could be investigated scientifically: as a consequence, an increasing number of scientists began to search for its anatomical and functional basis and its links with other such cognitive systems. The relatively recent introduction of neuroimaging tools, such as PET and fMRI, has brought rapid and groundbreaking developments to the field of Neurolinguistics.

In this book, Denes harnesses these advances to adopt a biolinguistic approach to the study of a subject that increasingly sees the collaboration of linguists, experimental psychologists, neuroscientists and clinicians. *Talking Heads* reviews the latest research on the nature, structure and origin of language to provide a concise analysis of the multifaceted aspects of language which focuses both on theoretical aspects and physical implementation.

Following an up-to-date description of acquired language disorders, and their contribution to the design of a functional architecture of language, the book illustrates the neurological process involved in the production and comprehension of spoken and written language, as well as investigating the neurological and functional systems responsible for sign language production and first and second language acquisition.

With a glossary of the anatomical and linguistic terms, this book provides an invaluable resource to undergraduate and graduate students of psychology, psycholinguistics and linguistics. It will also be of interest to neurologists, speech therapists and anyone interested in the mind–brain problem.

Gianfranco Denes teaches neurolinguistics and neuropsychology at the Universities of Padua and Venice, Italy. Former Associate professor of Neuropsychology and Head of the Neurology Unit, City Hospital in Venice, his research field spans many aspects of neuropsychology, focusing on aphasia and acquired language impairments.

Talking Heads

The neuroscience of language

Gianfranco Denes

Authorized translation from Italian language
edition published by Zanichelli.

Ψ **Psychology Press**
Taylor & Francis Group

HOVE AND NEW YORK

First published 2009 by Zanichelli, Italy
Title of the original Italian edition: Parlare con la Testa

First published in the UK 2011
by Psychology Press
27 Church Road, Hove, East Sussex BN3 2FA

Simultaneously published in the USA and Canada
by Psychology Press
711 Third Avenue, New York, NY 10017

Translated by Philippa Venturelli Smith

Psychology Press is an imprint of the Taylor & Francis Group, an Informa business

© Zanichelli 2009
English translation © 2011 Psychology Press

Typeset in Times by RefineCatch Ltd, Bungay, Suffolk
Printed and bound in Great Britain by TJ International Ltd, Padstow, Cornwall
Cover design by Hybert Design

This publication has been produced with paper manufactured to strict environmental standards and
with pulp derived from sustainable forests.

British Library Cataloguing in Publication Data
A catalogue record for this book is available from the British Library

Library of Congress Cataloging in Publication Data
Denes, G.
  [Parlare con la testa. English]
  Talking heads : the neuroscience of language / Gianfranco Denes.
    p. ; cm.
  Includes bibliographical references and index.
   ISBN 978-1-84872-039-8 (hbk.)
  1. Neurolinguistics.   2. Language disorders.   3. Psycholinguistics. I. Title.
  [DNLM: 1. Language.   2. Brain—physiology.   3. Language Disorders.   4. Linguistics. P 107]
  QP399.D8513 2011
  612.8'2336—dc22   2010033676

ISBN: 978-1-84872-039-8 (hbk)

For Maria

All reasonable efforts have been made to contact copyright holders but in some cases this was not possible. Any omissions brought to the attention of Routledge will be remedied in future editions.

Contents

Preface　　　　　　　　　　　　　　　　　　　　　　　　xi

1　Defining language　　　　　　　　　　　　　　　　　1

Notes　8
References　8

2　The origin and evolution of language and words　　　11

Notes　17
References　18

3　The anatomy of language　　　　　　　　　　　　　21

The anatomo-clinical method　22
A new anatomy of language? The contribution of neuroimaging　29
Forgetting Wernicke? New neurological models of language　36
Cognitive neuropsychology　39
Language and hemispheric specialization　44
The right hemisphere and language　46
Notes　47
References　48

4　Acquired language disorders: The aphasias　　　　　55

Recovery from aphasia　62
Living with aphasia　65
Notes　65
References　65

**5   The sounds of language: The production and
      comprehension of words**   69

Production of language sounds   72
Perception and comprehension of language sounds   80
Neurological bases and functional mechanisms of word repetition   86
Prosodic aspects of language   87
Foreign accent syndrome   87
Notes   88
References   88

**6   The words to say it: The functional and neurological
      architecture of the lexical system**   93

Defining the lexicon   93
Error analysis and evaluation of models of processing of the lexicon   96
Organization of the mental lexicon   99
From the conceptual system to articulation: Lexical access   101
Factors that influence lexical access   106
*The content of the lexical-syntactic system: Semantic categories and
    grammatical classes   108*
Grammatical classes   114
*Beyond literal meaning: Comprehension of connotations,
    metaphors and idioms   116*
*The origin of semantic-lexical deficits: Loss of information
    or access deficit   117*
Neurological correlates of the lexical-semantic system   118
Notes   121
References   121

7   The trains of language: Syntax and morphology   129

Agrammatism   132
Interpreting agrammatism: Neurolinguistic theories   136
Morphological deficits in aphasia   138
Neurological bases of morphology and syntax   140
Notes   142
References   143

**8   The neurological bases and functional architecture
      of written language**   149

Orthographic systems   150
Anatomical and functional models of written language processing   151

Cognitive models of reading 154
Computational models of reading 156
Components of the two-route model 157
Diagnosis and cognitive classification of the dyslexias 161
Cognitive models of writing 165
Structure of the orthographic form 166
Reading by touch: The neuropsychology of Braille 169
Learning to read and developmental dyslexia 170
Notes 173
References 174

9 The neurological bases and functional architecture of bilingualism 179

Aphasia in bilinguals 179
Neuroimaging studies 181
*Anatomical correlates of differences between individuals in
    the ability to learn a second language 184*
Linguistic differences and genes 185
Lexical access in bilinguals 185
Notes 189
References 189

10 Speaking with our hands: Sign language 193

Aphasia in the signing population 194
Experimental studies 195
The system of mirror neurons and sign language 197
References 198

11 Language acquisition and developmental language disorders 201

Neurological bases of language development 201
Lexical-semantic processing 204
Syntactic processing 205
Specific language disorders 205
Language acquisition and development in special populations 206
References 207

Appendix: Outlines of neuroanatomy 211

The nerve cell 211
Macroscopic and functional anatomy of the nervous system 212
Neural routes of visual and acoustic perception 219
Note 225
References 225

Glossary   227
Author index   231
Subject index   241

Preface

Over the past one and a half centuries the idea has gradually developed that language, like the other cognitive faculties that unite to form the mind, can be considered the final product of a 'mental organ' (Chomsky, 1986; Pinker, 1994) specific to the human species and with a dedicated physical structure located within the central nervous system. Consequently, as with other biological systems (for example respiration, blood circulation), language can be investigated scientifically in its anatomical and functional components (Lenneberg, 1967). This biolinguistic approach calls for interdisciplinary investigation involving linguists, experimental psychologists, neuropsychologists and neuroscientists. As a result there has been the progressive development of a new discipline, termed *Neurolinguistics*, which aims to research the following areas:

- the nature and representations of the components of the language system at the cerebral level;
- how these structures develop and operate at the level of language production and comprehension;
- which components within the cognitive and neurological architecture of language are specific to language and which, on the other hand, are shared with other biological systems;
- the relationship between language and other systems and cognitive faculties that do not require linguistic mediation, such as the ability to think in images (Rizzi, 2004).

The biolinguistic approach has also allowed what may be considered to be the central problem in the study of language to be addressed: whether language, on a par with other biological systems, represents the end point of a complex adaptation for communication that evolved through the natural selection of traits already present in other animal species (Pinker & Jackendoff, 2005), or whether it is a species-specific ability distinct from other forms of animal communication (Chomsky, 1989). As a corollary a third question may be asked: whether language evolved through a process of gradual modification of previously existing communication systems, or whether it emerged through adaptation of characteristics of other abilities, such as those necessary for spatial navigation or numerical reasoning, unrelated to communication systems (Hauser, Chomsky, & Fitch, 2002).

The first studies dedicated to the search for the neurological bases of language emerged from and developed within the field of medicine on the basis of observation of language deficits following cerebral lesion (aphasia), with the combined aims of benefiting both research and clinical practice. The correlation between the language deficit presented by a patient and the cerebral lesion identified at post-mortem (anatomo-clinical method) permitted the construction of a neurological model of language organization and, from a clinical point of view, allowed the identification of the site of the cerebral lesion *in vivo* through examination of the aphasic symptoms of a patient. Defining the nature of the language deficit was of clinical benefit as it then guided speech and language therapy intervention.

Only later, and with a certain reticence,[1] did psychologists and linguists realize just how important the study of aphasic deficit was in that it allowed their theoretical models to be verified experimentally. Every aphasic patient is, in fact, an experiment of nature. The cerebral lesion causing the aphasia often affects, partially or totally, one of the components of language, thus offering an invaluable source for the study of the structure of language and its anatomical and functional organization. Language, like other biological functions, is not made up of a monolithic structure, impervious to experimental investigation, but has several distinct components (*modules*, Fodor, 1983; Coltheart, 1999) which, combined, form 'a functional and anatomical architecture' that can be investigated experimentally.

It soon became clear that the study of aphasic symptoms represents a 'window' that permits the nature of the deficit to be revealed, as well as the functional and anatomical organization of language processes. From a theoretical viewpoint the notion was gradually asserted that the study of language, 'if carried out with a certain level of abstraction…can bring about the discovery of how these abstract units are realized in physical mechanisms more fundamental in nature and how these principles find their foundation' (Chomsky, 1980, p. 31). Until thirty years ago the main, or rather the only tool for addressing the neurological correlates of cognitive and language functions was anatomo-clinical observations, relating the observed cognitive deficit *in vivo* to the site of anatomical damage at post-mortem examination.

The introduction of neuroimaging methods of investigation such as computerized axial tomography (CAT scan) and magnetic resonance (MR) extended anatomo-clinical method to living subjects, allowing determination of the site and extension of the cerebral lesion and its alteration over time.

The application of methods of investigation that are functional in nature, such as the recording of event-related evoked responses, positron emission tomography (PET) and functional magnetic resonance imaging (fMRI), allows investigation of variations of electrical activity (event-related potentials), metabolic activity (PET) and blood flow (fMRI) in subjects engaged in language tasks. It has thus been possible to identify, sometimes with surprising accuracy, the specific neural circuits dedicated to the elaboration of the lexical, semantic, morphosyntactic and phonological aspects of language, which unite to constitute a sentence.

To conclude, the introduction of methods of cognitive psychology (cognitive neuropsychology) into the field of neurolinguistics and its integration with anatomical data obtained through new investigative procedures, has allowed the construction and validation of hypotheses regarding the nature of aphasic symptoms and, equally important, the functional and anatomical organization of language processes.

This volume, which originates from my experience as a clinical neuropsychologist and a teacher within the Faculty of Medicine and on a Language Sciences degree course at the Universities of Padua and Venice, addresses the following subjects:

- The first two chapters are dedicated to a definition of language, its evolution and characteristics and a comparison to other communication systems.
- In Chapter 3 the anatomy of language is described from the starting point of the earliest observations of deficits following cerebral lesion and the construction of neurological models of language.
- Chapter 4 illustrates the clinical picture of aphasia, with particular focus on the qualitative analysis of language deficits and their contribution to clarifying the nature of language components.
- Chapter 5 illustrates processes underlying the perception and production of language sounds.
- Chapter 6 also has a neuropsychological approach and is dedicated to the mental and neurological structure of the lexicon.
- The study of words, how they are formed and combined in sentences made up of groups of words (morphology and syntax), is addressed in Chapter 7 using data collected from studies of patients with morphological or syntactic deficits (agrammatism).
- Language is not limited to use of the mother tongue and oral–auditory communication: it is, in fact, possible to communicate through writing, in different languages and using sign language. Chapters 8, 9 and 10 therefore address the neuropsychology of written language, bilingualism, sign language and Braille.
- The final chapter explains the acquisition process of the mother tongue and investigates specific learning difficulties.
- To complete the volume there is an Appendix giving a summary of the anatomical and functional structure of the central nervous system, and a glossary of neuroanatomical and linguistic terms used in the book.

Many friends and colleagues have revised and commented on the various chapters with patience and competence: to Anna Basso, Paola Benincà, Guglielmo Cinque, Anna Cardinaletti, Chiata Lavorato, Claudio Luzzatti, Michele Miozzo, Emanuela Magno Caldognetto, Francesca Meneghello, Daniela Perani, Maria Rosser, Carlo Semenza, Laura Vanelli and Virginia Volterrra my warmest thanks. Eleanora Rossi, PhD in Neurolinguistics, deserves the merit for the chapter on morphology and syntax. Marta Peretto has patiently assisted me in drawing up the references.

Note

1 '...it is the sad truth that remarkably little has been learned about the psychology of language problems in normal individuals over a hundred years of aphasia study; on the other hand, the contribution of psycholinguistics to the understanding of the neurological realization of language has been non-existent' (Fodor, Bever, & Garrett, 1974).

References

Chomsky, N. (1980). *Rules and representations*. New York: Columbia University Press.

Chomsky, N. (1986). *Knowledge of language: Its nature, origin, and use*. New York: Praeger.

Coltheart, M. (1999). Modularity and cognition. *Trends in Cognitive Sciences, 3* (3), 115–120.

Fodor, J. A. (1983). *The modularity of mind*. Cambridge, MA: MIT Press.

Fodor, J. A., Bever, T., & Garrett, M. (1974). *The psychology of language*. New York: McGraw-Hill.

Hauser, M. D., Chomsky, N., & Fitch, W. T. (2002). The faculty of language: What is it, who has it, and how did it evolve. *Science, 298* (5598), 1569–1579.

Lennenberg, E. H. (1967). *Biological foundations of language*, New York: John Wiley & Sons.

Pinker S. (1994). *The language instinct: How the mind creates language*. New York: HarperCollins.

Pinker, S., & Jackendoff, R. (2005). The faculty of language: What's special about it? *Cognition, 95* (2), 201–236.

Rizzi, L. (2004). On the study of language faculty: Results, developments, and perspective. *The Linguistic Review, 21*, 323–344.

1 Defining language

> ... his ability to talk, his words – the gift of expression, the bewildering, the illuminating, the most exalted and the most contemptible, the pulsating stream of light, or the deceitful flow from the heart of an impenetrable darkness.
>
> (Conrad, 1988, *Heart of Darkness*)

Often the terms 'speech' and 'language' are considered synonymous, however they actually define very different concepts.

While speech can be simply defined as communication through spoken words, for many linguists the term language delineates an abstract nucleus, independent of other forms of communication and with computational operations specific to the human species (Chomsky, 1986). These mechanisms organize the elements of certain subsystems (distinctive features, phonemes, syllables, morphemes, words, idioms) to form elements of a higher order (syntagms, phrases, sentences) that can then be expressed through different means: gestures, written signs and, finally, words, which are considered the product of that unique auditory–vocal instrument that, during evolution, developed to allow optimum communication through language.

From a different point of view, biologists and psychologists define language as a communication system unique to the human species, constructed essentially of sound and meaning and with the faculty of allowing us to associate the sound representations to their meaning. The production and reception of sounds with linguistic value and their association to meaning are sustained by anatomical and functional systems, some specific to human language, others shared with other biological systems, both species-specific and common to other animal species.

Unlike the sometimes highly sophisticated communication systems used by other animal species (an example is the bee dance), human language, or simply language, possesses two characteristics, decomposition or dissociation and combinatory abilities. Language is *dissociated* in that its constituent elements are characterized by the fact that they are actually separate units that can be isolated within the continuum of language production. In physical reality, the boundaries between the various representative units cannot be identified objectively (such as boundaries between words and between phonemes); for example /p/ and /b/ can be articulated in an infinite number of ways, with more or less voicing, with no perceivable interval between the two. It is the presence of the mental image of /p/ or /b/ that allows attribution to one or the other of the concrete production of the sound. Dissociation or decomposition also regards the fact that, at different levels, the representational units can be broken down into lower level units: for example, the phonemes /p/ and /b/ can be broken down into features and share all features (in fact they are both bilabial plosive consonants) except for voicing (present in /b/, absent in /p/). Lexical elements can also be broken down into morphological elements (and these perhaps into more basic morphological elements, but research on this issue is currently underway) and then subsequently into phonemes and so on.

In non-verbal communication, such as the bee dance, it is possible to specify the communicative signal through rhythm or duration. In the bee dance it is obviously impossible to deconstruct every meaningful movement (for example the distance from the food source) into smaller movements that are insignificant but can mark the difference in meaning between one movement and another. This type of communication system, then, works on a continuum. On the other hand, as previously mentioned, in language every element (word, phoneme) can be broken down into smaller elements (distinctive features, phonemes) intrinsically devoid of meaning, but which can, if substituted within a larger element, differentiate sound and meaning (for example the difference between *pay* and *bay* is obtained by changing one component of the initial phoneme, the voicing feature, present in /b/ and absent in /p/.

Through *combinatory ability*, meaningless elements carrying linguistic value (vowel or consonant phonemes, morphemes, etc.) combine to form words and these, in turn, combine to form phrases and sentences that, in theory, can become infinitely complex.

In a hugely influential article, Hauser, Chomsky, and Fitch (2002) proposed, within the faculty of language, a distinction between language faculty in the 'narrow' sense and language faculty in the 'broad' sense, which is made up of several components, the first dedicated to the perception and production of language sounds, the second involving a conceptual system and other possible systems (Figure 1.1).

For Hauser et al. neither the perception nor the production of language sounds have underlying mechanisms that are species-specific. As far as the perception of language is concerned, it has been recently shown that other animal species possess a 'categorical' type of perception (see Chapter 5) and can discriminate between different languages on the basis of rhythmical differences. Even animals far lower down the evolutionary scale than humans produce and perceive sounds that can, like human language, be analysed in formants, the resonant frequencies of the vocal tract shapes (Ramus, Nespor, & Mehler, 2000). Finally, some anatomical characteristics of the vocal tract that were considered specific to the human species, in that they are necessary for the production of the sounds of language (such as the lowering of the larynx, see Chapter 2) are present, though in a reduced manner, in other animal species, casting doubt therefore on the

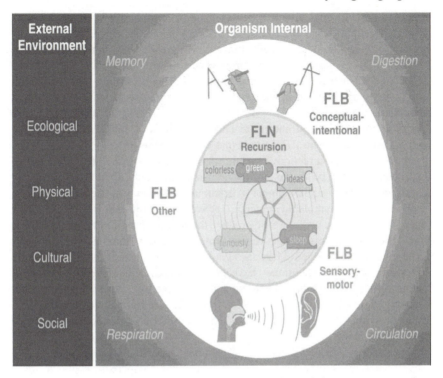

Figure 1.1 A schematic representation of external and internal factors to an organism that are related to the faculty of language. FLB includes sensory-motor, conceptual-intentional, and other possible systems. FLN includes the core grammatical computations that we suggest are limited to recursion. See text for more complete discussion 'Colorless green ideas sleep furiously', Chomsky, 1957, p. 15. (From Hauser et al., 2002). Reproduced with permission of Dr Marc Hauser.

specificity of the sensory-motor system for the elaboration of language. According to Hauser et al., therefore, it appears evident that there were no important evolutionary modifications in the system of sound production and reception that played a critical role in the emergence of language.

Hauser et al. also discussed the specificity of the human species for certain characteristics of the conceptual system. Many animals in fact appear to possess a rich variety of conceptual representations (Shettleworth, 1998), and are even able to understand the intentions of others (*Theory of Mind* or the ability to understand the thoughts and intentions of communicative partners: Frith & Frith, 2003).

Thus the broad language component is formed of elements shared with other functional and anatomical systems, and the narrow language component is principally, if not solely, made up of the mechanism for recursion. This ability allows us to make almost infinite use, within a language constituent, of other similar constituents. Within language the most evident use of recursion is with regard to syntax, which allows lexical elements to form higher level entities, such as sentences that can be freely extended: it is possible, for example, to construct a sentence that is then transformed into a new sentence when other sentences are inserted into the original, and this process can continue infinitely. A limit to the length of the sentence will be determined by the properties of the more peripheral components of language in the broad sense, such as respiratory capacity and short-term memory.

Unlike the syntactic structures that form the basis of animal communication and are made up of an *AB pattern* that can be repeated $(AB)^n$, a context-free grammar[1] based on a recursive system of the type *AB, AABB, AAABBB*, and so on, is considered to be the basis of the human language ability in that it allows the construction of an infinite number of grammatically correct sentences.

If we take for example the sentence 'the weather is fine' and we place it within the phrase 'Paul knows', we thus produce the phrase 'Paul knows the weather is fine'. The result of this process can, in turn, be placed within the sentence 'Mary says', in order to produce 'Mary says Paul knows the weather is fine', and so on.

Various recursive techniques have been adopted in the different models of language inspired by Chomsky, to which the reader can refer for more in-depth understanding (Chomsky, 1957, 1986, 1995). The end product of the recursive process is, finally, interfaced with the sensory-motor and conceptual-intentional interfaces.

From an experimental point of view the human specificity of the recursive faculty of language is upheld by a series of studies that compare the syntactic structure of animal communication with human language: Fitch and Hauser (2004) have recently demonstrated that cotton top tamarin monkeys are able to learn spontaneously acoustic structures of the $(AB)'$ type, but are not able to discriminate or learn type $A'B'$ recursive acoustic structures. This inability seems to be the result of a fundamental computational limitation that does not allow recognition or memorization of acoustic structures that are organized in a hierarchical manner.

An outcome of research that appears to contradict the hypothesis that recursive ability is species-specific comes from a recent study carried out on a species of European starlings (*Sturnus vulgaris*) by Gentner, Fenn, Margoliash, and Nusbaum (2006). These birds, following lengthy training, are able not only to recognize an acoustic structure defined by a recursive pattern, but also to distinguish whether new acoustic patterns are recursive in type or belong to finite state grammatical patterns. However, as Marcus (2006) underlines, the discovery of this characteristic is open to several interpretations. The first, which is methodological, underlines the fact that, while the primates studied by Fitch and Hauser (2004) did not undergo specific training, the subjects used by Gentner et al. (2006) underwent lengthy training, excluding therefore the possibility that in different conditions from those found in nature the tamarin monkeys or other animal species can spontaneously develop and use context-free grammatical structures. A further hypothesis underlying the difference between primates and birds could be the fact that the faculty to recognize recursive type acoustic patterns is established only in those species that are capable of acquiring new vocalization structures, such as songbirds, the human species and perhaps cetaceans.

In addition, the hypothesis that the recursive rules apply only to language has been abandoned within the minimalist programme of research in linguistics (see Chapter 7): recursive rules apply to other cognitive domains, including music (Patel, 2003), action control (Conway & Christiansen, 2001) and visuospatial processing (Byrne & Russon, 1998).

According to Hauser et al. (2002) the recursive property is supported by a specific module which did not emerge in the human species within the communication system. During the evolutionary process the recursive faculty emerged and developed as an independent module, impervious to other systems and dedicated to the solution of tasks such as navigation or numerical quantification. Later, however, this module became penetrable and could be used for other tasks through a mechanism of exaptation (Gould & Vrba, 1982), meaning a shift in function without changes in anatomical structure (Darwin used the term 'preadaptation'). Therefore the human species has applied this module to the communicative faculty and, using it as an interface between the sensory-motor and conceptual apparatus, has thus allowed the emergence of language in its entirety. Belonging to a biological system, the faculty of language, both in its broad and narrow senses, is implemented by the nervous system in the same way as other cognitive systems and is bound by the same biophysical, developmental and computational structural ties.

In conclusion then, according to this hypothesis, language, precisely because of the presence and the fundamental role of the recursive faculty, cannot be considered the end product of the evolutionary process of communication, but rather it must be viewed as a species-specific faculty that arose for other functions and was attributed by Chomsky (1988, p. 170) to a genetic mutation, and which exists alongside other aspects of communication. The peripheral components of the language faculty are, on the other hand, located within the evolutionary process, with a transition from simple functional and anatomical structures to more evolved structures, and therefore not requiring structures dedicated specifically to these functions.

Various scholars (Premack, 1971, 1985; Gardner & Gardner, 1969) have tried at length to teach a communication system to animals close to man on the phylogenetic scale (chimpanzees, bonobos) based on the same principles on which language is built, while overcoming the difficulties caused by anatomical differences such as the structure of the vocal tract. They used systems similar to sign language, or other visual non-verbal communication systems such as the Bliss System (a graphic symbolic system) which requires objects to be placed in a certain order that corresponds to the structure of a specific sentence. On the whole, results have been disappointing: at the height of training the animals were able to produce, at the most, the equivalent of simple sentences, while showing no sign of having learnt the process of recursion. In contrast every child, with surprising regularity of time scale and independently of the language to which he or she is exposed, develops normal language both in terms of its peripheral components (decoding and production of language sounds) and in terms of syntactic abilities. What is more, as far as the lexicon is concerned, the differences between non-human primates and human species are huge: even the most 'educated' laboratory-raised chimpanzee is unable to learn more than a hundred or so words, while a preschool aged child acquires, purely through exposure and with no specific training, a vocabulary of tens of thousands of words (Wallman, 1992). According to Hauser et al. (2002), words possess some properties that appear to be specifically human, in terms of the range and precision of the concepts that they can express (concrete and abstract words, open and closed class, etc.). Despite these properties, Hauser et al. (2002) do not consider the lexicon to be part of the language faculty in the narrow sense, attributing its development to a more general, not word-specific, learning mechanism.

A demonstration that language development is not solely the result of exposure to an oral–acoustic language environment is provided by Senghas, Kita, and Ozyürek (2004) on the basis of a series of observations carried out in Nicaragua on a group of preverbal deaf subjects. Until 1970 in Nicaragua there were no educational structures for people affected by congenital deafness, and non-hearing individuals had no contact with each other and communicated only with hearing individuals. When an expanded elementary school for special education was opened, social interaction began and the hearing-impaired people attending the school started to communicate with each other using gestures, both during school hours and within the daily routine. When social interaction increased, it became evident that from a simple gestural system such as that used by a hearing-impaired child within his or her family, the students moved on, with no specific instruction or exposure, to the use of a proper sign language, made up of single gestures that were combined grammatically and governed by the same rules underlying spoken language.[2] This is in accordance with the hypothesis of the existence of a 'language instinct' (Pinker, 1994), which can be expressed in different modalities and does not require explicit training.

The hypothesis that the recursive faculty, and consequently the emergence of language, is not the fruit of an evolutionary process determined by natural selection, not only reinforces the notion that language, in its most specific component, is a natural product distinct from communication, but also raises the question of its function. In fact according to Chomsky (2000), faculty of language in narrow sense cannot simply be conceived to be a system for communicating information, but rather a means of expressing thoughts, as, for example, in internal language or childhood monologue. The phonological component of internal language intervenes to focus attention on particular thought content or to increase short-term memory ability (Fitch, Hauser, & Chomsky, 2005).

Chomsky's theory that separates language from communication and fails to place it in an evolutionary perspective has not, however, received universal consensus and has been subjected to rigorous criticism, which maintains that language, on the contrary, like other biological systems, is made up of a set of characteristics that, through the evolutionary selection process, have co-adapted and united in order to allow communication of complex propositions.

Pinker and Jackendoff (2005), for example, confute the hypothesis that there are no substantial qualitative differences between the peripheral components (the conceptual and sensory-motor systems) of language and animal communication, but only quantitative differences. According to these authors, the claim of Hauser et al. (2002) that there is no species-specific module for the perception of oral language (Liberman, Cooper, Shankweiler, & Studdert-Kennedy, 1967; Liberman & Mattingly, 1985; see Chapter 5) is cast into doubt by some experimental evidence from both adults and newborns. The latter, in fact, listen more willingly to speech sounds than non-speech sounds that however possess spectral and temporal properties similar to speech sounds (Vouloumanos & Werker, 2004). From an anatomical viewpoint, both adults (Hickok & Pöppel, 2000) and newborns (Peña, Bedore, & Rappazzo, 2003) possess cerebral areas that are specific to the perception and analysis of speech sounds. Finally, unlike humans, primates are not able to categorize consonants according to place of articulation, using formant transitions.

As far as production is concerned, here too there are numerous examples that prove the phono-articulatory organs are adapted specifically for language. For example, the complexity of the motor programmes necessary for the articulation of language sounds is not found in any other animal species. Similarly, the modification of both the larynx and the upper vocal tract seems to have developed with the aim of rendering language possible and is not shared with other animal species.

At a conceptual level, there is limited proof that even the most evolutionarily advanced primates, such as chimpanzees, are capable of developing abilities such as the Theory of Mind. In addition, the ability to use other conceptual systems, for example, the ability to use instruments made up of various components, or the paternal instinct, appear to be present only in the human species. Finally, according to Jackendoff (1996), there are concepts, such as the notion of time periods (e.g. the notion of a week) which cannot immediately be perceived without language mediation. It seems, therefore, that in the human species, alongside the evolution of a conceptual system shared with other animal species, there exist concepts that have developed thanks to the pre-existing presence of linguistic expressions.

Pinker and Jackendoff's criticism of the hypothesis of Hauser et al. extends also to the function and specificity of recursive ability. If it is true that the process of recursion is present in cognitive tasks distinct from language, it is within language that it finds its *raison d'être*, that is the need to express recursive-type complex thoughts. In addition, according to Pinker and Jackendoff, the hypothesis that the recursive faculty belonging to language emerges from recursive abilities used in other cognitive operations such as numerical manipulation and calculus does not hold up to criticism. Most human cultures quantify objects using one of two systems: the first by analogy, similar to the way in which we judge whether the water level is the same in two glasses of water, and the second using a system to categorize rapidly small numbers of objects, usually not more than 4 (subitizing; Butterworth, 1999; Dehaene, 1997). The recursive system of numeration (not universally present), seems, on the other hand, to have developed through a process of adaptation borrowed from the language system. Lastly, recursive theory cannot be applied to some characteristics specific to the human species, such as the richness and variety of the lexicon.

To conclude, despite substantial differences between the various theories, the notion of human specificity of language and its multicomponential structure, is firmly established, while leaving unresolved for now the question of whether language represents the final step in an evolutionary process that adapts pre-existing systems in a species-specific fashion, or whether the faculty of language emerged from the adaptation of systems not originally linked to communication.

Notes

1   In computer sciences and in linguistics, a context-free grammar is a formal grammar in which every rule of derivation is of the type V → w where V is a non-terminal symbol and w is a sequence of terminal and non-terminal symbols. The term 'context-free' refers to the fact that the non-terminal symbol V can always be substituted by w, independently of the symbols that precede or follow it. A formal language is called context-free if it is generated by a context-free grammar.
2   However, as Russo and Volterra (2005) pointed out, the subjects of this study did not grow up in communicative isolation but communicated from birth with people using language, even if only a gestural system, thereby being able to acquire some elements of language prior to the emergence of a sign language.

References

Butterworth, B. (1999). *The mathematical brain*. Basingstoke, UK: Macmillan.

Byrne, R. W., & Russon, A. E. (1998). Learning by imitation: A hierarchical approach. *Behavioral and Brain Sciences, 21* (5), 667–684.

Chomsky, N. (1957). *Syntactic structures*. The Hague: Mouton.

Chomsky, N. (1986). *Knowledge of language: Its nature, origin, and use*. New York: Praeger.

Chomsky, N. (1988). *Language and problems of knowledge. The Managua lectures*. Cambridge, MA: MIT Press.

Chomsky, N. (1995). *The minimalist program*. Cambridge, MA: MIT Press.

Chomsky, N. (2000). *New horizons in the study of language and mind*. Cambridge, UK: Cambridge University Press.

Conrad, J. (1988). *Heart of darkness and other stories*. Ware, UK: Wordsworth Editions.

Conway, C. M., & Christiansen, M. H. (2001). Sequential learning in non-human primates. *Trends in Cognitive Sciences, 5* (12), 539–546.

Dehaene, S. (1997). *The number sense: How the mind creates mathematics*. New York: Oxford University Press.

Fitch, W. T., & Hauser, M. D. (2004), Computational constraints on syntactic processing in a nonhuman primate. *Science, 303* (5656), 377–380.

Fitch, W. T., Hauser, M. D., & Chomsky, N. (2005). The evolution of the language faculty: clarifications and implications. *Cognition, 97* (2), 179–210; Discussion 211–225.

Frith, U., & Frith, C. D. (2003). Development and neurophysiology of mentalizing. *Philosophical Transactions of the Royal Society of London, Series B: Biological Sciences, 358* (1431), 459–473.

Gardner, R. A., & Gardner, B. T. (1969). Teaching sign language to a chimpanzee. *Science, 165* (894), 664–672.

Gentner, T. Q., Fenn, K. M., Margoliash, D., & Nusbaum, H. C. (2006). Recursive syntactic pattern learning by songbirds. *Nature, 440* (7088), 1204–1207.

Gould, S. J., & Vrba, E. S. (1982). Exaptation – a missing term in the science of form. *Palebiology, 8*, 4–15.

Hauser, M. D., Chomsky, N., & Fitch, W. (2002). The faculty of language: What is it, who has it, and how did it evolve. *Science, 298* (5598), 1569–1579.

Hickok, G., & Pöppel, D. (2000). Towards a functional neuroanatomy of speech perception. *Trends in Cognitive Sciences, 4* (4), 131–138.

Jackendoff, R. (1996). *Languages of the mind: Essays on mental representation*, Cambridge, MA: MIT Press.

Liberman, A. M., Cooper, F. S., Shankweiler, D., & Studdert-Kennedy, M. (1967). Perception of the speech code. *Psychological Review, 74*, 431–461.

Liberman, A. M., & Mattingly, I. G. (1985). The motor theory of speech perception revised. *Cognition, 21*, 1–36.

Marcus, G. (2006). Startling starlings. *Nature, 440*, 1117–1118.

Patel, A. D. (2003). Language, music, syntax and the brain. *Nature Neuroscience, 6* (7), 674–681.

Peña, E., Bedore, L. M., & Rappazzo, C. (2003). Comparison of Spanish, English, and bilingual children's performance across semantic tasks, *Language, Speech, and Hearing Services in Schools, 34* (1), 5–16.

Pinker, S. (1994). *The language instinct: How the mind creates language*. New York: HarperCollins.

Pinker, S., & Jackendoff, R. (2005). The faculty of language: What's special about it? *Cognition, 95* (2), 201–236.

Premack, D. (1971). Language in chimpanzee? *Science, 172*, 808–822.

Premack, D. (1985). 'Gavagai!' or the future history of the animal language controversy. *Cognition, 19* (3), 207–296.

Ramus, F., Nespor, M., & Mehler, J. (2000). Correlates of linguistic rhythm in the speech signal. *Cognition, 75* (1), AD3–AD30.

Russo, T., & Volterra, V. (2005). Comment on 'Children creating core properties of language: Evidence from an emerging sign language in Nicaragua'. *Science, 309* (5731), 56.

Senghas, A., Kita, S., & Ozyürek, A. (2004). Children creating core properties of language: Evidence from an emerging sign language in Nicaragua. *Science, 305* (5691), 1779–1782.

Shettleworth, S. J. (1998). *Cognition, evolution, and behavior*. New York: Oxford University Press.

Vouloumanos, A., & Werker, J. F. (2004). Tuned to the signal: The privileged status of speech for young infants. *Developmental Science, 7* (3), 270–276.

Wallman, J. (1992). *Aping language*. Cambridge, UK: Cambridge University Press.

2 The origin and evolution of language and words

The notion that language is specific to the human species has given rise, since ancient times, to a multitude of theories regarding its origin and evolution (for a review see Ruhlen, 1994). None of these, however, satisfy modern scientific criteria. In 1886, the influential Linguistic Society of Paris expressly forbade the question of the origin and evolution of language to be addressed by its members: '*la societé n'admit aucune communication concernant l'origine du language*'.

A few years later, Saussure (1916) explained why this edict had been made:

> the act in which the names of things were given ... cannot be conceived by us, but this act has never been questioned ... For this reason, the problem of the origin of language is not of the importance that is attributed to it, indeed, it is a question which should not even be asked: the only real object of linguistics is the normal and regular life of an already established idiom.

The question of the origin of evolution of language has only recently been considered a subject worthy of scientific interest, following the advancement in both neurosciences and cognitive sciences and the integration of these disciplines.

From an evolutionary perspective, language can be considered as resulting from the interfacing of three separate systems of adaptation: individual learning, cultural transmission and biological evolution. These systems are based on different temporal scales: years for individual learning, thousands of years for the appearance of language in the human species and hundreds of thousands of years for the evolution of the species. The task of such systems is to transform information in such a way as to adapt it to a specific function and thereby bring about a major transition within the evolutionary process.

At the level of biological evolution this process is natural selection. Natural selection favours and transmits, within the genotype, those variations that allow production of the phenotype most suited to the needs of the species.

In a similar way, individual learning can be considered the result of a process of adaptation of the genetic and cultural patrimony.

The notion of adaptation through cultural transmission is less obvious. Knowledge of a particular language persists in time through constant use, generating a set of linguistic data that is then passed down through successive generations.

Finally, every member of the human species possesses the ability to learn language naturally, needing no specific instruction. This is as a result of a mechanism of genetic assimilation (*Baldwin effect*; Baldwin, 1896) which means that every individual is able to adapt optimally to the environment in which he or she lives thanks to the plasticity of his or her phenotype. Individuals are able to reinforce or modify certain innate physical or behavioural characteristics, allowing therefore the learning process to become innate.

A major consideration when addressing the problem of the origin and evolution of language is the divergence of opinions regarding the nature of language (see Chapter 1). While some scholars believe that language is the product of a species-specific *mental organ* (Chomsky, 1986; Hauser, Chomsky, & Fitch, 2002), independent from more general communication processes, others believe that language is the end product of a generalized learning process, with underlying neurological and functional mechanisms that are partly shared with other cognitive and neurological systems and found in other species (Pinker & Jackendoff, 2005).

Despite these controversies, it seems clear that certain forms of preadaptation developed prior to the emergence of language in the human species. The most obvious of these is the ability to form stable connections between a sign (or gesture) and a concept (or perceived object). This symbolic ability appears to be present in a reduced form in some primates, the most widely known example being vocal alarm signals to signify danger (usually a predator) produced by some primate species, for example, the green vervet monkey (*Chlorocebus pygerythrus*). These signals, emitted by the colony's 'sentry', seem to be interpreted by the rest of the colony as a sign of imminent danger and provoke a flight response. However it is unclear whether the signals refer symbolically to the predator or whether they elicit a conditioned flight response associated with the presence of a predator (Cheney & Seyfarth, 1990).

An important factor differentiating words from the manual or vocal signs produced by other animal species is that words are not situation specific. When a child says 'cat' he may be referring to the cat in front of him, expressing the desire to own a cat, asking where the cat is, pointing to the bowl in front of him that belongs to the cat and so on. Animals, on the other hand, do not possess this property unless specifically taught. In the presence of food or the danger a sign is only given when the food is found or the danger is spotted; it never indicates searching or anticipation.

A second example of a system of preadaptation to language is the human ability to imitate complex motor sequences of the vocal tract and limbs with communicative intent. In primates the ability to imitate vocalizations is almost absent and can be found only in some species of birds belonging to the passerine family. These birds learn the song characteristics of an adult male of the same species through a two-stage mechanism involving an initial period of memorization of the sound followed by development of vocalization. Singing ability has a specific underlying neural system which is different from that used for general motor learning (Bolhuis & Gahr, 2006) and there seems, therefore, to be a marked similarity between a bird's acquisition of song and the process of word acquisition in humans even though the two species are phylogenetically very distant.

At a cognitive level, various other mechanisms for preadaptation to language have been proposed, such as sustained attention and long- and short-term memory for sound sequences. These systems are also encountered to a lesser degree in animal species.

Questions remain, however, regarding the evolution of grammatical structures (e.g. universal grammar). One line of thought is that grammar has been established through an evolutionary process of the natural selection of an innate grammatical structure. This has produced a system that allows increasingly complex propositional information to be coded, such as that conveyed by closed class words (pronouns, adverbs, etc.). It also allows an exchange of information within a 'cognitive niche' (Pinker, 2003) relating to individuals, objects or events not immediately visually perceived.

A second line of thought is that the emergence of a grammatical structure, rather than being the product of biological adaptation, is the effect of the cultural transmission of language through hundreds or thousands of generations. The structure of language has become ever more complex, passing through the filter put in place by language learning mechanisms in early childhood. This theory is supported by examples from different sources, for example the analysis of the development of sign language in profoundly hearing-impaired subjects in the absence of specific learning (Senghas, Kita, & Ozyürek, 2004) or the results of computer simulation of cultural transmission.

There is also debate about the way in which language emerged within the evolutionary process: did language emerge via the vocal channel from the outset or was there a preceding stage of manual language transmission?

Gentilucci and Corballis (2006) present neurophysiological data supporting the idea of a progressive evolution from gestural to vocal communication: in their review they show that the transition from primarily manual to primarily vocal language was a gradual process, and is best understood if it is supposed that speech itself is a gestural system rather than an acoustic system, an idea captured by the motor theory of speech perception and articulatory phonology. Studies of primate premotor cortex, and, in particular, of the so-called 'mirror neuron system' (see later in this chapter) suggest a double hand/mouth command system that may have evolved initially in the context of taking in food, and later formed a platform for combined manual and vocal communication. In humans, speech is typically accompanied by manual gesture, speech production itself is influenced by executing or observing hand movements, and manual actions also play an important role in the development of speech, from the babbling stage onwards. The final stage at which speech became relatively autonomous may have occurred late in hominid evolution, perhaps with a mutation of the *FOXP2* gene (Lai, Fisher, Hurst, Vargha-Khadem, & Monaco, 2001; see below) around 100,000 years ago. Non-human primates do not show cortical control of the vocalization process, so that gesture is used for communication, and vocalizations are essentially affective in nature, composed of inarticulate sounds such as grunts or cries. The sounds produced by the human species during crying, laughter or in response to pain may therefore represent the 'fossils' of a communication system common to humans and primates. A cortical system for the voluntary control of the muscles of the vocal cords (Kent, 2004) has emerged through natural selection in the human species only, allowing development of the phonetic and phonological system. Consequently, attempts to teach the rudiments of human language to primates through the vocal channel have been ineffective; only when primates are taught to use manual signs or to match visual symbols to an object or request (Bliss System, see Chapter 1)[1] can some rudiments of language appear.

It appears, therefore, that the preadaptation system for the development of communication shared by the ancestor common to both humans and primates was based on gesture rather than sound. This may have originated around 6 million years ago, when, through the natural selection process, hominids evolved from the quadrupedal to bipedal position, allowing the upper limbs to be used not only for manipulating objects but also for communication. The transition from gesture to sounds would have come about when the increasing manual manipulation of objects and tools conflicted with the use of the hands as a communicative instrument. Furthermore, a major disadvantage of gestural communication lies in the fact that speakers must be in visual contact with each other, they can communicate only in a lit atmosphere and they are unable to communicate and manipulate objects simultaneously.

The notion of a primitively gestural origin of language is supported by the recent discovery of the mirror-neuron system in monkeys (for a review see Rizzolatti & Craighero, 2004). Neurons situated in the frontal premotor cortex (area 5) are found to activate during the execution and observation of actions. A broader mirror system involving the parietal lobes as well as the frontal regions was later identified in monkeys and humans. This system has been found to represent the anatomical substrate for the perception and interpretation of gestures linked to biological movement. Functional neuroimaging studies (fMRI) in humans have shown selective activation of specific areas of the premotor cortex during observation of hand, mouth and foot movements. These correspond to the areas activated during the execution of the observed movements or during the production of sounds that correspond to the oral movements (Buccino, Riggio, Melli, Binkofski, Gallese, & Rizzolatti, 2001; Kohler, Keysers, Umiltà, Fogassi, Gallese, & Rizzolatti, 2002). It is, therefore, not unreasonable to hypothesize that the origin of communication was gestural, with an underlying system of mirror neurons, and subsequently developed into oral language.[2] This demonstration of the involvement of the motor system in language perception gives experimental support to the motor theory of speech perception (Liberman, Cooper, Shankweiler, & Studdert-Kennedy, 1967), which suggests that language perception is based on the activation of the neuromotor programmes of the articulators (tongue, lips and vocal cords) corresponding to the phonemes perceived (see Chapter 5).

The next step is to attempt to define the transition from gestures to auditory–oral communication in temporal and functional terms. The most plausible hypothesis is that of a gradual transition, through successive mutations, from one modality to another with orofacial movements being progressively introduced for communication purposes and culminating in vocalization. Present-day humans still use manual gestures synchronized with words for communication purposes as if providing a reminder of their common origin (McNeill, 1992).

MacNeilage (1998) has pointed out a strong similarity between facial movements during the production of words and the facial gestures produced by primates in conjunction with the production of sounds such as lip smacking, tongue clicking or teeth chattering. Finally, Studdert-Kennedy (2000), underlines the fact that basic syllable structure derives from the series of opening and closing movements of the mouth used in the mastication and swallowing of food, suggesting that these movements then evolved into phonatory type gestures.

The transition from gestural to oral communication could therefore be a result of the appearance of new mutations occurring alongside increasing cognitive development and through a process of natural selection that allowed the processing of an ever increasing number of symbols. Gestures, like the other vocal signs produced by primates, are made up of determined forms organized into a whole (*Gestalt*) that cannot be broken down into smaller units. Therefore the processing (production, perception and understanding) of a large number of Gestalt gestures is practically impossible. Words, on the other hand, are made up from a small repertory of sounds of different categories (phonemes) that in themselves are meaningless but that can be combined to form an almost infinite number of meaningful units, known as words.

According to Lieberman (1991), vocal communication in the human species originated progressively. The form of the vocal tract in Neanderthals was less developed than that of humans today, allowing them to produce a protophonology, made up of a small number of elements evolving over time to reach the present stage. There may have been an intermediate developmental stage with the introduction of base units such as syllables. Syllables are formed by means of a set of articulatory acts organized into lip opening and closing movements to allow the production of vowels or consonants. It is thus possible that in the first stages of vocal communication a syllabary developed (Levelt & Wheeldon, 1994) composed of protosyllables, each one made up of holistic vocal sets.

Subsequently, as cognitive abilities developed, so too did phonological competence as successive modifications of the vocal tract (the descent of the larynx,[3] Nishimura, 2003) allowed the production of an increasing number of syllables that can be broken down into their constituent elements (phonemes), culminating in the phonetic and phonological competence found today.

The production of words required not only modification of the vocal tract to allow the production of a huge number of formant configurations (*patterns*) but also a sophisticated checking system necessary for the control and synchronization of the vocal articulators (tongue, lips, velum).

According to Kimura (1993), left hemisphere specialization for language (see Chapter 3) stems from the fact that the left hemisphere is involved in complex motor processing in general, including the processing essential for language production. Clinical data demonstrate, however, that an acquired deficit of motor programming of the limbs (apraxia) is not always accompanied by an articulatory impairment of language (verbal apraxia) and aphasia (for a review see Papagno, Della Salla, & Basso, 1993), and consequently, that these three conditions can be functionally and anatomically disassociated. Arbib (2006) however, suggests that a process of duplication of the motor circuit may have arisen during the evolutionary process, with the copy circuit specializing in the motor control of the phonatory apparatus and gesture (facial and manual) associated with language production. Arbib also points out that articulatory processes and processes for assembling words in grammatically correct sequences require two separate mechanisms.

It is important to note that vocal learning is a rare characteristic, found only in three species of phylogenetically distant mammals (humans, bats and cetaceans) and in three groups of phylogenetically distant birds (parrots, humming-birds and songbirds). Songbirds, in particular, are able to learn the song of another bird species as long as contact occurs during a specific developmental period. Moreover, some species as well as being able to imitate the song of another species can also imitate sounds produced by instruments such as the ringtone of a telephone and even the human voice (Pepperberg, 1991).

A comparative study of the nervous structures involved in vocalization has demonstrated a clear difference between species. The three species of songbird possess similar cerebral nuclei for vocalization, which are distributed along two pathways, one posterior and one anterior. Nervous control of vocalization in humans has two underlying circuits: a posterior tract, which includes projections from the motor cortex corresponding to the face down to the vocal nuclei of the brainstem, and an anterior tract, which includes part of the premotor cortex and some subcortical formations such as the basal ganglia and the thalamus.

This neural organization is found neither in songbirds nor in mammals that do not use vocalization, but is similar to the neuronal circuits used for a different type of learning.

According to Jarvis (2004), therefore, it is possible to hypothesize that the process of vocal learning evolved separately in birds and humans under the control of narrow genetic ties determined by the presence of a neural circuit that pre-existed in the nervous system of vertebrates.

Alongside the question of the origin of spoken language and its differentiation from other forms of communication, a series of studies has tried to establish the exact way in which the spoken word evolved, from its emergence to its present stage of development (linguistic fossils, for a review see Bickerton, 1990 and Jackendoff, 1999).

According to Bickerton (1990) today's language (that is, the combination of the historical-natural general properties of the species, known for thousands of years) evolved from a protolanguage. This protolanguage, when compared with language in use today, was characterized by the lack of development of syntactic components. According to Bickerton, traces of protolanguage are evident in language acquisition and consist of isolated symbolic vocalizations, which increase in number and speed of learning in a way that is not witnessed in other animal species. There then follows a process of concatenation of the single vocal emissions into longer utterances to form a protosyntax that later develops into complete syntactic competence (according to Jackendoff, 1999, compound words such as *hairdryer* or *spokesman* could be considered as examples of syntax-free language).

A further example of linguistic fossils is provided by studies of second language learning during a post-critical age in subjects not exposed to school-type learning (Klein & Perdue, 1997). The language of these subjects (the basic variety) is characterized by an adequate level of lexical competence, while there is seriously inadequate use of flexible morphology and a lack of subordination (relative phrases and direct discourse are absent). These findings are, of course, relevant only to languages possessing the above mentioned characteristics.

Finally, some authors consider the agrammatical production of some aphasic patients (Piñango, 1999) or the learning of a language in a period following the critical stage resulting in near normal lexical development but profoundly deficient language use, as regression or an interruption at the stage of protolanguage (e.g. the story of Genie, a normally hearing child who had no exposure to language in the first years of her life, Curtiss, 1977).

It is probable that future studies into the human genome will give rise to new theories regarding the origin and evolution of language and that increasing knowledge of the genetic bases of language will modify current theories; however at the present time data are limited. An example of this type of research is the discovery of the *FOXP2* gene, situated on chromosome 7 (Lai et al., 2001). The mutation of this gene is transmitted by an autosomal dominant route and is seen to cause severe disturbance of language development characterized by articulatory and syntactic deficits (Gopnik, 1990, see Chapter 11). The discovery of this gene has been used to support different theories on the origin and evolution of language. For example, some authors believe that this discovery confirms the appearance of gestural communication prior to vocal communication, or, on the other hand, a primitively vocal communication (for a review see Christiansen & Kirby, 2003).

There is more certainty regarding results of genetic analysis that places the emergence of language between 100 and 200,000 years ago (Enard et al., 2002), coinciding with a genetic mutation that differentiated man from chimpanzee. The *FOXP2* gene appears very early in phylogenesis and humans differ from the chimpanzee by only 3 points. Two of these three mutations appeared in humans following their separation from other primates (e.g. the chimpanzee and the bonobo), supporting the hypothesis that articulated language appeared relatively recently and at the moment at which humans became distinct from other primates.

Notes

1   Recently, further evidence for the hypothesis that language evolved from a phyloge-netically ancient form of communication involving gestures, has emerged from the observation of facial–vocal signs and arm–facial gestures produced by chimpanzees and bonobos, the nearest primates to the human species and the only species of monkey to use gestures for communicative purposes in a way similar to humans (Pollick & de Waal, 2007). Although facial–vocal expressions are the same for both species, bonobos make more use of gesture and are also able to use gesture with greater flexibility (the

same gesture assumes different meanings in different contexts). By combining gesture with vocal expressions, bonobos demonstrate the ability to use multimodal communication.

2 Buccino et al. (2005) provide further data to support the involvement of the mirror neuron system in language processing. Modulation of the motor system was seen by these authors when subjects listened to phrases describing actions performed by the limbs or orofacial musculature.

3 At birth the position of the human larynx is the same as in other mammals, but there is gradual lowering of the larynx in the postnatal period and the definitive position is reached in adolescence. This phenomenon is species-specific and not present even in non-human primates. In terms of acoustic physics, the combination of this laryngeal position and tongue movements allows production of the sounds and voicing contrasts typical of the human voice.

4 Krause et al. (2007) discovered that Neanderthals and present-day humans share two evolutionary mutations of the *FOXP2* gene, supporting the hypothesis of an earlier appearance of some form of language (300–400,000 years ago).

References

Arbib, M. A. (2006). Aphasia, apraxia and the evolution of the language ready brain. *Aphasiology*, *20* (9/10/11), 1125–1155.

Baldwin, J. M. (1896). A new factor in evolution. *American Naturalist*, *30*, 441–541.

Bickerton, D. (1990). *Language and species*. Chicago: University of Chicago Press.

Bolhuis, J. J., & Gahr, M. (2006). Neural mechanisms of birdsong memory. *Nature Reviews Neuroscience*, *7*, 347–357.

Buccino, G., Riggio, L., Melli, G., Binkofski, F., Gallese, V., & Rizzolatti, G. (2005). Listening to action-related sentences modulates the activity of the motor system: A combined TMS and behavioral study. *Brain Research: Cognitive Brain Research*, *24* (3), 355–363.

Cheney, D. L., & Seyfarth, R. M. (1990). The representation of social relations by monkeys. *Cognition*, *37* (1–2), 167–196.

Chomsky, N. (1986). *Knowledge of language: Its nature, origin, and use*. New York: Praeger.

Christiansen, M. H., & Kirby, S. (2003). Language evolution: Consensus and controversies. *Trends in Cognitive Sciences*, *7* (7): 300–307.

Curtiss, S. (1977). *Genie: A psycholinguistic study of a modern-day 'wild child'*. New York: Academic Press.

Enard, W., Przeworski, M., Fisher, S. E., Lai, C. S., Wiebe, V., Kitano, T., et al. (2002). Molecular evolution of *FOXP2*, a gene involved in speech and language. *Nature*, *418* (6900), 869–872.

Gentilucci, M., & Corballis, M. C. (2006). From manual gesture to speech: A gradual transition. *Neuroscience and Biobehavioral Reviews*, *30* (7), 949–960.

Gopnik, M. (1990). Genetic basis of grammar defect. *Nature*, *347* (6288), 26.

Hauser, M. D., Chomsky, N., & Fitch, W. T. (2002). The faculty of language: What is it, who has it, and how did it evolve? *Science*, *298* (5598), 1569–1579.

Jackendoff, R. (1999). Possible stages in the evolution of the language capacity. *Trends in Cognitive Sciences*, *3* (7), 272–279.

Jarvis, E. D. (2004). Learned bird song and the neurobiology of human language. *Annals of the New York Academy of Sciences*, *1016*, 749–777.

Kent, R. D. (2004). The uniqueness of speech among motor systems. *Clinical Linguistics and Phonetics*, *18* (6–8), 495–505.

Kimura, D. (1993). *Neuromotor mechanisms in human communication.* Oxford, UK: Oxford University Press.

Klein, W., & Perdue, C. (1997). The basic variety. *Second Language Research, 13,* 301–347.

Kohler, E., Keysers, C., Umiltà, M. A., Fogassi, L., Gallese, V., & Rizzolatti, G. (2002). Hearing sounds, understanding actions: Action representation in mirror neurons. *Science, 297* (5582), 846–848.

Krause, J., Lalueza-Fox, C., Orlando, L., Enard, W., Green, R. E., Burbano, H. B., et al. (2007). The derived *FOXP2* variant of modern humans was shared with Neanderthals. *Current Biology, 17* (21), 1908–1912.

Lai, C. S., Fisher, S. E., Hurst, J. A., Vargha-Khadem, F., & Monaco, A. P. (2001). A forkhead-domain gene is mutated in a severe speech and language disorder. *Nature, 413* (6855), 465–466.

Levelt, W. J., & Wheeldon, L. (1994). Do speakers have access to a mental syllabary? *Cognition, 50* (1–3), 239–269.

Liberman, A. M., Cooper, F. S., Shankweiler, D. P., & Studdert-Kennedy, M. (1967). Perception of the speech code. *Psychological Review, 74* (6), 431–461.

Lieberman, P. (1991). The evolution of human speech: Its anatomical and neural bases. *Current Anthropology, 48* (1), 39.

MacNeilage, P. F. (1998). The frame/content theory of evolution of speech production. *Behavioral and Brain Sciences, 21* (4), 499–511; Discussion 511–546.

McNeill, D. (1992). *Hand and mind: What gestures reveal about thought.* Chicago: University of Chicago Press.

Nishimura, T. (2003). Comparative morphology of the hyo-laryngeal complex in anthropoids: Two steps in the evolution of the descent of the larynx. *Primates, 44* (1), 41–49.

Papagno, C., Della Sala, S., & Basso, A. (1993). Ideomotor apraxia without aphasia and aphasia without apraxia: The anatomical support for a double dissociation. *Journal of Neurology, Neurosurgery, and Psychiatry, 56* (3), 286–289.

Pepperberg, I. M. (1991). Learning to communicate: The effects of social interaction. In P. H. Klopfer & P. P. G. Bateson (Eds.), *Perspectives in ethology.* New York: Plenum.

Piñango, M. M. (1999). Syntactic displacement in Broca's aphasia comprehension. In Y. Grodzinsky & R. Bastiaanse (Eds.), *Grammatical disorders in aphasia: A neurolinguistic perspective* (pp. 75–87). London: Whurr Publishers.

Pinker, S. (2003). Are your genes to blame? *Time, 161* (3), 98–100.

Pinker, S., & Jackendoff, R. (2005). The faculty of language: What's special about it? *Cognition, 95* (2), 201–236.

Pollick, A. S., & de Waal, F. B. (2007). Ape gestures and language evolution. *Proceedings of the National Academy of Sciences, 104* (19), 8184–8189.

Rizzolatti, G., & Craighero, L. (2004). The mirror-neuron system. *Annual Review of Neuroscience, 27,* 169–192.

Ruhlen, M. (1994). *On the origin of languages: Studies in linguistic taxonomy,* Stanford, CA: Stanford University Press.

Saussure, F. de (1916). *Cours de linguistique générale.* Payot: Parigi.

Senghas, A., Kita, S., & Ozyürek, A. (2004). Children creating core properties of language: Evidence from an emerging sign language in Nicaragua. *Science, 305* (5691), 1779–1782.

Studdert-Kennedy, M. (2000). Imitation and the emergence of segments. *Phonetica, 57* (2–4), 275–283.

3   The anatomy of language

Until the eighteenth century the issue of the nature and origin of language was mainly a philosophical or religious question. It was only towards the end of that century that the scientific milieu had accepted the idea that cognitive functions or 'faculties' were represented in the brain by specific neural structures.

As a consequence, these faculties were considered to be biological systems, open to experimental investigation of their anatomical and functional substrate.

A pivotal role was played by the wide diffusion of phrenological theories, particularly in France and Germany. These theories proposed a neurological base for the moral and cognitive faculties, which, according to the phrenologists (Gall, Spurzheim) were innate faculties, their physical bases being located in specific sites in the cerebral cortex (Gall, 1825). The phrenologists also asserted that individual differences (an individual may have a faculty that is more or less developed relative to the mean) were proportionally related to the development of the specific areas designated for single functions. They affirmed, what is more, that investigation of cranial bosses (the protruding parts of the cranial bones covering the cerebral cortex) allowed deduction of the size of the underlying cerebral area and its level of functioning. Gall and Spurzheim believed that the bases of at least thirty faculties (moral sense, friendship, religiousness, conjugal love, etc.) could be located with precision in the cerebral cortex. Their main assumption was therefore that the mind, rather than being a single faculty, was made up of separate faculties, each with its own anatomical base.

As far as language was concerned, Gall postulated that memory for words, or the lexicon (*Wortsinn*) was located in the cerebral area behind the left orbit (sic!) and that the motor component of language (*Sprachsinn*) could be found in an area immediately above this. Although phrenology lacked scientific status because it lacked experimental support, the diffusion of Gall's ideas was fundamental for promoting research into the neurological bases of language.

The anatomo-clinical approach (Bouillaud, 1825, for a review see Luzzatti & Whitaker, 2001) was the first to promote a scientific methodology in the search for neurological bases of cognitive faculties and to propose 'neurological models' of cognitive processes.

More recently, sophisticated neuroimaging techniques have been introduced into clinical practice and research, so that clinical data have been combined with the data obtained from normal subjects.

The anatomo-clinical method

The most compelling evidence for anatomo-functional division of cognitive operations started in France with the observation of patients with specific cognitive impairments following localized brain lesions (the anatomo-clinical method). The cognitive deficits evident in a patient during clinical observation were correlated to the site of cerebral lesion found at post-mortem. It was thus deduced that the area of the lesion formed the neurological base of the damaged cognitive system or subsystem as revealed during clinical observation.

According to the phrenologists, the cognitive supremacy of the human species was a result of greater development of the frontal lobes, which therefore constituted a 'site of intelligence', with language being its highest expression.

In 1861, the French neurologist P. P. Broca made a fundamental contribution to the localizationalist hypothesis. At a meeting of the Anthropological Society of Paris, Broca presented the anatomo-clinical observations of a patient who died for extracranial reasons at the age of 51 and who, 30 years previously had lost the ability to speak (the patient replied to every question with the stereotype *tan tan*, and was unable to repeat any word). The patient, however, communicated fairly efficiently through gestures, or by varying the intonation of the monosyllable he used. When listeners were unable to understand his communicative attempts, he became angry and added a single, colourful curse to his vocabulary (*Sacrè Nom de Dieu!*).

His auditory comprehension, in contrast, was clinically normal and he displayed no motor deficit in the movements of phono-articulatory muscles during non-verbal tasks such as chewing and swallowing. His intellectual status was considered normal. Monsieur Leborgne died for reasons that were not associated with his brain damage. At post-mortem, Broca found a large lesion of the cerebral hemisphere (Figure 3.1), centred on the frontal lobe and in particular at the base of the third frontal gyrus. He identified the same site of lesion during autopsy of a second patient, who, subsequent to a stroke occurring the year before his death, was able to speak only five words, *oui, non, toujours, tois* (a distortion of *trios*, three, which he used to express any number) and *Lelo*, a mispronunciation of his name, *Lelong*. He added that the patient's articulatory difficulties were not caused by any motor deficit, but by the impairment of 'a particular type of memory, which is not memory for words, but for the movements necessary for articulating words' (Broca, 1861).

Broca (1864) presented two additional cases to a meeting of the French Anatomical Society, stating: '... the integrity of the third frontal gyrus (and perhaps the second) seems indispensable to the articulation of language'.

In subsequent years, Broca's observations led him to a further fundamental discovery: aphemia (a word that was substituted a few years later with the term aphasia, which we still use today, or the less frequently used dysphasia) only occurred following a lesion of the left hemisphere. This led him to affirm: *nous parlons avec l'hemisphère gauche* (We speak with the left hemisphere).

Some years later, Fritsch and Hitzig (1870) demonstrated, in dogs, that electrical stimulation of the frontal area of one hemisphere produced isolated limb movement

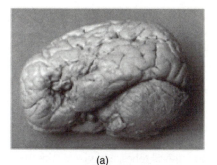
(a)

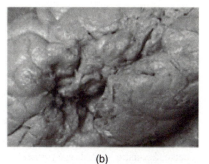
(b)

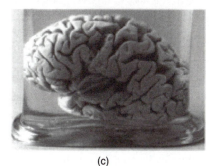
(c)

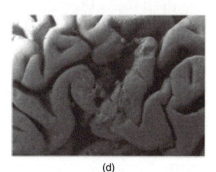
(d)

Figure 3.1 Photographs of the brains of Leborgne and Lelong, Broca's first aphasic patients. (a) The lateral surface of the first patient, Leborgne. The lesion is clearly visible at the height of the inferior section of the frontal lobe. The softening of surrounding superior and posterior regions suggests further cortical and subcortical involvement. (b) Enlargement of Leborgne's cerebral lesion. (c) The lateral surface of the second patient, Lelong. The size of the frontal, temporal and parietal lobes is reduced because of atrophy, allowing the insula to be seen. (d) Enlargement of Leborgne's cerebral lesion. It can be seen that the lesion is limited to the posterior area of what we now call Broca's area, while the anterior area is undamaged (from Dronkers et al., 2007). Reproduced with permission of Oxford University Press.

on the opposite side of the body. There was, moreover, constant correspondence between the area of the cortex undergoing stimulation and the location of the resulting movement. This effect was not witnessed when posterior areas of the cortex were stimulated. In the years that followed, experiments on dogs and other mammals demonstrated that auditory and visual deficits followed lesions to the occipital and temporal lobes. These findings led to the development and consolidation of the notion of cerebral localization of sensory and motor functions.

Finally, the fact that around 90% of people show a right-handed preference (Annett, 1982, 1985) under the control of the left hemisphere, led to the conclusion that the left hemisphere is dominant over the controlateral right or 'minor' hemisphere, controlling two species-specific skills, language and handedness. It was only later discovered that the right hemisphere was critical for processing a variety of non-verbal cognitive skills (for a review see Denes & Pizzamiglio, 1999).

The most important contribution to the development of a neurological model of language was made by a German neurologist, Karl Wernicke, who, in 1874, published a monograph with an extremely significant title: *The Aphasic Symptom Complex: A Psychological Study on an Anatomical Basis*. Wernicke propounded a model of neurological language processing based on the principles of the functional and anatomical organization of the cerebral cortex proposed by his mentor Theodor H. Meynert: motor functions are represented in the frontal and prefrontal anterior areas of the cerebral cortex, while the processing of sensory stimuli takes place in the parietal, temporal and occipital lobes. To be more precise, acoustic stimuli are processed in the temporal lobes, and visual stimuli in the occipital lobes, while the parietal lobes have the task of analysing thermal, tactile and pain stimuli. Meynert also divided the primary areas from secondary, or association, areas. Each sensory modality projects to a specific primary cortical area where information from the sensory receptors is perceived. The product of this initial analysis is then sent to the specific association areas where it is stored. In this way recognition is possible, through a match between information elaborated in the primary areas and images deposited in the specific association areas. The same procedure occurs for motor functions: the specific patterns for the various motor acts are deposited in the motor association area and are transmitted, when needed, to the primary motor area for execution. The complex of secondary areas can, therefore, be seen as the store for culturally learned information, which reaches the highest level of development in the human species (Figure 3.2). The association areas are also connected to each other, so that a stimulus processed in a sensory modality (e.g. a visual stimulus), can activate a corresponding image stored in another sensory modality (e.g. acoustic).

On this basis, Wernicke conceived the following model of the neurological organization of language: Broca's area is situated in front of the primary motor area corresponding to the representation of the phono-articulatory muscles and located in the posterior part of the left inferior frontal gyrus (area 44 in Brodmann's classification[1]) and it is here that the motor programmes necessary for word articulation are stored. The decoding process of language occurs in the acoustic association area (Brodmann's area 22), situated in the posterior part of the left superior temporal gyrus, and in close connection with the primary acoustic area, allowing auditory stimuli to be transformed into linguistic units[2] (Figure 3.3).

Wernicke hypothesized the existence of a connection between the two areas through the activation of a reflex arc active during the process of language acquisition. The perception of a word or a syllable brings about simultaneous articulation of that word or syllable through reflexive imitation, so that there is contemporaneous activation of motor and sensory images of the word in the cortex. This association becomes stable through a direct cortical connection, which Wernicke postulated as existing at the level of the insula and Geschwind (1965) subsequently demonstrated to be located at the level of the internal arcuate fasciculus.

According to this model, which was then elaborated by Lichtheim (1885) (Figure 3.4) and more recently by Geschwind (1965) and Catani, Jones, and

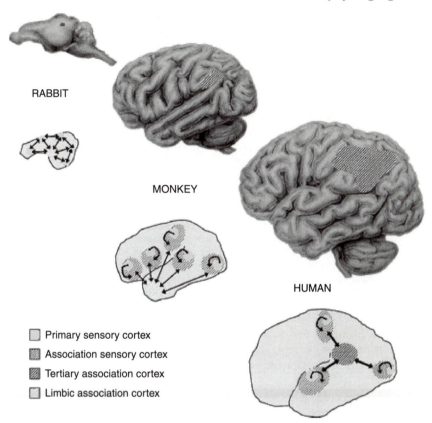

RABBIT

MONKEY

HUMAN

☐ Primary sensory cortex
▨ Association sensory cortex
▨ Tertiary association cortex
☐ Limbic association cortex

Figure 3.2 Geschwind's (1965) view of the evolution of cross-modality associations. For simplicity only sensory cortex is illustrated. The top diagonal sequence shows the expansion of inferior parietal cortex from rabbit through monkey to human, considered by Geschwind as central for the development of language. The bottom diagonal sequence shows the differences in brain circuitry between the species. In the rabbit, Flechsig's rule does not apply and the primary cortices of different sensory modalities are connected directly to one another as well as through limbic cortex. In the monkey, primary cortices connect only to their association cortices with intermodality connections mediated by the limbic cortex. In humans, the majority of intermodality connections are mediated by higher order association cortex in the parietal lobe (from Catani et al., 2005). Reproduced with permission of Oxford University Press.

ffytche (2005), language comprehension is possible through the activation of the acoustic image of a word, which, in turn, activates a set of sensory and motor images that, as a whole, form the specific conceptual representations of the word. Spontaneous speech production stems from the activation of a conceptual representation, which, in turn initiates parallel activation of the motor and sensory images associated with the concept.

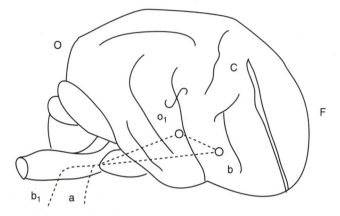

Figure 3.3 Wernicke's (1874) model of language processing: *a*, the central termination of the acoustic nerve; *b*, location of the representation of movements in the cerebral cortex that are necessary for the production of sound, connected to *a* by association fibres *ab* (note that, inexplicably, Wernicke drew his model on the right hemisphere!).

According to Wernicke, the parallel activation of sensory images during word production facilitates and simultaneously binds selection of the motor image corresponding to the concept. The route followed is therefore: concept→ sensory image→ motor image (for recent experimental support see Hickok & Pöppel, 2004).

In addition, according to Geschwind, the naming process comes about through a series of stable cortico–cortical associations between different sensory modalities. In the human species there is an area of the cerebral cortex (the angular gyrus) located at the intersection of the temporal, parietal and occipital lobes, where the fibres from the various association areas converge, thus allowing a swift connection between sensory images (visual, tactile, auditory, etc.) and the corresponding acoustic image (in contemporary terminology, the phonological representation).

Finally, written language production and comprehension come about through an intermediate pathway between the visual–graphic centres (for reading) situated in the occipital lobe and the graphic motor (frontal lobe), auditory–verbal and verbal–motor centres, so that processing of graphemes (e.g. letters (*f*) or combinations of letters (*ph*) corresponding to a single phoneme /*ff*/) is possible through a process of grapheme–phoneme transcoding.

In England, J. H. Jackson (1878) and in France, Pierre Marie (1906) proposed a different approach to that of the 'diagram makers', a term used by Head (1926) to define the followers of Wernicke and the Lichtheim approach. An initial criticism of the classic model concerned its inadequacy to understand the nature of some aphasic symptoms, such as syntactic disturbances (Jackson) and the lack of anatomical precision regarding the areas involved in the production of language (Marie). Jackson's interest, rather than focusing on the search for specific centres for the various language functions, started from the interpretation of a phenomenon

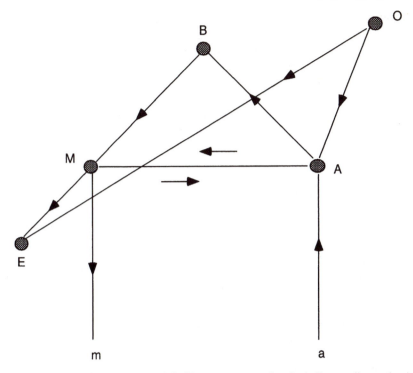

Figure 3.4 Lichtheim's (1885) model of language processing, including reading and writing: the afferent component '*a*' transmits acoustic impressions to the auditory
image centre *A*, connected to the motor image centre *B*; the motor images are
transmitted through *m* to the organs of articulation. Reading requires a visual
centre *O*, connected to *A* in order to link existing auditory impressions to the
written symbols of words. Writing requires an executive centre *E*. Lichtheim
illustrates the theoretical authority of his diagram by suggesting that reading
aloud involves the pathway *O A M m*, and intelligent writing must connect *B*
with *E*.

that is often found in aphasia, that of automatic–voluntary dissociation. Even in
relatively severe forms of aphasia in which spontaneous production is seriously
compromised, when given a cue by the examiner the patient is often able to
produce serial speech, such as numbers, prayers and the days of the week. In the
same way, though spontaneous language is virtually non-existent, the patient is
often able to produce some stereotyped phrases (Leborgne's famous *tan tan*) or
colourful oaths. An example often cited in the literature is that of the patient who,
when asked to say 'no', replied *no, no, I cannot say no*. According to Jackson,
therefore, aphasia does not represent a loss of language *tout court*, but instead
represents an inability to use language in a voluntary, propositional manner.
Jackson explained this phenomenon in evolutionary terms, postulating that during
phylogenetic and ontogenetic development there is a shift from automatic to
voluntary behaviour and the extent of the shift is proportional to the level of

development of the cerebral hemispheres. A cerebral lesion brings about lower level functioning with loss of the voluntary and declarative aspects of language and the consequential emergence of automatic stereotyped speech.

In 1906 Marie published an article with a provocative title, 'Révision de la question de l'aphasie: la troisième circonvolution frontale gauche ne joue aucun rôle spécial dans la fonction du langage'. According to Marie, there is only one type of aphasia, Wernicke's aphasia, whose central feature is a non-language specific comprehension impairment, which represents the most obvious aspect of a greater cognitive deficit, the loss of ability to associate meaning to a signifier (cultural or, in modern terms, semantic memory). Therefore, according to Marie, there is no specific language area, nor is language an autonomous function, but part of a specialized form of culturally learned intelligence. Production difficulties observed in Broca's aphasia are not the expression of damaged language (loss of the motor images of words), but rather the consequence of a mechanical disorder of the articulation of speech (anarthria).

The contrasts between the localizationalists (Wernicke, Lichtheim, Dejérine, Geschwind) and scientists of the holistic school (Marie, Head, Goldstein and Bay) continued for years, particularly in the medical environment, which was more concerned with ideas regarding localization than with research into the 'nature' of the language disturbance following cerebral lesion.

In Russia, Luria (1966) proposed a different approach to the interpretation of aphasic disorders. In his view a cognitive function, however complex, is not represented in a single cerebral 'site', but is, instead, the expression of a complex system, involving different cerebral areas acting in synchrony to process specific aspects of information. According to Luria, the anterior part of the cerebral cortex controls and programmes motor behaviour, the posterior area controls and programmes receptive aspects, while the limbic system regulates attention and vigilance. A lesion in any one of the three systems will cause language disturbance, with the characteristics of the disturbance differing according to the subsystem affected. Therefore, according to Luria, in order to understand the relationship between the nervous system and language, before searching for anatomo-functional correlations, a theory of language should be drawn up, specifying both the deep components of language and components of language use. This theory would allow a hypothesis to be made regarding the effects on language of damage to one of these systems. A disturbance of articulation can arise following lesions to different parts of the cerebral cortex, although clinical characteristics will differ according to the functional system affected. Some articulatory deficits will be characterized by difficulty in pronouncing single speech sounds (kinesthetic motor aphasia) or by inability to organize the sequence of movements that allow rapid transition from one articulatory position to another (kinetic motor aphasia).

Roman Jakobson (1964), one of the first linguists to be deeply interested in acquired language impairments, suggested that aphasic syndromes arise when two specific processes underlying the elaboration of language are put out of use, namely, the process of selection and the process of combination. Selection allows the choice of a specific linguistic unit (phoneme or lexeme) from all those belonging to the same linguistic set. On the other side, combination allows the chosen unit (phoneme, word) to be combined with other units of the same level. According to Jakobson, different aphasic syndromes, in particular Broca's and Wernicke's aphasias, arise when these two specific processes are put out of use. In Broca's aphasia there is the effect of a deficit of contiguity, while in Wernicke's aphasia there is an underlying selection deficit, with the patient no longer being able to choose between semantically similar words. This deficit leads to the production of semantic paraphasias (words belonging to the same or superordinate category, for example *dog* or *animal* for *cat*) and passepartout words (for example, *thing*, instead of *pen*).

A new anatomy of language? The contribution of neuroimaging

In the years following the pioneering observations of the French and German neurologists, it became more and more evident that the anatomo-clinical method based on post-mortem studies showed severe limitations, the greatest of which was the impossibility to correlate the anatomical lesion to the language deficit 'in real time'. As will be discussed later, aphasia is not a constant deficit, but often decreases in severity post-onset and may evolve qualitatively because of spontaneous recovery and/or speech therapy, while the anatomical lesion does not change over time. The weight of various factors, such as age (aphasia usually affects older people), gender and educational level had not been sufficiently considered in the construction of models based on an anatomo-clinical approach. Last but not least, the study of the effects of a particular lesion was often centred on the areas deemed to be necessary for language processing but did not take into account the fact that language is part of a complex neuronal and functional circuit.

From a theoretical perspective, moreover, a neurological model of language based solely on the existence of three processes (comprehension, production and conceptualization) did not take into account the weight of its components, such as syntax, phonology and semantics within these processes.

The last thirty years, therefore, have witnessed the development of a new 'anatomy of language' involving more sophisticated models resulting from the introduction of bioimaging instruments into both clinical practice and research.

Bioimaging methods

Methods of morphological investigation

In recent times computers have been employed to process information obtained using highly sophisticated radiological tools that allow the site of a cerebral lesion to be diagnosed *in vivo* and with surprising accuracy.

Computerized axial tomography (CAT) was developed in 1973 and immediately introduced into clinical practice. Today it is still the commonest and fastest way to identify the presence of a cerebral lesion. The image is obtained when an X-ray beam is transmitted through a thin section of the brain. The grade of attenuation of the X-ray beam varies according to tissue type (attenuation is low when the X-ray beam passes through cerebrospinal fluid, considerably higher when it passes through bone tissue and intermediate when it passes through nervous tissue) and can be measured by external detectors. The data obtained from this procedure are integrated and a computer image generated. When the data obtained are compared with the pattern of normal subjects congenital malformations and acquired lesions can be identified. In most cases not only the site but also the nature of the lesion can be identified (e.g. vascular, neoplastic).

Magnetic resonance imaging (MRI) is a more recent innovation. It provides a more precise image of nervous structures than the CAT scan and does not require the use of X-rays. The examination is performed by placing the subject within a powerful magnetic field. In this condition endogenous atomic nuclei of the cerebral tissue and cerebrospinal fluid align with the longitudinal orientation of the magnetic field. The application of radio waves of definite length modifies the axis of alignment of the atoms, shifting them from a longitudinal to a transverse plane. When the radio impulse stops, the atoms return to their original alignment and the energy absorbed and subsequently released produces an identifiable magnetic signal. By repeating the radio impulse and measuring the signals emitted after the application of each impulse, a matrix of data is formed which then undergoes computer analysis providing an image of the cerebral structures. In comparison with CAT, MRI provides superior resolution and allows images to be obtained in any plane desired, whether orthogonal or oblique (Figure 3.5).

Methods of functional investigation (PET, fMRI)

In parallel with the development of tools of morphological investigation, various techniques of functional investigation have been produced. These techniques allow, with surprising precision, spatial identification of specific cerebral regional activity occurring during the execution of particular cognitive tasks performed by both patients and normal participants. Two such techniques are Positron Emission Tomography (PET) and functional magnetic resonance imaging (fMRI). The guiding principles of functional neuroimaging investigations are the functional segregation and integration of brain organization. The first principle refers to modular deployment of functional specialization within cerebral regions (see later in this chapter). Furthermore, following the path of the *box and arrows* models of language processing of Wernicke–Lipmann (Catani & ffytche, 2005), the different brain areas may be characterized in terms of anatomical and functional connectivity.

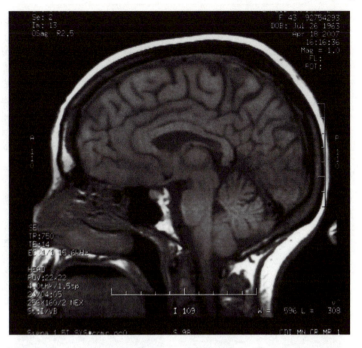

Figure 3.5 MR image of the brain (sagittal section, median view) showing white and grey matter, corpus callosum, lateral ventricle, thalamus, pons and cerebellum. © Mark Herreid, iStockphoto.

The logic of functional neuroimaging

Both PET and fMRI studies are based on the assumption of serial processing of information, so that the addition or subtraction of a component on presentation of a multiple component task does not interfere with the functioning of other operations involved in the task. The basic model (using subtraction) adopts the following logic: during the execution of a cognitive task involving a specific procedure (x), measurement of metabolic activity (PET) or blood flow (fMRI) is carried out in specific cerebral areas. The data obtained during the execution of task x are subtracted from data obtained in a baseline condition (usually at rest), or when the subject is engaged in a task that shares all operations with the experimental procedure, except that which is presumed to be carried out by procedure x. It is therefore possible, albeit with some limitations, to identify the regional cerebral activity occurring during performance of various cognitive tasks, such as reading concrete and abstract nouns and verbs for lexical decision (Perani et al., 1999; Figure 3.6).

In an experiment that is still today considered a milestone, Petersen, Fox, Posner, and Raichle (1988) performed a PET study aimed at identifying which parts of the cerebral cortex are activated during the different stages of word processing presented through the auditory and visual modality. The experiment

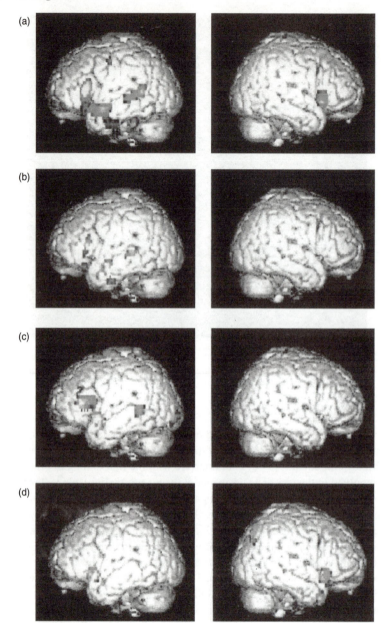

Figure 3.6 PET images of the lateral surface of the left hemisphere in lexical decision
tasks, showing commonalities and differences between the different word
classes. (A) The areas activated when all lexical conditions pooled together are
compared with the letter string baseline. Within these areas, the commonalities
(i.e. regions equally activated by all stimuli, irrespective of word class or concreteness) (B), the regions specifically associated with the processing of verbs
(C) or abstract words (D) are shown (from Perani et al., 1999). Reproduced
with permission of Oxford University Press.

consisted of a series of hierarchically organized steps, each of which was matched to the step preceding it, with the functional maps obtained being subtracted at each stage. The baseline condition, which was shared by both modalities of stimulus presentation, involved the participant being asked to stare at a light point in the centre of a screen. This condition was followed by a phase of presentation of verbal stimuli (nouns) either visually or through headphones (phase of sensory processing). The next phase consisted of the reading aloud or repetition of the same words in order to investigate phonological coding and articulatory programming. The final phase, semantic processing, involved the participants being asked to produce a verb semantically linked to the presented words. The results obtained in the first two conditions, subtracted from the metabolic pattern seen in the baseline condition, were fairly predictable and in line with data obtained through clinical methods: bilateral activation, though more pronounced on the left, of the posterior temporal cortex and of the cingulate gyrus[3] for stimuli presented through the auditory channel, and activation of the medial occipital areas for visually presented stimuli. Bilateral activation of the frontal opercular areas (precentral gyrus, Broca's area, supplementary motor area) and insula was evident in production tasks (reading aloud and repetition). The results of the last subtraction, which required a semantic elaboration of the stimuli, were, on the other hand, quite unexpected and differed from clinical findings: there was activation of an area of the left hemisphere anterior to Broca's area and of a small area of the anterior cingulate gyrus. The activation of these areas was interpreted as being a result of the 'intentionality' of the task, rather than a specific effect of the semantic elaboration of the stimuli.

It must, however, be mentioned that the latency between the presentation of the stimuli and the hemodynamic response corresponding to the expected brain activation is in the order of a few seconds, representing the limit of temporal resolution of this technique, which remains far removed from the time window of other neurophysiological techniques such as EEG or ERP (see later in this chapter).

Intracranial registration and stimulation

The electrical stimulation of areas of the cerebral cortex during surgery performed on awake patients has been used for clinical purposes in order to localize the cerebral areas involved in language functions so as to avoid their ablation during surgical removal of epileptic foci (Penfield & Jasper, 1954). The application of an electrical current to specific parts of the cortex can, in fact, elicit vocalization or cause a complete arrest of ongoing speech (Penfield & Roberts, 1959) and can also interfere significantly with some linguistic processes (Ojemann, 1983).

A significant development was attained in recent years with the use of a grid of electrodes implanted on the outermost covering membrane of the cerebral cortex (dura mater), which can be used to interfere with specific cognitive tasks with extreme spatial precision.

It should be pointed out, however, that most of the patients undergoing these studies had suffered from epilepsy for many years and their cerebral organization may, therefore, have differed from that of healthy subjects.

Transcranial magnetic stimulation (TMS)

Over the last 20 years a non-invasive technique of brain interference, Transcranial Magnetic Stimulation (TMS, Barker, Jalinous, & Freeston, 1985) has been introduced. This technique, used in healthy subjects, consists of the application of a strong magnetic field to an area of the skull lying above specific cerebral areas, leading to temporary inactivation ('virtual lesions') or, on the contrary, enhancement, of the underlying cerebral activity. If the participant undergoing TMS, shows a change in performance of a cognitive task in comparison with the baseline condition, it can be inferred that the activity of the stimulated region is critical in performing the task. The technique has a spatial resolution of about 1 cm and therefore permits observation of the function of small cerebral areas before cortical reorganization takes place (the length of the stimulation does not exceed 200 ms).

The first applications of this technique (Pascual-Leone, Gates, & Dhuna, 1991) demonstrated a specific effect on articulatory ability following stimulation of Broca's area ('I could move my mouth and I knew what I should say, but the words didn't come out'. Pascual-Leone et al., 1991, p. 699).

The temporary application of a magnetic field can also modify the level of cerebral excitability during the execution of cognitive tasks. Sakai, Noguchi, Takeuchi, and Watanabe (2002) showed that magnetic stimulation of Broca's area improves the ability to identify syntactic anomalies in sentences presented through the auditory modality. This effect was specific to syntax, in that there was no improvement seen in tasks involving detection of semantic anomalies.

Cappa, Sandrini, Rossini, Sosta, and Miniussi (2002) found that TMS applied to Broca's area facilitated recall of verbs but not nouns. Similarly Buccino et al. (2005) were able to demonstrate that when subjects listened to phrases describing actions (*washing windows*) different cerebral areas were activated compared with those activated when the subjects listened to abstract phrases (*he loved his fatherland*).

In conclusion, this technique promises to improve knowledge of the anatomical bases of language and the functional relationships between areas involved in different language tasks, especially when used in combination with other neuro-imaging techniques (for a review see Devlin & Watkins, 2007).

Electroencephalography (EEG) and event-related
potentials (ERPs)

Electroencephalography (EEG) is the recording of electrical activity produced by the firing of neurons within the brain, as recorded from multiple electrodes placed on the scalp. In neurology, the main diagnostic application of EEG is in the case of epilepsy, as epileptic activity can produce an abnormal electrical pattern on a standard EEG study. The EEG is typically described in terms of rhythmic and transient activities. The rhythmic activity is divided into bands by frequency (α, β, δ) that can vary according to the participant's state (rest, sustained attention, sleep), the locus of registration and the presence of brain damage. Its temporal resolution is very high (on the level of a single millisecond) but spatial resolution is poor. Still in use in clinical practice (detection of epileptic focuses) its importance in cognitive research has been severely reduced by the adoption of neuroimaging techniques.

Derivatives of the EEG technique include the recording of event-related potentials (ERPs). This is a non-invasive and inexpensive technique visualizing the changes in electrical cerebral activity compared with the resting state during the performance of cognitive tasks, such as the presentation of a word. A number of surface electrodes are painlessly applied to the participant's scalp. The synchronization of the electrical signals underlying the electrodes is recorded in different parts of the cortex during the processing of simple or complex stimuli. Despite poor spatial resolution, ERP recordings have shown to be the best tool for detecting *on line* the different neurological and functional stages of language comprehension.

The graphic representation of ERPs is a continuous wave, developing over time. Peaks of positive or negative deflection can be identified, when compared with the baseline activity. Early and late components are related to different stages of stimulus processing. The late component N400 is of particular interest as it is observed following the presentation of linguistic and other meaningful stimuli. It is characterized by a negative deflexion distributed bilaterally over the central-parietal areas and appears about 400 ms after stimulus presentation (for a review see Kutas & Federmeier, 2000). The N400 component is often associated with semantic processing and implicit (unconscious) language analysis, such as the processing of stimuli presented in their second language to bilingual subjects (Thierry & Wu, 2007).

The amplitude of N400 is generally proportional to the difficulty of the semantic integration of a stimulus. For example, in a context that predicts the word 'glass', as in the sentence 'I drink water from a ...', the presentation of the word 'plate' brings about an N400 deflexion of greater width than that produced by the word 'glass', but of less width than that produced by the word 'bicycle'.

Magnetoencephalography (MEG)

This technique measures the magnetic fields generated by the neuronal activity of the brain. The magnetic field passes unaffected through brain tissue and the skull, so it can be externally recorded. MEG has a very high temporal resolution: events with time scales in the order of milliseconds can be recorded, with an obvious advantage over fMRI and PET, which have much longer time scales.

The spatial distributions of the magnetic fields can be analysed to localize the sources of the activity within the brain, and the locations of the sources are superimposed on anatomical images, such as MRI, to provide information about the temporal and spatial time course of information processing. For example, in a seminal study, Salmelin, Hari, Lounasmaa, and Sams (1994) showed that, during a picture naming task, the conversion from visual to symbolic representation progressed bilaterally from the occipital visual cortex towards temporal and frontal lobes.

Multimodal fusion

As outlined above, no functional or anatomical brain investigation method is faultless: while PET and fMRI allow precise spatial correlation between the regions of activity of the normal brain engaged in cognitive tasks, they are, as said before, poor in temporal correlation. On the other hand, EEG and MEG studies do not offer satisfactory spatial correlation.

As a consequence, some 'fusion' methods of brain investigation are being developed with the aim of complementing the spatial resolution of fMR (*where it is*) with the temporal precision of EEG and MEG (*when it is*). However, despite the progress of technology, reliable results from multimodal integration techniques are not available at the present time: perhaps 'because there are many questions about functional anatomy that do not need bilateral spatial and temporal precision' (Friston, 2009).

Forgetting Wernicke? New neurological models of language

Modern investigation of lesions through brain imaging has allowed the internal organization of classic language areas (Wernicke's and Broca's) and their integration with the other subcortical and cortical areas to form a large neural network, to be drawn up and, in part, validated. It has also provided experimental support for new neurological models of language abilities.

For example, a more complex picture of the role played by Broca's area in the language domain has been provided: several clinical studies have demonstrated that Broca's aphasics, in addition to their deficits in production are also impaired in speech comprehension, mostly when submitted to syntactic comprehension tasks (see Chapter 7).

Schäffler and colleagues (1993, 1996) showed that electrical stimulation of Broca's area in non-aphasic neurosurgical patients may elicit deficits in the comprehension of complex verbal commands. Sahin, Pinker, Cash, Schomer, and Halgren (2009) recorded local field potentials from populations of neurons using electrodes implanted in Broca's area in neurosurgical patients engaged in language production tasks (silent reading or silent production of the inflected forms of nouns and verbs in accordance with a syntactic requirement). Similarly, a pattern of distinct neuronal activity in Broca's area was found for lexical, phonological and grammatical activity, suggesting that this region is involved in unification operations at word and sentence level (Hagoort & Levelt, 2009).

Language-related studies aside, several recent works have found activation of Broca's area in other cognitive domains (for a review, see Fadiga, Craighero, & Roy, 2006), such as the observation, execution and imitation of actions (for a review see Fazio et al., 2009). These data have been considered to provide empirical support for the existence of a mirror-like system in humans, mapping execution and observation of actions onto the same neural substrate (see later in this chapter).

On the other hand, the site of the 'sensory speech centre' (Wernicke, 1874) is, at present, far from being firmly established. A number of recent studies (for a review see Petkov, Logothetis, & Obleser, 2009) have shown that a number of cortical areas outside the classical language centre, such as the posterior stretches of the superior and middle temporal lobes, are involved in a variety of speech- and language-related processes. Wernicke's area may comprise the unimodal auditory association cortex located in the left superior temporal anterior gyrus up to the primary auditory cortex in Heschl's gyrus (HG), processing the acoustic–phonetic features of speech (Démonet et al., 1992). Additionally, it may extend to the heteromodal cortex, involving three architectonic zones in the left temporal and parietal lobes, where the output from both heard and written word form systems converges (Mesulam, 1998). According to Wise et al. (2001), the posterior superior temporal cortex has a role in processing the mimicry of sounds, including repetition, with a specific role of the posterior left superior temporal sulcus in the transient representation of phonetic sequences.

In a recent fMRI study by Gitelman, Nobre, Sonty, Parrish, and Mesulam (2005), a group of normal participants performed a word processing task involving two presentation conditions (auditory and written) and three different types of analysis (semantic, phonological and orthographic). The first task required the participant to decide whether the words were synonyms (*biro–pen*); in the second task the participant had to decide whether the words rhymed (*cap–tap*). The third condition involved judging whether both words contained the same letters (*post–stop*). A common pattern of activation was revealed for all the tasks and included the ventrolateral area, the supplementary motor area, the occipito-temporal parietal area of the left hemisphere, the insula and the right lobe of the cerebellum.

The semantic task, on the other hand, activated the anterior part of the left frontal lobe and the lateral area of the temporal cortex, while frontal posterior activation was evident during phonological analysis tasks. Finally, the left parietal lobe was found to be active in orthographic analysis.

The authors therefore proposed the existence of a common neural network underlying the different lexical tasks, while single areas process specific aspects of information. The resulting model of language foresees both integration and segregation of specific neural aggregates.

The declarative-procedural model underlying memory processing developed Schacter and Tulving (1994)[4] has been applied to language by Ullman (2001). It is based on two types of competence, the mental lexicon and a computational device, the 'mental grammar'.

The mental lexicon is mostly made up of a set of information composed of sound–meaning pairs (lexical forms). Other specific verbal information such as the knowledge that certain verbs require a particular argument or have irregular inflections is also contained within the mental lexicon. Learning and recall of lexical forms is a conscious, context-dependent, process and shares learning mechanisms with other non-verbal mechanisms based on the same basic principles.

In addition language consists of the learning and use of specific rules applied to components of the language system, including syntax, morphology and phonology (for example prosodic phonology or phonotaxis, which defines the rules regarding phoneme combination). The learning and use of such rules is implicit, beyond voluntary control, obeys the same rules governing procedural memory and is based on the same neurological system. On this basis, according to Ullman, it is not unreasonable to suppose the existence of dedicated subsystems, processing grammar, with a further distinction between morphology and syntax, and supported by neuronal circuits located between the basal ganglia and the frontal lobes: the declarative memory system underlies the mental lexicon, while grammar is supported by a rule-governed procedural system.

Language, therefore, in its declarative and procedural components, is part of a larger memory system that contains specific neuronal and functional subsystems that are dedicated to linguistic functions and obey the same general principles as memory.[5]

Ullman puts forward various examples drawn from neurological pathology to support his model: morphological and syntactic disturbances follow, in most cases, lesions to the anterior part of the left hemisphere including Broca's area, while lexical deficit is observed following temporal lobe lesions. During the performance of semantic and lexical processing tasks, functional neuroimaging techniques have shown activation of the temporal areas (Damasio et al., 1996), while activation of anterior areas has been shown during the execution of experimental syntactic tasks (Moro et al., 2001). These data have been confirmed in a recent fMR study carried out by Friederici, Rüschmeyer, Hahne, and Fiebach (2003), which required detection of syntactic or semantic violation in auditorily presented sentences. Activation of the superior temporal region was noted during tasks requiring detection of semantic anomalies, while anterior areas were activated during 'syntactic' tasks, including Broca's area and the left basal ganglia.

From the clinical and neuroimaging studies so far reviewed, the existence of a modular organization of language clearly emerges at both an anatomical and a functional level.

A different approach, however, has been proposed in other psycholinguistic models. Liberman and colleagues (1967, 2000) postulated a link between motor representation and perception of language. The motor theory of language perception claims that speech perception occurs through a link between the perceived phonemes and their motor representation. Since speaking implies simultaneous motor and sensory activity for sound production, a synchronous pattern of activity is formed in both motor and auditory systems with the construction of specific articulatory–auditory circuits. Experimental confirmation of this theory was recently provided by Pulvermüller et al. (2006) who, in an fMR study performed on normal participants, demonstrated simultaneous activation at the level of the auditory areas of the temporal lobe and the precentral motor areas during a listening task involving the bilabial plosive /p/ and the alveolar plosive /t/. There was further specification according to whether there was lip movement for /p/ or tongue movement for /t/.

The role of the basal ganglia and cerebellum in language processing

Before new methods of morphological and functional neuroimaging were introduced, it was commonly thought that the basal ganglia and cerebellum were essential to processes of control and motor planning, with no significant role in cognitive functions. This view was however recently challenged by a number of clinical and experimental observations, suggesting that these structures may play an active role in language and memory tasks.

In a PET study of normal subjects, Paulesu, Frith, and Frackowiak (1993) demonstrated that the cerebellum is part of a cortical–subcortical network active during short-term memory and verbal memory tasks (phonological output buffer). On the clinical side, Silveri and colleagues (1994, 1998) reported two patients affected by cerebellar ischemic damage, who exhibited a specific (if transitory) deficit of short-term verbal memory which, in the second case, was accompanied by a modest receptive agrammatism (i.e. difficulty in understanding syntactically complex phrases, see Chapter 7). According to Silveri the syntactic deficit could be seen as part of the disturbance of short-term verbal memory giving rise to a deficit in storing phonological/morphological components before syntactic implementation of the sentence.

A similar role has been hypothesized for the basal ganglia (Booth, Wood, Lu, Houk, & Bitan, 2007; see Chapter 4 for examples of language disturbance following basal ganglion lesions).

Cognitive neuropsychology

The major contribution to neurolinguistics provided by the application of anatomo-clinical methods and by neuroimaging techniques has certainly been to allow the areas dedicated to the processing of the various linguistic operations to be defined with increasing precision.

Some authors, however (Coltheart, 2006, but for a different viewpoint see Umiltà, 2006 and Vallar, 2006) claim that the contribution of these techniques to the construction of a 'functional architecture' of the mind and the validation of psychological theories underlying cognitive function is limited or even non-existent. They have, therefore, focused their interest on the 'functional' nature of the language deficit, both developmental and acquired, neglecting the underlying anatomical substrate and interpreting neuropsychological data in the light of sophisticated theoretical models of language processing.

The aphasic patient is considered an 'experiment of nature', in that the cerebral lesion can cause specific components of a single linguistic function to be put out of use. The study of the resulting deficit thus allows a theoretical model of language to be validated, modified or rejected, independently of its physical location. For the dedicated supporters of these theories, the discovery that language is localized in our big toe rather than the left hemisphere would therefore be of no importance at a theoretical level! For them, the vital issue is not *where* the deficit originates, but lies in the search for the nature and representation of the mental processes underlying language through examination of the aphasic deficit.

Cognitive neuropsychology adopts the principles and methods of cognitive psychology. This, in turn, bases itself on the concept of the brain as a machine that, like a computer, processes information serially according to specific programmes that are pre-established and independent of external influences.

Cognitive neuropsychology is based on two principles: 'modularity' and 'transparency'.

According to the principle of modularity, every cognitive function, including language, is made up of a series of subcomponents or 'modules' (Fodor, 1983), which are small, specialized and virtually independent of each other (Marr, 1982), and of central processes that handle complex cognitive operations, such as memory and reasoning. There is no modular organization for these systems but they possess a diffuse neural support and are therefore, according to Fodor, not suited to a scientific approach (for a critical review see Shallice, 1988).

These modules were originally conceived as innate, genetically determined mechanisms lacking individual variation (universality assumption) and acting rapidly, automatically and independently with no influence from other components of the cognitive system, such as memory (computationally autonomous and informationally encapsulated). They operate on specific representations, reacting only to one particular type of input (domain specificity) and are linked to dedicated neural structures. Their task is to codify and recognize perceptual input (Fodor, 1983). Examples of these modules are those for phonological analysis and colour perception.

At variance with Fodor's original assumption, Moscovitch and Umiltà (1990) claim the existence of complex and in part culturally transmitted modules. These were produced during the processes of evolution and cultural development and are made up of groups of simple modules. Their task is to handle complex information, for example, facial recognition or the processing of written material (reading and writing).

In a modular approach to cognitive neuropsychological research, a further assumption must be adopted, the principle of constancy or transparency (Caramazza, 1986). The principle of constancy assumes that after a focal cerebral lesion, the underlying cognitive processes do not undergo global and random disruption of their efficiency, leading to functional reorganization of new components or new connections. It postulates that, on the contrary, the resulting cognitive deficit is the expression of a cognitive system that is substantially intact, but deprived of some specific components that have been partially destroyed or have become inaccessible. According to this principle, therefore, it is possible to infer the role played by the damaged component within the cognitive process being examined, and to gain insight into the nature and functioning of the undamaged processes. In normal participants, these processes are not 'transparent' in that they are part of a complex system which is difficult to penetrate: only a cerebral lesion 'opens a window', allowing the scientist to know how cognitive processes are organized.

Experimental investigation of cognitive deficits requires, therefore, first, the construction of a theoretical model assumed to be at the base of the functions under investigation, and second, the drawing up and administration of a series of tests based on this theoretical model. Finally, the patient's responses are analysed in qualitative and quantitative terms and compared with the responses of a control group matched for age and educational level. It is thus possible to define and analyse the nature of the computational processes to which the information is submitted, independently of neurological implementation (Jackendoff, 1987).

The first, and in many ways most important, contribution to the development of the cognitive neuropsychology of language, dates back to 1973 when two English neuropsychologists, John Marshall and Frida Newcombe, published a work entitled 'Patterns of paralexia'. In this study they described three types of acquired dyslexia (reading difficulty following cerebral damage): visual dyslexia, surface dyslexia and deep dyslexia. The critical feature of this work lies, on one hand, in the description of a multicomponential model of reading and, on the other, in the interpretation of the three types of dyslexia as being caused by a specific deficit within the model. The model contains a mechanism for the identification of single letters, and once identification has taken place, the information passes via a lexical–semantic route for the processing of known words, or via a sublexical route, which activates during tasks involving the reading of unfamiliar words or non-words to break up the string of graphemes and transform them into their corresponding phonemes (Chapter 8).

Marshall and Newcombe's paper was soon followed by the description of a series of neuropsychological deficits to be defined and interpreted in the light of the principles of cognitive neuropsychology: writing (Beauvois & Dérouesné, 1981), calculation (McCloskey, Caramazza, & Basili, 1985) and face recognition disorders (Bruce & Young, 1986).

Cognitive models of language processing

According to most cognitive models of single word processing, the first step consists of activation of mechanisms specific to word recognition, one for heard words (phonological input lexicon) and another for written words (orthographic input lexicon) (Figure 3.7).

For written words, input to these mechanisms derives from an abstract system of letter identification (Polk & Farah, 1997), described in detail in Chapter 8, while auditory identification of words comes about *on line*, moment by moment, as the specific information regarding the single words reaches the system (Tyler, 1985). Once the word has been recognized in its orthographical or phonological form, the information is transferred to a common semantic system dedicated to the comprehension of both heard and written words as well as meaningful non-verbal information (such a meaningful non-verbal sounds or objects and drawings).[6]

From the semantic system (for details see Chapter 6), the information is transmitted to two independent output systems, a phonological output system and an orthographic output system, where phonological and orthographic forms are stored in order to activate the specific representation corresponding to the semantic information. The selected orthographic or phonological form is then transferred to

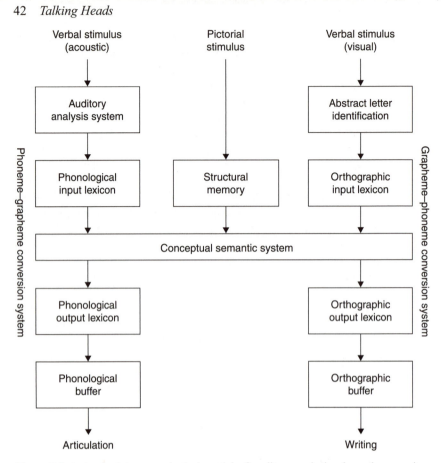

Figure 3.7 A standard two-way lexical model of auditory and visual word processing, including lexical and sublexical mechanisms (from Denes & Pizzamiglio, 1999). Copyright © 1999, Psychology Press, reproduced with permission of Taylor & Francis.

a temporary store (phonological and orthographic buffer), where it is held for as long as necessary before oral or written production. The independence of the phonological and orthographic lexicons is demonstrated by the fact that it is not always possible to obtain the correct orthographic form through a process of phoneme–grapheme transcoding, particularly in languages such as English or French whose orthography is not transparent (see Chapter 8).

The lexical–semantic route can, obviously, only be used for words that are auditorily or graphically familiar. Unfamiliar words or non-words must be processed sublexically. In the visual modality (non-word reading) the phonemes that form the string must be recognized and broken down, transcoded into their corresponding phonemes and finally reassembled in the phonological buffer. Interruptions to this route cause a specific deficit in the reading of non-words with preserved ability to read real words (phonological dyslexia, see Chapter 8).

Similarly, a non-word repetition task requires activation of an acoustic to phonological conversion mechanism. This mechanism differentiates and identifies the phonemes making up the string and subsequently translates and stores them at the level of the phonological buffer for the time needed to process the articulatory programme. The existence of this route has been documented by means of assessing patients who displayed a severe and specific deficit in non-word repetition tasks (McCarthy & Warrington, 1984; Beauvois, Dérouesné, & Bastard, 1980). This pattern could not be attributed to a deficit in auditory discrimination or auditory short-term memory given the absence of phonological errors in word repetition.

Finally, since some patients have been described who are able to read both regular and irregular words (irregular words cannot be read through the sublexical route) but are unable to understand their meaning, a third lexical, non-semantic route has been proposed. This route connects the visual input and phonological output systems, bypassing semantic processing.

It should be noted that the same criticisms have been put forward regarding the modular approach to the study of the mind:

1   It is not possible to understand the nature and representation of 'higher' processes such as planning or reasoning given that, by definition, they are non-modular.
2   In order for the data obtained from clinical analysis to have theoretical value, it must be assumed that the participant's performance reflects the functioning of a normal system without a damaged subsystem and which has not yet undergone functional reorganization. However, after damage to a specific component, patients can develop alternative strategies, which are not used by normal subjects. Also in this case, the transparency principle remains valid, provided that such strategies are part of the behavioural repertoire available to normal participants and based on the work of components that are part of the system spared by the cerebral lesion (Caramazza, 1988).
3   From a clinical point of view, it must be remembered that a cerebral lesion rarely affects a single system or a single component of this system but often the extensive anatomical damage means that several functional components are affected. Despite this caveat, cognitive neuropsychology has been found to be the best, or perhaps the only, possible method of investigating the structure of cognitive processes (Rosenthal, 1988).

Connectionist modelling of language processing

Cognitive methods of language processing are based on the computer analogy, which involves serial treatment of information with the presence of temporary stores or buffers, and specific information underlying the physical computations is not taken into account.

In the last twenty years or so the 'computer metaphor' of mental architecture has been substituted with models compatible with the principles of cerebral activity ('brain metaphor').

The use of a modular approach also allows the development of computational models of the various language functions that are far more detailed than models based on clinical practice. The models can also be implemented with specific stimuli and experimentally 'damaged' in order to reproduce specific cognitive deficits (see Coltheart, Curtis, Atkins, & Haller, 1993; Zorzi, 2006).

Language and hemispheric specialization

Unlike other species, even those phylogenetically close to humans such as monkeys, humans display a clear pattern of cerebral functional asymmetry, the most patent example being handedness, which occurs irrespectively of gender, education and social milieu. About 90% of individuals prefer to use their right hand for fine manual activity, with the remaining 10% being left handed. Monkeys and every other animal species show random hand preference, although monkeys raised in captivity show a slight right-handed preference, which is only evident in pointing and not in other tasks. Right-handed manual preference is genetic in origin in most cases (Annett, 1982, 2001).[7] It is controlled by the left hemisphere, which has, since Broca's time, been recognized as the neurological basis of language. For this reason, as far as cerebral dominance is concerned, the left hemisphere has been labelled the 'dominant' hemisphere and the right hemisphere has been given a secondary role. It is only since the birth of neuropsychology that the right hemisphere has been shown to have a critical role in the processing of both verbal and non-verbal information (see Denes & Pizzamiglio, 1999).

Until 30 years ago, it was common belief that left-handed individuals had right hemisphere dominance not only for handedness but also for language, showing a mirror-like cerebral pattern of lateralization, in comparison with right-handed people. Studies of left-handed aphasic patients, however (Basso & Scarpa, 1990) and of normal left-handed participants have shown that, in the majority of cases, the left hemisphere is dominant for language (Annett, 1985). Results from normal participants using experimental techniques such as *dichotic listening* (simultaneous presentation of different verbal or non-verbal stimuli to both ears) and *tachistoscopic presentation* of visual stimuli to a visual hemifield have confirmed data obtained from brain damaged patients suggesting that left hemisphere specialization for language dates from the first months of life. It cannot, however, be excluded that there is a gradual segregation of language functions. A left hemisphere lesion, even of considerable size, occurring in childhood may delay language development, but does not cause major language deficit, unlike adult onset of aphasia (Bates & Roe, 2001).

This discovery of hemispheric specialization in humans regarding manual preference and language has prompted a series of studies aimed at researching the nature of this association. One theory states that the association is a result of a single genetic mutation (for a review see Corballis, 1997), but this assumption is contradicted by the fact that asymmetry for vocalization occurs further down the phylogenetic scale than hemispherical asymmetry for hand preference. Left-sided dominance for vocalization has been found in many animal species, ranging from frogs to birds. Experiments performed on some species of adult canary demonstrate that sectioning of the left hypoglossal nerve, which controls movements involved in the production of song, renders the bird unable to sing. However the role of vocalization in non-human species remains doubtful in that the sounds produced appear to express emotion, similar to crying or laughter, rather than having a specific communicative intent (Deacon, 1997). What is more, neurophysiological data show that non-human primates have no cortical control over vocalization. In experimental conditions, vocalization in monkeys is produced by the stimulation of phylogenetically ancient areas linked to the processing of emotions, in particular the anterior cingulate cortex which appears to have the role of modulating vocalization according to the emotions experienced (Hauser, 1996).

A series of more recent studies has, on the other hand, tried to link the emergence of language in humans to the progressive transition from gesture to vocal communication. In the course of evolution there has been gradual development of a neocortical system for fine motor control (including movements of the vocal tract in humans) localized in the premotor area and including Broca's area. In primates, this area exerts no control over vocal tract movements but activation is seen, however, during manual grasping. This area also contains mirror neurons (Rizzolatti & Luppino, 2001), a particular type of nerve cell that codifies both the production and the perception of gestural movements. While this system is bilateral in monkeys, in humans it seems to be located prevalently in the left hemisphere, which therefore has been hypothesized to control both the production and the perception of vocalization and gesture (Baumgaertner, Buccino, Lange, McNamara, & Binkofski, 2007).

Left cerebral hemisphere dominance for language could, therefore, derive from the role that this hemisphere exerts on handedness. According to Kimura (1977) and Corballis (2003) all complex motor acts, both vocal and manual, requiring fine motor control for the production of precise, sequential movements of a certain duration, must be under left hemisphere control. In addition, according to McNeill (1985) there is a precise synchronization process between gestures and words, seen as part of a single integrated system, in which the vocal component conveys mostly the syntactic aspects, while gestures communicate the iconic, mimetic components.

The most obvious demonstration of the use of gesture to convey language is the use of sign language by the preverbal deaf population (see Chapter 9).

From a different point of view, left hemisphere specialization for language depends on the form or code in which the information requiring processing is presented or on the way in which it is processed. All stimuli requiring or allowing linguistic-propositional analysis are processed by the left hemisphere, while stimuli requiring analogic elaboration are handled by the right hemisphere (Berlucchi, 1982).

The discovery that certain childhood language disorders, such as developmental dyslexia (Chapter 11) and stammering, affect prevalently male children has led to the investigation of possible gender-related differences in cerebral organization (McGlone, 1978).

Studies of normal participants through lateralized presentation of stimuli, or more recently, using PET (Pugh et al., 1996; Shaywitz et al., 1995), have suggested a higher level of left-sided language lateralization in males compared with women. On the other hand, no certain data have emerged from clinical group studies, in which site of lesion (left or right), incidence, severity and the recovery from aphasia have been correlated for males and females.

As far as possible, anatomical asymmetries between the two cerebral hemi-spheres associated with cerebral dominance, post-mortem, CAT and MRI studies have revealed an enlarged left *planum temporale* (which includes Wernicke's area and the primary auditory area) on the left (Geschwind & Levitsky, 1968; Musiek & Reeves, 1990; Shapleske, Rossell, Woodruff, & David, 1999); in the two thirds of the brain examined.

Chiarello, Kacinik, Manowitz, Otto, and Leonard (2004) correlated the degrees of anatomical and functional asymmetry. Participants who were shown by MRI to have a more developed left *planum temporale* displayed greater functional asymmetry during a test of word recognition (in favour of the left hemisphere) than subjects who were seen to have less anatomical asymmetry. This appears to suggest that variations between individuals in hemispheric specialization may be linked to differences in neuroanatomy.

The right hemisphere and language

Once the dominant role of the left hemisphere in language had been established within the scientific community, the search for possible involvement of the right hemisphere in language was neglected for many years, with it being relegated to the role of 'support' in the event of improvement in language following a left hemisphere lesion.

While the right hemisphere does not normally have much responsibility for linguistic processes such as phonology, morphology and syntax, it plays, however, an important role in mediating a set of paralinguistic or pragmatic phenomena that accompany the words of an utterance. Attitudes, emotions and mood are communicated via the intonation contour by pitch, loudness and voice quality, and the right hemisphere seems to be better suited to process-ing these facets of paralinguistic meaning (for a review see Van Lancker Sitdis, 2008).

The role of the right hemisphere in the interpretation of figurative aspects of language such as metaphors was further investigated by Bottini et al. (1994) in normal volunteers using PET. They found that, in addition to left hemisphere activation, the comprehension of metaphors activated a number of regions in the right hemisphere, suggesting the presence of a wide network of cerebral regions simultaneously at work in processing both strictly linguistic and paralinguistic facets of language.

On the other hand, following extensive damage to the left hemisphere sustained in early childhood, language functions are likely to reorganize and develop in the right hemisphere, especially if the lesion affects the classical Broca's or Wernicke's language areas. To account for this picture it has been postulated that the right hemisphere shows a considerable degree of functional plasticity in childhood, which allows it to develop functions such as language to which it is not genetically dedicated (Varga-Khadem, O'Gorman, & Watters, 1985). Plasticity does, however, decline with age: functional neuroimaging studies carried out on right handed aphasic patients following left hemisphere lesion have not supported the hypothesis of a prominent role of the right hemisphere in the recovery process (for a review see Kinsbourne, 1998). Of greater interest are the few studies of aphasic patients whose language performance improves during the chronic stage in comparison to performance in the acute stage, but then worsens considerably following a second stroke affecting the right hemisphere (Basso, Gardelli, Grassi, & Mariotti, 1989; Cappa, Miozzo, & Frugoni, 1994).

From an experimental point of view, a notable contribution to the investigation of right hemisphere language abilities has emerged from studies performed on 'split brain' patients.

In order to better control their drug-resistant epilepsy these patients have successfully undergone sectioning of the corpus callosum, the large band of fibres connecting the two cerebral hemispheres. These patients are, therefore, unable to transfer information between the two hemispheres. The contribution made by the cerebral hemispheres to the processing of both verbal and non-verbal information can therefore be studied in isolation using specific techniques (presentation of visual, tactile and auditory stimuli) that exploit the anatomical peculiarity of the patients (the right visual hemifield projects to the left hemisphere and vice versa; stimuli presented to one ear are prevalently analysed by the opposite cerebral hemisphere). It has been observed that the right hemisphere is endowed with good semantic ability, in both auditory and visual modes, while its phonological and syntactic abilities are very limited (Zaidel, 1998).

Notes

1 At the beginning of the last century, the anatomist, Brodmann, subdivided and classified the cerebral cortex into homogeneous areas according to the appearance of its layers, beginning with 1 and continuing to add numbers each time a new configuration was discovered.

2 According to this model, the primary and association auditory areas are unimodal, that is, specific to the processing of auditory stimuli. A series of recent studies has, however, revealed that these areas can be involved in non-auditory tasks. MacSweeney et al. (2001) found activation of the auditory cortex during lip reading in normal subjects. Haist et al. (2001) revealed similar activation in a single word reading task. The role of the auditory areas in the elaboration of sign language will be explored in Chapter 10.

3 The cingulate cortex is situated on the medial surface of the cerebral hemispheres around the corpus callosum and is part of the limbic system, which is phylogenetically ancient and linked to the handling of emotions.

4 In the multicomponential model, memory is organized into two subsystems, declarative memory and procedural memory, which are, to a great extent, functionally and anatomically independent of each other. Declarative memory is active in the learning, manipulation and recall of encyclopaedic knowledge, such as word significance

(semantic memory) and in episodes with spatial-temporal connotations, often autobiographical (episodic memory). This type of memory is explicit in nature (the memories
are conscious) and is vital for forming connections between elements that are arbitrar-
ily related (for example, the association of a phonological form to a specific meaning
or a fact to a certain context). The neurological substrate is in part made up of phylogenetically ancient formations, such as the medial section of the temporal lobes, including
the hippocampus, in turn connected to the neocortical temporal and temporal-parietal
regions in the lateral part of the cerebral hemispheres. The former are active in processes of consolidation and (perhaps) recall of stored data, although a role that is independent of neocortical formations in the learning of new memories cannot be excluded.
Through procedural memory, on the other hand, it is possible to learn motor tasks and
to control their performance (for example, learning to drive a car or use a computer
keyboard). Learning and memory are largely implicit, with no process of conscious
recall. The neurological areas involved in this type of memory include the lateral portion of the frontal areas (including Broca's area) and some subcortical formations such
as the basal nuclei and cerebellum.

5   According to Ullman, explicit learning of the syntactic component of language is
found in bilinguals who learn a second language after learning their mother tongue
(Chapter 9).

6   An alternative hypothesis is that rather than a single amodal system, there are specific
semantic systems, one a verbal system for the comprehension of written and spoken
words, the other visual, for the comprehension of objects and figures (Warrington &
Shallice, 1984; Shallice, 1988 and, for a critical review, Caramazza, Hillis, Rapp, &
Romani, 1990).

7   Only recently has it been shown that lateralization seems to be widespread among vertebrates, and is not at all unique to the human brain. For example, Vallortigara (2006)
points out that, in various non-human species, the left side of the brain in specialized in
processing complex auditory signals.

References

Annett, M. (1982). Handedness. In J. G. Beaumont (Ed.), *Divided visual field studies of
cerebral organization*. London: Academic Press.

Annett, M. (1985). *Left, right, hand and brain: The right shift theory*. Hillsdale, NJ:
Lawrence Erlbaum Associates, Inc.

Annett, M. (2001). *Handedness and brain asymmetry. The right shift theory*. Hove, UK:
Psychology Press.

Barker, A. T., Jalinous, R., & Freeston, I .L. (1985). Non-invasive magnetic stimulation of
human motor cortex. *Lancet, 1* (8437), 1106–1107.

Basso, A., Gardelli, M., Grassi, M. P., & Mariotti, M. (1989). The role of the right
hemisphere in recovery from aphasia. Two case studies. *Cortex, 25* (4), 555–566.

Basso, A., & Scarpa, M. (1990). Traumatic aphasia in children and adults: A comparison
of clinical features and evolution. *Cortex, 26* (4), 501–514.

Bates, E., & Roe, K. (2001). Language development in children with unilateral brain injury.
In C. A. Nelson & M. Luciana (Eds.), *Handbook of developmental cognitive neuroscience*
(pp. 281–307), Cambridge, MA: MIT Press.

Baumgaertner, A., Buccino, G., Lange, R., McNamara, A., & Binkofski, F. (2007).
Polymodal conceptual processing of human biological actions in the left inferior frontal
lobe. *European Journal of Neuroscience, 25* (3), 881–889.

Beauvois, M. F., & Dérouesné, J. (1981). Lexical or orthographic agraphia. *Brain, 104*
(Pt 1), 21–49.

Beauvois, M. F., Dérouesné, J., & Bastard, V. (1980). *Auditory parallel to phonologic alexia*. Paper presented to the third European Conference of the International Neuropsychological Society, Chianciano, Italy.

Berlucchi, C. (1982). Una ipotesi neurofisiologica sulle asimmetrie funzionali degli emisferi cerebrali nell'uomo. In C. Umiltà (Ed.), *Neuropsicologia sperimentale* (pp. 95–133). Milano: F. Angeli.

Booth, J. R., Wood, L., Lu, D., Houk, J. C., & Bitan, T. (2007). The role of the basal ganglia and cerebellum in language processing. *Brain Research, 1133* (1), 136–144.

Bottini, G., Corcoran, R., Sterzi, R., Paulesu, E., Schenone, P., Scarpa, P., et al. (1994). The role of the right hemisphere in the interpretation of figurative aspects of language. A positron emission tomography activation study. *Brain, 117* (Pt 6), 1241–1253.

Bouillaud, J. B. (1825). Recherches cliniques propre à démontrer que la perte de la parole correspond à la lésion des lobules antérieurs du cerveau, et à confirmer l'opinion de M.Gall, sur la siège de l'organe du langage articulé (Mémoire lu à l'Académie royale de Médicine, le 21 février 1825). *Archives Générales de Médicine, 3* (8), 25–45.

Broca, P. (1861). Perte de la parole, ramollissement chronique et destruction partielle du lobe antérieur gauche [Sur le siège de la faculté du langage]. *Bulletin de la Société d'Anthropologie, II*, 235–238.

Broca, P. (1864). Remarques sur le siège de la faculté du langage articulé, suivies d'une observation d'aphémie. *Bulletin de la Société Anatomique, XXXVI*, 330–357.

Bruce, V., & Young, A. (1986). Understanding face recognition. *British Journal of Psychology, 77* (3), 305–327.

Buccino, G., Riggio, L., Melli, G., Binkofski, F., Gallese, V., & Rizzolatti, G. (2005). Listening to action-related sentences modulates the activity of the motor system: A combined TMS and behavioral study. *Brain Research: Cognitive Brain Research, 24* (3), 355–363.

Cappa, S. F., Miozzo, A., & Frugoni, M. (1994). Glossolalic jargon after a right hemispheric stroke in a patient with Wernicke's aphasia. *Aphasiology, 8* (1), 83–87.

Cappa, S. F., Sandrini, M., Rossini, P. M., Sosta, K., & Miniussi, C. (2002). The role of the left frontal lobe in action naming: rTMS evidence. *Neurology, 59* (5), 720–723.

Caramazza, A. (1986). On drawing inferences about the structure of normal cognitive systems from the analysis of patterns of impaired performance: The case for single-patient studies. *Brain and Cognition, 5* (1), 41–66.

Caramazza, A. (1988). Some aspects of language processing revealed through the analysis of acquired aphasia: The lexical system. *Annual Review of Neuroscience, 11*, 395–421.

Caramazza, A., Hillis, A. E., Rapp, B. C., & Romani, C. (1990). The multiple semantics hypothesis: Multiple confusions? *Cognitive Neuropsychology, 7*, 161–190.

Caramazza, A., & McCloskey, M. (1988). The case for single-patient studies. *Cognitive Neuropsychology, 5*, 517.

Catani. M., & ffytche, D. H. (2005). The rises and falls of disconnection syndromes. *Brain. 128* (10), 2224–2239.

Catani, M., Jones, D. K., & ffytche, D. H. (2005). Perisylvian language networks of the human brain. *Annals of Neurology, 57* (1), 8–16.

Chiarello, C., Kacinik, N., Manowitz, B., Otto, R., & Leonard, C. (2004). Cerebral asymmetries for language: Evidence for structural–behavioral correlations. *Neuropsychology, 18* (2), 219–231.

Coltheart, M. (2006). What has functional neuroimaging told us about the mind (so far)? *Cortex, 42* (3), 323–331.

Coltheart, M., Curtis, B., Atkins, P., & Haller, M. (1993). Models of reading aloud: Dual-route and parallel distributed processing approach. *Psychological Review, 100*, 589–608.

Corballis, M. C. (1997). The genetics and evolution of handedness. *Psychological Review, 104* (4), 714–727.

Corballis, M. C. (2003). *From hand to mouth. The origin of language*. Princeton, NJ: Princeton University Press.

Damasio, H., Grabowski, T. J., Tranel, D., Hichwa, R. D., & Damasio, A. R. (1996). A neural basis for lexical retrieval. *Nature, 380* (6574), 499–505; Erratum in *Nature, 381* (6595), 810.

Deacon, T. W. (1997). *The symbolic species: The co-evolution of language and the brain*. New York: Norton.

Démonet, J. F., Chollet, F., Ramsay, S., Cardebat, D., Nespoulous, J. L., Wise, R., et al. (1992). The anatomy of phonological and semantic processing in normal subjects. *Brain, 115* (Pt 6), 1753–1768.

Denes, G., & Pizzamiglio, L. (1999). *Handbook of clinical and experimental neuropsychology*. Hove, UK: Psychology Press.

Devlin, J. T., & Watkins, K. E. (2007). Stimulating language: insights from TMS. *Brain, 130* (Pt 3), 610–622.

Dronkers, N. F., Plaisant, O., Iba-Zizen, M. T., & Cabanis, E. A. (2007). Paul Broca's historic cases: High resolution MR imaging of the brains of Leborgne and Lelon. *Brain, 130*, 1432–1441.

Fadiga, L., Craighero, L., & Roy, A. C. (2006). Broca. In Y. Grodzinsky & K. Amunts (Eds.), *Broca's region* (pp. 137–152). New York: Oxford University Press.

Fazio, P., Cantagallo, A., Craighero, L., D'Ausilio, A., Roy, A. C., Pozzo, T., et al. (2009). Encoding of human action in Broca's area. *Brain, 132* (Pt 7), 1980–1988.

Fodor, J. A. (1983). *The modularity of mind. An essay on faculty psychology*. Cambridge, MA: MIT Press.

Friederici, A. D., Rüschemeyer, S. A., Hahne, A., & Fiebach, C. J. (2003). The role of left inferior frontal and superior temporal cortex in sentence comprehension: Localizing syntactic and semantic processes. *Cerebral Cortex, 13* (2), 170–177.

Friston, K. J. (2009). Modalities, modes, and models in functional neuroimaging. *Science, 326* (5951), 399–403.

Fritsch, G., & Hitzig, E. (1870). Uber die elektrische Erregbarkeit des Grosshirns. *Archives of Anatomy and Physiology, 37*, 300–332.

Gall, F. J. (1825). *Sur les fonctions du cerveau et sur celles de chacune de ses parties, avec des observations sur la possibilité de reconnaître les instincts, les penchans, les talens, our les dispositions morales et intellectuelles des hommes et des animaux*. Paris: J. B. Baillière.

Geschwind, N. (1965). Disconnexion syndromes in animals and man, I. *Brain, 88* (2), 237–294; II. *Brain, 88* (3), 585–644.

Geschwind, N., & Levitsky, W. (1968). Human brain: Left–right asymmetries in temporal speech regions. *Science, 161* (3837), 186–187.

Gitelman, D. R., Nobre, A. C., Sonty, S., Parrish, T. B., & Mesulam, M. M. (2005). Language network specializations: An analysis with parallel task designs and functional magnetic resonance imaging. *Neuroimage, 26* (4), 975–985.

Hagoort, P., & Levelt, W. J. (2009). Neuroscience. The speaking brain, *Science, 326* (5951), 372–373.

Haist, F., Song, A. W., Wild, K., Faber, T. L., Popp, C. A., & Morris, R. D. (2001). Linking sight and sound: fMRI evidence of primary auditory cortex activation during visual word recognition. *Brain and Language, 76* (3), 340–350.

Hauser, M. D. (1996). *The evolution of communication.* Cambridge, MA: MIT Press.

Head, H. (1926). *Aphasia and kindred disorders of speech* (Vols 1 & 2). London: Cambridge University Press.

Hickok, G., & Pöppel, D. (2004). Dorsal and ventral streams: A framework for understanding aspects of the functional anatomy of language. *Cognition, 92* (1–2), 67–99.

Jackendoff, R. (1987). *Consciousness and the computational mind.* Cambridge, MA: MIT Press.

Jackson, J. H. (1878). On affections of speech from disease of the brain. *Brain, 1,* 304–330.

Jakobson, R. (1964). Toward a linguistic typology of aphasic impairments. In A. V. A. De Reuck & M. O'Connor (Eds.), *Disorders of language.* London: Churchill.

Kimura, D. (1977). Acquisition of a motor skill after left-hemisphere damage. *Brain, 100* (3), 527–542.

Kinsbourne, M. (1998). *Taking the project seriously. The unconscious in neuroscience perspective. Annals of the New York Academy of Sciences, 843,* 111–115.

Kutas, M., & Federmeier, K. D. (2000). Electrophysiology reveals semantic memory use in language comprehension. *Trends in Cognitive Sciences, 4* (12), 463–470.

Liberman, A. M., Cooper, F. S., Shankweiler, D. P., & Studdert-Kennedy, M. (1967). Perception of the speech code. *Psychological Review, 74* (6), 431–461.

Liberman, A. M., & Whalen, D. H. (2000). On the relation of speech to language. *Trends in Cognitive Sciences, 4* (5), 187–196.

Lichtheim, L. (1885). On aphasia. *Brain, 7,* 433–484.

Luria, A. R. (1966). *Higher cortical functions in man.* New York: Basic Books.

Luzzatti, C., & Whitaker, H. (2001). Jean-Baptiste Bouillaud, Claude-François Lallemand, and the role of the frontal lobe: Location and mislocation of language in the early 19th century. *Archives of Neurology, 58* (7), 1157–1162.

MacSweeney, M., Campbell, R., Calvert, G. A., McGuire, P. K., David, A. S., Suckling, J., et al. (2001). Dispersed activation in the left temporal cortex for speech-reading in congenitally deaf people. *Proceedings of the Royal Society of London, Series B: Biological Sciences, 268* (1466), 451–457.

Marie, P. (1906). Révision de la question de l'aphasie: La troisième circonvolution frontale gauche ne joue aucun rôle spécial dans la fonction du langage. *Semaine Médicale, 26,* 241–247.

Marr, D. (1982). *Vision.* San Francisco: W. H. Freeman.

Marshall, J. C., & Newcombe, F. (1973). Patterns of paralexia: A psycholinguistic approach. *Journal of Psycholinguistic Research, 2* (3), 175–199.

McCarthy, R., & Warrington, E. K. (1984). A two-route model of speech production. Evidence from aphasia. *Brain, 107* (Pt 2), 463–485.

McCloskey, M., Caramazza, A., & Basili, A. (1985). Cognitive mechanisms in number processing and calculation: Evidence from dyscalculia. *Brain and Cognition, 4* (2), 171–196.

McGlone, J. (1978). Sex differences in functional brain asymmetry. *Cortex, 14* (1), 122–128.

McNeill, D. (1985). So you think gestures are nonverbal? *Psychological Review, 92* (3), 350–371.

Mesulam, M. M. (1988). From sensation to cognition. *Brain, 121* (Pt 6), 1013–1052.

Moro, A., Tettamanti, M., Perani, D., Donati, C., Cappa, S. F., & Fazio, F. (2001). Syntax and the brain: Disentangling grammar by selective anomalies. *Neuroimage, 13* (1), 110–118.

Moscovitch, M., & Umiltà, C. (1990). Modularity and neuropsychology. In M. F. Schwartz (Ed.), *Modular deficits in Alzheimer-type dementia* (pp. 1–59). Cambridge, MA: MIT Press.

Musiek, F. E., & Reeves, A. G. (1990). Asymmetries of the auditory areas of the cerebrum. *Journal of the American Academy of Audiology, 1* (4), 240–245.

Ojemann, G. A. (1983). Neurosurgical management of epilepsy: A personal perspective in 1983. *Applied Neurophysiology, 46* (1–4), 11–18.

Pascual-Leone, A., Gates, J. R., & Dhuna, A. (1991). Induction of speech arrest and counting errors with rapid-rate transcranial magnetic stimulation. *Neurology, 41* (5), 697–702.

Paulesu, E., Frith, C. D., & Frackowiak, R. S. (1993). The neural correlates of the verbal component of working memory. *Nature, 362* (6418), 342–345.

Penfield, W., & Jasper, H. (1954). *The functional anatomy of the human brain*. Boston: Little, Brown & Co.

Penfield, W., & Roberts, L. (1959). *Speech and brain mechanisms*, Princeton, NJ: Princeton University Press.

Perani, D., Cappa, S. F., Schnur, T., Tettamanti. M., Collina, S., Rosa, M. M., et al. (1999). The neural correlates of verb and noun processing: A PET study. *Brain, 122*, 2337–2344.

Petersen, S. E., Fox, P. T., Posner, M. I., & Raichle, M. E. (1988). Positron emission tomographic studies of the cortical anatomy of single-word processing. *Nature, 331*, 585–589.

Petkov, C. I., Logothetis, N. K., & Obleser, J. (2009). Where are the human speech and voice regions, and do other animals have anything like them? *Neuroscientist, 15* (5), 419–429.

Polk, T. A., & Farah, M. J. (1997). A simple common contexts explanation for the development of abstract letter identities. *Neural Computation, 9* (6), 1277–1289.

Pugh, K. R., Offywitz, B. A., Shaywitz, S. E., Fulbright, R. K., Byrd, D., Skudlarski, P., et al. (1996). Auditory selective attention: An fMRI investigation. *Neuroimage, 4* (3, Pt 1), 159–173.

Pulvermüller, F., Huss, M., Kherif, F., Moscoso del Prado Martin, F., Hauk, O., & Shtyrov, Y. (2006). Motor cortex maps articulatory features of speech sounds. *Proceedings of the National Academy of Sciences, 103* (20), 7865–7870.

Rizzolatti, G., & Luppino, G. (2001). The cortical motor system. *Neuron, 31* (6), 889–901.

Rosenthal, V. (1988). Does it rattle when you shake it? Modularity of mind and the epistemology of cognitive research. In G. Denes, C. Semenza, & P. Bisiacchi (Eds.), *Perspectives on cognitive neuropsychology*. Hove, UK: Lawrence Erlbaum Associates Ltd.

Sahin, N. T., Pinker, S., Cash, S. S., Schomer, D., & Halgren, E. (2009). Sequential processing of lexical, grammatical, and phonological information within Broca's area. *Science, 326* (5951), 445–449.

Sakai, K. L., Noguchi, Y., Takeuchi, T., & Watanabe, E. (2002). Selective priming of syntactic processing by event-related transcranial magnetic stimulation of Broca's area. *Neuron, 35* (6), 1177–1182.

Salmelin, R., Hari, R., Lounasmaa, O. V., & Sams, M. (1994). Dynamics of brain activation during picture naming. *Nature, 368* (6470), 463–465.

Schacter, D. L., & Tulving, E. (Eds.). (1994). *Memory systems*. Cambridge, MA: MIT Press.

Schäffler, L., Lüders, H. O., & Beck, G. J. (1996). Quantitative comparison of language deficits produced by extraoperative electrical stimulation of Broca's, Wernicke's, and basal temporal language areas. *Epilepsia, 37*, 463–475.

Schäffler, L., Lüders, H. O., Dinner, D. S., Lesser, R. P., & Chelune, G. J. (1993). Comprehension deficits elicited by electrical stimulation of Broca's area. *Brain, 116*, 695–715.

Shallice, T. (1988). *From neuropsychology to mental structure.* Cambridge, UK: Cambridge University Press.

Shapleske. J., Rossell, S. L., Woodruff, P. W., & David, A. S. (1999). The planum temporale: A systematic, quantitative review of its structural, functional and clinical significance. *Brain Research Reviews, 29* (1), 26–49.

Shaywitz, B. A., Shaywitz, S. E., Pugh, K. R., Constable, R. T., Skudlarski, P., Fulbright, R. K., et al. (1995). Sex differences in the functional organization of the brain for language. *Nature, 373,* 607–609.

Silveri, M. C., Di Betta, A. M., Filippini, V., Leggio, M. G., & Molinari, M. (1998). Verbal short-term store-rehearsal system and the cerebellum. Evidence from a patient with a right cerebellar lesion. *Brain, 121* (Pt 11), 2175–2187.

Silveri, M. C., Leggio, M. G., & Molinari, M. (1994). The cerebellum contributes to linguistic production: A case of agrammatic speech following right cerebellar lesion. *Neurology, 44,* 2047–2050.

Thierry, G., & Wu, Y. J. (2007). Brain potentials reveal unconscious translation during foreign-language comprehension. *Proceedings of the National Academy of Sciences, USA, 104* (30), 12530–12535.

Tyler, L. K. (1985). Real-time comprehension processes in agrammatism: A case study. *Brain and Language, 26* (2), 259–275.

Ullman, M. T. (2001). A neurocognitive perspective on language: The declarative/procedural model. *Nature Reviews Neuroscience, 2,* 717–726.

Umiltà, C. (2006). Localization of cognitive functions in the brain does allow one to distinguish between psychological theories. *Cortex, 42* (3), 399–401; Discussion 422–427.

Vallar, G. (2006). Mind, brain, and functional neuroimaging. *Cortex, 42* (3), 402–405; Discussion 422–427.

Vallortigara, G. (2006). The evolutionary psychology of left and right: Costs and benefits of lateralization. *Developmental Psychobiology, 48* (6), 418–427.

Van Lancker Sitdis, D. (2008). The relation of human language to human emotion. In B. Stemmer & H. A. Whitaker (Eds.), *Handbook of the neuroscience of language* (pp. 199–208). New York: Academic Press.

Vargha-Khadem, F., O'Gorman, A. M., & Watters, G. V. (1985). Aphasia and handedness in relation to hemispheric side, age at injury and severity of cerebral lesion during childhood. *Brain, 108* (Pt 3), 677–696.

Warrington, E. K., & Shallice, T. (1984). Category specific semantic impairments. *Brain, 107* (Pt 3), 829–854.

Wernicke, K. (1874). *'Der aphasische Symptomencomplex'. Eine Psychologische Studie auf Anatomischer Basis.* Breslau: M. Cohn und Weigart.

Wise, R. J., Scott, S. K., Blank, S. C., Mummery, C. J., Murphy, K., & Warburton, E. A. (2001). Separate neural subsystems within 'Wernicke's area'. *Brain, 124* (Pt 1), 83–95.

Zaidel, E. (1988). Language in the disconnected right hemisphere. In G. Adelman (Ed.), *Encyclopedia of neuroscience* (Vol. 1, pp. 563–564). Boston: Birkhauser.

Zorzi, M. (2006). L'approccio computazionale in psicologia cognitiva. *Giornale Italiano di Psicologia, 33* (2), 225–245.

4 Acquired language disorders: The aphasias

In the years following the observations of Broca and Wernicke, neurologists interested in language noticed the frequent association, in most aphasic patients, between different types of language impairment. It was observed, for example, that a lesion of Broca's area not only affected single word production but was often linked to a syntactic deficit, present in both sentence production and comprehension (agrammatism, Pick, 1913).

Similarly, the comprehension deficit following a lesion of Wernicke's area was often associated with a lexical deficit affecting the production of single words and a specific impairment in sentence construction (paragrammatism).

The study of the association of aphasic symptoms had a main role in the building up of the taxonomy of the aphasic syndromes, denotating a cluster of symptoms that tend to co-occur and are related by some anatomical or functional peculiarity.

The concept of an aphasic syndrome has assumed both anatomical and functional valence. When considering anatomy, it is suggested that the association of symptoms is a consequence of the fact that certain areas are anatomical neighbours and share a blood supply (*weak syndrome*). To give an example, the association of phonetic and phonological disorders to agrammatism could be because the neural substrates of articulatory programming and syntactic processing, although independent, are supplied by the same cerebral artery which, when occluded, will put both systems out of use.

Conversely, according to the functional hypothesis, the aphasic syndrome reflects the effects of a lesion to a single anatomo-functional mechanism that serves different tasks (*strong syndrome*). Jakobson (1964), for example, claimed that the association between agrammatism and articulatory disturbances in Broca's aphasia could be a result of a deficit in the process of contiguity or combination, so that the patient is no longer able to organize a sequence of words to form a sentence and cannot rapidly programme and sequence the phonatory movements to articulate single words. While in the weak syndromes variations in cerebral blood flow or the extension of the lesion can cause dissociated deficits (for example, production deficits in the absence of syntactic deficits or vice versa), in the case of strong syndromes the association of symptoms is constant (for a review see Vallar, 1999).

Among neurologists the notion of an aphasic syndrome was warmly welcomed, regardless of its underlying philosophy, as it seemed to allow them to easily qualify the type of language deficit as well as to infer *in vivo* the site of lesion.

As a consequence, several classifications were proposed, the best known being along the lines of the Wernicke–Lichtheim model, revised and updated a century later by Geschwind (1965).

The collaboration of psychologists in the study of aphasic deficits allowed statistical methods of evaluation to be implemented. Studies were made of large groups of patients, their performances being compared both within the aphasic groups and with non-language impaired participants, matched for age and education level. As a result, numerous test batteries were published and widely used, since they allowed, or at least that was the proposers' intention, detection of the presence, type and severity of the aphasic deficit (*Boston Diagnostic Aphasia Examination*, Goodglass & Kaplan, 1972; *Aachener Aphasie Test*, Huber, Poeck, Weniger, & Willmes, 1983).

Using the Wernicke–Lichtheim model for the neural organization of language in its updated form (Figure 4.1), Goodglass and Kaplan proposed a classification that made an initial distinction between non-fluent aphasias, resulting from lesions to the anterior regions of the left hemisphere, and fluent aphasias, resulting from lesions to the retrolandic (posterior) areas.

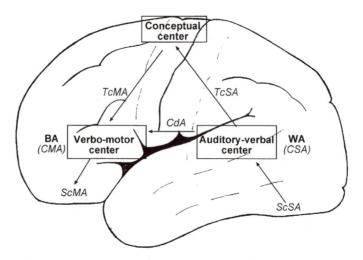

Figure 4.1 Image centres (represented within boxes, associationistic pathways (represented with arrows connecting these boxes) and aphasic syndromes resulting from disruption of these centres or pathways according to the Lichtheim model. ScSA = subcortical sensory aphasia; WA(CSA) = Wernicke's aphasia (cortical sensory aphasia); CdA = conduction aphasia; TcSA = transcortical sensory aphasia; TcMA = transcortical motor aphasia; BA (CMA) = Broca's aphasia (cortical motor aphasia); ScMA = subcortical motor aphasia (from Denes & Pizzamiglio, 1999). Copyright © 1999, Psychology Press, reproduced with permission of Taylor & Francis.

Table 4.1 Examples of language produced by aphasic patients

Broca's aphasia:
Stroke. Nine years ago. And hospital … Talking … No! … Walking … No! Therapy, …
 six months … Better
(*Responses by a Broca's patient to a question about his illness*)

Wernicke's aphasia:
I drove him when the straightway from he guards and place, I forgot to talker, what,
 where the name of the police I told where the place there. We were in on the job with
 the crowbar I caught one lot of van, yes, one two …

A non-fluent aphasia is characterized by articulatory disorders, with effortful production, the tendency to produce sentences that are shorter than normal, and dysprosody. Spontaneous language is therefore poor, with frequent interruptions and composed of single words, mostly nouns. In contrast, the oral production characteristic of fluent aphasias contains long sequences of words with normal articulation and a range of grammatical constructions, but showing severe lexical difficulty, relating especially to open class words (Table 4.1).

Within the category of non-fluent aphasias a further distinction is made between Broca's aphasia, global aphasia and transcortical motor aphasia.

Broca's aphasia is characterized by a deficit in oral production, which, in the severest cases and above all in the first stages of the illness, may be practically absent (anarthria) or reduced to monosyllables. Most patients have articulatory and phonological difficulties (Chapter 5). Repetition and reading aloud, although compromised, are less affected than spontaneous speech, while writing difficulties are on a par with, or worse than, those evident in spontaneous speech. The patient is unable to produce grammatically correct sentences and has difficulty with agreements, for example, between subject and verb. 'Grammatical words' such as free morphemes (closed class words, such as articles, prepositions, clitics, etc.) are often omitted and substituted with unstressed forms. Since in highly inflected language such as Italian, the omission of a bound morpheme produces a non-word, in these languages morphemes are substituted rather than omitted. On the contrary, in languages like English, the omission of the verbal flexion (*loved* → *love*) coincides with the phonological form of the infinitive (*to love*). Production in Broca's aphasia has in the past been labelled *telegraphic* and seen as the product of an adaptation to an articulatory deficit resulting from economy of effort (speech is tiresome and the patient prefers to use short sentences).

In these patients phonological and phonetic difficulties are sometimes reduced, or may even disappear, during recital of memorized sequences, such as the alphabet, numbers, prayers, and so on. At the lexical level, closed class words and verbs are most severely affected, while nouns are relatively preserved.

Auditory comprehension was for a long time considered normal, but on closer scrutiny, a deficit in the comprehension of sentences that are syntactically complex is often observed (see Chapter 7).

Transcortical motor aphasia along with transcortical sensory aphasia is caused, according to the associationalist model, by a disconnection, rather than by destruction of Broca and Wernicke's areas. In the case of transcortical sensory aphasia, Broca's area is disconnected from the area relating to concepts. Therefore the patient tends to be mute and does not initiate communication, but repetition and reading aloud are normal, in contrast to Broca's aphasia.

In global aphasia, following a lesion of the entire language area, there is a severe deficit in oral production, which is often reduced to a single recurrent phrase. This is accompanied by a severe deficit in auditory and reading comprehension.

Fluent aphasias include Wernicke's aphasia, conduction aphasia, anomic aphasia and finally, transcortical sensory aphasia.

Spontaneous production in Wernicke's aphasia is fluent, with normal phrase length, articulation and prosody. When the content of the speech output is analysed, however, numerous errors are evident: anomias, phonological and semantic paraphasias and neologisms occur. There is a lack of open class words compared to closed class words and they are often substituted by passepartout words ('thing', 'that one there'), perseverations and circumlocutions. From a syntactic point of view, the principal anomalies are difficulties with noun–verb agreement, the substitution of one preposition by another and errors in the gender and pronoun case (paragrammatism). Reading aloud and writing display the same characteristics. Some patients maintain a relatively well preserved ability to read aloud but are unable to understand what they have read. The characteristic feature of Wernicke's aphasia is, however, a comprehension deficit at both single word and sentence level, which reflects a phonological, but more frequently lexical-semantic deficit. Finally, the patient's lack of awareness and insight into his or her problems is often characteristic of Wernicke's aphasia. A person affected by Wernicke's aphasia may demonstrate open denial of the illness, blaming the listener for not being able or not wanting to understand what he or she has said.

Conduction aphasia is attributed (Geschwind, 1965) to a lesion of the internal arcuate fasciculus, at the level of the supramarginal gyrus, which carries information from Wernicke's area to Broca's area.[1] The characteristic of this type of aphasia is a dissociation between disproportionately severely impaired repetition in relation to the level of fluency in spontaneous speech and good auditory comprehension. Spontaneous speech is characterized by frequent phonological paraphasias and *conduits d'approche* (repeated phonological approximations to untangle the sound of the target word). Similar characteristics are found in reading aloud, naming and repetition. Writing, both to dictation and copying a text, is characterized by correct production at the level of single graphemes but is disrupted by the presence of literal paraphasias to the extent of creating neologisms.

Anomic aphasia (amnesic aphasia) is a form of fluent aphasia characterized by a specific lexical deficit for open class words, particularly nouns, with relative sparing of verbs and, above all, closed class words. There is sometimes dissociation between written and oral production and there are examples in the literature of the sparing of a single modality. It differs from Wernicke's aphasia in that comprehension and repetition are good, and from Broca's aphasia in that production is fluent. Attempts to overcome the lexical deficit cause the patient to resort to circumlocutions such as 'the thing we use for cutting' for 'knife' or passepartout words ('thing', 'that thing there'). Semantic and phonological paraphasias are seldom present.

This aphasia is rarely found in its pure form and is attributed to a lesion at the level of the left angular gyrus. At times it represents the only residual symptom of an improved aphasia. It is important to emphasize, however, that lexical disturbances are frequent in every type of aphasia and do not indicate the location of the lesion. It is also important to remember that significant lexical disturbances (not an occasional difficulty in remembering a word!) may be the first symptom, alongside memory deficits, of degenerative cerebral pathologies, such as Alzheimer's disease.

Transcortical sensory aphasia usually occurs following a large retrolandic lesion of the left hemisphere or generalized anoxic brain damage (following, for example, cardiac arrest). Language is fluent, paraphasic, with little meaningful content and often echolalic (the patient tends to repeat the examiner's questions). The feature that differentiates this aphasia from Wernicke's aphasia is the dissociation between seriously compromised auditory comprehension and good ability to repeat, which is an almost compulsive behaviour in these patients. Single word reading may be relatively spared (though manifesting elements of surface dyslexia, see Chapter 8), but reading comprehension is absent (Table 4.2).

Since the introduction of non-invasive neuroimaging techniques, such as CAT scans and MRI, into clinical practice, cases of aphasia following lesions to the thalamus or basal ganglia, anatomical structures without a specific role according to the classical language models, have been observed. In general the symptoms are similar to those of transcortical aphasias, but are of less severity and their prognosis is better.

There are two possible explanations for an aphasia caused by damage to these structures: the first is based on the phenomenon of diaschisis; that is, a sudden loss of function in a portion of the brain (for example, language cortical areas) that is at a distance from the site of injury (subcortical structures), but is connected to it by neurons (see below).

The second interpretation postulates that the thalamus plays an active part in the processing of language, being part of a thalamic–cortical circuit at the base of semantic-lexical language components.

Functional neuroimaging studies (PET, fMRI) in normal participants have shown a pattern of activation of the basal ganglia in phonological processing tasks, through connections with the left frontal and temporal cortex. More recently, Teichmann et al. (2008) in a study of patients suffering from Huntington's disease (a degenerative illness that selectively affects the basal ganglion), hypothesized a specific role of these structures in some syntactic operations, which, according to generative theory, involve movement.

Finally, the application of methods of functional neuroimaging has revealed an active role of the cerebellum in articulatory control and short-term memory (Booth, Wood, Lu, Houk, & Bitan, 2007).

Table 4.2 Clinical characteristics of aphasias according to the Wernicke-Geschwind model

Type of aphasia	Production	Repetition	Auditory comprehension	Naming	Site of lesion
Broca	Non-fluent, agrammatical	Compromised	Clinically good	Fair (nouns > verbs)	Areas 44, 45, base of the third frontal convolution
Global	Non-fluent	Compromised	Compromised	Compromised	Left frontal-temporal-parietal
Wernicke	Fluent, poor content	Compromised	Compromised	Compromised, with phonological and semantic paraphasias and neologisms	Posterior area of the superior temporal convolution (area 22)
Conduction	Fluent, paraphasic	Compromised	Good	Fair, with phonological paraphasias	Parietal lobe (arcuate fasciculus)
Anomic	Fluent, anomic	Good	Good	Compromised	Angular gyrus
Transcortical motor	Non-fluent	Good	Good	Compromised	White matter around Broca's area
Transcortical sensory	Fluent	Good	Compromised	Compromised	Parietal-temporal-occipital junction

Standardized tests have tended to be widely used in assessing language rehabilitation. When a standardized test is performed at regular intervals during the course of rehabilitation, it allows objective evaluation of global improvement and improvement of individual language components. Aphasia, following a stroke, does not produce a uniform and constant picture, but improves over time, to some extent as a result of spontaneous recovery and speech therapy intervention, which should begin once the clinical picture has been carefully evaluated (Basso, 2003).

It was evident, however, that these evaluation procedures have their drawbacks. A large number of patients defy classification in that their deficit is on the borderline between types, for example, lying somewhere between Broca's aphasia and a mild global aphasia, or between an anomic aphasia and Wernicke's aphasia.

On the other hand, the use of neuroimaging tools has allowed the site of the lesion responsible for the aphasic deficit to be specified with ever increasing accuracy. In a large number of cases it was found that the site of the lesion surmised from clinical investigation, did not, in fact, correspond to the site of damage revealed through instrumental investigation.

A lesion limited to Broca's area, for example, gives rise only to an anarthria, which is sometimes temporary (Mohr, Sidman, Stoddard, Leicester, & Rosenberger, 1973). Conduction aphasia is not always caused by an anatomical disconnection between anterior and posterior areas of the left cerebral hemisphere (Hickok et al., 2000) and Wernicke's aphasia is not always caused by a lesion to the posterior superior area of the left temporal lobe. The tests have also been criticized by the increasing number of psycholinguists looking at the field of aphasia: they claim that the classical model of language processing, based on the existence of only three processes (comprehension, production and conceptualization) is too coarse and does not take into account that comprehension and production are made up of different dominions such as syntax, phonology and semantics. Moreover, the evaluation of language deficits has not always been sufficiently refined for research purposes, resulting in patients being grouped into the same diagnostic category while in fact their deficits were very different in nature.

Accordingly, a series of test batteries has been devised with the aim of providing more detailed qualitative assessment of a patient's deficit (*The Psycholinguistic Assessment of Language Processing in Aphasia, PALPA.* Kay, Coltheart, & Lesser, 1992).

Patients were defined according to the presence of a deficit of a single language component: phonology, syntax or the lexicon. To perform these test batteries, participants were divided into apparently homogeneous groups for evaluation of a given deficit. However, this method too was soon rejected, although some researchers still upheld its validity. For example, some authors (Grodzinsky, 1986, 1990) defended the value of group studies, considering, for example, that agrammatic patients were homogeneous and affected by the same deficit, while according to other authors (Caramazza & McCloskey, 1988), a superficially similar deficit such as agrammatism present in a group of patients may well be very different in nature, in that functionally different syntactic mechanisms may have been put out of use. In a thorough review of the value of aphasic syndromes,

Marshall (1986) concluded that aphasia studies based on clinical taxonomies did not provide scientifically relevant data.

Despite these criticisms, the neuropsychology of language, has, over the last thirty years, become the leading discipline in attracting a huge number of academics intent on researching the neural basis and functional structure of language through the use of different perspectives and methods. The results obtained through anatomo-clinical correlation combined with the data from morphological and functional neuroimaging techniques with a view to inferring models of normal *cognitive* functioning have produced remarkable developments. Together with the diffusion of the methods of cognitive psychology to the study of aphasic deficits, group studies have been progressively replaced by single case studies coupled with a sound theoretical base as a reference. Information is therefore obtained through rigorous analysis of the stimuli and patient response, allowing valid inferences to be made concerning the functioning of normal cognitive processes (Caramazza & McCloskey, 1988). Obviously, the single case study approach has also been criticized, the most obvious criticism being the impossibility, in most cases, of replicating the data obtained from an individual patient. It is, of course, practically impossible to find a second patient affected by precisely the same cerebral lesion and presenting an identical functional deficit. This criticism can be addressed if the patients undergo the same tests during different assessments and their response patterns do not significantly change across sessions. Finally, as Vallar (1999) rightly points out, both single case and group studies can contribute to the development of knowledge of the neural and functional substrates of language, one approach being, in specific circumstances, more appropriate than the other: a compromise position does exist by carrying out group studies of single patients who, on the basis of a theory of normal language processing, are affected by the same deficit (multiple case studies).

Recovery from aphasia

In the majority of cases, aphasia is caused by non-progressive damage to the cerebral cortex that may be due to trauma, but more often is vascular in origin, for example, haemorrhage or ischemic occlusion (thrombosis) of an artery supplying the left hemisphere. In most cases there is a recovery period following stabilization of the ictus, which may result in total or, more usually, partial recovery of language processes as a result of both spontaneous recovery and speech and language rehabilitation (Basso, Capitani, & Vignolo, 1979).

The anatomical and functional bases of this process have not yet been defined. Unlike other organs and tissues (for example, muscle or skin), nervous tissue possesses poor ability to regenerate. For this reason two hypotheses, which are not mutually exclusive, have been formulated to explain improvement of aphasia: the regression of the diaschisis (von Monakow, 1914) and the takeover of language functions by the nervous structures that have remained intact.

According to the first hypothesis, an acute cerebral injury may produce a functional, but reversible, depression in distant, but connected, regions in both the damaged and controlateral hemisphere. As a rule, regression of the functional depression takes place spontaneously in the first months after onset of the acute lesion. The contribution of the areas affected by diaschisis remains however to be assessed.

The second hypothesis assumes that most of the improvement in the aphasia, particularly in the post-acute period, can be attributed to the transfer of language functions to the right hemisphere (Gowers, 1895), through a process of activation of language abilities that are inactive when the brain is functioning normally.

Clinical support for the theory of transfer of functions comes from the observation of worsening of the clinical picture in patients with an existing left hemisphere lesion who are subsequently affected by a second right hemisphere ictus (Cappa, Miozzo, & Frugoni, 1994).

The introduction of new neuroimaging techniques in the study of the mechanism of recovery from aphasia (Cappa, 2000; Pizzamiglio, Galati, & Committeri, 2001) has not provided a definitive clarification of the neural bases of improvement. During the initial phase of recovery a reduction in the hypometabolism of the areas of the left hemisphere surrounding the lesion has been documented, alongside language improvement, which supports the hypothesis of a reduction in the diaschisis, However, functional neuroimaging studies carried out in post-acute aphasic patients have shown greater activation of right hemisphere regions during the execution of language tasks compared to the patern observed in non-brain damaged subjects.

Crosson et al. (2007) have tried to summarize results obtained using fMRI studies to investigate the neural bases of recovery from aphasia. In general, a small lesion is a predictor of good recovery generated by the left hemisphere. On the other hand, when there is extensive left hemisphere damage, the corresponding areas of the right hemisphere intervene in the recovery process.

As far as specific effects of speech and language rehabilitation are concerned in the activation of the right hemisphere, Thulborn, Carpenter, and Just (1999), using MRI, have found progressive activation of the right hemisphere, proportional to the amount of clinical improvement.

Several studies have been set up to search for factors influencing recovery from aphasia and have attempted to identify which language components tend to show most recovery, both spontaneously and following speech therapy.

As far as spontaneous recovery (or rather, recovery in the absence of direct therapeutic intervention[2]) is concerned, many variables have been taken into consideration, such as age, gender, manual preference, size and site of lesion (Basso, 1992). None of these, except the size of the underlying anatomical damage, has shown to have a critical influence on the regression of the aphasia. Furthermore, personal factors such as patient motivation and the presence of affective disorders (often aphasia is accompanied by mood disorders) can play an important role in both spontaneous and therapeutically achieved recovery.

The linguistic parameter that improves most in the absence of specific treatment is that of auditory comprehension, followed by oral expression, reading and writing (Basso, Faglioni, & Vignolo, 1975). In the best outcome, the only residual sign is often a lexical deficit (anomia).

It is usually considered that spontaneous recovery occurs during the first 6 months post-onset, although many patients, for reasons which are not clear, continue to display slow and progressive improvement after this time.

The study that provided the greatest contribution to the effect of therapy was carried out by Basso et al. (1979). A large number of aphasic patients underwent a cycle of speech and language therapy (three sessions a week) and their improvement was evaluated using serial controls. Improvement was defined as an increase of at least two points on a five-point scale that considered production (oral and written) and comprehension (auditory and written). Comparing results obtained from treated patients with those of a similar group of patients who had not received speech and language therapy, Basso et al. revealed a significant improvement in the treated group in all four verbal behaviours, with length of therapy being a crucial factor in this study.

As far as the therapeutic approach is concerned, individual treatment therapy is more beneficial than group therapy, particularly in the acute phase of the illness, and second, treatment carried out by a speech and language therapist, preferably in collaboration with a psychologist or clinical linguist, produces a significantly better outcome than therapy performed by a volunteer with no specific training. Therapy was shown to have been effective on all the parameters investigated, with benefit directly proportional to length and intensity of therapy (Denes, Perazzolo, Piani, & Piccione, 1996).

Data regarding type of therapy are more uncertain. The various approaches are heterogeneous and so are difficult to compare in terms of efficacy (Holland & Forbes, 1993).

With the introduction of cognitive neuropsychology into the study of aphasic deficits, there have been numerous attempts to apply these methods and principles to language rehabilitation, or rather to rehabilitation of certain elements of a language disorder, for example lexical deficits (Greenwald, Raymer, Richardson, & Rothi, 1995), reading deficits (Berndt & Mitchum, 1994) and writing disorders (Carlomagno & Parlato, 1989). This method can be applied only to single cases and involves definition of the mechanism underlying the specific deficit based on a theoretical model of normal language processes. It involves a rigorous treatment procedure, based on the construction of a therapeutic model centred on the nature of the deficit and characterized by the administration of specific treatment materials.

De Partz (1995), for example, described a treatment method carried out on a dysgraphic patient, whose errors were sensitive to word length caused, in all probability, by a post-lexical deficit at the level of the graphemic buffer. The patient was visually presented with a set of words which he then studied and subsequently auto-dictated. Some words contained a second, embedded word (for example, the word *cravache*, 'whip', contains the word *vache* 'cow', while others matched for length and frequency did not contain a lexical segment, for example, *cramique*, 'sweet bread roll'. The two types of word were presented to the patient with the lexical segment and the corresponding non-lexical segment underlined (*cra vache*, *cra mique*). The patient's task was to observe how the words had been divided, before writing them without the help of the model. The treatment involved five sessions, with improvement evident primarily in the writing of words containing lexical segments, but improvement was also evident, although to a lesser extent, in the writing of the words with no lexical segment. There were also signs of generalization to words not contained within the experimental set but containing a lexical segment.

The advantage of this type of rehabilitative approach, centred on the nature of the deficit, is evident. On the other hand it is not totally clear if the improvement obtained occurs only with stimuli presented during therapy or whether this improvement then generalizes to other stimuli.

Finally, it must be remembered that it is rare for a patient to be affected by a single deficit and so a more global approach is usually necessary, and that it is often difficult to transfer a single approach from one patient to another.

Living with aphasia

Aphasia does not only mean the loss of language. In most cases there are changes to the patient's work, social and family life. The patient becomes isolated, unable to communicate, and may become depressed to the extent of refusing therapy, deeming it to be useless.

The aphasia obviously has consequences for the whole family, with a change of roles and possible impact on the economic and emotional life of the family unit. For this reason, self-help organizations have been established, with aphasic individuals, their families and volunteers as members. The aim of these organizations is to spread knowledge of aphasia and help aphasic people to rediscover their role within the family and integrate into society.

Notes

1 More recent studies have, however, shown that conduction aphasia can follow a partial or total lesion of a vast cortical–subcortical area that includes the parietal and temporal lobes of the left hemisphere.
2 As Anna Basso (2003) rightly underlines, the term 'spontaneous' is ambiguous. There is no such thing as spontaneous recovery given that the language community in which the patient lives provides language stimulation.

References

Basso, A. (1992). Prognostic factors in aphasia. *Aphasiology*, *6*, 337–348.

Basso, A. (2003). *Aphasia and its therapy*. Oxford, UK: Oxford University Press.

Basso, A., Capitani, E., & Vignolo, L. A. (1979). Influence of rehabilitation on language skills in aphasic patients. A controlled study. *Archives of Neurology*, *36*, 190–196.

Basso, A., Faglioni, P., & Vignolo, L. A. (1975). Etude controlèe de la rèèducation du language dans l'aphasie: Comparaison entre aphasiques traitès et non-traitès. *Revue Neurologique*, *131*, 607–614.

Berndt, R., & Mitchum, C. (1994). Approaches to the rehabilitation of 'phonological assembly': Elaborating the model of nonlexical reading. In G. W. Humphreys & M. J. Riddoch (Eds.), *Cognitive neuropsychology and cognitive rehabilitation*. Hove, UK: Lawrence Erlbaum Associates Ltd.

Booth, J. R., Wood, L., Lu, D., Houk, J. C., & Bitan, T. (2007). The role of the basal ganglia and cerebellum in language processing. *Brain Research, 1133* (1), 136–144.

Cappa, S. F. (2000). Recovery from aphasia: Why and how? *Brain and Language, 71* (1), 39–41.

Cappa, S. F., Miozzo, A., & Frugoni, M. (1994). Glossolalic jargon after a right hemispheric stroke in a patient with Wernicke's aphasia. *Aphasiology, 8* (1), 83–87.

Caramazza, A., & McCloskey, M. (1988). The case for single-patient studies. *Cognitive Neuropsychology, 5*, 517.

Carlomagno, S., & Parlato, V. (1989). Writing rehabilitation in brain-damaged adult aphasics: A cognitive approach. In X. Seron & G. Deloche (Eds.), *Cognitive approaches in neuropsychological rehabilitation* (pp. 175–209). Hillsdale, NJ: Lawrence Erlbaum Associates, Inc.

Crosson, B., McGregor, K., Gopinath, K. S., Conway, T. W., Benjamin, M., Chang, Y.L., et al. (2007). Functional MRI of language in aphasia: A review of the literature and the methodological challenges. *Neuropsychology Review, 17* (2), 157–177.

De Partz, M. P. (1995). Deficit of the graphemic buffer: Effects of a written lexical segmentation strategy. *Neuropsychological Rehabilitation, 5*, 129–147.

Denes, G., Perazzolo, C., Piani, A., & Piccione, F. (1996). Intensive versus regular speech therapy in global aphasia: A controlled study. *Aphasiology, 10* (4), 385–394.

Denes, G., & Pizzamiglio, L. (1999). *Handbook of clinical and experimental neuropsychology*. Hove, UK: Psychology Press.

Geschwind, N. (1965). Disconnexion syndromes in animals and man, I. *Brain, 88* (2), 237–294; II. *Brain, 88* (3), 585–644.

Goodglass, H. & Kaplan, E. (1972). *The assesment of aphasia and related disorders*. Philadelphia: Lea & Febiger.

Gowers, W. (1895). A manual of diseases of the nervous system (2nd ed., Blakiston, Vol. 1, p. 407). London: J. &. A. Churchill.

Greenwald, M. L., Raymer, A. M., Richardson, M. E., & Rothi, L. J. G. (1995). Contrasting treatments for severe impairments of picture naming. *Neuropsychological Rehabilitation, 5* (1&2), 17–49.

Grodzinsky, Y. (1986). Language deficits and the theory of syntax. *Brain and Language, 27* (1), 135–159.

Grodzinsky, Y. (1990). *Theoretical perspectives on language deficits*. Cambridge, MA: MIT Press.

Hickok, G., Erhard, P., Kassubek, J., Helms-Tillery, A. K., Naeve-Velguth, S., Strupp, J. P., et al. (2000). A functional magnetic resonance imaging study of the role of left posterior superior temporal gyrus in speech production: Implications for the explanation of conduction aphasia. *Neuroscience Letters, 287* (2), 156–160.

Holland, A., & Forbes, M. (1993). *Aphasia treatment: World perspectives*. London: Chapman & Hall.

Huber, W., Poeck, K., Weniger, D., & Willmes, K. (1983). *Aachener Aphasie Test (AAT)*. Göttingen: Hogrefe.

Jakobson, R. (1964). Toward a linguistic typology of aphasic impairments. In A. V. A. De Reuck & M. O'Connor (Eds.), *Disorders of language*. London: Churchill.

Kay, J., Coltheart, M., & Lesser R. (1992). *PALPA: Psycholinguistic assessment of language processing in aphasia*. Hove, UK: Lawrence Erlbaum Associates Ltd.

Marshall, J. C. (1986). The description and interpretation of aphasic language disorder. *Neuropsychologia, 24*, 5–24.

Mohr, J. P., Sidman, M., Stoddard, L. T., Leicester, J., & Rosenberger, P. B. (1973). Evolution of the deficit in total aphasia. *Neurology, 23* (12), 1302–1312.

Pick, A. (1913). *Die aggrammatischen Sprachstorungen*. Berlin: Springer Verlag.

Pizzamiglio, L., Galati, G., & Committeri, G. (2001). The contribution of functional neuroimaging to recovery after brain damage: A review. *Cortex, 37*, 11–21.

Teichmann, M., Gaura, V., Démonet, J. F., Supiot, F., Delliaux, M., Verny, C., et al. (2008). Language processing within the striatum: Evidence from a PET correlation study in Huntington's disease. *Brain, 131*, 1046–1056.

Thulborn, K. R., Carpenter, P. A., & Just, M. A. (1999). Plasticity of language-related brain function during recovery from stroke. *Stroke, 30* (4), 746–754.

Vallar, G. (1999). The methodological foundations of neuropsychology. In G. Denes & L. Pizzamiglio (Eds.), *Handbook of clinical and experimental neuropsychology* (pp. 95–134). Hove, UK: Psychology Press.

Von Monakow, C. (1914) *Die Lokalisation im Grosshirn und der Abbau der function durch kortikale Herde*. Wiesbaden: Bergman.

5 The sounds of language: The production and comprehension of words

'What do you read, my lord?'

(*Hamlet*, 2.2.191)

'Words, words, words.'

(2.2.192)

Spoken language is made up of groups of sounds (phonological forms) that express meaning (words). The groups are, in turn, made up of combinations of meaningless sounds (phonemes) that are divided into two categories based on their acoustic and articulatory characteristics: vowels and consonants. In all languages consonants (C) are more numerous than vowels (V). This is a consequence of the particular anatomy of speech tract (see later) that allows a larger variety of consonants rather than vocalic segments to be produced by human articulators. For example, in Italian the proportion is 24C:7V; in Arabic 29C:3V. Cases like Swedish with 16 consonants and 17 vowels are rare, while, on the contrary, there are languages like Arabic of Greenlandic with only 3 vowels. Maddieson (1984) analysed 317 spoken languages and established that the 5-vowel systems are the most common, and the majority of systems have over 20 consonants. From a functional point of view, in all linguistic systems, consonants, being more numerous than vowels, bear the brunt for distinguishing between lexical items.

The possible combination of phonemes in any language is specified by its set of rules (phonotactics or prosodic phonology) and allows the construction of an infinite number of words. For example, an averagely well educated individual is thought to possess a lexicon composed of between 60,000 and 100,000 words (Pinker, 1994).

All language sounds are the product of a combination of about twenty simple elements, or 'phonological features'. These elements serve as the crucial distinguishing mark, both in production and perception, between two phonemes, such as the distinctive feature of voicing, which distinguishes /b/ from /p/ in English, or nasality, which distinguishes /m/ from /b/ and /p/ (see Table 5.1).

Some features such as [rounding], [anterior], [posterior], [high], [nasal], and so on, refer to specific articulators (lips, tip or blade of tongue, soft palate), other

Table 5.1

Manner	Bilabial	Labiodental	Dental	Alveolar	Post-alveolar	Velar
			Place			
Plosive: Total closure in the vocal tract, followed by a sudden release	p b			t d		k g
Nasal: Complete closure of the vocal tract, with lowering of soft palate so air is forced through the nose	m			n		ŋ
Fricative: Narrowing of the vocal tract, causing air turbulence as a jet of air hits the teeth		f v	θ ð	s z	ʃ ʒ	

features, such as [consonant], [lateral], [continuous] can be realized by various articulators (Figure 5.1). The characteristic of language that allows the production of an almost infinite number of words using a limited number of elements, was labelled 'double articulation' by the French linguist Martinet (1960). It is species-specific, being absent, as seen in Chapter 2, in the communicative systems of other animal species.

The link between the sound produced and the meaning expressed by the sounds is completely arbitrary, apart from onomatopoeic words whose sounds reproduce or are evocative of natural sounds or noises. Within all the possible sound combinations allowed by the rules of phonotactics, the link between sound and meaning is essentially fortuitous. To give an example, the Italian word '*formaggio*', the French word '*fromage*' and the English word '*cheese*' are made up of completely different sound sequences, but correspond, with some minor variation (bearing in mind the uncountable variety of French or Italian cheese!), to the same concept. Only some aspects of the phonological form are predictable because of the sound sequence into which they are inserted. In English, for example, through a process of assimilation, a segment adopts partially or totally the characteristics of the segment that precedes or follows it. Consider the /d/ contained in the word 'broadcast' which is replaced by a /g/ because of the influence of the neighbouring /k/.

The collection of phonological forms possessed by the speaker makes up the mental lexicon. Speech production then involves selection from the lexicon of the phonological forms corresponding to the set of words necessary to transmit

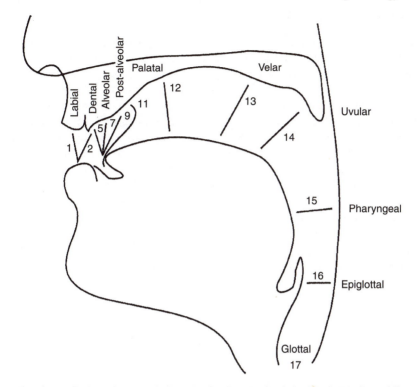

Figure 5.1 The nine regions of the vocal tract that can be considered the target areas for the moveable articulators. The numbered lines show some of the 17 named articulatory gestures (from Ladefoged & Maddieson, 1996). Reproduced with permission of John Wiley and Sons Ltd.

a message. The next stage consists of the elaboration of a mental plan necessary for word production (*phonological planning*), which will, in the final stage, be implemented through movements of the vocal tract.

Language perception, on the other hand, consists of extracting the phonological forms from the acoustic signals produced by the conversational partner and attributing meaning to them. According to this scheme, therefore, the phonological elements known to the speaker are the abstract phonological representation or units of action for the production of speech as well as the objects of language perception. There is, therefore, a fundamental equality of the basic elements of language production and perception, so that the vocal tract produces signals of phonological value, which are, in turn, decoded into phonological elements through the auditory tract.

This chapter illustrates one of the current models of the production and perception of spoken language along with a description of their neurological base and an analysis of the phonetic and phonological deficits arising subsequent to a cerebral lesion.

Production of language sounds

Human speech is produced by the vocal tract, which may be viewed as a set of resonating cavities bounded by anatomical structures that are either fixed or moveable (Figure 5.2). The main energy source is the lungs together with the diaphragm. When speaking, the airflow is forced through the glottis between the vocal cords and the larynx to the three main cavities of the vocal tract, the pharynx and the oral and nasal cavities. From the oral and nasal cavities the airflow exits through the mouth and nose, respectively. The V-shaped opening between the vocal cords, called the glottis, is the most important sound source in the vocal system. The vocal cords may act in several different ways during speech. The most important function is to modulate the airflow by rapidly opening and closing, causing a buzzing sound from which vowels and voiced consonants are produced. The fundamental frequency of vibration (F0, see this chapter) depends on the mass and tension and is about 110 Hz, 200 Hz and 300 Hz for men, women and children, respectively. With stop consonants the vocal cords may shift suddenly from a completely closed position in which they cut off the airflow completely, to a totally

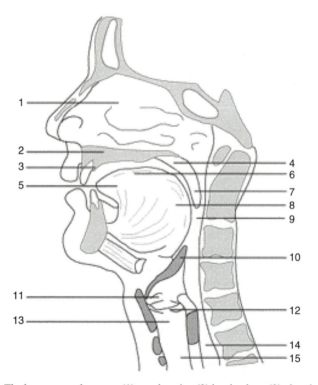

Figure 5.2 The human vocal organs. (1) nasal cavity, (2) hard palate, (3) alveolar ridge, (4) soft palate (velum), (5) tip of the tongue (apex), (6) dorsum, (7) uvula, (8) radix, (9) pharynx, (10) epiglottis, (11) false vocal cords, (12) vocal cords, (13) larynx, (14) oesophagus, and (15) trachea (from Ladefoged & Maddieson, 1996). Reproduced with permission of John Wiley and Sons Ltd.

open position producing a light cough or a glottal stop. On the other hand, with unvoiced consonants, such as /s/ or /f/, they may be completely open. An intermediate position may also occur with, for example, phonemes like /h/.

The pharynx connects the larynx to the oral cavity. It has almost fixed dimensions, but its length may be changed slightly by raising or lowering the larynx at one end and the soft palate at the other end. The soft palate also isolates or connects the route from the nasal cavity to the pharynx. At the bottom of the pharynx are the epiglottis and false vocal cords, which prevent food reaching the larynx and isolate the oesophagus from the vocal tract. The epiglottis, the false vocal cords and the vocal cords are closed during swallowing and open during normal breathing.

The oral cavity is one of the most important parts of the vocal tract. Its size, shape and acoustics can be varied by the movements of the palate, the tongue, the lips, the cheeks and the teeth. The tongue is especially flexible, the tip and the edges can be moved independently and the entire tongue can move forwards, backwards, up and down. The lips control the size and shape of the mouth opening through which speech sound is radiated. Unlike the oral cavity, the nasal cavity has fixed dimensions and shape. Its length is about 12 cm and its volume 60 cm^3. The airstream to the nasal cavity is controlled by the soft palate.

The loudness of speech is determined largely by the intensity of vibration of the vocal cords (Fant, 1960; Stevens, 1983). This, in turn, depends on subglottic pressure, in that an increase in pressure causes the air to flow more rapidly through the vocal cords (for a review see Levelt, 1989).

The acoustic wave generated by the vocal cords then passes through the vocal or supralaryngeal tract (the pharyngeal, oral and nasal cavities which act as resonators) where it is filtered and finally emitted through the lips or nostrils. This process, which is essential for the differentiation of single language sounds, comes about through a series of band pass filters that modify the wave form, allowing the passage of specific frequencies and blocking others. This concentration of sound energy is determined by the dimension and shape of the vocal tract, which changes constantly and rapidly through movements of the articulators (tongue, lips, palate).

It is possible to identify and visualize the various acoustic components of language through spectrographic analysis.[1] Using this procedure, a single component that is linked to the vibration of the vocal cords has been identified (fundamental frequency, F0), as well as a series of components (the formants F1, F2 and F3) that depend on the configuration of the supralaryngeal vocal tract (Figure 5.3).

It is important to underline the relative independence of the formants F1, F2 and F3 from F0. This latter is determined by the frequency of vibration of the vocal cords (the source of sound emission), while the other formants are determined by the vocal tract configurations (filters).

Formants have a fundamental role in the process of word production and comprehension, as demonstrated by our ability to understand whispered speech, which is produced in the absence of vocal cord vibration, but with normal configuration of the vocal tract.

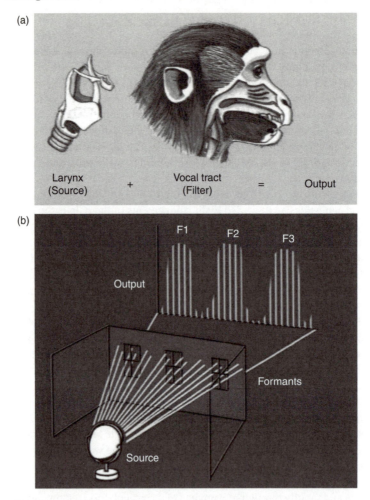

(a)

Larynx   +   Vocal tract   =   Output
(Source)   (Filter)

(b)

F1   F2   F3

Output

Formants

Source

Figure 5.3 The source/filter theory of vocal production, proposed initially for speech, appears to apply to vocal production in all mammals. The theory holds that vocalization results from the product of a sound source (usually localized in the larynx), combined with a filter placed within the vocal tract (consisting of various formants) (a). The formants, or resonances of the vocal tract, function as band pass filters that allow the passage of only specific frequencies while blocking others (b). The filtering action applies to all sounds (language and non-language) produced at the larynx (from Hauser et al., 2002). Reproduced with permission of Dr Marc Hauser.

In Chomsky and Halle's system (1968), words are made up of a sequence of separate sounds, or phonemes, represented as groups of features with distinctive characteristics and with binary value (+ or −), and identified with articulatory labels regarding voicing (± voice), tongue height (± high, low), manner (± continuous) and place of articulation (± frontal, posterior). These features can essentially be considered to be instructions to the articulatory organs, while naturally possessing acoustic correlates.

Jakobson, Fant, and Halle (1952), on the other hand, consider that the distinctive features are characterized by acoustic–perceptive labels that depend on place of articulation and the presence or absence of vocal cord vibration.

The production of these signals requires nervous system coordination of the activity of the anatomical structures of the vocal tract (lips, jaw, tongue, soft palate, vocal cords) as well as temporal organization of their movements. The degree of oral cavity closure depends on the type of consonant to be produced: for example, in the process of production of apicodental stop consonants (/t/, /d/), the rapid tongue movements must be synchronized with the movements of other articulators, such as the lips, soft palate and vibrations of the glottis. Similarly, the distinction between the sound /p/ (not voiced) and /b/ (voiced) is determined by the different time interval between onset of vocal cord vibration and the moment of release of lip closure. This difference (*voice onset time*, VOT) is enough to differentiate between the two sounds. For the consonant /p/, vocal cord vibration commences around 30 ms after lip opening, while for the consonant /b/, the time interval is much reduced, around 10 ms, with some considerable variation between languages.

Specific neural organization is responsible for the control of these motor programmes, which differs from that of more generalized motor learning. Analogously, the muscles involved show peculiar properties: craniofacial and laryngeal muscles differ from other muscles of the body in that they possess particular types of muscle fibres which allows the rapid and varied muscle contractions necessary to sustain the biomechanical apparatus specific for the movements involved in phonation (Kent, 2005).

The sounds of language can be classified into vowels, consonants, voiced consonants and semiconsonants (or semivowels). This distinction has an articulatory basis: during phonation the airflow generated by the lungs causes the vocal cords to vibrate, closing and opening in a cyclical manner. The airflow is then filtered within the oral cavity. Vowels are produced through a particular configuration of the oral tract, obtained by placing the tongue towards the back of the cavity (for /u/), or centrally (for /a/), near the soft palate (for /i/) or distant from it (for /a/), with lip rounding (/u/), or relaxed (/a/). To produce vowel sounds, therefore, it is the vibration of the air inside the oral cavity that causes the acoustic effect, without the intervention of the articulators. The production time for vowels is greater (150 ms) than the time necessary to produce consonants (< 100 ms), consonants being formed by rapid modifications or *transitions* of the frequencies making up the sound. Vowels have therefore always been considered to be 'closer', both from an articulatory and perceptive point of view, to non-language sounds and more resistant to neurological damage in terms of both production and comprehension.

In the formation of consonants the airstream through the vocal tract is obstructed, completely or partially at different points (lips, alveolar ridge and soft palate), producing explosion or friction. In voiced sounds there is both the noise of the consonant and sound resulting from the emission of a large quantity of air from the nose or parts of the mouth combined with spontaneous vibration of the vocal cords.

The articulators, in turn, can be separated into organs that have a role in sound production simply because they are anatomically present (palate, superior dental arch, posterior pharyngeal wall, cheeks and nasal cavity) and others that require active movement (inferior dental arch, lips, tongue, soft palate and pharynx).

The movements of the phono-articulatory organs when producing a target consonant or vowel are extremely variable because of the effect of contiguity between the elements making up the phonic sequence. A process of coarticulation arises when there is transition from one target sound to another, as well as elements of anticipation or perseveration with consequent modification of the vocal tract or supraglottic cavity. Common examples from English are: eight [eɪt] vs. eighth [eɪt̪θ] keep [k₊ʲip] vs. cool [kʷul] where the /t/ in 'eighth' is dental (here transcribed [t̪]) when followed by the dental fricative [θ], and the /k/ of 'keep' has a front-of-velar (transcribed [k₊]), palatalized articulation when followed by the high front vowel [i]. The /k/ of 'cool' is not so advanced, and is labialized.

Two competing theories debate the boundaries between consonant and vowels sounds: while modern phonology theory assumes separate representation and processing of consonants (Clements & Keyser, 1983; Durand, 1990; Goldsmith, 1990), the other view (MacNeilage, 1998) is that the distinction between consonant and vowel sounds is only a way of labelling sounds that, in fact, exist on a *continuum*, with vowels representing the highest level of the correlation with voicing (the degree of opening of the vocal cords during phonation).

Recently, Caramazza, Chialant, Capasso, and Miceli (2000) described two patients suffering from conduction aphasia who displayed double dissociation in a word repetition task. In one case the errors particularly affected vowels (the Italian verb *salire* was replaced by *solire*) rather than consonants, while the second patient showed an opposite picture (*salire* being replaced by *savite*). The distribution of errors within the consonant category did not involve voicing, neither did it depend on the acoustic characteristics that differentiate vowels from consonants. According to Caramazza et al., therefore, consonants and vowels are not only elaborated by different neural mechanisms, but have independent status within language production processes. The aphasic patient described by Semenza et al. (2007) also displayed errors affecting mainly production of vowels, with lexical frequency and grammatical class having no effect, except for number words (*three, eight*) which were produced correctly.[2]

Speech production disorders

Phonetic and phonological errors are an almost constant finding in the output of aphasic patients. Their analysis is fundamental for at least two reasons: for the speech pathologists to understand whether the speech production process is impaired at the level of articulatory implementation or, on the contrary, whether there is inability to access and maintain correct phonological representation during the production process.

On the other hand, studies of anatomical–clinical correlation, supported by an ever increasing amount of data obtained from neuroimaging studies, have allowed the neural circuits involved in word production to be outlined with greater precision.

Phonetic impairments

Articulatory deficits have been the hallmark of Broca's aphasia since its first decriptions. It was only in 1939, however, that, thanks to the collaboration between a neurologist (Alajouanine), a psychologist (Ombredane) and a linguist (Durand), both the acute pattern and their evolution were defined in a monograph entitled *Le Syndrome de Désintégration Phonetique dans l'aphasie* (phonetic disintegration syndrome, PDS). From an initial stage of *anarthria* (inability to articulate sounds of linguistic value), the patient passes to a *paretic* stage, followed by a *dystonic* stage. Sound distortion can occur to such an extent that another sound is produced, which can be interpreted as a phonological paraphasia (see later). On further analysis of similar cases, it emerged that the speech impairment does not follow damage to the phono-articulatory system and that the errors, unlike those observed in peripheral dysarthrias, are variable and unreliable. It follows, then, that the deficit arises from poor control of articulatory planning, so that articulation rather than being automatic becomes effortful, slow and controlled. The pattern is clearly described in the report of Lecours and Lhermitte's patient (1976, p. 93):

> In the normal state, thought is expressed through words automatically and the process of articulation is without effort, mechanical. On the contrary, my articulation is no longer automatic but needs to be ordered, directed. I have to think how to pronounce every word I wish to say. If I want to say '*bonjour*' I am unable to do so and I say '*beaus*'. If I want to say '*le*' or '*la*', if I am not careful I say '*de*' or '*da*'. For this reason I must articulate every vowel, every consonant, every syllable.

In an analysis of the phonetic characteristics of PDS, Lecours and Lhermitte (1976) and La Pointe and Johns (1975) describe the following consonant transformations: *devoicing* (/b/→ /p/), *fricative to non fricative* (/f/→ /p/), *denasalization* (/n/→ /d/), *delateralization* (/l/ →/d/). Sometimes more than one transformation is present, giving rise to more complex transformations. In general, articulatory difficulties are greater when production requires synchronization of two independent articulators, for example, the production of a nasal consonant (/m/, /n/) requires the synchronization of two articulators: the release of oral cavity closure and the lowering of the palate.

It should be noted, however, that the deficit in temporal coordination in the oral production of aphasic patients is not total. The length of fricative production is normal and processes of coarticulation have an almost normal pattern, for example, when producing the syllable /su/, aphasic patients anticipate the closed vowel /u/ in the preceding /s/ in the same way as control subjects (Katz, 1988).

The nature of the phonetic deficit in aphasia is not always the same. According to some authors, beginning with Darley, Aronson, and Brown (1975), the deficit is not primarily linguistic, but apraxic in type, limited to articulatory programming (*apraxia of speech*), as a result of lack of planning and control of the articulatory process.

According to Martin (1974), on the other hand, the term verbal apraxia reflects an outdated model of language processing. Every aphasic person, in fact, shows inefficient processing of linguistic units at different levels. Consequently, PDS is the result of the effect of an altered process of selection and combination of the linguistic units at a phonological level. To support the idea that the PDS is primarily linguistic in nature, it should be mentioned that the deficit spares serial speech (for example, prayers, days of the week) and may vary according to production conditions (spontaneous speech, repetition).

A substantial similarity between phonetic deficits consequent to aphasia has been demonstrated in various cross-studies of language. For example, the finding of altered voice onset time (VOT) in the production of word-initial occlusive consonants, described by Blumstein and colleagues (1980) has also been seen in aphasic patients speaking different languages, including tonal languages[3] (for a review see Gandour, Wong, & Hutchins, 1998).

Anatomical correlations

The area most frequently affected by PDS and, more generally, in aphasias in which phonetic deficits are prevalent, is Broca's area, as recently shown by Hillis et al. (2004) who investigated 40 aphasic patients affected by PDS.

Similarly, the results of a PET study carried out on normal subjects during word production tasks showed activation of Broca's area and the neighbouring precentral sulcus during repetition and reading aloud of words (Price, Moore, & Frackowiak, 1996).

Phonological output impairments

In a series of papers, Sheila Blumstein (for a review see Blumstein, 1994, 2001) convincingly demonstrated that phonological errors with similar characteristics can be found in all types of aphasia and in all languages.

Analysis of the oral production of aphasic patients reveals errors of *selection*, for example, the substitution of phonemes (*cat* → *bat*), or errors of planning because of an inability to maintain the correct order of phonemes within the phonological string (*black* → *balck*). The substitutions usually affect a single feature only, for example, voicing, with the production of a voiceless consonant in place of a voiced consonant and vice versa. Usually consonants are more affected than vowels. A further characteristic of phonological errors in aphasia is their unpredictable nature. A patient who has committed a phonological error in the pronunciation of a word may later produce the same word correctly, and the voiced–voiceless substitution (/d/ /t/) is as frequent as the inverse substitution (/t/ /d/).

The influence of the syllabic structure of the target word on the type of errors made during the process of feature selection still needs to be identified. In fact, phonemic substitution is more frequent within a syllable containing a single consonant (for example, the /f/ of 'far'), rather than a syllable that contains the same phoneme within a consonant cluster (for example, the /f/ of 'flow').

From a different point of view, the phonological errors of aphasic patients have been divided into coding errors at the *lexical* stage and at the post-lexical stage. Beland, Caplan, and Nespoulous (1990), for example, have interpreted errors that are sensitive to syllable structure as being a result of damage to the post-lexical system, in that the phonological lexical representation does not contain information specifying the syllabic structure.

More recently, Goldrick and Rapp (2007) made a detailed analysis of errors committed in spontaneous naming and repetition by two patients, the first affected by a deficit in phonological representation at the lexical level, and the second at post-lexical level. In the first patient, the errors were present only in naming tasks, with repetition of the same words being significantly better and the presence of semantic paraphasias (*shirt* → *skirt*), and morpheme substitution (*butterfly* → *butterflower*). The patient also showed better production of high rather than low frequency words. The second patient, in contrast, displayed errors in naming and repetition that were quantitatively similar but were sensitive to the complexity of the phonological structure, such as phoneme frequency, place of articulation and the position of the syllable within the word.

Finally, a clinical picture compatible with damage to the buffer system has been described in some patients (Bisiacchi, Cipolotti, & Denes, 1989; Bub, Black, Howell, & Kertesz, 1987; Caramazza, Miceli, & Villa, 1986). The production of non-words in tasks of repetition, reading aloud and writing (tasks that require the phonological representation to be maintained, without semantic help, for the time required for conversion between input and output) was compromised to the same degree. On qualitative analysis, the picture was characterized by the presence of phonological errors such as substitution, omission and transposition. Similarly, the patient described by Caramazza et al. (2000), showed phonological errors in all oral output modalities (picture naming, repetition, reading).

Anatomical correlations

In one of the first correlation studies between error type in naming and site of lesion determined by CAT, Cappa, Cavallotti, and Vignolo (1981) hypothesized that the phonological aspects of a word are processed in the perisylvian areas of the left hemisphere, while the marginal areas, distant from the Sylvian fissure, process the semantic-lexical aspects.

More recently, Levelt and Indefrey (2000) summarized the results of functional neuroimaging studies (fMRI and PET) carried out on normal subjects during tasks of word production (picture naming, reading aloud). The process of lemma selection (the meaning and the syntax of a lexical item – see Chapter 6) activates the central part of the second left temporal convolution. Wernicke's area is activated in all tasks requiring recall of a specific phonological code (naming, reading aloud). Finally, the processes of phonetic coding, articulation and syllabification, activate the anterior prerolandic areas, including Broca's area.

Perception and comprehension of language sounds

Within the process of comprehension of spoken language the following stages can be identified:

- A sublexical auditory phonological stage, the end product being the identification of phonemes in order to obtain the phonological form of the words.
- A lexical stage, where the content, semantically rich words and the morphosyntactic elements are processed.
- A suprasegmental stage, allowing the processing of intonation, which marks separation of the different constituents of the verbal message and word stress, so that the prosodic aspects of output are understood.

The process of phoneme recognition and identification is the first stage of the language process, consisting of the ability to differentiate between language sounds on the basis of their phonetic characteristics (Pisoni & Luce, 1987). It is still not clear, however, to what extent this mechanism is separate from the more generalized processes of auditory perception, nor are the mechanisms through which some acoustic signals are perceived as phonemes and their neurological bases clearly established.

There are three hypotheses regarding the nature of phonetic perception. The first proposes the existence of a specific mechanism for language processing, active from the moment at which the speech sound enters the cerebral cortex (Liberman & Whalen, 2000). According to this hypothesis, the process of phoneme perception comes about through activation of the neuromotor programmes of the articulators (tongue, lips, vocal cords) corresponding to the phonemes perceived, so that a phonetic code with motor characteristics is activated (*motor theory of language perception*, Liberman et al., 1967). The basis of this theory is the concept that the objects of language perception must be constant within the group of distinctive features and without acoustic–phonetic variability: this need can only be satisfied through the activation of neuromotor programmes, which do not take into consideration individual variations in production.

According to articulatory phonology (Browman & Goldstein, 1995), spoken language is not considered primarily a system for the production of sounds, but instead a system specific to the production of articulatory gestures through the work of six articulators: lips, soft palate, larynx, tongue (body, tip and root). At the base of this approach lies the fact that the smallest units of spoken language, phonemes, do not exist as distinct and constant units in the acoustic signal. In fact the acoustic signals corresponding to a single phoneme vary constantly depending on the context in which they are spoken (coarticulation). In particular, the formant transitions of a phoneme can vary according to the phonemes that precede or follow it. However, despite these variations, phonemic perception occurs at a frequency that exceeds 10–15 phonemes per second, a fact that conflicts with a theory that foresees a series of context-dependent transformations. It should also be underlined that non-language, simple sounds, such as tones or noise, cannot be perceived at such speed, further proof of the existence of mechanisms dedicated to language perception.

Therefore the hypothesis that oral speech is fundamentally a gesture seems to overcome these difficulties in that, as Studdert-Kennedy (2005) points out, during the process of coarticulation, the specific articulatory gestures for the single phonemes overlap in time, allowing a rapid process of production and perception.

The recent discovery of activation of the same motor areas (Broca's area and other neighbouring areas), during both a passive listening task and a production of monosyllables (Wilson, Saygin, Sereno, & Iacoboni, 2004), is open to two interpretations. According to the first interpretation, there are echo neurons in Broca's area that mediate the process of imitation of verbal sounds; that is, they have a similar role to that of mirror neurons in the visual modality (for a summary see Rizzolatti & Craighero, 2004). Alternatively, these data reinforce the hypothesis of active participation of the motor system in the passage from acoustic impulse to a phonetic-phonological code, in agreement with the motor theory of language perception.

Pulvermüller et al. (2006) found that when normal subjects listen silently to syllables that include the stop consonants /p/ and /t/ there is parallel activation of the left superior temporal cortex and the motor areas corresponding to movements of the lips and tongue specific to the production of the same syllables (Figure 5.4). These data reinforce the hypothesis of active participation of the motor cortex in tasks of phonemic perception, supporting the existence of a direct connection between phonological mechanisms of production and comprehension.

According to Fowler (1981), on the other hand, the movements of specific portions of the vocal tract, rather than neuromotor commands, lie at the base of the processes of spoken language perception, with a specific phonetic correlate. Unlike proponents of the motor theory of language perception, Fowler maintains that language perception does not have underlying specialized species-specific mechanisms, but obeys the same general principles underlying other perceptual abilities.

According to Diehl, Lotto, and Holt (2004) the first stages of word perception are based on the same functional and anatomical systems that process other classes of acoustic environmental symbols. Divergence comes about only when the linguistic signal comes into contact with semantic-lexical representations (Stevens, 1983). This theory, therefore, assumes that word perception is retrieved from the acoustic signals (distinctive features, phonemes, words and linguistic units

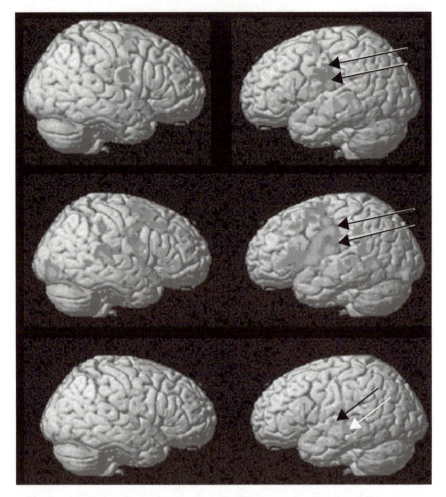

Figure 5.4 Activation elicited by actions and perceptions related to the lips and tongue. (Top) Repetitive lip movements (black arrow) and tongue movements (white arrow) tested against rest as a baseline ($P < .05$, family-wise-error-corrected). (Middle) Repetitive silent articulation of syllables including the lip-related phoneme [p] (black arrow) and the tongue-related phoneme [t] (white arrow) tested against rest ($p < .05$, false-discovery-rate-corrected). (Bottom) Listening to spoken syllables, including the lip-related phoneme [p] (black arrow) and the tongue-related phoneme [t] (white arrow) tested against listening to noise with spectrotemporal characteristics that matched those of the syllables ($p < .05$, family-wise-error-corrected) (from Pulvermüller et al., 2006). Copyright © 2006, National Academy of Sciences, reproduced with permission.

of higher order), without the intermediation of the perception of gestures or corresponding motor programmes. Once the acoustic information has been extracted and coded, such as the spectral structures, the FO and the length of signal, the acoustic representations are translated into distinctive features, conceived as perceptual abstract codes that represent both a group of acoustic attributes and their articulatory correlates. The final step consists of phonological processing, which allows phonemes to be discriminated and identified as the specific sounds of the various spoken languages (for a review see Remez, 2001).

A characteristic of phonological perception is the fact that it is categorical: categorical perception (CP) means that a change in some variable along a continuum is perceived, not as gradual but in terms of discrete categories. While it is difficult to discriminate between two acoustically different stimuli belonging to the same category (allophones of the same phonemes[4]), it is easy to discriminate between phonemes belonging to different categories (/p/ and /t/) even if, from an acoustic point of view, pairs of stimuli belonging to different categories differ as much as pairs of stimuli belonging to the same category (Liberman et al., 1967).

In an already classical experiment, Liberman et al. (1967) asked normal participants to identify synthetic syllables in which the second formant transition was varied in equal steps.[5] Depending on the precise parameter values, the resulting sounds were perceived as 'ba', 'da' or 'ga'. Although in this experiment the change is gradual, this is not the way it is perceived. Participants regularly perceive the different stimuli as being instances of one of the three syllable types, 'ba', 'da' or 'ga'.

Along the same lines, in a task of discrimination of syllables pairs varying in the same parameters, performance is at *chance* when the stimuli belong to the same category, but almost perfect for couples belonging to different categories of the same phoneme (Liberman et al., 1967).

CP was for a long time considered a species-specific characteristic, innate and occurring only for language sounds. Later, however, CP was found also to be present for non-language sounds (Miller, Wier, Pastore, Kelly, & Dooling, 1976; Pisoni, 1977) and in other species. Some animals, in fact (chinchillas, macaques), if trained, demonstrate CP for language sounds similar to those of human speakers.

These results seem to cast doubt on the idea that the perception of spoken language is supported by a speech mode. It would seem, in fact, that language coding comes about through a non-specialized auditory mechanism, active in the processing of both linguistic and non-linguistic signals.

Anatomical correlations

Data provided by functional neuroimaging studies (PET and fMRI, for a review see Benson, Richardson, Whalen, & Lai, 2006) have revealed two distinct patterns of cerebral activation during phonological perception. The first, present in passive listening tasks, is characterized by bilateral activation of the superior temporal lobes, including the primary acoustic areas. In more complex tasks, on the other hand, such as phoneme discrimination or making judgements about rhyme, there is activation of a neural circuit involving the left frontal lobe. This different pattern of activation is obviously linked to the different characteristics of the tasks. The first task is more automatic in nature, while the second task requires not only a process of phonological perception but greater attentional resources and the involvement of the short-term memory system.

However, it is clinical neurolinguistics that has provided the most significant data in the drawing up of the functional architecture and the anatomical bases of phonetic perception. The greatest contribution comes from the study of patients affected by a selective central auditory disorder, while their peripheral hearing is normal. Sometimes the deficit affects processing of both verbal signals and non-verbal signals (acoustic agnosia), whereas in other cases it is limited to language (word deafness).

The traditional neurological interpretation of this condition is that it reflects the effect of a lesion that disconnects both of the acoustic primary areas from Wernicke's area.

Pure word deafness is characterized by an almost complete loss of spoken language comprehension. The patient is able to hear the sounds, but is unable to repeat or understand what has been said. Vowel sounds are perceived better than consonants (vowels are considered, as said before in this chapter, to be 'closer' to non-language sounds than consonants). The comprehension of the prosodic aspects of language is preserved and the patient is able to judge when the speaker is using the patient's own language or a foreign language (Denes & Semenza, 1975). This sparing may be the result of greater 'resistance' to cerebral damage of the functional structures dedicated to prosodic analysis, in that prosodic analysis does not require an analysis of acoustic-articulatory features.

The case of patient CS (Denes, Balliello, Volterra, & Pelegrini, 1986), affected by Landau-Kleffner syndrome (for a review see Denes, 2008) has been considered important in clarifying the relationship between deficits of phonemic perception and language processing. This rare syndrome affects normally developing children between 4 and 7 and is characterized by epilepsy and regression to the point of the disappearance of language comprehension and production. Peripheral hearing and intelligence are normal. In all tests of perception and identification of phonemes CS displayed chance performance, which precluded any form of speech and language therapy rehabilitation. Surprisingly, however, the child learnt written language and was able to communicate effectively through this. Perez and Davidoff (2001) described the case of a patient with similar symptoms who managed to learn and communicate through sign language. It can, therefore, be assumed that in most cases of verbal deafness, the comprehension deficit is a result of a specific disturbance of phoneme decoding, leaving the other language components unimpaired and accessible through written or visual channels.

At times verbal deafness is accompanied by an acoustic agnosia. The interpretation of this disorder is controversial. Some authors consider it to have an underlying psycho-acoustic deficit, with preservation of the mechanisms of linguistic processing of the acoustic signal. For others, however (Vignolo, 1982), the acoustic agnosia is simply the epiphenomenon of a more general conceptual-semantic deficit following aphasia. This hypothesis was recently confirmed by Saygin, Dick, Wilson, Dronkers, and Bates (2003). In a task involving the matching of environmental sounds and corresponding sentences to pictures, Broca's and

Wernicke's aphasics were the most impaired, while anomic and right hemisphere-damaged patients showed less severe deficits. Impairments in verbal and non-verbal domains went hand in hand. These results suggest that, at least in some cases, aphasia is not a pure linguistic deficit and that language may share neural resources utilized for the processing of meaningful information across cognitive domains.

Phonological processing deficits are present in all types of aphasia. Basso, Casati, and Vignolo (1977) and Blumstein, Tartter, Nigro, and Statlender (1984) submitted aphasic individuals to tasks of discrimination and identification of pairs of syllables varying in voicing and place of articulation. In general, the patients were unimpaired in discrimination tasks, but showed significant difficulty in the identification tasks. These findings suggest that the difficulties in phonological perception are not because of an inability to perceive the acoustic dimensions of the stimulus, but rather represent an inability to connect information obtained from the perceptual analysis to the abstract phonological representation.

It is of particular interest that no correlation has been found between poor performance on sublexical tests of phoneme identification and tests of word comprehension: many studies (Basso et al., 1977; Blumstein, Cooper, Zurif, & Caramazza, 1977; Miceli, Gainotti, Caltagirone, & Fasullo, 1980) have found a pattern of double dissociation between phoneme and word comprehension. Some patients, in fact, performed poorly on tests of syllable identification, while word comprehension was good. Other patients demonstrated the opposite trend. Similarly, in multiple choice tasks of word–picture matching, where foils were either semantically similar to the target (for example, if the test word was 'dog', the semantic distracter was 'cat') or phonologically similar (for example 'fog'), the aphasics errors were mainly semantic, showing that the deficit of language comprehension in aphasia is not phonological but is prevalently semantic-lexical in nature (Gainotti, Miceli, Silveri, & Villa, 1982).

These findings, therefore, support a theory that considers word understanding to be an expression of two separate processes, one being phonological, sublexical, the other lexical. The clinical demonstration of this theory is offered, according to Hickok and Pöppel (2004), by conduction aphasia. The feature that distinguishes this type of aphasia from other forms of fluent aphasia (see Chapter 4) is the dissociation between good word comprehension and impaired repetition. According to Hickok and Pöppel (2004), conduction aphasia represents an example of selective sparing of the lexical comprehension route, in part perhaps supported by the linguistic abilities of the right hemisphere, while the lesion of the left temporal lobe puts the system of phonological analysis and its interface with the articulatory system out of use. Phonological paraphasias are interpreted as the consequence of a lack of control of the temporal lobe over the phonological aspects of production.

The opposite picture is seen in transcortical sensory aphasia, characterized by good repetition of both words and non-words, but virtually absent language comprehension. The patient does not understand the meaning of the words that he or she is able to repeat correctly, sometimes to the point of becoming echolalic. In this case it is can be hypothesized that there is a disconnection between the phonological system and the lexical system, with sparing of the former. Repetition is preserved because the auditory-motor circuit is intact, while there is a loss of the interface between sound and meaning (Hickok & Pöppel, 2004). From an anatomical point of view, the lesion, as has already been stated, spares Wernicke's area but affects the surrounding areas, that is, the posterior section of the left temporal lobe.

Neurological bases and functional mechanisms of word repetition

In general, word repetition is considered easier than other oral production tasks such as naming or reading aloud, in that it does not require activation of conceptual or phonological representations and, from an articulatory point of view, it is easier to plan a string of phonemes when the auditory form has already been provided.

A selective repetition deficit can occur, as said before, only when there is disconnection between Broca's and Wernicke's areas because of an interruption of the internal arcuate fasciculus. In parallel with the anatomical model, the process of repetition foresees, from a functional point of view, the existence of a sublexical mechanism that converts the product of acoustic analysis into phonemes that, in turn, will be transmitted to Broca's area for subsequent articulatory planning.

More recently, however, two different types of repetition deficit have been described, the first characterized by a disorder of reproduction and the other by a disorder of repetition. The reproduction disorder consists of difficulty in repeating single words, but above all, non-words, with the presence of phonological paraphasias. In the second disorder, the patient has no difficulty in repeating isolated words but has greater difficulty as the number of words to be repeated increases.

Described for the first time by Warrington and Shallice (1969) and replicated by many authors (for a summary see Vallar & Shallice, 1990), the reproduction deficit has been interpreted as the result of a specific deficit in verbal short-term memory rather than being a primarily linguistic deficit.

A different interpretation has been attributed to the repetition impairment described by Michel and Andreewsky (1983) and by Howard and Franklin (1987). Error analysis has revealed semantic errors, with a marked effect on grammatical class and imageability, so that nouns are repeated better than verbs and high frequency words are repeated better than low frequency words or non-words (Beauvois, Dérouesné, & Bastard, 1980). This group of symptoms, similar to those present in deep dyslexia (see Chapter 8), suggests the existence of a two routes at work in repetition tasks, one sublexical, active in non-word processing, and a second, semantic-lexical, specific for word processing. If the first is damaged, there is a resulting inability to repeat non-words. If, on the other hand, the damage to the sublexical system is associated with a deficit of the semantic system, the clinical picture will be characterized by inability to repeat non-words together with the production of semantic paraphasias in word repetition (deep dysphasia, see Katz & Goodglass, 1990).

Prosodic aspects of language

Through prosody (from the Greek προσῳδία, the patterns of stress and intonation in a language), it is possible to communicate and understand the suprasegmental characteristics of language related to stress, pitch and intonation, and obtained by variations of the fundamental frequency (F0), intensity and temporal rhythm conveyed by pauses and syllable length. Prosody conveys paralinguistic and emotional information. While for languages like English the difference between a question and a statement is marked not only by a change in intonation but also by a different superficial structure (*John left – Did John leave?*), for languages such as Italian it is sometimes only through the use of specific prosodic patterns that it is possible to differentiate between questions and a statements. For example, F0 decreases towards the end of the sentence in a statement and rises in a question. Moreover, prosodic markers define syntactic boundaries, such as those that delimit syntagmatic groups in the sequence of connected words (for example, 'will you haveI marmalade IorI jam?'), through modification of temporal rhythm (Price, Ostendorf, Shattuck-Hufnagel, & Fong, 1991). On the other hand, the processing of rhythmic and melodic components of speech allows the emotive state of the speaker to be signalled and understood.

In a review of the anatomical bases underlying prosody, Baum and Pell (1999) propose two different hypotheses. According to the hypothesis of functional lateralization, prosodic information carrying linguistic information is processed in the left hemisphere, while the right hemisphere processes the affective contents of prosody. A second hypothesis based on the processing of acoustic indices suggests that prosodic temporal indices are processed by the left hemisphere, while spectral indices are processed by the right hemisphere (Van Lancker & Sidtis, 1992).

Shah, Baum, and Dwivedi (2006) found left hemisphere damaged subjects were selectively impaired in using the prosodic modifications necessary to distinguish between sentences containing prosodic boundaries. In contrast, patients with right hemisphere damage were impaired in discriminating and identifying the emotional content of semantically anomalous phrases (Pell, 2007).

In conclusion, it can be affirmed that the right hemisphere controls the emotional characteristics of prosodic stimuli, while it is the left hemisphere's task to process prosodic representations, bestowing on them value as signals within the language content.

Foreign accent syndrome

Specific phonetic and phonological contrasts characterize the different languages. The acquisition of these contrasts occurs in the first stages of language development, through a process of synchronization of the perceptual and motor systems of the native language. In this way the child, at around 2 years old, will speak with an 'accent', which, despite prolonged exposure to other languages, he or she will wholly or partially maintain throughout life.

A left hemisphere lesion can, in some rare cases (Blumstein, Alexander, Ryalls, Katz, & Dworetzky, 1987; Fridriksson et al., 2005) modify the accent, so that the patient seems to have lost his or her native accent and acquired a different type of accent, which is perceived by the listener as being foreign. An example of this is the case of a Norwegian patient who seemed to have acquired a German accent, or a Dutch patient who spoke with a French accent. In general the patient's production is perceived as 'foreign' with no specific language being identifiable (foreign accent syndrome).

Analysis of the phonological characteristics of these patients reveals the presence of prosodic and segmental disorders, varying in each patient but differing from the segmental and prosodic disorders seen in fluent aphasia or dysarthria. Instrumental analysis of oral production has excluded the hypothesis that patients affected with this disorder have acquired the characteristics of the accent of another language community. It is more likely that their cerebral damage has caused them to produce a variety of phonetic characteristics that do not belong to their native language, so that the listener presumes their accent is foreign. The nature of this single disorder is not completely clear at the present time. It could represent the effect of a compensatory strategy for defective control of the motor regulation of oral production (for a review, see Gurd & Coleman, 2006).

Notes

1   The spectrograph is an instrument that converts a sound wave into a spectrogram, made up of a graph in which the vertical scale represents the frequencies of the components of the sound and the horizontal scale represents decibel intensity. The spectrograph is frequently used in acoustic physics but is slowly being replaced by the system of numerical analysis of sound.
2   Cubelli (1991) has described a similar pattern in the written modality.
3   In tonal languages, for example Chinese, the same syllable can be produced in four different tones with a different meaning corresponding to each different realization. In other languages, a syllable can be produced at a different pitch (high or low), with no difference in meaning.
4   An allophone is a phonic variation of a phoneme, tied to a specific context and with no distinctive power. An example of this in English is the different [*l*] sounds in the word *clearly*, although both are perceived as belonging to the same category and represent the same phoneme.
5   Spectrographic interpretation of occlusive consonants is based not so much on the consonant segment itself but rather on the vowels that precede or follow it. Their formants, in fact, present clear deviations, known as *formant transitions*, which represent the visible trace of the rapid variations in vocal behaviour (that is, the position of the organs inside the mouth) at the moment at which they change during the passage from one phoneme to the next.

References

Alajouanine, T., Ombredane, A., & Durand, M. (1939), *Le syndrome de la désintégration phonétique dans l'aphasie*. Paris: Masson.
Basso, A., Casati, G., & Vignolo L. A. (1977). Phonemic identification defect in aphasia. *Cortex*, *13*, 84–95.
Baum, S. R., & Pell, M. D. (1999). The neural bases of prosody: Insights from lesion studies and neuroimaging. *Aphasiology*, *13* (8), 581–608.

Beauvois, M. F., Dérouesné, J., & Bastard, V. (1980). Auditory parallel to phonologic alexia. Paper presented at the third European Conference of the International Neuropsychological Society, Chianciano, Italy.

Beland, R., Caplan, D., & Nespoulous, J. L. (1990). The role of abstract phonological representations in word production: Evidence from phonetic paraphasias. *Journal of Neurolinguistics*, *5*, 125–164.

Benson, R. R., Richardson, M., Whalen, D. H., & Lai, S. (2006). Phonetic processing areas revealed by sinewave speech and acoustically similar non-speech. *Neuroimage*, *31* (1), 342–353.

Bisiacchi, P. S., Cipolotti, L., & Denes, G. (1989). Impairment in processing meaningless verbal material in several modalities: The relationship between short-term memory and phonological skills. *Quarterly Journal of Experimental Psychology*, *41A*, 293–319.

Blumstein, S. E. (1994). The neurobiology of the sound structure of language. In M. S. Gazzaniga (Ed.), *The cognitive neurosciences* (pp. 915–929). Cambridge, MA: MIT Press.

Blumstein, S. E. (2001). Deficits of speech production and speech perception in aphasia. In R. S. Berndt (Ed.), *Handbook of neuropsychology* (pp. 95–113). Amsterdam: Elsevier.

Blumstein, S. E., Alexander, M., Ryalls, J., Katz, W., & Dworetzky, B. (1987). On the nature of the foreign accent syndrome: A case study. *Brain and Language*, *31*, 215–244.

Blumstein, S. E., Cooper, W. E., Goodglass, H., Statlender, S., & Gottlieb, J. (1980). Production deficits in aphasia: A voice-onset time analysis. *Brain and Language*, *9*, 153–170.

Blumstein, S. E., Cooper, W. E., Zurif, E. G., & Caramazza, A. (1977). The perception and production of voice-onset time in aphasia. *Neuropsychologia*, *15* (3), 371–383.

Blumstein, S. E., Tartter, V. C., Nigro, G., & Statlender, S. (1984). Acoustic cues for the perception of place of articulation in aphasia. *Brain and Language*, *22*, 128–149.

Browman, C. P., & Goldstein, L. (1995). Dynamics and articulatory phonology. In R. F. Port & T. van Gelder (Eds.), *Mind as motion* (pp. 175–194). Cambridge, MA: MIT Press.

Bub, D., Black, S., Howell, J., & Kertesz, A. (1987). Damage to input and output buffers. What's a lexicality effect doing in a place like that? In E. Keller & M. Gopnik (Eds.), *Motor and sensory processes of language*. Hillsdale, NJ: Lawrence Erlbaum Associates, Inc.

Cappa, S. F., Cavalliotti, G., & Vignolo, L. A. (1981). Phonemic and lexical errors in fluent aphasia correlation with lesion site. *Neuropsychologia*, *19*, 171–177.

Caramazza, A., Chialant, D., Capasso, R., & Miceli, G. (2000). Separable processing of consonants and vowels. *Nature*, *403* (6768), 428–430.

Caramazza, A., Miceli, G., & Villa, G. (1986). The role of the (output) phonological buffer in spelling, writing and repetition. *Cognitive Neuropsychology*, *3*, 37–76.

Chomsky, N., & Halle, M. (1968). *The sound pattern of English*. New York: Harper & Row.

Clements, G. N., & Keyser, S. (1983). *CV phonology: A generative theory of the syllable*. Cambridge, MA: MIT Press.

Cubelli, R. (1991). A selective deficit for writing vowels in acquired dysgraphia. *Nature*, *353* (6341), 258–260.

Darley, F. L., Aronson, A. E., & Brown, J. R. (1975). *Motor speech disorders*. Philadelphia: W. B. Saunders.

Denes, G. (2008). Acquired epileptiform aphasia or Landau-Kleffner syndrome: Clinical and linguistic aspects. In B. Stemmer & H. A. Whitaker (Eds.), *Handbook of neuroscience of language* (pp. 361–367). London: Academic Press.

Denes, G., Balliello, S., Volterra, V., & Pellegrini, A. (1986). Oral and written language in a case of childhood phonemic deafness. *Brain and Language, 29*, 252–267.

Denes, G., & Semenza, C. (1975). Auditory modality-specific anomia: Evidence from a case of pure word deafness. *Cortex, 11*, 401–411.

Diehl, R. L., Lotto, A. J., & Holt, L. L. (2004). Speech perception. *Annual Review of Psychology, 55*, 149–179.

Durand, J. (1990). *Generative and non-linear phonology*. London: Longman.

Fant, G. (1960). *Acoustic theory of speech production*. The Hague: Mouton.

Fowler, C. A. (1981). Production and perception of coarticulation among stressed and unstressed vowels. *Journal of Speech and Hearing Research, 24* (1), 127–139.

Fridriksson, J., Ryalls, J., Rorden, C., Morgan, P. S., George, M. S., & Baylis, G. C. (2005). Brain damage and cortical compensation in foreign accent syndrome. *Neurocase, 11* (5), 319–324.

Gainotti, G., Miceli, G., Silveri, M. C., & Villa, G. (1982). Some anatomo-clinical aspects of phonemic and semantic comprehension disorders in aphasia. *Acta Neurologica Scandinavica, 66* (6), 652–665.

Gandour, J., Wong, D., & Hutchins, G. (1998). Pitch processing in the human brain is influenced by language experience. *Neuroreport, 9* (9), 2115–2119.

Goldrick, M., & Rapp, B. (2007). Lexical and post-lexical phonological representations in spoken production, *Cognition, 102* (2), 219–260.

Goldsmith, J. (1990). *Autosegmental and metrical phonology*. Oxford, UK: Blackwell.

Gurd, J. M., & Coleman, J. S. (2006). Foreign accent syndrome: Best practice, theoretical issues and outstanding questions. *Journal of Neurolinguistics, 19*, 424–429.

Hauser, M. D., Chomsky, N., & Fitch, W. T. (2002). The faculty of language: What is it, who has it, and how did it evolve? *Science, 298* (5598), 1569–1579.

Hickok, G., & Pöppel, D. (2004). Dorsal and ventral streams: A framework for understanding aspects of the functional anatomy of language. *Cognition, 92* (1–2), 67–99.

Hillis, A. E., Work, M., Barker, P. B., Jacobs, M. A., Breese, E. L., & Maurer, K. (2004). Re-examining the brain regions crucial for orchestrating speech articulation. *Brain, 127*, 1479–1487.

Howard, D., & Franklin, S. (1987). Three ways for understanding written words and their use in two contrasting cases of surface dyslexia. In A. Allport, D. Mackay, W. Prinz, & E. Scheerer (Eds.), *Language perception and production*. London: Academic Press.

Jakobson, R., Fant, G., & Halle, M. (1952). *Preliminaries to speech analysis*. Cambridge, MA: MIT Press.

Katz, R. B., & Goodglass, H. (1990). Deep dysphasia: Analysis of a rare form of repetition disorder. *Brain and Language, 39* (1), 153–185.

Katz, W. F. (1988). Anticipatory coarticulation in aphasia: Acoustic and perceptual data. *Brain and Language, 35*, 340–368.

Kent, R. D. (2005). The uniqueness of speech among motor systems. *Clinical Linguistics and Phonetics, 18*, 495–505.

La Pointe, L. L., & Johns, D. F. (1975). Some phonemic characteristics in apraxia of speech. *Journal of Communication Disorders, 8* (3), 259–269.

Ladefoged, P., & Maddieson, I. (1996). *The sounds of the world's languages*. Oxford, UK: Blackwell.

Lecours, A. R., & Lhermitte, F. (1976). The pure form of the phonetic disintegration syndrome (pure anarthria): Anatomo-clinical report of an historical case. *Brain and Language, 3*, 88–113.

Levelt, W. J. M. (1989). *Speaking: From intention to articulation*. Cambridge, MA: MIT Press.

Levelt, W., & Indefrey, P. (2000). The speaking mind/brain. In A. Marantz, Y. Miyashita, & W. O'Neil (Eds.), *Image, language, brain* (pp. 77–93). London: MIT Press.

Liberman, A. M., Cooper, F. S., Shankweiler, D., & Studdert-Kennedy, M. (1967). Perception of the speech code. *Psychological Review, 74*, 431–461.

Liberman, A. M., & Whalen, D. H. (2000). On the relation of speech to language. *Trends in Cognitive Sciences, 4* (5), 187–196.

MacNeilage, P. F. (1998). The frame/content theory of evolution of speech production. *Behavioral and Brain Sciences, 21*, 499–546.

Maddieson, I. (1984). *Patterns of sounds*. Cambridge, UK: Cambridge University Press.

Martin, A. D. (1974). Some objections to the term apraxia of speech. *Journal of Speech and Hearing Disorders, 39* (1), 53–64.

Martinet, A. (1960). *Eléments de linguistique générale*. Paris: Librairie Armand Colin.

Miceli, G., Gainotti, G., Calatagirone, C., & Fasullo, C. (1980). Some aspects of phonological impairment in aphasia. *Brain and Language, 11*, 159–169.

Michel, F., & Andreewsky, E. (1983). Deep dyslexia: An analogue of deep dyslexia in the auditory modality. *Brain and Language, 18*, 212–223.

Miller, J. D., Wier, C. C., Pastore, R. E., Kelly, W. J., & Dooling, R. J. (1976). Discrimination and labelling of noise-buzz sequences with varying noise-lead times: An example of categorical perception. *Journal of the Acoustical Society of America, 60*, 410–417.

Pell, M. D. (2007). Reduced sensitivity to prosodic attitudes in adults with focal right hemisphere brain damage. *Brain and Language, 101* (1), 64–79.

Perez, E. R., & Davidoff, V. (2001). Sign language in childhood epileptic aphasia (Landau-Kleffner syndrome). *Developmental Medicine and Child Neurology, 43* (11), 739–744.

Pinker, S. (1994). *The language instinct*. Cambridge, MA: MIT Press.

Pisoni, D. B. (1977). Identification and discrimination of the relative onset time of two component tones: Implications for voicing perception in stops. *Journal of the Acoustical Society of America, 61* (5), 1352–1361.

Pisoni, D. B., & Luce, P. A. (1987). Acoustic–phonetic representations in word recognition. *Cognition, 25* (1–2), 21–52.

Price, C. J., Moore, C. J., & Frackowiak, R. S. J. (1996). The effect of varying stimulus rate and duration on brain activity during reading. *NeuroImage, 3*, 40–52.

Price, P. J., Ostendorf, S., Shattuck-Hufnagel, S., & Fong, C. (1991). Use of prosody in syntactic disambiguation. *Journal of the Acoustical Society of America, 90*, 2956–2970.

Pulvermüller, F., Huss, M., Kherif, F., Moscoso del Prado Martin, F., Hauk, O., & Shtyrov, Y. (2006). Motor cortex maps articulatory features of speech sounds. *Proceedings of the National Academy of Sciences, USA, 103* (20), 7865–7870.

Remez, R. E. (2001). The interchange of phonology and perception considered from the perspective of organization. In E. V. Hume & K. A. Johnson (Eds.), *The role of speech perception phenomena in phonology* (pp. 27–52). San Diego, CA: Academic Press.

Rizzolatti, G., & Craighero, L. (2004). The mirror-neuron system. *Annual Review of Neuroscience, 27*, 169–192.

Saygin, A. P., Dick, F., Wilson, S. M., Dronkers, N. F., & Bates, E. (2003). Neural resources for processing language and environmental sounds: Evidence from aphasia. *Brain, 126* (4), 928–945.

Semenza, C., Bencini, G. M., Bertella, L., Mori, I., Pignatti, R., Ceriani, F., et al. (2007). A dedicated neural mechanism for vowel selection: A case of relative vowel deficit sparing the number lexicon. *Neuropsychologia, 45* (2), 425–430.

Shah, A. P., Baum, S. R., & Dwivedi, V. D. (2006). Neural substrates of linguistic prosody: Evidence from syntactic disambiguation in the productions of brain-damaged patients *Brain and Language*, *96*, 78–89.

Stevens, K. N. (1983). Design features of speech sound systems. In P. F. MacNeilage (Ed.), *The production of speech*. New York: Springer.

Studdert-Kennedy, M. (2005). How did language go discrete? In M. Tallerman (Ed.), *Language origins: Perspectives on evolution*. Oxford, UK: Oxford University Press.

Vallar, G., & Shallice, T. (1990). *Neuropsychological impairments of short-term memory*. New York: Cambridge University Press.

Van Lancker, D., & Sidtis, J. J. (1992). The identification of affective-prosodic stimuli by left- and right-hemisphere-damaged subjects: All errors are not created equal. *Journal of Speech and Hearing Research*, *35* (5), 963–970; Comment. (1993). *Journal of Speech and Hearing Research*, *36* (6), 1191.

Vignolo, L. A. (1982). Auditory agnosia. *Philosophical Transactions of the Royal Society of London, B*, *298*, 49–57.

Warrington, E. K., & Shallice, T. (1969). The selective impairment of auditory verbal short-term memory. *Brain*, *92*, 885.

Wilson, S. M., Saygin, A. P., Sereno, M. I., & Iacoboni, M. (2004). Listening to speech activates motor areas involved in speech production. *Nature Neuroscience*, *7* (7), 701–702.

6 The words to say it: The functional and neurological architecture of the lexical system

'When I use a word, it means just what I choose it to mean, neither more nor less.'
(Lewis Carroll, *Alice's Adventures in Wonderland*)

For many reasons the lexicon can be thought of as the bricks supporting the structure of language. Speaking constitutes the end product of a mechanism that allows concepts to be mapped onto lexical forms, the words. Words are then combined according to specific rules to form sentences of different degrees of complexity. It is not, therefore, surprising that in recent years an increasing number of studies exploring the lexicon have been carried out by different disciplines (for a review see Levelt, 1989, 2001; Rapp, 2001). These studies aim to:

- draw up a functional architecture of the lexical system, specifying the components that are active in the various operations and modalities of both production and comprehension, while distinguishing the 'central' from the 'peripheral' components, active in pre- or post-lexical tasks;
- clarify the organization of the content of its single components and the way in which the content is processed;
- specify the neurological base of the lexicon.

This chapter has an essentially neuropsychological bias. Its contents are based on the analysis of data collected from patients affected by cerebral lesions who present with a deficit of a single lexical component either at content level or at the level of processing. The chapter addresses the study methods adopted in cognitive neuropsychology, and an explanation of current models of the organization of the lexicon will follow.

Defining the lexicon

Every adult person (although his or her educational level, interests and social background may create some differences) possesses a patrimony of more than fifty thousand words (Levelt, 1989). These words constitute an individual's mental lexicon, that is to say, a 'store' containing the set of information (semantic, syntactic, morphological and phonological) relating to the words of known languages. For literate people, there must, in addition, be storage of information regarding the written form of words.

Access to this repertory, for both word production and comprehension, is extremely efficient and rapid. We can, in fact, process three to four words every second, whatever our level of education or the language spoken. The acquisition of the lexicon is equally easy. Already before the age of 1, a baby starts to understand words and shortly after he/she starts to produce single words (mostly content words and routines used in social interactions such as *bye bye* and *hello*). At the age of 6 the lexicon already exceeds ten thousand words, with a notable and rapid increase in the years that follow (see Chapter 11).

The lexical system of a language is made up of the set of lexical entries known by a person. A lexical entry can be considered a structure that contains a series of information which can be grouped into the following components (Levelt, 1989, 2001):

- A *semantic form*, consisting of the contribution made by the lexical entry in determining the meaning of a complex proposition containing that specific word.
- A *grammatical form*, made up of the set of characteristics that determine the syntactic properties of the lexical items. For example it may determine whether the word belongs to the open class or closed class category (see later) and, if it is a closed class word, whether it belongs to the category of nouns, verbs or adjectives.
- A *morphological form*, conceived as the knowledge of the internal structure or form of a word. Words, in fact, can be simple (*why*, *each*) and non-segmentable, in that they cannot be broken down into smaller meaningful units (*morphemes*), or they may be complex, made up of a root and an inflection that, according to the language spoken, specifies its case (singular or plural), its gender (masculine, feminine, neutral) and, in the case of verbs, the tense and mood. Finally, there are words that contain a *prefix* or *suffix* (see later).
- A *phonological form*, made up of a variety of phonological traits that specify the segmental units and the units of prosody and intonation.
- An *orthographic form*, made up of the set of single graphemes forming the graphic structure.

Bierwisch and Schreuder (1992) add an argument structure to these components, which specifies the number and type of complement that the lexical item requires.

It must be underlined, however, that not all words can be considered lexical entries. For example, the various inflections that a verb or noun can assume (*look*, *looking*, *looked*; *dog*, *dogs*) are elements bound by a relationship within the same lexical entry; the presence of diacritic features, such as those for person, number and tense, determine the correct choice from within the lexical entry.

Traditional grammars classify words according to semantic criteria, so that the class of nouns is made up of words indicating entities or objects, while the class of verbs contains action-related words. On closer scrutiny, however, it is evident that a classification based solely on semantic criteria is not always sufficient. For example, there are nouns that portray actions or processes, such as *handstand* or *somersault*, while words communicating states can belong to the class of verbs, such as *to dream* or *to suffer*.

The distinction between open class words and closed class words represents a focus of particular interest to neuropsychologists. The former, which include nouns, verbs, adjectives and adverbs is a class in constant movement in that words may disappear from the class and others may be added. On the contrary, the class of closed words, made up of articles, pronouns, prepositions and conjunctions, contains a finite number of members and does not change over time. Within open class words, the presence or absence of common features or characteristics determines the inclusion of the word in various subcategories. For example, for nouns, the living (animal, vegetable) non-living (tool, mineral), common-proper, concrete-abstract, countable (which take the plural form) and uncountable, or mass (for example, *blood, mercury*) features characterize different groups.

Finally, there are the compound nouns, which may be made up of words belonging to the same class, for example two nouns (*dishwasher*), or a verb and a noun (*pickpocket*) or two adjectives (*bittersweet*). The characteristics of the formation and processing of compound words will be discussed in Chapter 7.

The relationship between the lexical entries may be *intrinsic* or *extrinsic* (Levelt, 1989). Intrinsic relationships derive from the characteristics possessed by each lexical entry, so that one lexical entry can be connected to another through meaning (for example *dog → animal, dog → tramp*, etc.). These semantically linked lexical items form a *semantic field*, for example that of dogs, animals or colours. Other forms of intrinsic relationship exist between words that share a root (for example, *draw → drawing*), are similar phonologically (*cat → bat*) or belong to the same grammatical class (for example, proper nouns or verbs).

The extrinsic relationship between lexical items is determined by factors such as the frequency of co-occurrence of words, for example the word *death* is often found in the same context as the word *war*, or by antonym relationships (for example, the relationship between the words *right* and *left*).

As we will see later, experimental demonstration of the reality, both in terms of functional and neurological substratum, of word classes and lexical connections has been provided mostly by the analysis of selective lexical deficits and sparing following cerebral damage, and, more recently, by data collected from functional neuroimaging studies.

Study methods

Within the different language components, there is no doubt that the study of the lexicon is one of the major focuses of interest for scholars from various disciplines. There are many reasons for this, the first and most obvious being the importance of the subject and the second the fact that the lexicon is (apparently!) easier to study than other components of language. The construction of tests (comprehension or production of single words), the possibility of exploring the different modalities of production (oral and written naming, repetition and reading) and comprehension (auditory, visual), the possibility of carrying out a precise assessment of both the type of stimulus making up the test (for example, lexical frequency, grammatical and semantic class, etc.) and the response (latency of response, analysis of error type) are tasks that are apparently more simple than those required by the study of other components of language. Finally, the huge contribution made by both neuroimaging studies and above all reports of patients presenting categorical lexical deficits has allowed greater progress to be made in this field compared with other sectors of language sciences.

The current approaches towards studies of the lexicon are, however, subject to criticism. The principal criticism is that studies of the lexicon are 'artificial' because they do not reflect an authentic speaking situation. Studies of the lexicon, in fact, apart from a few cases, are based on the processing of single words, isolated from both linguistic and environmental contexts, whereas language, on the other hand, is made up of combinations of words in grammatically correct sequences that are sensitive to context.

Information gathered from studies on normal subjects is obtained using techniques that investigate the different speed of response during the processing of words belonging to different grammatical or lexical categories (measurement of reaction times, RT, the elapsed time between the presentation of a sensory stimulus and the subsequent behavioural response). The assumption is that speed of reaction is directly proportional to the difficulty of the task. It has thus been possible to evaluate, for example, time differences during the processing of concrete versus abstract words in tasks of lexical access, or the effects of phonological or semantic foils in picture naming tasks (Roelofs, 1992). RT measurements also allows investigation of the relationship between words, through the results of the *priming effect* (the positive or negative influence that a semantically or phonologically similar word presented prior to presentation of the target word can exert on recognition times of the target word compared with a neutral word, Marslen-Wilson & Tyler, 1997; Dell & O'Seaghdha, 1992).

More recently, the use of neuroimaging techniques, such as fMRI and PET (described in Chapter 3) has not only allowed the sites dedicated to lexical processing to be mapped with increasing accuracy, but, more importantly, has allowed integration of anatomical and cognitive approaches, thereby providing essential data to validate the theoretical models underlying the lexicon.

Error analysis and evaluation of models of processing of the lexicon

The greatest contribution to understanding the structure and organization of the lexicon has been provided by analysis of slips of the tongue (involuntary and non-habitual deviations from the speaker's intended language, Bloomer & Laver,

1973) made by normal subjects and by analysis of errors committed by brain-damaged subjects in tasks of word production (*paraphasias*) and comprehension.

Errors of production and comprehension can, in fact be considered 'cracks' through which it is possible to glimpse intrapsychic dynamic mechanisms and, from a linguistic point of view, the functional organization of the cognitive processes underlying language.

Errors made by normal individuals in everyday verbal activities (conversation, conference speech, etc.) are very rare and do not exceed, according to Fromkin (1973), one or two per two thousand words. Half of them are lexical errors and are caused by diverse factors such as attentional deficits (Freud, 1904), rather than originating from a dysfunction of the language system.

Aphasic errors, on the other hand, in the great majority of cases reflect an impairment of specific subcomponents of the mental lexicon. Errors may consist of the production of words that are semantically close to the target word (semantic paraphasias, for example, *cat* → *dog*), in other cases a word or, more rarely, a non-word (known as a neologism and consisting of a meaningless sequence of phonemes, for example '*stumple*') is produced, which is acoustically similar to the desired word (phonological or phonemic paraphasias, e.g. '*tat*' for '*cat*'). Finally, the substitution may involve a single component of a word leading to morphological type errors (e.g. '*they have six childrens*' '*She read two book*') or there may be a combination of different types of error, for example morphological–phonological errors (Table 6.1).

In both normal speakers and aphasic patients the deficit of lexical access is rarely constant and does not usually compromise the entire knowledge of the word. It is a daily experience, in fact, that the name we are unable to recall becomes accessible a few seconds later and, moreover, we are usually able to access knowledge of some of the phonological characteristics of the word we are trying to recall. For example, we can often remember the first syllable, the length of the word or perhaps a word that rhymes with the desired word (Tip of the Tongue phenomenon, TOT, James, 1890/1981). The following is an example

Table 6.1 Examples of errors in the word production of aphasic patients

Type of error	Stimulus	Response
Anomia	Table	–
Anomia with circumlocution	Pen	You need it to write
Neologism	Lamp	Trang
Verbal paraphasia	Cherry	Bicycle
Conduite d'approche	Yellow	Black no, black … red … yellow … white
Morphological error	Two dogs	Two dog
Semantic paraphasia	Table	Chair
	Nest	Egg
	Artichoke	Vegetable … cabbage
Perseveration	Dog	Green (reply from the preceding stimulus)

provided by a French patient (Henaff Gonon, Bruckert, & Michel, 1989) who was asked to name a picture of a birdcage (*volière*): '… it begins with v … can fly … it begins with vol … in museums … birds fly inside it … it is feminine in gender, I'm sure, there's another word which comes to mind when I think of this one, *Voilier* (sailing boat) …'. It is evident that, despite the patient's inability to retrieve the phonological form, he knew a huge amount of phonological, semantic and morphological information regarding the word.

More systematic studies (Badecker, Miozzo, & Zanuttini, 1995) have confirmed these anedoctal reports showing, for example, that aphasic patients, while unable to remember the number of syllables and the phonemes that make up a particular word, can, however, retrieve the word's gender (i.e. masculine or feminine).

The analysis of the errors made by aphasic patients in processing mass nouns as opposed to numerable or count nouns has been extremely important in clarifying how the complete representation of the words is obtained. The former represent concepts that refer to substances or states (*water*, *sugar*, *happiness*) that are not differentiated within the whole, while count nouns denote concepts that are made up of distinct units (*dogs*, *books*, *girls*). Count nouns have various diacritics (singular, plural) and can be preceded by the definite and indefinite article, whereas mass nouns are commonly used in the singular form only preceded by the definite article. It follows that the choice of the syntactic elements making up the phrase is guided by the lexicon (Levelt, 1989).

A patient described by Semenza, Mondini, and Cappelletti (1997) showed a specific deficit in the processing of mass nouns ('*there's a sand in the sea*'), while a patient studied by Mondini, Jarema, and Liguori (2004) showed the opposite pattern, with normal processing of the mass/count noun distinction in the context of a generalized syntactic deficit. Finally, Vigliocco, Vinson, Martin, and Garrett (1999) described a patient who, despite his severe anomia, was able to apply syntactic rules relative to count and mass nouns.

As far as lexical comprehension deficits are concerned, the errors reflect those in production, being semantic or phonological, with the patient matching an object or a picture with a name that is semantically or phonologically similar to the target word produced by the examiner (for example, the patient matches the word *match* to a picture of a *mat*, a phonological foil, or to a picture of a *fire*, a semantic foil).

Phonological paraphasias reflect a deficit of accessing and coding of the phonological form of the word within the phonological lexicon. They are characterized by omissions, perseveration and substitution of one or more phonemes within a word (/*pun*/ instead of /*spun*/; /*tevilision*/ for /*television*/). In some cases the entire word is produced incorrectly. If the final product is a non-word it is termed a neologism. An analysis of phonological errors committed by both normal individuals (Levelt, 1999), and aphasic patients (Blumstein, 1973, 1994) has demonstrated that different factors can influence phonological coding, such as phonological similarity (in general, errors differ from the target word by only one distinctive feature so that, for example, a voiced stop phoneme is substituted by its voiceless counterpart),[1] phonotactics, syllabic complexity, word length, metric structure (for a summary see Nickels, 2001) and finally, the vowel–consonant status. Semenza et al. (2007), for example, described the case of a patient affected by Wernicke's aphasia whose phonological errors were prevalently vowel substitutions.

Another type of patient error consists of the substitution of target word with another word (*verbal paraphasias*). There are two types of verbal paraphasias: within category, known as semantic paraphasias, and errors that involve the substitutions of a word not related to the target word, as in *sink*/*dog*.

Semantic paraphasias can be present in both spontaneous language and, as we shall see in Chapter 8, in reading aloud (*semantic paralexias*). Semantic paraphasias may share the same syntactic category and some semantic characteristics as the target word, for example, the paraphasia *cat* in the place of the correct word *dog* shares both lexical class (both are nouns) and the fact that they are domestic animals. On other occasions, the relationship is associative, for example *drive* for *car*, or of a higher or lower order (*animal* for *cow* or *flower* for *plant*).

Semantic paraphasias may result from damage to different parts of the system. In some cases they are caused by damage inside the semantic system, resulting in inability to access a complete or adequately specified semantic representation (Goodglass & Wingfield, 1997). In other cases the semantic paraphasias reflect a deficit of access or damage to the output lexicon (Caramazza & Hillis, 1990). In the case of a semantic deficit, the error is evident in both comprehension and production, so, for example, the patient will read the word 'cat' as 'dog' while pointing to the picture of a dog. On the other hand, when the deficit affects the lexicon, comprehension of the word will be preserved: the patient will read the word *grey* as *blue* but will define it as *the colour of hair when you get old*. In some cases the deficit at output level will involve both written and oral naming, while in others it will affect a single modality. PW, for example, a patient described by Rapp and Caramazza (1997), had normal word comprehension in both written and auditory modalities but committed different types of errors when naming or writing words, so that, for example, when presented with the picture of a brush he wrote the word correctly, but named it 'comb'.

Organization of the mental lexicon

Lexical models currently proposed are essentially of two types, one being more general and concerning all the lexical components, and a second type that deals with specific aspects such as the production or recognition of words in the different oral and written modalities.

Some models, as we will see, hypothesize serial treatment of information by parts of subsystems known as modules, which have specific functions and can be judged in isolation. Others are interactive, postulating the existence of interactive processes of language processing.

The simplest and in many ways the most influential model of the structure of the lexicon was devised by Morton (1969, 1970): in this model a key part is attributed to the logogen, a device which accepts information from the sensory analysis mechanisms concerning properties of linguistic stimuli and from

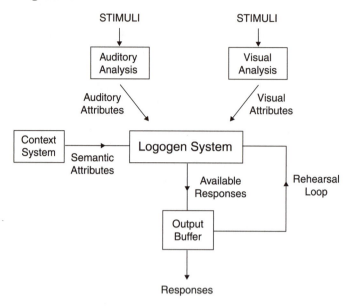

Figure 6.1 Morton's original model of word processing (from Morton, 1969).

context-producing mechanisms. When the logogen has accumulated more than a certain amount of information, a response (a word) is made available (Morton, 1969, see Figure 6.1).

The processing of information proceeds in a serial manner, so that the selection of the entry within each single level (semantic, lexical or phonological) occurs prior to activation of the subsequent level. These models postulate the existence of a peripheral component where the phonological forms of the known words are stored, and which can be activated by auditory, orthographic and visual input. The central component identifies with an amodal lexical-semantic system that allows comprehension of the meaning of each word as well as its relationship with other words within the lexicon. The latter can be considered part of the larger system of semantic memory, which includes the set of verbal and extra-verbal knowledge making up a thesaurus common to all those belonging to a specific society. During the production process a connection is activated between the semantic system and the peripheral component, while a connection in the opposite direction occurs in comprehension. Processing of the written form of the word comes about through a sublexical process that transcodes phonemes into graphemes during the process of reading aloud and vice versa in the writing process. This model, praiseworthy for its simplicity, cannot cope with the selective sparing or deficits observed in some brain-damaged subjects. Dissociation between written and oral naming has, in fact, been found in some patients consisting of selective sparing of a single modality. The patient described by Hier and Mohr (1977) made semantic errors only in oral naming, while written naming was good, suggesting a specific deficit at the level of the phonological output lexicon. Similarly, the patient described by

Caramazza and Hillis (1990) named a shell *octopus*, but was able to write its name correctly. These cases are important in that they allow the functional architecture of written language to be outlined as they provide the demonstration that the written form can be accessed without preceding phonological mediation (see Chapter 8).

Other patients have demonstrated the existence of functional and anatomical independence between the phonological input and output lexicons. Patients affected by word deafness (Auerbach, Allard, Naeser, Alexander, & Albert, 1982; Denes & Semenza, 1975), although possessing normal peripheral hearing, display an almost total inability to understand spoken language, while comprehension of written language and oral and written naming are within the norm.

Finally, the dissociation between sparing or deficits of recall of the form of the word and comprehension of the same word has made a definitive contribution to the construction of a more detailed multistage model of the lexico-semantic component that has, at least partially, had neurological support from the results of clinical observations and functional neuroimaging studies. Goodglass and Baker (1976) and Gainotti (1976), for example, after examination of a large sample of errors produced by aphasic subjects during word production or comprehension tasks, have identified two different types of lexical deficit. Some patients showed a selective difficulty in naming tasks with preserved comprehension, while others performed poorly in both tasks. These results are compatible with the existence of two independent components within the system: a more central system that is active in both production and comprehension tasks, and a second more peripheral component comprising a 'store' of phonological forms.

Up-to-date models of lexical processing include a semantic-conceptual system and four lexicons, namely two input lexicons, one phonological, the other ortho-graphic, with two corresponding output lexicons. The lexicons are linked to the conceptual system that is activated in the input phase during tasks of auditory or visual comprehension, while the peripheral lexicons are activated during produc-tion tasks.

Finally, access to the input lexicons is preceded by a stage of phonological or orthographic analysis. During the production process, on the other hand, there is a connection with the interface systems, namely the phonological and orthographic buffers, which are essentially short-term memory stores that hold information for the necessary length of time prior to activation of the articulatory or graphic plan (Figure 6.2).

From the conceptual system to articulation: Lexical access

Naming an object or person in front of us, expressing desires, in other words finding and producing the words that form language, is an operation we carry out an endless number of times during the day in a rapid and efficient manner.

If, however, we try to analyse the underlying mechanism, its complexity becomes immediately apparent: the process that starts with conceptual specifica-tion and concludes with evocation of the group of phonemes that are specified for

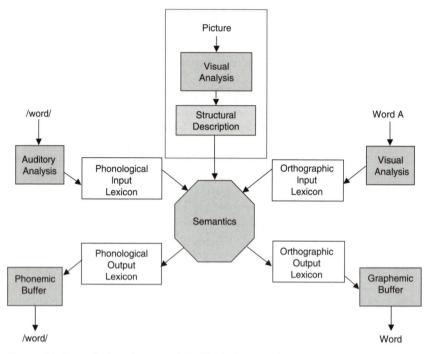

Figure 6.2 A standard two-way model of lexical processing, including lexical and non-lexical processing.

order and metrical and lexical organization, constitutes what is known as **lexical access**.

Morton (1970) conceived a direct route from the preverbal conceptual-semantic representations to a 'store' where the phonological forms are deposited until they are physically produced through the evocation of a neuromotor plan preceding articulation (Figure 6.3a). Butterworth (1989, 1992), on the other hand, foresees the presence of an intermediate step, consisting of a lexical-semantic representation located between the conceptual representation and the phonological form (Figure 6.3b).

Levelt (1989; Levelt et al., 1991) and with some modifications, Dell (1986), have proposed a theory that specifies the steps from the *evocation of the concept* the speaker wants to express to the operation of s*yllabification* preceding articulation. It involves a process of unification through the retrieval of different types of information from semantics, syntax and phonology and their combination into larger structures. This theory is supported by data obtained measuring reaction times during different tasks of lexical production and by analysis of the errors produced during spontaneous conversation. A computational implementation of the theory was carried out by Roelofs (1992, 1997), and this can be consulted for further details. The first step (Figure 6.3c) consists of the selection of the item corresponding to the concept to be expressed from within the mental lexicon,

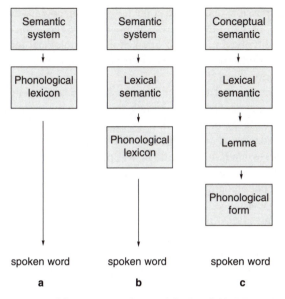

Figure 6.3 Access to word forms: competing models. Panel (a): Morton's original model (1970); Panel (b): lexical-semantic mediation (Butterworth, 1989); Panel (c): syntactic (lemma) mediation (Levelt, 1989) (adapted from Morton, 1970; Butterworth 1989; Levelt 1989).

bearing in mind that the chosen phonological form must correspond to a particular communicative intent. In Levelt's example (2001), the drawing of a horse can be named *animal*, *horse* or *stallion* according to the level of specification required. It follows that different lexical forms can be associated with the same concept and are activated to make further choices (for more details see Levinson, 1983).

The transition from conceptual representation to specific phonological form is not direct, but, according to Levelt, requires passage through an intermediate grammatical stage, the lemma. In fact the specific lexical form for each concept includes not only a phonological representation but also an abstract amodal representation of the syntactic form (lemma), which specifies its category (noun, verb) and the possible diacritic variants (singular, plural, masculine, feminine). To give an example, the lemma of *cat* specifies that it belongs to the class of nouns, and that it can be singular or plural (in some languages a further distinction is made according to gender: in Italian, for example, the male cat is termed *gatto*, while the female cat is *gatta*). Normally, moreover, semantic traits are also active, such as [animate, non-human], and these influence syntactic processes. With the selection of the lemma, the syntactic characteristics necessary for further processing become available as well. The grammatical codification for the construction of phrases, propositions and sentences depends on information provided by the lemma.

The hypothesis that there is an obligatory passage through the stage of the lemma during the process of word production gives rise to two corollaries. The first concerns a possible distinction, at the level of both cognitive and anatomical implementation, between the processes implicit in the evocation of grammatical class and those involved in the evocation of the phonological form. The second concerns the relationship between the course of activation of the lemma and the phonological form.

If we consider the first question, neuropsychological evidence allows us to establish independence between knowledge of the phonological form and grammatical knowledge of the word to be produced. Dante, the aphasic patient described by Badecker et al. (1995), was able to name correctly only 112 out of 200 drawings shown to him. Of the 88 he was not able to name, he was, however, able to correctly judge their gender (male or female), although he was not able to remember their phonological characteristics, such as word length, or the first or last letter of the word.

Badecker et al. (1995) provide evidence that the evocation of the phonological or orthographic form must follow the stage of the lemma: their patient committed morphological errors in written and oral naming and in reading aloud, as if there were a specific deficit at the level of an amodal representation of the lemma.

Once the process of selection of the lexical concept and the lemma has been completed, the next stage consists of activation of the corresponding phonological form or lexeme, composed of the morphemes that form the word. For example, the word 'tables' contains a root form *tab/le/* and the morpheme *s*, which specifies the plural. An operation of insertion at positional level is therefore carried out, which foresees the specification of the morphological and prosodic structure (for example, syllable organization) of the segments making up the word.

A syllable can be considered to be the unit of organization of articulatory movements, since the execution of these movements varies according to the position they occupy within the syllable. It consists of a *nucleus* (the vowel), an *onset*, which includes any consonants that precede the nuclear element, and a consonant or semivowel that closes the syllable, known as a *coda*, though this is not always present (Davenport & Hannahs, 2005). During speech, the syllable structure is recalled from a store as well as being constructed 'on line' (Ramus & Mehler, 1999). This on-line process is necessary because syllabification involves connected speech, not just single words. Accordingly, syllable boundaries do not always respect boundaries between words: for example, when a British speaker says *the car is running*, the sequence *car is* becomes resyllabified as [ka-riz], the /r/ of car is now syllable initial and thus becomes pronounced (Levelt, 1989).

The procedure by which a recalled word passes from a long-term memory store containing the abstract phonological form to phonological codifying is carried out by a mechanism of selection and copying (Buckingham, 1986). The task of this mechanism is to select the phonemes of the lexeme to be produced and place them in their own segmental box within the phonological structure. The result of the coding process is an *abstract representation* (phonetic plan) of how the utterance should be produced. According to Goldrick and Rapp (2007), the phonological representation is carried out in two stages, the first being lexical, the second post-lexical. The first stage is sensitive to the lexical properties of the target word, such as lexical frequency or the presence within the lexicon of words that are semantically or phonologically similar to the target word, but it does not specify all the syllabic information. The post-lexical representation, on the other hand, contains the syllabic structure and is sensitive to strictly phonological factors, such as the frequency of the phonemes within the target word and the syllable structure (see later in this chapter).

Once obtained, the phonetic plan must be placed in a temporary store (buffer) that holds the contents of the abstract phonological representation and is where the information obtained undergoes articulatory implementation before being produced as language sounds (Caramazza, Miceli, & Villa, 1986), or undergoes further phonological specification (Caplan, Vanier, & Baker, 1986).

From the articulatory buffer, therefore, the motor units (phonetic plan) necessary for articulation are retrieved. The time required for their retrieval depends on the total number of units stored in the buffer (Stemberger, 1985). The final stage consists of motor commands being sent to the neuromotor circuits to implement movements of the muscles of the phono-articulatory tract.

The interactive model proposed by Dell (1986) and applied to the study of aphasic disorders by Martin and Saffran (1990) postulates the existence of phonological, semantic and lexical 'nodes'. The course of activation of each node depends on two parameters, the strength of connection and the index of decay. During the naming process, for example, there is activation of a series of semantic

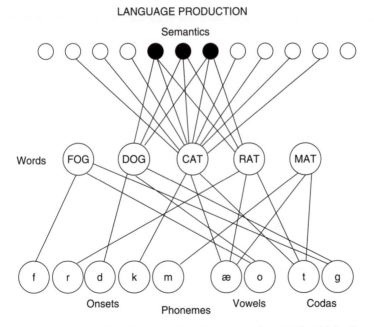

Figure 6.4 Interactive model of word retrieval: (see text from Dell, 1986). Copyright © 1986, American Psychological Association, reproduced with permission.

Table 6.2 List of factors influencing lexical access

Age of acquisition and lexical frequency: See text.

Perceptual qualities of the referent: Concrete words are more accessible than abstract words.

Grammatical class: Dissociations have been described between nouns and verbs and between open class words compared to closed class words, simple words compared to compound words, etc.

Emotional content of the word: Emotionally rich words (swear words) that can be more easily retrieved in operatively rich contexts.

Operativity: Words that denote 'operative' objects that can be handled and have distinctive perceptual boundaries that are more easily processed.

Mode of presentation: Difficulty in naming items presented in a specific modality (visual, tactile, auditory).

---

nodes, which then, in turn, activate the lexical nodes corresponding not only to the stimulus but also to other semantically similar stimuli. The process continues until the most activated node is selected, although neighbouring lexical entries are not totally blocked. The next step corresponds to the activation of the specific phonological nodes, which, in turn, inhibit or activate overlying nodes until there is the final selection of the most active phonological form. Activation is assumed to decay exponentially (over time) towards zero (Figure 6.4).

The connectionist type models are derived from studies of computer simulation and are applied mostly to reading processes and their disorders. Perry, Ziegler, and Zorzi (2007) postulate distributed activation of input and output units connected to semantic units through intermediate layers in the context of a neural network.

Factors that influence lexical access

Every speaker is able to select the phonological form corresponding to the concept he or she wishes to express from within his/her mental lexicon. Speakers can also use the lexicon to understand the meaning of a word presented to them either visually or through the auditory modality. This process, however, is sensitive to various factors such as the age of acquisition of the word, its lexical frequency and semantic and grammatical class (Table 6.2).

Some of the most significant factors influencing access to lexical knowledge in both normal speakers and aphasic speakers are listed below.

Age of acquisition and lexical frequency

Words acquired early in life are recognized and produced faster than words acquired later in life (for a review see Morrison & Ellis, 2000). This is true for all languages, and many studies have demonstrated that the age of acquisition of a noun, particularly when combined with the parameter of lexical frequency, represents an important index of prediction of the accuracy and speed of recall and comprehension (Ghyselink, Custers, & Brysbaert, 2004). Similarly, these factors play a significant role in the lexical recall abilities of both aphasic patients (Kay,

Hanley, & Miles, 2001; Cuetos, Aguado, Izura, & Ellis, 2002) and patients affected by other forms of cognitive damage, such as Alzheimer's disease (Silveri, Monteleone, Burani, & Tabossi, 2000) and semantic dementia (see later, Lambon Ralph, Graham, Ellis, & Hodges, 1998).

It is still not totally clear, however, why words acquired early in life are more easily recalled by normal subjects and prove more resistant to cerebral damage.

Ellis and Lambon Ralph (2000) instructed a simple neural network to associate patterns presented in input to other patterns in output. Some of these (known as 'early' patterns) were inserted into the system from the beginning of the training, while others (known as 'late' patterns) were presented only after the system had learnt to associate the patterns presented in the early stage. The training then continued until all stimuli had been learnt. Despite the fact that the frequency of training was adjusted to equalize the total number of times the network underwent training of the two classes of stimuli, the final representation of the early patterns was stronger than that of the late patterns. The late patterns, moreover, were less resistant to the effects of damage to the system. Ellis and Lambon Ralph hypothesize, therefore, that the *locus* of the effect of age of acquisition and lexical frequency is situated at the same level as the connections between different types of representation (semantic and phonological). The strength of these connections will depend on the moment at which the entry initiates training and the frequency which with the connection is activated, with a cumulative effect. As learning proceeds, the network will become more rigid and less plastic, with the consequence that words introduced late in training will be more difficult to learn than words introduced earlier.

The age of acquisition factor can be applied to dominions other than word acquisition. For example, both normal and brain-damaged subjects find it easier to recognize the faces of famous people they knew in the past compared with contemporary personalities (Moore, Valentine, & Turner, 1999).

The introduction of neuroimaging techniques has allowed investigation into the question of whether recall of words learned at different ages activates different neural systems. Ellis, Burani, Izura, Bromiley, and Venneri (2006), for example, have used fMRI to demonstrate specific activation of the occipital and left temporal pole during silent reading of words acquired early in life. In contrast, activation of the fusiform gyrus and the middle occipital convolution was observed in tasks of processing words learnt later in life. These two patterns of activation may reflect, according to Ellis et al., different mechanisms of representation linked to the age of learning of words. The activation of the occipital poles and the temporal pole reflects a more detailed semantic and visual representation. On the other hand, words learnt later in life require a more complex mapping process between visual and semantic representation, and require more resources.

Similarly to age of acquisition, lexical frequency plays an important role in the ability to retrieve and understand words. In particular, most studies of word retrieval speed have located frequency at the stage of phonological (or word-form) access in contrast to the word (or 'lemma') access stage (Kittredge, Dell, & Schwartz, 2006). Frequency has a major effect on normal and aphasic phonological speech errors. In anomic aphasia, the frequency effect is increased and, despite fluent and well articulated spontaneous output, language will consist principally of closed class words, which, according to dictionaries of frequency, are those most frequently used (Marshall, 1977). Finally, frequency effects in aphasia may interact with phonological similarity or tendency to perseveration.

The content of the lexical-syntactic system: Semantic categories and grammatical classes

Within the long-term memory system, Tulving (1972) distinguished a system of Semantic Memory (SM) from an Episodic or autobiographical memory (AB). AB stores records concerning events and their spatial and temporal relationship (for example, remembering where and with whom we went to dinner last week). SM, on the other hand, has been conceived by Tulving as a type of mental thesaurus, organized knowledge a person possesses about words and other verbal symbols, their meaning and referents, the relations about them (Tulving, 1972).

In the following years, the term SM assumed a wider meaning, including a system of more generalized knowledge, which comprehends both the meaning of words and knowledge of the world, such as, for example, all the information we possess regarding animals, tools, rules of behaviour and so on. Within this system and at the level of both neurological and cognitive representation, however, the distinction between the meaning of the words and world knowledge is not totally clear, including representations of concepts that cannot be expressed verbally, such as *body awareness*, understood as the implicit knowledge of the spatial relationships between various body parts or, on the other hand, concepts linked to verbal mediation only (for example, the concept of a week).

The distinction between general semantic knowledge and verbal semantic knowledge can be better understood by examining the difference in the way aphasic patients access world knowledge compared with patients affected by a particular form of cognitive deterioration known as semantic dementia (Jefferies & Lambon Ralph, 2006), characterized by a general amodal deficit of knowledge that extends beyond the comprehension and production of words to the knowledge and use of objects, and in which objects may be used by the patients in an inappropriate manner (for example, attempting to light a cigarette with a pen).

On the other hand, aphasic patients rarely display this type of behaviour, even in the presence of an almost total inability to understand and produce language. For example, although they may use the name *knife* for a *fork*, and may indicate the fork when the examiner asks them to pick up the knife, they continue to cut meat with a knife and bring it to their mouth with a fork.

It is therefore possible to postulate the existence of two anatomically and functionally neighbouring systems, one linked to knowledge of the world and the other to the phonological and orthographic representation of words, joined through lexical semantics. The latter may be restricted to the semantic information necessary for applying the correct verbal label (the name) to an object or person and deciding whether a phonological or orthographic string corresponds to the object or person in front of us.

Following the group study performed by Goodglass, Klein, Carey, and Jones (1966), which showed that not all aphasic patients presented a homogeneous deficit of the processing of words belonging to different semantic or grammatical categories, the reports of most single case studies presenting deficits or sparing of comprehension and naming restricted to single lexical and semantic categories (Warrington & McCarthy, 1983, 1987; Warrington & Shallice, 1984) has led to the development of the hypothesis of a categorical organization of the conceptual and lexical systems at various levels of processing. Further specification has been made between amodal deficits, characterized by inability to process the information at both conceptual and lexical levels, and deficits restricted to a specific input or output modality (for a review see Saffran & Schwartz, 1994; Rapp & Goldrick, 2006; Caramazza & Mahon, 2006) (see Table 6.3).

At the same time, countless functional neuroimaging studies have been carried out with the aim of investigating the neurological organization of the conceptual-semantic system (for a review see Damasio et al., 2004; DeLeon et al., 2007).

Four semantic categories in particular have demonstrated the greatest specificity in terms of both cognitive processing and neurological base: living organisms (animals and vegetables), inanimate objects (mostly objects that can be manipulated), unique entities defined by a proper name (people and geographical locations) and numbers. As far as grammatical classes are concerned, the best known distinction is that between nouns and verbs.

Living organisms and objects

Warrington and Shallice (1984) described four patients affected by a bilateral temporal lesion following herpes simplex encephalitis, who demonstrated a selective inability to understand the meaning of words corresponding to animals, vegetables and food, alongside normal processing of words corresponding to objects in common use. The patient SBY, for example, defined a 'towel' as a *material that you use to dry yourself*, a 'submarine' as a *ship which goes under water*. In contrast, he defined 'wasp' as a *bird which flies* and 'holly' as a *drink*.

Table 6.3 Deficits and selective sparing of specific lexical-semantic categories following cerebral damage

Selective comprehension disorders	Colours, household objects, concrete words, biological categories compared to inanimate objects, and vice versa
Selective naming disorders	Body parts, proper nouns and geographical locations, letters of the alphabet, numbers, animals, common nouns and verbs
Selectively spared comprehension	Geographical locations
Selectively spared naming	Colours, letters, body parts, proper nouns

Source: Taken from Denes, G. (1999). *Neuropsicologia del linguaggio in frontiera della vita*, Vol. 3. Rome: Istituto dell'Enciclopedia Italian.

In two patients whose aphasic deficit did not permit evaluation of language production, performance in non-verbal tasks, such as matching words to drawings, produced a similar dissociation. At around the same time, aphasic patients were described who showed the opposite picture, presenting a specific disorder in the knowledge of 'inanimate' compared with 'animate' concepts (Warrington & McCarthy, 1983, 1987).

According to Warrington and Shallice (1984), the selective deficit for living organisms on one hand and tools on the other reflects an organization of knowledge according to different types of critical information, in particular their perceptual and functional attributes. It is the sensory characteristics (size, colour, taste, etc.) of both animals and vegetables that allow differentiation between members of the same category: for example, differences in taste and colour are features that allow differentiation between a courgette and an aubergine. In the same way, a donkey and a zebra are characterized and differentiated by the colour of their coat.

In contrast, functional attributes are probably more important than perceptual characteristics for identification of artefacts, such as tools. The colour or design of the tool is irrelevant. Confirmation of the different importance of these two types of information in world knowledge comes, according to Warrington and Shallice (1984), from a more detailed analysis of deficits present in patients demonstrating dissociation between animate and inanimate entities. The first group of patients presented difficulty in recognizing living things but also showed difficulty in recognizing musical instruments and precious stones. The members of these latter categories are differentiated by their perceptual characteristics (sound and colour). On the other hand, patients with a deficit in recognizing tools were impaired in defining the function of different parts of the body (Warrington & McCarthy, 1987).

Caramazza and colleagues (Caramazza & Shelton, 1998; Caramazza & Mahon, 2006) maintain, on the other hand, that world knowledge is organized into domains that possess specific underlying neural circuits that were established during the course of evolution through a process of natural selection. The necessity of being able to rapidly and efficiently judge the potential utility or dangerousness of biological items such as animals and plants led to the development of specific, anatomically separate neural circuits that allow us to distinguish whether a vegetable is edible or poisonous, whether an animal is a predator or prey, and finally, whether the person in front of us is a friend or potential killer. In support of this hypothesis, there have been descriptions of patients who, within the 'biological' category, presented a conceptual or lexical deficit restricted to animals, with no simultaneous deficit of semantic-lexical processing for food and musical instruments (Caramazza & Shelton, 1998; Hart & Gordon, 1992). Other patients have been described with a lexical deficit limited to plants, or to the comprehension and naming of body parts (for a review see Semenza, 2002).

In favour of an evolutionary basis underlying the categorical organization of concepts, Capitani and Laiacona (Capitani, Laiacona, Mahon, & Caramazza, 2003; Laiacona, Barbarotto, & Capitani, 2006) report that patients affected by a conceptual deficit for biological categories show a difference in frequency according to gender. The vast majority of patients affected by a deficit in knowledge of plants are males, while it is females who are most affected by a lexical deficit restricted to animal categories (Gainotti, 2005). These data could be interpreted in the light of the model of 'task division' proposed by Silverman and Eals (1992). During the evolutionary process the male specialized in hunting, while the task of females was to recognize and select fruit, herbs and edible plants. Accordingly, females have developed a cognitive and neurological system for knowledge of the plant world that is more efficient and resistant to cerebral damage than that of the male, whose principal task was hunting.

According to Gainotti (2005), however, these differences relating to gender may have a cultural origin, in that women are more familiar with the category of plants and men with tools and animals. Normal males, in fact, name artefacts and different types of birds more easily than females, while females name plants and fruit more fluently (McKenna & Parry, 1994; Barbarotto, Laiacona, Macchi, & Capitani, 2002: Marra, Ferraccioli, & Gainotti, 2007). Consequently, it is the element of familiarity arising from social factors that determines the gender difference in the processing of tools and living organisms. A further contribution to the hypothesis that differences linked to gender are of cultural origin rather than the result of a putting out of use of a specific field of knowledge, derives from the analysis of the site of lesion in patients with deficits restricted to the knowledge of animals and vegetables. In both cases the lesion is localized at the anterior temporal level and in the temporal-occipital portions of the system of visual processing (Ungerleider & Mishkin, 1982), necessary for the identification of living organisms. Obviously, it could be that there is neural segregation of the neurological systems dedicated to the knowledge of plants or animals. Certain systems could have their neurological base in neighbouring areas of the cerebral cortex, which, in the case of simultaneous damage, gives rise to deficits in both categories. Finally, individual factors, such as hobby preferences, could play a role. For example, a love of cooking or gardening may lead to a more detailed cognitive representation for plants that is more resistant to cerebral damage than other semantic categories.

Proper nouns

All grammars distinguish common nouns from proper nouns. These can be defined as the noun words that have an exclusively 'referential' value (Frege, 1892; Kripke, 1980). They are used (like personal and demonstrative pronouns) only to 'refer to' or name people, geographical places or brand names. Unlike common nouns, for example *table* or *potato*, proper nouns refer to a single item within a category and have no descriptive content on the basis of which we can identify the referent. While the noun 'table' designates a category possessing a series of recurring attributes (*it has a top, four legs, it is round, rectangular or square*) on the basis of which it is possible to identify the referent (Semenza, 2006), for proper nouns the sense of a term consists in the definite description that speakers associate with it: it is a sort of original naming act that does not allow, however, definition of the attributes of the noun. The name *John Brown* tells us only that we are referring to a male, without specifying his age, his height or profession, and so on.

An unexpected and transitory difficulty in retrieving the name of someone we know is a common phenomenon. The hypothesis that the process of recall of proper names is more difficult than the recall of common names is therefore commonly accepted, without taking into consideration other factors such as familiarity and lexical frequency. It is also a fact that being unable to remember the name of the person in front of us is certainly a more embarrassing experience and so more often remembered than an inability to recall a common noun, which is often overcome with circomlocution.

The best known experimental evidence that proper nouns are indeed more difficult to remember than common nouns derives from the observations of McWeeny, Young, Hay, and Ellis (1987) on the 'baker paradox'. The word *baker* in English is, of course, both a common noun and a common surname. The task of matching the word to an unknown face is more difficult when the person being tested is told that *Baker* is a surname rather than the name of the person's occupation. Since the phonological form is identical in both conditions and the lexical frequency of the surname is the same as that of the occupation, it is obvious that it is the different lexical category that determines the difference.

In general, in aphasia there is a lexical deficit for both proper and common nouns, but some (rare) cases have been described of sparing or, more frequently, of a selective deficit for proper nouns compared with common nouns (for a review see Semenza, 2006), which has allowed a model of the processing of proper nouns to be drawn up at both a theoretical level and the level of neurological implementation. The lexical deficit may include both names of people and geographical terms, or it may be limited to names of people.

Anomia for proper nouns does not have a single underlying mechanism. In some cases there is an underlying selective inability to access the phonological and orthographical forms corresponding to a person or geographical place from within the output lexicon, while semantic knowledge is preserved. The sparing of semantic knowledge is demonstrated by the correct matching of the photo to a noun spoken by the examiner during a multiple choice task and the ability to provide information about that person or place corresponding to the name we are unable to retrieve. A phonological cue (providing the initial sound of the word) is not always helpful in retrieving the noun, which, however, when spoken by the examiner, is correctly repeated. In other cases, the deficit for proper nouns has an underlying semantic deficit, for example, APA, the patient described by Miceli et al. (2000) was not able to provide an adequate conceptual description of the person whose name he could not recall.

Finally, cases of prosopanomia are of interest. Prosopanomia, the inability to recall the name of a person presented visually, differs from prosopagnosia, which is the inability to recognize familiar faces. The patient VI (Semenza, Sartori, & D'Andrea, 2003) was able to recognize the famous person whose photo he was shown, but was not able to name him or her; however, when this same person was

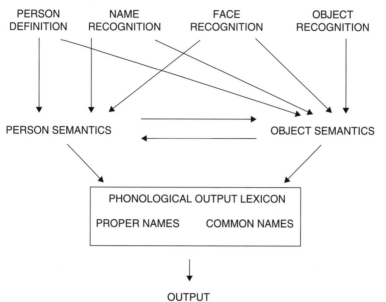

Figure 6.5 A model of proper noun processing derived from neuropsychological studies (from Semenza, 2006). Reproduced with permission of University of Edinburgh.

described verbally to him (*tell me the name of the famous Italian director who has directed the following films ...*) his performance improved considerably.

A model of functional organization at the basis of the processing of the single entities or conspecifics (Caramazza & Mahon, 2006) defined by proper nouns can be envisaged. The model postulates a distinction within the semantic system between concepts related to objects and those relating to people, accessible through different modalities (in the case of a person, face, voice, verbal description). Once the conceptual representation has been obtained, the corresponding phonological form is activated and is deposited within the output lexicon, which, in turn contains a distinction between common nouns and proper nouns (see Figure 6.5).

The lexicon of numbers

An increasing body of neuropsychological studies, starting from the seminal report of Anderson, Damasio, and Damasio (1990) whose patient showed a dissociation between preserved reading and writing of numbers and impaired processing of written words, suggests that numerical knowledge is independently represented in the brain and can dissociate from non-numerical knowledge at the level of semantic and lexical processing.

Cipolotti, Butterworth, and Denes (1991) described a patient who, after left parietal lobe damage, manifested almost total inability to understand any number higher than 4. She could not associate the word 'seven' with the corresponding number, define its corresponding numerosity, or name the number preceding or following it. On the other hand, her semantic-lexical knowledge of other classes of words, when tested through naming and comprehension tasks, was found to be within normal limits. Cappelletti, Butterworth, and Kopelman (2001) described the opposite pattern: their patient, affected by semantic dementia, was severely impaired in naming and reading or writing non-number words, as well as in a variety of verbal and pictorial semantic tasks, yet he showed no comparable impairments for numerical material.

Analogously, neuropsychological evidence suggests that, even at the lexical level, numerals require specific processing mechanisms. Marangolo, Piras, and Fias (2005) assumed that their patient, with impaired oral production of number words and relatively spared production of words, was unable to access number words inside the phonological output lexicon. Denes and Signorini (2001) described a patient, who, following a left parietal lesion, was unable to read numbers in either alphabetic or Arabic form. In contrast, repetition and comprehension of series of numbers was within normal limits, suggesting that the underlying deficit was either an inability to access the phonological lexicon from the semantic system, or specific damage to the number words within the phonological output lexicon (see also Chapter 8).

Grammatical classes

Nouns and verbs

'Amongst us lives an honest man, touched by a very grave apoplexy, who spoke nouns and wholly forgot verbs ...'. Thus Vico, in his work *Principles of New Science* (1744), describes the first reported case in literature of a specific lexical deficit for verbs following an acquired cerebral lesion. Vico's interest however, was not the search for the neurological bases of the lexicon, but rather the verification of his theory on the origin and development of language (Denes & Dalla Barba, 1998).

Only since the 1960s have numerous studies been published regarding groups of patients or single cases presenting a double dissociation, with sparing or selective deficit of nouns compared with verbs in tasks of reading aloud (Marshall & Newcombe, 1966), naming (Damasio & Tranel, 1993; Caramazza & Hillis, 1991) and auditory comprehension (Damasio et al., 2004). In the case of *deep dyslexia* (Chapter 8), for example, nouns are read more accurately than verbs, which are read better than adjectives, and adjectives are read better than function words.

In Broca's aphasia, nouns are more easily produced than verbs, while on the contrary, in fluent aphasias, verbs are more easily produced than nouns (Zingeser & Berndt, 1988; Denes et al., 1996, but for a contrasting view see Berlingeri et al., 2008; Luzzati, Aggujaro, & Crepaldi, 2006).

In other cases, the noun–verb dissociation is evident in one output modality only. The patient described by Caramazza and Hillis (1991) displayed selective difficulty in producing verbs compared with nouns only when writing, while another patient (Hillis & Caramazza, 1995) had more difficulty in the oral production of verbs than when verbs were tested using other modalities. Three hypotheses have been proposed to explain the differences in processing of the two grammatical classes. The first is a semantic type hypothesis, the second is lexical in nature and the third a syntactic hypothesis, which places the selective deficit for verb processing within a picture of agrammatism.

According to Warrington and McCarthy (1987) the selective deficit in the comprehension and retrieval of nouns or verbs has a semantic, rather than lexical, origin. The meaning of many verbs is linked to the motor modality through the expression of actions, while, on the other hand, the meaning of nouns is prevalently linked to the visual modality.

It follows, then, from an associative perspective, that processing of different classes of words at a cortical level could be linked to the motor cortex for verbs (see later in this chapter) and perhaps to the mirror neuron system located close to Broca's area (but for a critical review see Arbib, 2010). On the other hand, the neurological substrate of concrete nouns may be found at the level of the visual cortex. According to Hebb (1949), in fact, the cerebral cortex can be considered to be composed of an associative memory, where the frequent co-activation of neurons leads to the formation of neuronal groups that are closely associated. Such cerebral aggregations can, in turn, form functional units localized in various parts of the cerebral cortex. It follows that when, in the course of learning, a word is frequently presented at the same time as a specific visual stimulus, thereby forming a link between signifier and signified (Saussure, 1916), there is simultaneous activation of the left perisylvian areas linked to processing of the phonemic string and the visual cortical areas. This in turn leads to the formation of neural aggregates distributed in the perisylvian cortex and in the temporal-occipital cortex. Such groups can reasonably represent the neural base for concrete nouns with a high degree of imaginability (the ability to imagine the meaning linked to a word, a factor that can influence aphasics, word retrieval), such as 'pear' or 'horse'.

The situation is different with verbs, which usually express an action such as 'write' or 'walk'. In this case, the word is frequently associated with a movement, thus forming stable neural associations between the language areas and those areas situated in proximity to the motor cortex that are dedicated to the processing and programming of body movements. In this perspective, therefore, the semantics rather than the grammatical class determine the different functional and anatomical bases of nouns and verbs.

A recent confirmation of the semantic hypothesis at the base of the noun–verb dissociation comes from Vigliocco et al. (2006). In a PET study carried out on normal subjects, activation of the motor areas of the left cerebral hemisphere was found in tasks of visual processing of words linked to movement ('dives', 'landing', 'shakes', 'gallop'), independent of grammatical class (noun or verb), lexical frequency or degree of imaginability. On the other hand, the processing of words with characteristics similar to those cited but expressing sensory qualities ('tickle', 'darkness', 'smells', 'sparkle') caused activation of the basal temporal and inferior frontal areas of the left hemisphere, independent of grammatical class (see below for further details).

Caramazza and colleagues (Caramazza & Hillis, 1991; Hillis & Caramazza, 1995; Rapp & Caramazza, 2002), in contrast, claim that the internal structure of the phonological and orthographic lexicons is independently organized in grammatical classes. This hypothesis is upheld by the performance of some patients who commit a greater number of semantic errors in naming verbs compared with nouns in the written modality only (Caramazza & Hillis, 1991; Hillis & Caramazza, 1995). In contrast, the patient EBA (Hillis & Caramazza, 1995) presented with specific difficulty for verbs in the oral modality only. In an opposite picture, many patients have been described whose naming of verbs is significantly superior to their ability to name nouns (Miceli, Silveri, Villa, & Caramazza, 1984; Zingeser & Berndt, 1990; Denes et al., 1996).

Finally, the selective deficit in verbs is claimed to be of syntactic origin. According to Saffran and Schwartz (1994), the verb processing deficit present in some Broca's aphasics, evident mostly in sentence production tasks, can be placed within a wider picture of damage to the morpho-syntactic system (agrammatism). Berndt and colleagues (1997a, 1997b) postulate the presence of damage at the level of the lemma, while for Friedmann (2000) a lesion of Broca's area leads to a pathological simplification of the syntactic tree so that verbs cannot be placed in their appropriate functional category or take on the correct morphological inflection. It is, however, necessary to underline that a purely 'syntactic' hypothesis is not sufficient to explain why some non-agrammatic patients show a verb processing deficit (Jonkers & Bastiaanse, 1998; Crepaldi et al., 2006).

In conclusion, there is probably no single factor at the basis of the difference in processing of nouns and verbs and, from a neuropsychological point of view, only an accurate analysis of the various components underlying the two lexical classes can clarify the nature of the selective deficits presented by patients.

Beyond literal meaning: Comprehension of connotation, metaphors and idioms

Alongside the denotative meaning of words, defined as the indissoluble relationship between a word and a specific referent (the dictionary definition), the meaning of a word is also based on looser associations. For example, the word 'girl' other than denoting a female person who is no longer a child but not yet an adult, has connotations of freshness and beauty, and so on. These aspects make up the connotative meaning of a word.

While, in normal speakers, the comprehension of the denotative and connotative aspects of meaning occurs simultaneously, the question of whether there may be dissociation of the two types of meaning in aphasic patients is not completely clear.

On one hand, if we consider that the connotative meaning is more subtle, abstract and perhaps has metalinguistic properties, we can therefore presume it is more sensitive to aphasic damage (Osgood & Miron, 1963). On the other hand, however, if we consider that comprehension of the connotative meaning is more primitive, general and pervasive, it may be more resistant than the denotative meaning, which requires a structured relationship between symbol and referent.

Using a modified version of the semantic differential of Osgood (1960), which requires the participant to match a word to an abstract drawing that represents the connotative meaning of the word (for example, the word 'intelligent' is paired more easily with an acute form than an obtuse form), Gardner and Denes (1973) carried out a test of word comprehension on a group of participants affected by cerebral damage. Both the denotative and the connotative meaning were tested. In aphasic patients, the comprehension of the two aspects of meaning correlated significantly for both concrete words and abstract words. Of particular interest was the performance of a small group of patients with right hemisphere lesions who displayed selective difficulty in understanding connotative meaning, leading to the deduction that the right hemisphere plays a role in the processes of metalinguistic comprehension of language.

Right hemisphere involvement has also been found in healthy individuals in processing the meaning of metaphors (rhetorical figures that are based on the figurative use of words), on the basis of partial similarity between the literal, declarative and figurative meaning (for example: my bag is very easy to carry, it's as light as a feather). In a PET study, Bottini et al. (1994) found activation of the right hemisphere areas during the process of comprehension of metaphors concomitant to widespread activation of the left hemisphere. More recently, Pobric, Mashal, Faust, and Lavidor (2008), in a study using repetitive transcranial magnetic stimulation (rTMS), have confirmed the involvement of the right hemisphere during both the comprehension of familiar metaphors (for which we can presume processing is similar to that used for the comprehension of conventional word combinations) and for new metaphorical expressions extracted from poetry texts.

Idioms are a group of words whose meaning cannot be deduced from the meaning of the constituent words, for example, the expressions *it was raining cats and dogs* or *kick the bucket*. Idioms have various dimensions, such as that of transparency/opacity and ambiguity, since some idioms can assume a literal significance (for example, 'break the ice'). Papagno, Tabossi, Colombo, and Zampetti (2004) have shown that the left temporal lobe plays a critical role in the process of comprehension of idioms, but not of metaphors, with additional involvement of the left prefrontal area both in the process of retrieving the figurative meaning from the semantic memory and in the inhibition of alternative, literal responses (Cacciari et al., 2006).

The origin of semantic-lexical deficits: Loss of information or access deficit

Both normal speakers and aphasics commit errors in word production and comprehension. While in normal subjects it is easy to argue that errors are the consequence of temporary difficulty in accessing the meaning or the correct phonological or orthographic form of a word (the name that 'slips our mind' is retrieved with no effort immediately after), it is more difficult to define whether the lexical-semantic failure seen in aphasics occurs as a result of loss of information following degradation of the lexical-semantic system at various levels of input or output, or of an inability to access these systems.

The first experimental contribution to the resolution of this problem came from application of the semantic priming technique[2] in aphasic patients submitted to lexical decision tasks (asked to classify stimuli as words or non-words). Milberg and colleagues (for a summary see Milberg, Blumstein, & Dworetzky, 1987) showed that Wernicke's aphasics affected by a word comprehension deficit, showed an associative priming effect similar to normal subjects, recognizing a target word more rapidly if it was preceded by a semantically related word. On this basis they proposed that the lexical semantic deficit in aphasic patients was not a result of degradation, but rather a problem in accessing lexical information. According to this theory then, in aphasia the process of automatic word retrieval is possible, while the use in explicit conditions is defective.

Shallice (1987) proposes five criteria that characterize disorders of degraded representation:

- A lack of priming effect.
- High frequency words are more resistant than low frequency words.
- Performance must be constant, in the sense that the patient must fail on the same entry in successive presentations.
- The superordinate information should be more resistant than attribute information: for example, it is easier to recall that a canary is a bird than to recall its colour.
- Rate of presentation: performance improves according to the length of time between the response to one stimulus and presentation of the successive stimulus (Warrington & McCarthy, 1983).

Neurological correlates of the lexical-semantic system

The first attempts to find a neurological basis for the lexicon date back to Geschwind (1965a, 1965b), based on a comparative study of the anatomy of the cerebral cortex. In comparison with other species, the temporal–parietal–occipital association areas of the human cortex are particularly developed. These areas are dedicated to the processing of information from different modalities (visual, auditory, tactile, somatosensory) and allow the association of information relative to various sensory attributes in specific areas of the cortex through a system of neural connections. One such area is the angular gyrus, located at the point at which the information processed in specific sensory areas converges to form cross-modal associations and acts to increase the capacity for the organization, labelling and multiple categorization of sensory-motor and conceptual events. According to an associationist perspective, in fact, concepts can be considered to be formed by the set of the functional and perceptive attributes of objects. From a similar viewpoint, this area is seen to underlie the naming process, in other words, the ability to associate names (or rather, the specific phonological forms) to concepts.

The introduction of neuroimaging techniques has allowed detailing of the neural base of the lexicon. In a pioneering study, Cappa, Cavallotti, and Vignolo (1981) correlated the site of lesion evident on CAT scan with the type of paraphasias (phonological and semantic) produced by aphasic patients during a naming task. They hypothesized that the perisylvian regions (the classic language areas) represent the neural correlate of the phonological aspects of language, while the marginal areas of the same hemisphere (distant from the Sylvian fissure) are critical in the processing of the semantic-lexical level of language.

This study was the first to experimentally highlight the fact that the processing of the lexicon involves a modular treatment of information that is carried out by cerebral areas not totally coinciding with the classical areas of linguistic processing. In the following years a number of neuroimaging studies were carried out on both patients and normal participants (Price et al., 1996), aimed at outlining a cognitive neuroanatomy underlying the lexical-semantic system. One of the most recent of these is the study of DeLeon et al. (2007), which is based on a serial model of lexical processing similar to that proposed in Figure 6.6.

The naming of a picture of a horse as 'horse' demands at least the following processes: (1) recognition of the visual stimulus as an instance of a familiar

Semantics:
Amodal general and
personal knowledge

Cowboys ride horses; horses can wear saddles, eat hay, like apples, native to US, race, can bite, are large; not eaten in the US; my horse is palomino; John's horse kicks

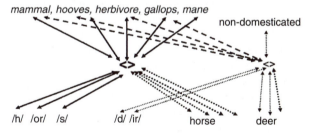

Figure 6.6 Schematic representation of the cognitive processes underlying picture naming. The representations that receive the most activation, and are therefore selected for output, are shown in bold. Solid lines indicate processes involved in oral naming; dashed lines indicate processes involved in written naming. More peripheral mechanisms for output (e.g. output buffers, mechanisms for motor programming of output) are not shown (from DeLeon et al., 2007). Reproduced with permission of Oxford University Press.

concept; (2) access to the meaning of horse (or what makes a horse a horse); (3) access to the phonological word form (the learned pronunciation of the word); and (4) motor programming and planning of articulation (as well as implementation of the movement sequences) to say the word. Although these functions may not be completely segregated anatomically, they can be individually impaired by brain damage. To test this hypothesis, DeLeon et al. evaluated 116 acute stroke patients using a battery of oral and written naming and other lexical tests and correlated the obtained data with RM images. The results of their study support the hypothesis of the existence of seven active cortical areas situated in the left area involved in single aspects of the mechanism of lexical processing of both specific aspects (for example, the retrieval of the phonological or orthographic form), and amodal tasks, such as the comprehension of the meaning of words, whatever the modality of presentation. The experimental evidence of a different neural role in processing the diverse aspects of lexical processing highlights, therefore, the existence of a complex network operating between different cerebral regions, the lesion of which will result in specific deficits.

Similarly, in an important study that combined lesion data from patients with semantic-lexical deficits and the results of activation studies (PET) in normal participants, Damasio et al. (2004) were able to identify cortical areas within the left hemisphere that are specific for the processing of concrete nouns, while processing of the corresponding concepts is the function of other areas located within the temporal lobe.

Finally, as far as the neurological substrate of proper nouns is concerned, both neuroimaging studies of normal participants (Damasio, Grabowski, Tranel, Hichwa, & Damasio, 1996; Gorno-Tempini et al., 1998) and data from patients postulate the existence of a neural circuit within the left hemisphere and centred on the temporal lobe, dedicated to the specific aspects of the processing of concepts and lexical forms of proper nouns (Yasuda, Beckmann, & Nakamura, 2000). This functional and neural segregation could, from an evolutionary perspective (Caramazza & Mahon, 2006) be particularly advantageous, in that it allows recognition of the identity of conspecifics and the ability to communicate with them precisely and rapidly.

In the majority of cases, the specific lexical deficit for verbs follows a lesion centred in the anterior language areas, including Broca's area, while, on the other hand, a deficit limited to the noun category has been described following left temporal cortex damage (Miceli et al., 1984, 1988; Damasio & Tranel, 1993; Caramazza & Hillis, 1991). Similarly, in a series of studies carried out on normal participants using various investigation techniques, different patterns of neural activation have been shown in tasks of verb and noun processing. In a PET study, Perani et al. (1999, see Figure 3.6) found neural activation of the frontal dorsolateral and left lateral temporal areas in tasks of verb processing, while processing of nouns is accompanied by diffuse prevalently left sided hemispheric activation. Federmeier, Segal, Lombrozo, and Kutas (2000), through the recording of evoked potentials, have found positivity specific to verbs in the left frontal region, while negativity in the left frontal-central region has been observed in tasks of noun processing.

Finally, repetitive transcranial magnetic stimulation (rTMS) applied to a left prefrontal region causes a delay (Shapiro et al., 2001) or facilitation (Cappa et al., 2002) in replies relating to verbs, but not nouns.

In conclusion, neuroimaging studies have revealed that a picture of involvement of mainly the posterior areas of the left hemisphere seems to emerge in tasks of noun processing, while verb processing, in particular processing of verbs depicting actions, is accompanied by activation of the more anterior frontal-parietal areas, suggesting a close relationship between the representation of verbs and the spatial knowledge linked to the action that the verbs express (Berlingeri et al., 2008).

Notes

1 It must, however, be noted that it is not always possible to define precisely the distance in features separating one phoneme from another. For example, adopting Chomsky and Halle's system, the phonemes /g/ and /d/ are distinguished by three features, while according to Jakobson, Fant, and Halle (1952) they are differentiated by a single feature only.
2 In a typical semantic priming experiment, participants have to identify a target word ('table') within a rapid serial sequence of distracters made up of words that are either semantically associated ('seat') or have no relationship to the target word ('bell'). The target word is more quickly recognized if it is preceded by a semantically associated word than when preceded by a non-associated word or a non-word.

References

Anderson, S. W., Damasio, A. R., & Damasio, H. (1990). Troubled letters but not numbers. Domain specific cognitive impairments following focal damage in frontal cortex. *Brain*, *113*, 749–766.

Arbib, M. A. (2010). Mirror system activity for action and language is embedded in the integration of dorsal and ventral pathways. *Brain and Language*, *112* (1), 12–24.

Auerbach, S. H., Allard, T., Naeser, M., Alexander, M. P., & Albert, M. L. (1982). Pure word deafness. Analysis of a case with bilateral lesions and a defect at the prephonemic level. *Brain*, *105* (2), 271–300.

Badecker, W., Miozzo, M., & Zanuttini, R. (1995). The two-stage model of lexical retrieval: Evidence from a case of anomia with selective preservation of grammatical gender. *Cognition*, *57* (2), 193–216.

Barbarotto, R., Laiacona, M., Macchi, V., & Capitani, E. (2002). Picture reality decision, semantic categories and gender. A new set of pictures, with norms and an experimental study. *Neuropsychologia*, *40* (10), 1637–1653.

Berlingeri, M., Crepaldi, D., Roberti, R., Scialfa, G., Luzzatti, C., & Paulesi, E. (2008). Nouns and verbs in the brain: Grammatical class and task specific effects as revealed by fMRI. *Cognitive Neuropsychology*, *25* (4), 528–558.

Berndt, R. S., Haendiges, A. N., & Wozniak, M. A. (1997a). Verb retrieval and sentence processing: Dissociation of an established symptom association. *Cortex*, *33* (1), 99–114.

Berndt, R. S., Mitchum, C. C., Haendiges, A. N., & Sandson, J. (1997b). Verb retrieval in aphasia, 1: Characterizing single word impairments. *Brain and Language, 56* (1), 68–106.

Bierwisch, M., & Schreuder, R. (1992). From concepts to lexical items. *Cognition, 42,* 23–60.

Bloomer, D. S., & Laver, J. M. (1973). Slips of the tongue. In V. Fromkin (Ed.), *Speech errors as linguistic evidence* (pp. 120–131). The Hague: Mouton de Gruyter.

Blumstein, S. E. (1973). *Phonological investigation of aphasic speech.* The Hague: Mouton de Gruyter.

Blumstein, S. E. (1994). Impairments of speech production and speech perception in aphasia. *Philosophical Transactions of the Royal Society of London, B: Biological Sciences, 346* (1315), 29–36.

Bottini, G., Corcoran, R., Sterzi, R., Paulesu, E., Schenone, P., Scarpa, P., et al. (1994). The role of the right hemisphere in the interpretation of figurative aspects of language. A positron emission tomography activation study. *Brain, 117,* 1241–1253.

Buckingham, H. W. (1986). The scan-copier mechanism and the positional level of language production: Evidence from phonemic paraphasia. *Cognitive Science, 10* (2), 195–217.

Butterworth, B. (1989). Lexical access in speech production. In W. Marslen-Wilson (Ed.), *Lexical representation and process.* Cambridge, MA: MIT Press.

Butterworth, B. (1992). Disorders of phonological encoding. *Cognition, 42,* 261–286.

Cacciari, C., Reati, F., Colombo, M. R., Padovani, R., Rizzo, S., & Papagno, C. (2006). The comprehension of ambiguous idioms in aphasic patients. *Neuropsychologia, 8,* 1305–1314.

Capitani, E., Laiacona, M., Mahon, B. Z., & Caramazza, A. (2003). What are the facts of semantic category-specific deficits? A critical review of the clinical evidence. *Cognitive Neuropsychology, 20,* 213–261.

Caplan, D., Vanier, M., & Baker, C. (1986). A case study of reproduction conduction aphasia II: Sentence comprehension. *Neuropsychology, 3* (1). 129–146.

Cappa, S., Cavallotti, G., & Vignolo, L. A. (1981). Phonemic and lexical errors in fluent aphasia: Correlation with lesion site. *Neuropsychologia, 19* (2), 171–177.

Cappa, S. F., Sandrini, M., Rossini, P. M., Sosta, K., & Miniussi, C. (2002). The role of the left frontal lobe in action naming: rTMS evidence. *Neurology, 59* (5), 720–723.

Cappelletti, M., Butterworth, B., & Kopelman, M. (2001). Spared numerical abilities in a case of semantic dementia. *Neuropsychologia, 39* (11), 1224–1239.

Caramazza, A., & Hillis, A. E. (1990). Where do semantic errors come from? *Cortex, 26* (1), 95–122.

Caramazza, A., & Hillis, A. E. (1991). Lexical organization of nouns and verbs in the brain. *Nature, 349,* 788–790.

Caramazza, A., & Mahon, B. Z. (2006). The organisation of conceptual knowledge in the brain: The future's past and some future directions. *Cognitive Neuropsychology, 23* (1), 13–38.

Caramazza, A., Miceli, G., & Villa, G. (1986). The role of the (output) phonological buffer in reading, writing, and repetition. *Cognitive Neuropsychology, 3,* 37–76.

Caramazza, A., & Shelton, J. R. (1998). Domain-specific knowledge systems in the brain: The animate–inanimate distinction. *Journal of Cognitive Neuroscience, 10* (1), 1–34.

Carroll, Lewis (1865). *Alice's adventures in wonderland.* London: Macmillan.

Cipolotti, L., Butterworth, B., & Denes, G. A. (1991). Specific deficit for numbers in a case of dense acalculia. *Brain, 114* (6), 2619–2637.

Crepaldi, D., Aggujaro, S., Arduino, L. S., Zonca, G., Ghirardi, G., Inzaghi, M. G., et al. (2006). Noun–verb dissociation in aphasia: The role of imageability and functional locus of the lesion. *Neuropsychologia, 44* (1), 73–89.

Cuetos, F., Aguado, G., Izura, C., & Ellis, A. W. (2002). Aphasic naming in Spanish: Predictors and errors. *Brain and Language, 82* (3), 344–365.

Damasio, H., Grabowski, T. J., Tranel, D., Hichwa, R. D., & Damasio, A. R. (1996). A neural basis for lexical retrieval. *Nature, 380* (6574), 499–505; Erratum in *Nature, 381* (6595), 810.

Damasio, A. R., & Tranel, D. (1993). Nouns and verbs are retrieved with differently distributed neural systems. *Proceedings of the National Academy of Sciences, USA, 90,* 4857–4960.

Damasio, H., Tranel, D., Grabowski, T., Adolphs, R., & Damasio, A. (2004). Neural systems behind word and concept retrieval. *Cognition, 92* (1–2), 179–229.

Davenport, M., & Hannahs, S. J. (2005). *Introducing phonetics and phonology* (2nd ed.). London: Hodder Arnold.

DeLeon, J., Gottesman, R. F., Kleinman, J. T., Newhart, M., Davis, C., Heidler-Gary, J., et al. (2007). Neural regions essential for distinct cognitive processes underlying picture naming. *Brain, 130* (5), 1408–1422.

Dell, G. S. (1986). A spreading activation theory of retrieval in sentence production, *Psychological Review, 93,* 283–321.

Dell, G. S., & O'Seaghdha, P. G. (1992). Stages of lexical access in language production. *Cognition, 42,* 287–314.

Denes, G., & Dalla Barba, G. (1998). Vico GB precursor of cognitive neuropsychology? The first reported case of noun–verb dissociation following brain damage. *Brain and Language, 6* (1), 29–33.

Denes, G., & Semenza, C. (1975). Auditory modality-specific anomia: Evidence from a case of pure word deafness. *Cortex, 11* (4), 401–411.

Denes, G., & Signorini, M. (2001). Door but not four and 4: A category specific transcoding deficit in a pure acalculic patient. *Cortex, 37* (2), 267–277.

Ellis, A. W., Burani, C., Izura, C., Bromiley, A., & Venneri, A. (2006). Traces of vocabulary acquisition in the brain: Evidence from covert object naming. *Neuroimage, 33* (3), 958–968.

Ellis, A. W., & Lambon Ralph, M. A. (2000). Age of acquisition effects in adult lexical processing reflect loss of plasticity in maturing systems: Insights from connectionist networks. *Journal of Experimental Psychology, Learning, Memory, and Cognition, 26* (5), 1103–1123.

Federmeier, K. D., Segal, J. B., Lombrozo, T., & Kutas, M. (2000). Brain responses to nouns, verbs and class-ambiguous words in context. *Brain, 123,* 2552–2566.

Frege, G. (1892). Über Sinn und Bedeutung. In Carlo Penco & Eva Picardi (Eds.). (2001). *G. Frege, Senso, funzione e concetto. Scritti filosofici.* Laterza: Bari.

Freud, S. (1904). *Psicopatologia della vita quotidiana. Dimenticanze, lapsus, sbatadaggini, superstizioni ed errori.* Torino: Bollati Boringhieri.

Friedmann, N. (2000). Moving verbs in agrammatic production. In R. Bastiaanse & Y. Grodzinsky (Eds.), *Grammatical disorders in aphasia: A neurolinguistic perspective* (pp. 152–170). London: Whurr.

Fromkin, V. (1973). *Speech errors as linguistic evidence.* The Hague: Mouton de Gruyter.

Gainotti, G. (1976). The relationship between semantic impairment in comprehension and naming in aphasic patients. *British Journal of Disorders of Communication, 11* (1), 57–61.

Gainotti, G. (2005). The influence of gender and lesion location on naming disorders for animals, plants and artefacts. *Neuropsychologia, 43* (11), 1633–1644.

Gardner, H., & Denes, G. (1973). Connotative judgements by aphasia patients on a pictorial adaptation of the semantic differential. *Cortex, 9*, 183–196.

Geschwind, N. (1965a). Disconnexion syndromes in animals and man, I. *Brain, 88* (2), 237–294.

Geschwind, N. (1965b). Disconnexion syndromes in animals and man, II. *Brain, 88* (3), 585–644.

Ghyselinck, M., Custers, R., & Brysbaert, M. (2004). The effect of age of acquisition in visual word processing: Further evidence for the semantic hypothesis. *Journal of Experimental Psychology, Learning, Memory, and Cognition, 30* (2), 550–554.

Goldrick, M., & Rapp, B. (2007). Lexical and post-lexical phonological representations in spoken production. *Cognition, 102* (2), 219–260.

Goodglass, H., & Baker, E. (1976). Semantic field, naming, and auditory comprehension in aphasia. *Brain and Language, 3* (3), 359–374.

Goodglass, H., Klein, B., Carey, P., & Jones, K. J. (1966). Specific semantic word categories in aphasia. *Cortex 8*, 191–212; *12*, 145–153.

Goodglass, H., & Wingfield, A. (1997). The changing relationship between anatomic and cognitive explanation in the neuropsychology of language. *Journal of Psycholinguistic Research, 27* (2), 147–165.

Gorno-Tempini, M. L., Price, C. J., Josephs, O., Vandenberghe, R., Cappa, S. F., Kapur, N., et al. (1998). The neural systems sustaining face and proper-name processing. *Brain, 121* (1), 2103–2118; Erratum in *Brain, 121* (12), 2402.

Hart, J., Jr., & Gordon, B. (1992). Neural subsystems for object knowledge. *Nature, 359* (6390), 60–64.

Hebb, D. O. (1949). *Organization of behavior: A neuropsychological theory*. New York: Wiley.

Henaff Gonon, M. A., Bruckert, R., & Michel, F. (1989). Lexicalization in an anomic patient. *Neuropsychologia, 27* (4), 391–407.

Hier, D. B, & Mohr, J. P. (1977). Incongruous oral and written naming. Evidence for a subdivision of the syndrome of Wernicke's aphasia. *Brain and Language, 4* (1), 115–126.

Hillis, A. E., & Caramazza, A. (1995). Representation of grammatical knowledge in the brain. *Journal of Cognitive Neuroscience, 7*, 396–407.

Jakobson, R., Fant, G., & Halle, M. (1952). *Preliminaries to speech analysis*. Cambridge, MA: MIT Press.

James, W. (1981). *The principles of psychology*. Cambridge, MA: Harvard University Press. (Original work published 1890)

Jefferies, E., & Lambon Ralph, M. A. (2006). Semantic impairment in stroke aphasia versus semantic dementia: A case-series comparison. *Brain, 129* (Pt 8), 2132–2147.

Jonkers, R., & Bastiaanse, R. (1998). How selective are selective word class deficits – 2 case-studies of action and object naming. *Aphasiology, 12* (3), 245–256.

Kay, J., Hanley, J. R., & Miles, R. (2001). Exploring the relationship between proper name anomia and word retrieval: A single case study. *Cortex, 37* (4), 501–517.

Kittredge, A. K., Dell, G. A., & Schwartz, M. F. (2006). Aphasic picture-naming errors reveal the influence of lexical variables on production stages. *Brain and Language, 99*, 1–2, 203–204.

Kripke, S. (1980). *Naming and necessity*. Cambridge, MA: Harvard University Press.

Laiacona, M., Barbarotto, R., & Capitani, E. (2006). Human evolution and the brain representation of semantic knowledge: Is there a role for sex differences? *Evolution and Human Behavior*, *27* (2), 168.

Lambon Ralph, M. A., Graham, K. S., Ellis, A. W., & Hodges, J. R. (1998). Naming in semantic dementia – what matters? *Neuropsychologia*, *36* (8), 775–784.

Levelt, W. J. (1999). Models of word production. *Trends in Cognitive Sciences*, *3* (6), 223–232.

Levelt, W. J. M. (1989). *Speaking. From intention to articulation*. Cambridge, MA: MIT Press.

Levelt, W. J. M. (2001). Spoken word production: A theory of lexical access. *Proceedings of the National Academy of Sciences*, *98* (23), 13464–13471.

Levelt, W. J. M., Schriefers, H., Vorberg, D., Meyer, A., Pechmann, T., & Havinga, J. (1991). The time course of lexical access in speech production: A study of picture naming. *Psychological Review*, *98*, 122–142.

Levinson, S. C. (1983). *Pragmatics*. Cambridge, UK: Cambridge University Press.

Luzzati, C., Aggujaro, S., & Crepaldi, D. (2006). Verb–noun double dissociation in aphasia: Theoretical and neuroanatomical foundations. *Cortex*, *42* (6), 875–883.

Marangolo, P., Piras, F., & Fias, W. (2005) 'I can write seven but I can't say it': A case of domain-specific phonological output deficit for numbers. *Neuropsychologia*, *43* (8), 1177–1188.

Marra, C., Ferraccioli, M., & Gainotti, G. (2007). Gender-related dissociations of categorical fluency in normal subjects and in subjects with Alzheimer's disease. *Neuropsychology*, *21* (2), 207–211.

Marshall, J. C. (1977). Disorders in the expression of language. In J. Morton & J. C. Marshall (Eds.), *Psycholinguistics Series 1*. London: Elek Science.

Marshall, J. C., & Newcombe, F. (1966). Syntactic and semantic errors in paralexia. *Neuropsychologia*, *4*, 169–176.

Marslen-Wilson, W. D., & Tyler, L. K. (1997). Dissociating types of mental computation. *Nature*, *387* (6633), 592–594.

Martin, N., & Saffran, E. M. (1990). Repetition and verbal STM in transcortical sensory aphasia: A case study. *Brain and Language*, *39* (2), 254–288.

McKenna, P., & Parry, R. (1994). Category specificity in the naming of natural and man-made objects: Normative data from adults and children. *Neuropsychological Rehabilitation*, *4*, 225–281.

McWeeny, K. H., Young, A. W., Hay, D. C., & Ellis, A. W. (1987). Putting names to faces. *British Journal of Psychology*, *78*, 143–149.

Miceli, G., Capasso, R., Daniele, A., Esposito T., Magarelli, M., & Tomaiuolo, F. (2000). Selective deficit for people's names following left temporal damage: An impairment of domain-specific knowledge. *Cognitive Neuropsychology*, *17*, 489–516.

Miceli, G., Silveri, M. C., Nocentini, U., & Caramazza, A. (1988). Patterns of dissociation in comprehension and production of nouns and verbs. *Aphasiology*, *2* (3/4), 351–358.

Miceli, G., Silveri, M. C., Villa, G., & Caramazza, A. (1984). On the basis for the agrammatic's difficulty in producing main verbs. *Cortex*, *20* (2), 207–220.

Milberg, W., Blumstein, S. E., & Dworetzky, B. (1987). Processing of lexical ambiguities in aphasia. *Brain and Language*, *31* (1), 138–150.

Mondini, S., Jarema, G., & Liguori, F. (2004). Semantic and syntax of mass and count nouns: Data from aphasia and dementia. *Brain and Language*, *91* (1), 138–139.

Moore V., Valentine, T., & Turner, J. (1999). Age-of-acquisition and cumulative frequency have independent effects. *Cognition, 72* (3), 305–309; Discussion, 311–316.

Morrison, C. M., & Ellis, A. W. (2000). Real age of acquisition effects in word naming and lexical decision. *British Journal of Psychology, 91* (Pt 2), 167–180.

Morton, J. (1969). Interaction of information in word recognition. *Psychological Review, 76* (2), 165–178.

Morton, J. (1970). A functional model of memory. In D. A. Norman (Ed.), *Models of human memory*. New York: Academic Press.

Nickels, L. A. (2001). Producing spoken words. In B. Rapp (Ed.), *The handbook of cognitive neuropsychology* (pp. 291–320). New York: Psychology Press.

Osgood, C. (1960). The cross-cultural generality of visual–verbal synesthetic tendencies. *Behavioral Science, 5*, 146–169.

Osgood, C., & Miron, M. (Eds.). (1963). *Approaches to the study of aphasia*. Urbana, IL: University of Illinois.

Papagno, C., Tabossi, P., Colombo, M., & Zampetti, P. (2004). Idiom comprehension in aphasia patients. *Brain and Langage, 89*, 226–234.

Perani, D., Cappa, S. F., Schur, T., Tettamanti, M., Collina, S., Rosa, M. M., et al. (1999). The neural correlates of verb and noun processing: A PET study. *Brain, 122*, 2337–2344.

Perry, C., Ziegler, J. C., & Zorzi, M. (2007). Nested incremental modeling in the development of computational theories: The CDP+ model of reading aloud. *Psychological Review, 114* (2), 273–315.

Pobric, G., Mashal, N., Faust, M., & Lavidor, M. (2008). The role of the right cerebral hemisphere in processing novel metaphoric expressions: A transcranial magnetic stimulation study. *Journal of Cognitive Neuroscience, 20* (1), 170–181.

Price, C. J., Wise, R. J. S., Warburton, E. A., Moore, C. J., Howard. D., Patterson, K., et al. (1996). Hearing and saying: The functional neuro-anatomy of auditory word processing. *Brain, 119*, 919–931.

Ramus, F., & Mehler, J. (1999). Language identification with suprasegmental cues: A study based on speech resynthesis. *Journal of the Acoustical Society of America, 105* (1), 512–521.

Rapp, B. (Ed.). (2001). *The handbook of cognitive neuropsychology*. Philadelphia: Psychology Press.

Rapp, B., & Caramazza, A. (2002). Selective difficulties with spoken nouns and written verbs: A single case study. *Journal of Neurolinguistics, 15* (3–5), 373–402.

Rapp, B., & Goldrick, M. (2006). Speaking words: Contributions of cognitive neuropsychological research. *Cognitive Neuropsychology, 23* (1), 39–73.

Rapp, B. C., & Caramazza, A. (1997). The modality specific organization of lexical categories: Evidence from impaired spoken and written sentence production. *Brain and Language, 56*, 248–286.

Roelofs, A. (1992). A spreading-activation theory of lemma retrieval in speaking. *Cognition, 42*, 107–142.

Roelofs, A. (1997). The WEAVER model of word-form encoding in speech production. *Cognition, 64* (3), 249–284.

Saffran, E. M., & Schwartz, M. F. (1994). Impairment of sentence comprehension. *Philosophical Transactions of the Royal Society of London, B: Biological Science, 346* (1315), 47–53.

Saussure, F. de (1916). *Cours de linguistique générale*. Payot: Parigi.

Semenza, C. (2002). Lexical-semantic disorders in aphasia. In G. Denes & L Pizzamiglio (Eds.), *Handbook of clinical and experimental neuropsychology* (pp. 215–244). Hove, UK: Psychology Press.

Semenza, C. (2006). Retrieval pathways for common and proper names. *Cortex, 42* (6), 884–891.

Semenza, C., Bencini, G. M., Bertella, L., Mori, I., Pignatti, R., Ceriani, F., et al. (2007). A dedicated neural mechanism for vowel selection: A case of relative vowel deficit sparing the number lexicon. *Neuropsychologia, 45* (2), 425–430.

Semenza, C., Mondini, S., & Cappelletti, M. (1997). The grammatical properties of mass nouns: An aphasia case study. *Neuropsychologia, 35* (5), 669–675.

Semenza, C., Sartori, G., & D'Andrea, J. (2003). He can tell which master craftsman blew a Venitian vase, but he can not name the Pope: A patient with a selective difficulty in naming faces. *Neuroscience Letters; 352*, 73–75.

Shallice, I. (1987). Impairments of semantic processing: Multiple dissociations. In M. Coltheart, G. Sartori, & R. Job (Eds.), *The cognitive neuropsycology of language* (pp. 111–128). Hillsdale, NJ: Lawrence Erlbaum Associates, Inc.

Shapiro, K. A., Pascual-Leone, A., Mottaghy, F. M., Gangitano, M., & Caramazza, A. (2001). Grammatical distinctions in the left frontal cortex. *Journal of Cognitive Neuroscience, 13*, 713–720.

Silveri, M. C., Monteleone, D., Burani, C., & Tabossi, P. (2000). Automatic semantic facilitation in Alzheimer's disease. *Journal of Clinical and Experimental Neuropsychology, 18* (3), 371–382.

Silverman, I., & Eals, M. (1992). Sex differences in spatial abilities: Evolutionary theory and data. In J. H. Barkow, L. Cosmides, & J. Tooby (Eds.), *The adapted mind* (pp. 533–549). New York: Oxford University Press.

Stemberger, J. P. (1985). An interactive activation model of language production. In A. W. Ellis (Ed.), *Progress in the psychology of language* (Vol. 1, pp. 143–186). Hove, UK: Lawrence Erlbaum Associates Ltd.

Tulving, E. (1972). Episodic and semantic memory. In E. Tulving & W. Donaldson (Eds.), *Organisation of memory*. London: Academic Press.

Ungerleider, L. G., & Mishkin, M. (1982). Two cortical visual systems. In D. J. Ingle, M. A. Goodale, & R. J. W. Mansfield (Eds.), *Analysis of visual behavior* (pp. 549–586). Cambridge, MA: MIT Press.

Vico, G. B. (1744). *Principi di scienza nuova d'intorno alla comune natura delle nazioni*. Napoli: Stamperia Muziana.

Vigliocco, G., Vinson, D. P., Martin, R. C., & Garrett, M. F. (1999). Is 'count' and 'mass' information available when the noun is not? An investigation of tip of the tongue phenomenon. *Journal of Memory and Language, 40*, 534–558.

Vigliocco, G., Warren, J., Siri, S., Arciuli, J., Scott, S., & Wise, R. (2006). The role of semantics and grammatical class in the neural representation of words. *Cerebral Cortex, 16* (12), 1790–1796.

Warrington, E. K., & McCarthy, R. (1983). Category specific access dysphasia. *Brain, 106* (4), 859–878.

Warrington, E. K., & McCarthy, R. A. (1987). Categories of knowledge. Further fractionations and an attempted integration. *Brain, 110* (5), 1273–1296.

Warrington, E. K., & Shallice, T. (1984). Category specific semantic impairments. *Brain, 107*, 829–853.

Yasuda, K., Beckmann, B., & Nakamura, T. (2000). Brain processing of proper names. *Aphasiology*, *14* (11), 1067–1089.

Zingeser, L. B., & Berndt, R. S. (1988). Grammatical class and context effects in a case of pure anomia: Implications for models of language production. *Cognitive Neuropsychology*, *5* (4), 473–516.

Zingeser, L. B., & Berndt, R. S. (1990). Retrieval of nouns and verbs in agrammatism and anomia. *Brain and Language*, *39* (1), 14–32.

7   The trains of language: Syntax and morphology

*Eleonora Rossi**

Language does not involve solely the production and comprehension of isolated words. It requires the processing of ordered strings of words (*sentences*). Sentences encode fundamental information about the type of action that is carried out, regarding who is the subject of the action (i.e. who performs the action), about who or what is on the receiving end of that action and, more generally, information regarding relationships between the elements of the sentence.

Words are the 'wagons' of language and are arranged and organized in 'trains' that respect the grammatical rules of a particular language. To quote one of Moro's examples (2008), if the lexicon supplies us with a sequence of words such as *Dante, Beatrice, day, one, amazed, was, met*, we may form several language trains, or sentences, some of which are possible, or grammatically correct, while others, though the words are the same, will not be grammatically correct. For example, the sentences 'One day Dante was amazed' or 'Beatrice met Dante' are correct, whereas sentences such as 'Amazed one day Dante was' or 'One Beatrice Dante met day' are grammatically incorrect, that is to say, made up of correct words that are however placed in the wrong order.

What are the rules that dictate the order of the elements in a sentence? As far as the English language is concerned (though this is not true for all languages),[1] the subject of the sentence is usually followed by a verb, which in turn is usually followed by the object. This linear order (so called subject–verb–object, SVO), however, is not always maintained. Consider the question 'What did John see?', in this case the word order changes and is replaced by the sequence object–subject–verb (OSV), which is derived from the previous one. Although the order is no longer canonical, the sentence is, however, grammatically correct. And what about the sentence 'The girl who is running is a friend of mine'? A complex sentence of this type provides two pieces of information and can be divided into two simpler sentences, namely 'A girl is running' and 'That girl is a friend of mine'. It is immediately noticeable that in the original sentence the two concepts are not expressed in a linear manner but that one sentence is 'embedded' within the other. If we wish to rewrite the sentence as a question using brackets to delineate the boundaries between the different parts of the sentence the result will

---

* Eleonora Rossi, PhD, is a post-doctoral researcher at Pennsylvania State University.

be: [[The girl [who is running] is a friend of mine]]. This example helps us to understand that one of the fundamental properties of languages is that of recursion (see Chapter 1) namely, the (virtually) infinite ability of a syntactic structure to repeat itself.

From the above examples it is obvious that there is a mechanism regulating the processes of sentence formation as well as the relationships between the various parts of the sentence. This mechanism, known as syntax (from the Greek συν- 'together' and τάξις 'sequence, order') is not immediately obvious, even to the trained eye.

The *minimalist programme* (Chomsky, 1993, 1995) puts forward the following organization of language. With the lexicon at the base of language, there are two abstract levels of representation, namely, the *logical form* (LF), which contains the abstract representation of the meaning of the possible sequences of words and the *phonological form* (PF), which corresponds to the abstract representation of the phonological form of these same sequences. The words are chosen from the lexicon and subsequently undergo a process of syntactic transformation through two fundamental operations, known as *merge* and *move*. At any stage of this derivation, the resulting word combination can be transferred to the phonological component in order to be spoken (a process known as *spell out*). Figure 7.1 illustrates a typical model of the minimalist programme.

As far as syntactic structure is concerned, linguistic theory proposes that the word order in sentences is subject to hierarchies between various macroelements that are larger than a word (even an inflected word) but smaller than a sentence.

These macroelements are known as phrases. In the field of linguistics, various types of phrases have been identified, including *nominal* phrase (NP), *prepositional* phrase (PP), *verbal* phrase (VP), *complementizer* phrase (CP), *agreement* phrase (AgrP), and *tense* phrase (TP).

Each single phrase is made up of a central part (called the *head of the phrase*), together with the *complement* of the phrase, found at the same level as the head, and an element at a level above the head known as its *specifier*. It follows that the internal structure of a phrase is asymmetrical, which is evident in the formal graphic notation that is commonly used.[2]

If we unite several phrases using a bottom to top process we build what is known as a *syntactic tree*. This is the formal linguistic representation of the

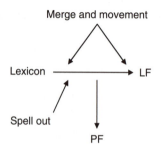

Figure 7.1 A model of the minimalist programme.

syntactic structure of a sentence, specifying the hierarchy between the various components and their relationship to each other. A sentence, therefore, is represented by the (non-linear) union between various phrases, which make up the building blocks of the syntactic structure of the sentences, combining to form a hierarchical structure.

In order for sentences to be grammatically correct, not only must the elements be placed in the correct order but rules influencing the form of the word within the sentence must also be respected, so that a 'morphological' relationship is established between the words forming the sentence.

A morpheme is the smallest meaningful element of language that cannot be further divided into smaller meaningful parts. Morphemes can be either *free* or *bound*. Free morphemes (articles, prepositions, pronouns, adverbs) carry meaning even when they appear in isolation, while bound morphemes must be connected to other units (lexical morpheme or root) to make up a word. An example of this is the inflectional morphemes added to verbs. If we consider, for example, the words *pens* or *books*, we can identify the following morphemes [*pen+s*] and [*book+s*]. The meaning of the root *pen-* is 'an object used for writing', the meaning of *book-* 'a collection of printed pages', while the addition of the morpheme -*s* lets us know that the words are plural. *Pen-* and *book-* are therefore *roots* or *lexical morphemes*, while -*s* is a *grammatical morpheme*.

Morphological processes are divided into *inflectional* and *derivational* processes. The first term denotes a process of word formation, the result of the union of two morphemes (usually a root and an inflected morpheme) and the consequent creation of a grammatically complex word. To give an example, verbs are composed of a root and an inflected morpheme. The inflectional morpheme allows us to define the tense and mood of the verb, and in (morphologically rich) languages such as Italian,[3] the inflectional morpheme also carries agreement with the characteristics of the subject (number and person agreement). Derivational processes, on the other hand, do not change the grammar of the word but can alter its lexical category, usually through the addition of an *affix* (prefix or suffix according to whether the derivational morpheme is applied to the left or right of the word). For example, the prefix *pre-* transforms the word *cook* into *precook* (belonging to the same grammatical category), while the suffix -*ly* transforms the adjective *slow* into the adverb *slowly*.

Another morphological process is *compounding*. In English, compound words can be made up from combining two nouns (*N–N* compound) for example, candlestick (*candle + stick*) or headscarf (*head + scarf*), or a noun and verb (*N–V* compound[4]), as for example, dishwasher (*dish + wash*). A third type of composition derives from the combination of an adjective and a noun (*A–N* compound), for example, hotdog (*hot + dog*). Another compound type can be found in Italian when two words are united by a preposition, for example *carta da parati* (wallpaper).

The distinction between morphological and syntactic processes is not, however, completely clear. According to some models (Kiparsky, 1982), morphological processes (inflectional, derivational and those specific to the formation of

compound words) are part of the lexical component of grammar, while according to others (Baker, 1988; Perlmutter, 1988), morphological processes are generated within the syntactic module. This concept applies particularly when the
morphological transformation comes about within a sentence, assuming, therefore,
morphosyntactic saliency. Another debated issue regards word representation;
that is, whether words are represented in a single unit at the level of the lexeme
(Bybee, 1988) or broken up into components with all the lexical roots separated
functionally from the grammatical morphemes (Caramazza, Laudanna, Capitani,
& Romani, 1988). However, most studies support an intermediate position.[5]
They postulate that alongside a mechanism based on the rules underlying
representative and productive processes for regular forms (for example, the
inflection of regular verbs: *loved, loving*, etc.) there also exists a mnemonic type
of learning system for the inflections of irregular verbs, for example, slept instead
of sleeped.

At this point we can consider some basic questions. What regulates the formation of language 'trains', or sentences, and, if such a mechanism exists, what are
its rules? What makes it possible, from both a functional and an anatomical point
of view, for every speaker, regardless of their educational level, to be able to produce grammatically correct sentences and judge the correctness of sentences they
read or hear, following their 'linguistic instinct' while possessing no specific linguistic notion of how the syntactic-grammatical structure of their native language
is organized? Moreover, and of greater importance for the subject matter of this
book:

1   Is there a specific linguistic mechanism underlying the knowledge and use of
     syntax (both at the functional and the neurological level), or is syntax
     supported by more general cognitive functions (for example, verbal working
     memory capacities)?
2   Is it possible that syntax is selectively damaged, leaving other language
     components intact?
3   Is it possible that syntax and morphology are processed by different functional
     and anatomical systems?
4   Last but not least, is it possible to obtain information through an investigation
     of errors committed by aphasic patients to help investigate the basis for a
     neurolinguistic theory of language?

In this chapter we will address each of these questions, trying to answer them
using mainly data collected from aphasic patients.

Agrammatism

Arnold Pick (1851–1924) was the first to write systematically about syntactic
disorders in aphasia, his first monograph dating from 1913. Pick not only
formulated a theoretical model of sentence production in which syntactic
processing precedes lexical selection, but he also founded the definition of

agrammatism as referring to a specific disorder of syntax. In his monograph Pick defined two subtypes of syntactic disorders. The first (*pseudoagrammatism*) is characterized by a general impoverishment of syntactic structures (which Pick considered secondary to articulatory difficulties and a reduction of verbal initiative). *True agrammatism* was defined as a disorder of grammatical formatives, independent of motor disorders, which results from an inability to produce the grammatical structures that correspond to the abstract sentence scheme generated by the subject. In most cases this is associated with a non-fluent aphasia of Broca's type. Subsequently Kleist (1916) introduced the term *paragrammatism* to indicate a disorder, often following a left temporal lesion, characterized by the presence of confused and erroneous syntax and associated with impaired comprehension typical of Wernicke's aphasia (for further details, see De Bleser, 1987).

For many years agrammatism has been considered a generalized disorder of grammar, and for many authors the term 'agrammatism' has meant a language disorder characterized by total loss of syntax and morphology, so that patients are forced, by default, to use semantic strategies during sentence production to make up for the grammatical deficit (Goodglass & Berko, 1960; Saffran, Schwartz, & Marin, 1980). However, such a sweeping notion is not in agreement with the literature both within and between languages that has gradually been accumulated. For example, Miceli, Silveri, Villa, and Caramazza (1984) highlighted that their Italian agrammatic patients committed many morphosyntactic errors but never created syntactically 'impossible' structures – for example, bare verbal roots lacking an inflected morpheme (even in the presence of an infinitival morpheme), such as *lav-* for *lavare* ('wash') and *bambin-* for *bambina* ('child'). They therefore hypothesized that the 'deep' knowledge of syntactic rules was not damaged and that the definition of agrammatism as a total loss of syntactic ability offered a limited vision of the phenomenon.

Over the years the scientific community began, therefore, to recognize that the study of agrammatic deficits required more detailed investigation. There was an evident need to define which components of grammar were compromised or spared and, above all, to investigate the similarities between agrammatic speech production and comprehension.

The analysis of agrammatic speech production has been undertaken in various languages.[6] Common characteristics of agrammatism are a reduction in mean length of utterance (MLU), slow and effortful speech, and compromised suprasegmental prosodic features. Agrammatism is also characterized by the prevalent use of open class words (nouns, adjectives, verbs) compared with closed class words (articles, pronouns, conjunctions), the omission or substitution of free or bound morphemes, and the frequent use of uninflected verbs (i.e. verbs in their infinitive form), which is particularly visible in languages featuring a rich inflectional morphology, like Italian. An example is provided below:

Ragazzo rompere$_\text{Verb inf.}$ bicchiere.
Boy break$_\text{Verb inf.}$ glass.
'The boy breaks the glass'.

Goodglass (2001) summarizes the characteristics of agrammatic speech production and comprehension in eight main points:

- the presence of fragmented and incomplete sentences;
- slow language and the loss of suprasegmental melodic features;
- omission and/or substitution of closed class words;
- substitution of verb roots or use of non-inflected verb forms in the place of inflected verb forms;
- simplified syntactic structure of the sentence (reduction in the use of coordinate and subordinate sentences);
- errors of inflectional and derivational morphology;
- loss of comprehension of inflectional morphology and grammatical functors;
- loss of comprehension of complex syntactic structures.

Table 7.1 contains examples of agrammatic language production, and Table 7.2 shows a comparison of the deficits presented by the patients in Table 7.1 according to the characteristics described by Goodglass. It is evident that all four patients share the principal characteristics defining agrammatic language: language production is effortful and slow, even in the absence of articulatory deficits, the syntactic structure of the sentences is simplified, grammatical functors are often omitted or substituted, verbs are often used in the infinitive form and there are errors of inflectional morphology.

Table 7.1 Examples of agrammatic speech production

P1: In this passage the patient is describing his job (Bar owner)

When 20 October 2002 … yes almost three years and a half ago … I saw the illness but I told I am strong. Later I was not strong as I think but … yes I had a lot of work, a bar. Maybe even two days in the car … then own three gyms, always mine, then coffee, coffee and then one vein explode.

P2: In this passage the patient explains his job (Art director)

Stage director … my work is to check everything … everything … and then … the maestros, singers, choir … the choir and that … look … story, story nice but sad and nice and sad and nice. Story … one person … many people. And then the orchestra directs the orchestra. The pianists do, the pianist do the choir … singers then the orchestra … the orchestra is everything.

P3: The patient is describing the 'Cookie Theft Picture'

Leeks the …. bathroom and leeks floor clean floors. Like this it does not matter. The material cleans. Children, girl, boy roll down from the door … no! Stool. And hear a … cookie. And then … child comes to ground.

P4: Another description of the 'Cookie Theft Picture'

The girl is … makes fall the cookies. Then the water on the ground. Wash then … cloth … clean … dry … then I made everything dirty.

Table 7.2 Characteristics of agrammatic speech

	Slower and fragmented speech	Simplified syntactic structure	Omission and/ or substitutions of closed-class particles	Use of non-inflected verbs	Errors in inflectional morphology
P1	+	+	−	+	+
P2	+	+	−	−	+
P3	+	+	+	+	−
P4	+	+	+	+	+

Even though the term 'agrammatism' was initially used to describe a production deficit, many studies subsequently demonstrated that agrammatic patients frequently presented similar deficits in comprehension. For example, agrammatic patients show difficulty in understanding grammatically complex sentences (such as passive sentences, subordinate sentences or sentences containing pronominal references) that require syntactic as well as semantic strategies for their interpretation (Caramazza & Zurif, 1976; Grodzinsky, 1995; Luzzati, Toraldo, & Guasti, 2001). To give an example, while agrammatic patients can correctly interpret semantically irreversible sentences such as 'The child eats the apple', they fail to understand semantically reversible sentences such as 'The man is chased by the woman'. In fact, the correct interpretation of semantically reversible sentences cannot solely rely on interpreting the sentence via semantic stategies, but requires the application of syntactic rules (which are critically impaired in agrammatism). For instance, for the example presented above, a pure semantic interpretation would not help much in determining who is the actor and who is the recipient of the action, in that it is equally possible that the woman chases the man or the man chases the woman. Instead, the application of syntactic rules is fundamental for correct interpretation.

According to Zurif et al. (1993) the difficulty that aphasic patients demonstrate in syntax comprehension is not a result of 'damage to a hypothetical syntactic processor', but rather a reduction in the necessary resources (for example, of short-term verbal memory). A similar conclusion is reached analysing the results of experiments investigating real-time comprehension of sentences with syntactic dependency, as in, for example, sentences containing unaccusative verbs[7] (Burkhardt, Piñango, & Wong, 2003), such as 'The man falls'. Results show that agrammatic patients understand these sentences correctly but at a reduced speed compared with normal subjects.

It should, however, be pointed out that agrammatism of production and comprehension is not a uniform phenomenon. From examination of the examples in Tables 7.1 and 7.2, it is evident that *P2* does not omit closed class words and uses verb inflections, even if they are used incorrectly. *P3*, on the other hand, omits functors and often fails to inflect verbs. From this and other examples a heated debate has arisen between proponents of agrammatism understood as a single syndrome of loss of a central mechanism of syntactic processing (Caramazza & Zurif, 1976; Drai & Grodzinsky, 1999, 2006; Grodzinsky, Piñango, Zurif, & Drai,

1999) and other authors who consider that agrammatic production is the result of loss of use of various cognitive systems, allowing, therefore, dissociated manifestations of agrammatism (Miceli & Mazzucchi, 1983; Miceli, Silveri, Romani, & Caramazza, 1989; Kolk & Vangrunsven, 1985). Miceli and Mazzucchi (1983), for example, present data pertaining to two agrammatic patients. The first (*C1*) omitted around 20% of lexical verbs (open class grammatical elements), while the other (*C2*) produced lexical verbs more frequently but in a non-finite form. Miceli and Mazzucchi propose that the different performance of these two patients demonstrates that agrammatism can be divided into two principal deficits, one prevalently syntactic (*C1*), the other morphological (*C2*). Kolk and Vangrunsven (1985) also described patients who committed mainly morphological errors while syntax was preserved. In contrast, Luzzatti and De Bleser (1996) described patients whose syntactic processing was more defective than their morphological processing. It follows that in order to understand the specific deficit and to draw inferences on the nature of the underlying processes, each single case must undergo in-depth analysis (Caramazza, 1986; Caramazza & Berndt, 1985).

An opposite point of view is that the analysis of groups of agrammatic patients provides larger quantities of data, allowing the characteristics of the deficit to be better defined (Grodzinsky et al., 1999; Drai & Grodzinsky, 2006). An intermediate position is that of Heeschen and Schegloff (1999) with their *adaptation theory*, according to which, the variability in agrammatic deficits is the result of the patient's use of different strategies to overcome a deficit that is fundamentally the same in all patients.

Interpreting agrammatism: Neurolinguistic theories

While in the literature there is almost unanimous agreement concerning the main characteristics of agrammatism, the debate is still open on how to explain agrammatic deficits in theoretical terms.

The neurolinguistic theories that have been developed to explain agrammatism can be divided into two subgroups. The first comprises theories that understand agrammatism as being derived from an underlying deficit of subcomponents of the cognitive system, for example a deficit in the verbal working memory resources that are necessary to support the processing of syntax (among others: Caplan & Waters, 1999; Waters & Caplan, 1996 for comprehension, Hartsuiker & Barkhuysen, 2006, for production). The second group, on the other hand, considers agrammatism to be the expression of either a deficit of linguistic (syntactic) representations (Friedmann & Grodzinsky, 1997; Friedmann, 2001, 2005 for production, Grodzinsky, 2000 for comprehension), or a deficit of syntactic operations, as proposed by Bastiaanse and van Zonneveld (2005), who suggest that agrammatic speakers are impaired in word order derivation. The *slow syntax theory* proposed by Piñango (2000), Burkhardt (2005) and Burkhardt et al. (2003, 2008) is an example of a cognitive-driven theory that proposes that agrammatism (at least, as far as comprehension is concerned[8]) is not a result of a disorder of the representation of the syntactic structure, but of a slowing of processing time. In particular, there is a slowing of the syntactic 'merge' operation; that is, the operation that combines two lexical elements to form a phrase. This suggested deficit does not prevent a priori the correct interpretation (and therefore, comprehension) of particular syntactic structures, such as, for example, reflexive pronouns, but slows their interpretation. The theory of *weak syntax*, proposed by Avrutin (2006) follows the same lines as that of slow syntax. In spite of the difference in terminology, the theory of weak syntax is also based on the idea that grammatical/syntactic access is slowed, but it also postulates that central to the agrammatic deficit is the inability to manage the competition between syntax and other grammatical operations. Finally, Caplan and Waters (1995), suggest that the real-time processing of syntactic operations is supported by short-term verbal memory. A deficit of verbal short-term memory will therefore compromise the correct processing of complex grammatical structures. Evidence for the role of verbal working memory in agrammatism comes from syntactic priming studies, which show that agrammatic speakers are indeed able to produce complex syntactic structures if they are primed to do so (Haarmann & Kolk, 1991, 1992), suggesting that when the hypothesized limitation in working memory resources is overcome, thanks to priming, agrammatic patients can produce relatively complex sentences.

Among linguistic accounts of agrammatism, the *trace deletion hypothesis* (TDH) has been proposed by Grodzinsky (2000) to account for agrammatic comprehension deficits. The TDH states that agrammatic speakers fail to correctly parse complex syntactic structures (for example passive sentences) because the syntactic representation of moved elements (i.e. 'traces') is deleted, making the interpretation of the moved grammatical elements impossible. Consider, for example, sentences such as 'I saw the man whom the woman chased', in which the object 'the man' moves from its canonical position (after the verb of the subordinate clause) to the second position in the main clause, leaving a trace in the original position. Grodzinsky showed that agrammatic speakers from different language backgrounds fail to correctly interpret these sentences, concluding that comprehension deficits in agrammatism arise from the deletion of the moved elements' traces. Luzzatti et al. (2001) found similar results in a group of 11 Italian agrammatic patients, who showed impaired comprehension both for passive sentences and clitic pronouns (for example, in the sentence 'Mary gives her a present' 'Maria *le* da un regalo'). The authors show however, that the pattern is not the same for all patients, suggesting that the TDH cannot be generalized to all agrammatic patients, in line with the *trade-off hypothesis* proposed by Linebarger, Schwartz, and Saffran (1983), which suggests that agrammatism can be linked to a general reduction in processing capacities.[9]

The *tree pruning hypothesis* (TPH, Friedmann & Grodzinsky, 1997; Friedmann, 2001, 2002) suggests a representational account for agrammatic production deficits. The TPH assumes that the syntactic tree is 'pruned' between the tense phrase and the agreement phrase,[10] and that the structures above the level of pruning are no longer accessible to agrammatic patients, while those below can still be accessed. In other words, agrammatic patients are more severely impaired in producing tense–verb agreement than verb–person agreement, or any other grammatical particles (like complementizers) that are assumed to be hosted in higher positions in the syntactic tree. For example, agrammatic patients are able to produce: 'John *eats* the apple' but have more difficulty producing the sentence: '*What* did John eat?' The TPH has been validated in a study with 18 agrammatic patients aiming at assessing the integrity of phrases within a syntactic tree. Friedmann (2005) distinguishes between two types of agrammatism: severe and moderate. In the first case, the tense phrase and all phrases above are under-represented. For example, a severely agrammatic patient will be unable to produce verbs with a correct tense agreement, while verbal agreement with the subject of the verb will be preserved. Thus a patient with severe agrammatism will not be able to correctly access the past tense form of verbs, because the tense phrase is not accessible. On the other hand, the same patient will be able to produce a correct subject agreement on the verb, as for example: 'Now the boy writes.'

A moderate agrammatic disorder, on the other hand, still allows access to the tense phrase projection but does not permit access to higher projections in the syntactic tree (for example, the *complementizer phrase*, CP). For example the production of relative and interrogative sentences such as 'John is eating some fruit. Maria wants to know what type. Mary asks John … [*what type of fruit are you eating?*] is defective or even impossible.

In the same study, Friedmann suggests that the pattern of improvement once agrammatic patients begin to recover language abilities follows the pattern of deficit described by the TPH in the reverse order; that is, agrammatic patients gradually regain access to the various projections, starting with the lower ones (agreement phrase), followed by the higher projections (tense phrase, and finally by the complementizer phrase), suggesting again that the higher portions of the syntactic tree seem to be the more vulnerable, and are the ones that are recovered later.

Morphological deficits in aphasia

Studies of morphological deficits present in aphasic patients have attempted to clarify:

- Whether morphological processes at the single word level are dissociable from morphological processes at the sentence level requiring an integration with syntax.
- Whether there are different mechanisms underlying derivational and inflectional morphological processes.
- The way in which compound words are processed.
- Whether morphological processing is the same for both language production and comprehension, and can be observable in other modalities (i.e. the written modality).

Caramazza and Hillis (1989) described a patient who produced a considerable number of inflectional errors both during oral and written description of events, and in repetition, reading and writing of dictated texts. This deficit, however, contrasted with a good level of inflectional processing at the single word level during spontaneous naming, reading and writing. The authors therefore hypothesized that the morphological deficit in agrammatism is located at the representational level, similar to the 'positional level' in Garrett's model (1982) of sentence production. In a cross-linguistic study (Italian and German), De Bleser, Bayer, and Luzzatti (1996) described a similar pattern of selective deficits of inflectional morphology within the structure of the sentence, while morphology at the lexical level was relatively spared, suggesting that even in cases of severe language deficit, the lexicon can remain largely intact, with a preserved ability to process inflectional aspects at a 'local' level. The results from these studies shed some light on the nature of morphological processes, which appear to be divided into local processes that happen at the lexical level, and more syntactic-driven processes that are embedded at a sentence level. Moreover, these studies suggest that agrammatism leads to a selective impairment of syntactic-driven morphological processes, leaving lexical-driven ones relatively intact.

Another set of studies investigated whether agrammatic patients show a dissociation between inflectional and derivational morphological operations at the single word level. Miceli and Caramazza (1988) provided data from one aphasic patient whose errors during a single word production task were mostly inflectional, with only a few being derivational in nature. The authors conclude that inflectional and derivational morphology are represented separately in the lexicon, and that every derived word is represented in its deconstructed form in the lexicon, separately from its inflectional variants.

Compound words are a special class of words that appear to be particularly useful for investigating morphological and syntactic operations at the interface between the lexicon and syntax, given that they are at the interface between words and sentences. The way in which compounds are created across languages can vary. However, morphologically rich languages, like Italian for example, display a particularly rich compounding system, which allows investigating with high precision the interface between lexical- and syntactic-driven morphology.

Luzzatti and De Bleser (1996) carried out a study using compound words that aimed at highlighting the existence of morphological dissociations in aphasic patients. Two agrammatic patients were asked to produce inflected morphemes (gender and number) for simple words, derived nouns, and compound nouns. Moreover, they were asked to produce the correct preposition in compound nouns that involved more than one word (*pasta [al] forno,* 'pasta [in] the oven') and finally, to produce adjectival-type derivational suffixes (*un'eruzione vulcan[ica]*, 'a vulcan[ic] eruption'). For both patients, inflectional and derivational morphology for simple words was preserved, however, the patients' performance was defective in tasks requiring formation of compound words. This appeared to be caused by an inability to perform a correct syntactic analysis of compound words, which resulted for example in errors in which patients determined the gender of the whole compound word only considering the final element of the word, leading to errors such la_{Fem} $piano_{Masc}$ $terra_{Fem}$. The authors conclude that the morphological deficit is evident only in those cases where there is simultaneous involvement of syntactic operations.

Mondini et al. (2005) assessed the production of various types of compounds in Italian aphasic speakers. They used several types of compound words, including prepositional compounds, and noun–preposition–noun compounds (N–P–N; for example '*canna da pesca*', meaning fishing rod, or '*gatto delle nevi*', meaning snowplough). The results show that one of the most frequent errors is the substitution of the preposition in prepositional compounds, for example, 'canna *di* pesca', or the simplification of the preposition, for example 'gatto *di* nevi'. This observation is confirmed even in cases in which N–P–N compounds have been classified as being 'strong' compounds, in other words, they cannot be 'split' by the insertion of an adjective. An example of this is the Italian word *capostazione* (station master), which cannot be divided, for example, into *capo abile stazione* (a good station master). This error pattern confirms that compound words are indeed decomposed at the morphosyntactic level. This idea is also confirmed by studies of verb–noun compounds (like *portafoglio* – wallet – which literally means 'carry bill') (Mondini et al., 2005), in which aphasic patients omit or selectively substitute the verbal element of the compound noun. This result is not solely to be attributed to the fact that the verb is the first constituent of the compound word, since (in the same experiment) subjects were also asked to produce noun–noun compound words, and in this case the component that was omitted or substituted was often the second constituent, as in *moto* for *motosega* (electric saw).

Other studies have highlighted how the morphological disorder could be restricted to a single output modality, such as reading or writing. For example, in deep dyslexia (Chapter 8) it is possible to observe that substitution errors for specific grammatical morphemes can be observed while reading. For example, patients will read 'enter' instead of 'entering' or 'he write' instead of 'he writes'. Badecker, Hillis, and Caramazza (1990) found a similar pattern in the writing domain, where a patient's written production errors were prevalently morphological in nature.

To conclude, having examined the various studies on morphological disorders in agrammatism, it is possible to state that morphological and syntactic processes are closely connected, leaving little room for an account that separates morphological and syntactic processes.

Neurological bases of morphology and syntax

For a long time, research into the neurological bases underlying the morphosyntactic processing of language has been mainly based on clinical studies. The recent introduction of neuroimaging techniques (as functional magnetic resonance imaging, fMRI, positron emission tomography, PET, and magnetoencephalography, MEG) has allowed broadening of the research perspectives by investigating syntactic processing in real time, allowing a more precise definition of the anatomical structures underlying syntactic processes.

One main question that researchers have been trying to answer for a long time is whether it is possible to pinpoint the 'locus of syntax', in other words to determine whether a specific brain area is involved during syntactic processing.

From a meta-analysis correlating patterns of syntactic deficit to cerebral lesions in aphasic patients, Caplan, Hildebrandt, and Makris (1996) and Mesulam (1998) suggest that the perisylvian cortex of the left hemisphere has a critical role during syntactic processing. This region includes the triangular and opercular region of the frontal lobe (Broca's area), the posterior portion of the superior temporal gyrus (Wernicke's area), the angular gyrus and the supramarginal gyrus. However, in a later study, Caplan et al. (2007) suggest that it is impossible to clearly determine the role of specific structures within the perisylvian cortex from clinical data only, and they propose that the neural substrate for syntactic processing is distributed over the entire perisylvian area, with possible variations between individuals.

The involvement of Broca's area in syntactic processing (both in production and in comprehension) has been demonstrated by several studies. Broca's area (BA44, BA45, BA46) has been found to be active during both overt (Haller et al., 2005; Musso et al., 2003; Tettamanti et al., 2001) and covert language processing both in sentence production (Indefrey et al., 2001), and comprehension (Just et al., 1996). Specifically, the left inferior frontal gyrus (BA45) has been found to be more active during the comprehension of syntactically complex sentences when compared with less complex ones (Stowe et al., 1998). Ben-Shachar and colleagues (2003, 2004) found that Broca's area is activated during both a grammaticality judgement and a sentence comprehension task. Similar findings come from Dapretto and Bookheimer (1999). Others performed experiments to try to determine whether specific syntactic operations could be supported by specific areas. Fiebach, Schlesewsky, and Friederici (2001) demonstrated that recognition of violations of 'local' syntactic operations activates the left ventral premotor area (BA 44/46), while recognition of violations of 'syntactic movement' activates Broca's area (BA 44/45).

In a PET study, Indefrey et al. (2001) created an experimental paradigm in an attempt to isolate the syntactic component of language processing. Participants were asked to produce sentences composed of strings of isolated words (nominal and verbal phrase), and in another condition to produce grammatically complex sentences. Comparing the areas activated during the production of single words and those activated during sentence production, the left rolandic operculum adjoining Broca's area (BA44) was activated, with a level of activation that was directly proportional to the complexity of the sentence produced.

In another PET study, Moro et al. (2001) analysed the cerebral activation of syntactic processes during comprehension, managing to isolate the morphosyntactic component from the semantic and phonological components. Results show activation of a common network for syntax and morphology occurring in the deep section of the circular sulcus of the left and right inferior frontal gyrus (areas 44 and 45). A specific area of activation, evident only for syntactic tasks, was found in the left caudate nucleus and in the insula. Moro et al. propose that syntactic tasks do not activate a single cerebral area but a network of cortical and subcortical areas. Recent studies suggest that other areas outside the perisylvian region may be involved during syntactic processing, as shown by Booth, Wood, Lu, Houk, and Bitan (2007), who demonstrated activation of the basal ganglia, and other studies (Ullman, 2001; Silveri, Leggio, & Molinari, 1994; Zettin et al., 1997) that demonstrated involvement of the cerebellum in tasks. Moreover, Broca's area has been reported to be particularly active during linguistic tasks in which verbal working memory load is enhanced, as is the case when manipulating verbal lists in alphabetical order (Barde & Thompson-Schill, 2002), or subvocal rehearsal of verbal material (Paulesu, Frith, & Frackowiack, 1993), as well as mental rotation judgement (Thomsen et al., 2000) and non-verbal motor planning (Binkofski et al., 2000), suggesting that Broca's area may be involved in supporting the processing of non-linguistic cognitive tasks. This idea has been recently supported by a study from Tettamanti et al. (2009) who show that Broca's area is active even during learning of non-linguistic material that followed non-rigid syntactic rules (which support the way in which all natural languages function).

To conclude, using both clinical data and neuroimaging data that investigate syntactic processes in real time, it can be deduced that there is no special brain area dedicated to grammatical processing, but rather it is possible to claim the existence of a 'network of activation for syntax' situated in the perisylvian regions of the left hemisphere. Within this network, Broca's area seems to be particularly active during the processing of both complex linguistic and non-linguistic syntactic operations based on a non-rigid syntax.

Notes

1 Word order varies according to language. An example is German and Dutch in which the basic word order (evident, for example, in subordinate phrases) is subject–object–verb: '*Ik denk dat Jan* [subject] *appels* [object] *eet* [verb]' ('I think Jan an apple is eating').

2 The formal graphic notation proposed by Jackendoff (1977) within the theory known as *X-bar* has been accepted as a notation common to all theoretical linguistics.

3 Morphology, like all other components of language, has different characteristics according to each language. Roughly speaking, languages such as English have a very poor inflective morphology of the nominal syntagma (for example, adjectives possess no inflective morpheme to denote gender). In contrast, other languages such as Italian, French and German, possess a rich morphology. German uses inflected morphemes to denote gender and number as well as to denote case, as occurs in Latin.

4 N–V type compound words are the most common.

5 Orsolini and Marslen-Wilson (1997), on the basis of a study of Italian participants using a priming technique, postulate the existence of a triple mechanism that assigns default, productive and idiosyncratic morphological processes to three different representational systems.

6 Through analysis of spontaneous speech and the results of specific experiments. English studies have been carried out by Bates et al. (Bates & Wulfeck, 1989; Bates, Wulfeck, & MacWhinney, 1991) and by Thompson, Shapiro, and Schendel (1995). Dutch studies have been carried out by Wagenaar, Snow, and Prins (1975) and by Vermeulen, Bastiaanse, and Van Wageningen (1989). Italian studies have been carried

out by Rossi and Bastiaanse (2007), Miceli and Mazzucchi (1983, 1990) and by Miceli and various colleagues (1984, 1989).

7   According to the classification proposed by Perlmutter (1983) and Burzio (1986), unaccusative verbs (also see Thompson, 2003) have the property of selecting their argument (which, however, in sentences containing unaccusative verbs, is in the position of the subject), with the property of being the 'recipient' of the action, as, for example, in the sentence 'the man falls'. According to this theory, the argument of the verb is generated in a post-verbal position and is then moved into the pre-verbal position.

8   Burkhardt et al. (2008) propose that an explanation in terms of slow syntax can also account for production deficits.

9   Caramazza, Capasso, Capitani, and Miceli (2005) supply data obtained from a group study of Italian patients affected by Broca's aphasia that do not confirm the pattern of deficits predicted by TDH.

10 Since Pollock (1989) the inflectional phrase (IP) is assumed to be divided into a tense phrase (TP) and an agreement phrase (AP).

References

Avrutin, S. (2006). Weak syntax. In Y. Grodzinsky & K. Amunts (Eds.), *Broca's region* (pp. 49–62). Oxford, UK: Oxford University Press.

Badecker, W., Hillis, A., & Caramazza, A. (1990). Lexical morphology and its role in the writing process: Evidence from a case of acquired dysgraphia. *Cognition, 35* (3), 205–243.

Baker, M. C. (1988). *Incorporation. A theory of grammatical function changing*. Chicago: University of Chicago Press.

Barde, L. H., & Thompson-Schill, S. L. (2002). Models of functional organization of the lateral prefrontal cortex in verbal working memory: Evidence in favor of the process model. *Journal of Cognitive Neuroscience, 14* (7), 1054–1063.

Bastiaanse, R., & van Zonneveld, R. (2005). Sentence production with verbs of alternating transitivity in agrammatic Broca's aphasia. *Journal of Neurolinguistics, 18*, 57–66.

Bates, E., & Wulfeck, B. (1989). Comparative aphasiology: A cross-linguistic approach to language breakdown. *Aphasiology, 3*, 111–142.

Bates, E., Wulfeck, B., & MacWhinney, B. (1991). Cross-linguistic research in aphasia: An overview. *Brain and Language, 41*, 123–148.

Ben-Shachar, M., Hendler, T., Kahn, I., Ben-Bashat, D., Grodzinsky, Y. (2003). The neural reality of syntactic transformations: Evidence from functional magnetic resonance imaging. *Psychological Science, 14* (5), 433–440.

Ben-Shachar, M., Palti, D., & Grodzinsky, Y. (2004). Neural correlates of syntactic movement: Converging evidence from two fMRI experiments. *Neuroimage, 21* (4), 1320–1336.

Binkofski, F., Amunts, K., Stephan, K. M., Posse, S., Schormann, T., Freund, H. J., Zilles, K., & Seitz, R. J. (2000). Broca's region subserves imagery of motion: A combined cytoarchitectonic and fMRI study. *Human Brain Mapping, 11* (4), 273–285.

Booth, J. R., Wood, L., Lu, D., Houk, J. C., & Bitan, T. (2007). The role of the basal ganglia and cerebellum in language processing. *Brain Research, 1133*, 136–144.

Burkhardt, P. (2005). *The syntax–discourse interface: Representing and interpreting dependencies*. Amsterdam & Philadelphia: John Benjamins.

Burkhardt, P., Avrutin, S., Piñango, M. M., & Ruigendijk, E. (2008). Slower-than-normal syntactic processing in agrammatic Broca's aphasia: Evidence from Dutch. *Journal of Neurolinguistics, 21* (2), 120–137.

Burkhardt, P., Piñango, M. M., & Wong, K. (2003). The role of the anterior left hemisphere in real-time sentence comprehension: Evidence from split intransitivity. *Brain and Language, 86*, 9–22.

Burzio, L. (1986). *Italian syntax: A government-binding approach*. Dordrecht: Reidel.

Bybee, J. L. (1988). Morphology as lexical organization. In M. Hammond & M. Noonan (Eds.), *Theoretical morphology: Approaches in modern linguistics* (pp. 119–141). San Diego, CA: Academic Press.

Caplan, D., Hildebrandt, N., & Makris, N. (1996). Location of lesions in stroke patients with deficits in syntactic processing in sentence comprehension. *Brain, 119* (Pt 3), 933–949.

Caplan, D., & Waters, G. S. (1995). Aphasic disorders of syntactic comprehension and working memory capacity. *Cognitive Neuropsychology, 12*, 637–649.

Caplan, D., & Waters, G. S. (1999). Verbal working memory and sentence comprehension. *Behavioral and Brain Sciences, 22*, 77–126.

Caplan, D., Waters, G., Kennedy, D., Alpert, N., Makris, N., Dede, G., et al. (2007). A study of syntactic processing in aphasia, II: Neurological aspects. *Brain and Language, 101*, 151–177.

Caramazza, A. (1986). On drawing inferences about the structure of normal cognitive systems from the analysis of patterns of impaired performance: The case for single-patient studies. *Brain and Cognition, 5* (1), 41–66.

Caramazza, A., & Berndt, R. S. (1985). Multicomponent deficit view of agrammatic Broca's aphasia. In M.-L. Kean (Ed.), *Agrammatism* (pp. 27–64). New York: Academic Press.

Caramazza, A., Capasso, R., Capitani, E., & Miceli, G. (2005). Patterns of comprehension performance in agrammatic Broca's aphasia: A test of the Trace Deletion Hypothesis, 1. *Brain and Language, 94*, 43–53.

Caramazza, A, & Hillis, A. E. (1989). The disruption of sentence production: Some dissociations. *Brain and Language, 36* (4), 625–650.

Caramazza, A., Laudanna, A., Capitani E., & Romani, C. (1988). Lexical access and inflectional morphology. *Cognition, 28*, 297–332.

Caramazza, A., & Zurif, E. B. (1976). Dissociation of algorithmic and heuristic processes in language comprehension: Evidence from aphasia. *Brain and Language, 3*, 572–582.

Chomsky, N. (1993). *A minimalist program for linguistic theory*. Cambridge, MA: MIT, Department of Linguistics and Philosophy.

Chomsky, N. (1995). *The minimalist program*. London: MIT Press.

Dapretto, M., & Bookheimer, S. Y. (1999). Form and content: dissociating syntax and semantics in sentence comprehension. *Neuron, 24* (2), 427–432.

De Bleser, R. (1987). From agrammatism to paragrammatism: German aphasiological traditions and grammatical disturbances. *Cognitive Neuropsychology, 4* (2), 187–256.

De Bleser, R., Bayer, J., & Luzzatti, C. (1996). Linguistic theory and morphosyntactic impairments in German and Italian aphasics. *Journal of Neurolinguistics, 9* (3), 175–185.

Drai, D., & Grodzinsky, Y. (1999). Comprehension regularity in Broca's aphasia? There's more of it than you ever imagined. *Brain and Language, 70*, 139–143.

Drai, D., & Grodzinsky, Y. (2006). A new empirical angle on the variability debate: Quantitative neurosyntactic analyses of a large data set from Broca's aphasia. *Brain and Language, 96*, 117–128.

Fiebach, C. J., Schlesewsky, M., & Friederici, A. D. (2001). Syntactic working memory and the establishment of filler-gap dependencies: Insights from ERPs and fMRI. *Journal of Psycholinguistic Research, 30*, 321–338.

Friedmann, N. (2001). Agrammatism and the psychological reality of the syntactic tree. *Journal of Psycholinguistic Research*, *30*, 71–90.

Friedmann, N. (2002). Question production in agrammatism: The tree pruning hypothesis. *Brain and Language*, *80*, 160–187.

Friedmann, N. (2005). Degrees of severity and recovery in agrammatism: Climbing up the syntactic tree. *Aphasiology*, *19*, 1037–1051.

Friedmann, N., & Grodzinsky, J. (1997). Tense and agreement in agrammatic production: Pruning the syntactic tree. *Brain and Language*, *56*, 397–425.

Garrett, M. F. (1982). Production of speech: Observations from normal and pathological language. In A. W. Ellis (Ed.), *Normality and pathology of cognitive functions*. New York: Academic Press.

Goodglass, H. (2001). *The assessment of aphasia and related disorders*. Austin, TX: Pro Ed.

Goodglass, H., & Berko, J. (1960). Agrammatism and inflectional morphology in English. *Journal of Speech and Hearing Research*, *3*, 257–267.

Grodzinsky, Y. (1995). Trace deletion, theta-roles, and cognitive strategies. *Brain and Language*, *51*, 469–497.

Grodzinsky, Y. (2000). The neurology of syntax: Language use without Broca's area. *Behavioral and Brain Sciences*, *23*, 1–71.

Grodzinsky, Y., Piñango, M. M., Zurif, E., & Drai, D. (1999). The critical role of group studies in neuropsychology: Comprehension regularities in Broca's aphasia. *Brain and Language*, *67*, 134–147.

Haarmann, H. J., & Kolk, H. H. J. (1991). Syntactic priming in Broca's aphasics: Evidence for slow activation. *Aphasiology*, *5*, 49–87.

Haarmann, H. J., & Kolk, H. H. J. (1992). The production of grammatical morphology in Broca's and Wernicke's aphasics: Speed and accuracy factors. *Cortex*, *28*, 97–112.

Haller, S., Radue, E. W., Erb, M., Grodd, W., & Kircher, T. (2005). Overt sentence production in event-related fMRI. *Neuropsychologia*, *43* (5), 807–814.

Hartsuiker, R. J., & Barkhuisen, P. N. (2006). Language production and working memory: The case of subject–verb agreement. *Language and Cognitive Processes*, *21*, 181–204.

Heeschen, C., & Schegloff, E. A. (1999). Agrammatism, adaptation theory, conversation analysis: On the role of so-called telegraphic style in talk-in-interaction. *Aphasiology*, *13*, 365–405.

Indefrey, P., Brown, C., Hellwig, F., Amunts, K., Herzog, H., & Seitzer, J. (2001). A neural correlate of syntactic encoding during speech production. *Proceedings of the National Academy of Sciences*, *98*, 5933–5936.

Jackendoff, R. (1977). *X/Syntax. A study of phrase structure*. Cambridge, MA: MIT Press.

Just, M. A., Carpenter, P. A., Keller, T. A., Eddy, W. F., & Thulborn, K. R. (1996). Brain activation modulated by sentence comprehension. *Science*, *274* (5284), 114–116.

Kiparsky, P. (1982). Lexical morphology and phonology. In The Linguistic Society of Korea (Ed.), *Linguistics in the morning calm*. Seoul: Hansin.

Kleist, K. (1916). Über Leistungsaphasie und grammatische Störungen, *Zeitschrift für Psychiatrie und Neurologie*, *40*, 118–199.

Kolk, H. H. J., & Vangrunsven, M. M. F. (1985). Agrammatism as a variable phenomenon. *Cognitive Neuropsychology*, *2*, 347–384.

Linebarger, M. C., Schwartz, M. F., & Saffran, E. M. (1983). Sensitivity to grammatical structure in so-called agrammatic aphasics. *Cognition*, *13*, 361–392.

Luzzatti, C., & De Bleser, R. (1996). Morphological processing in Italian agrammatic speakers: Eight experiments in lexical morphology. *Brain and Language*, *54*, 26–74.

Luzzatti, C., Toraldo, A., & Guasti, M. T. (2001). Comprehension of reversible active and passive sentences in agrammatism. *Aphasiology, 15,* 419–441.

Mesulam, M. M. (1998). From sensation to cognition. *Brain, 121* (Pt 6), 1013–1052.

Miceli, G., & Caramazza, A. (1988). Dissociation of inflectional and derivational morphology. *Brain and Language, 35,* 24–65.

Miceli, G., & Mazzucchi, A. (1983). Contrasting cases of Italian agrammatic aphasia without comprehension disorder. *Brain and Language, 19,* 65–97.

Miceli, G., & Mazzucchi, A. (1990). Agrammatism in Italian: Two case studies. In L. Menn & L. Obler (Eds.), *Agrammatic aphasia: A cross linguistic narrative sourcebook* (pp. 717–757). Amsterdam: Benjamins.

Miceli, G., Silveri, C., Romani, C., & Caramazza, A. (1989). Variation in the pattern of omissions and substitutions of grammatical morphemes in the spontaneous speech of so-called agrammatic patients. *Brain and Language, 36,* 447–492.

Miceli, G., Silveri, M. C., Villa, G., & Caramazza, A. (1984). On the basis for the agrammatic's difficulty in producing main verbs. *Cortex, 20,* 207–220.

Mondini, S., Luzzatti, C., Saletta, P., Allamano, N., & Semenza, C. (2005). Mental representation of prepositional compounds: Evidence from Italian agrammatic patients. *Brain and Language, 94* (2), 178–187.

Moro, A. (2008). *The boundaries of Babel: The brain and the enigma of impossible languages.* Cambridge, MA: MIT Press.

Moro, A., Tettamanti, M., Perani, D., Donati, C., Cappa, S. F., & Fazio, F. (2001). Syntax and the brain: Disentangling grammar by selective anomalies. *Neuroimage, 13,* 110–118.

Musso, M., Moro, A., Glauche, V., Rijntjes, M., Reichenbach, J., Buchel, C., et al. (2003). Broca's area and the language instinct. *Nature Neuroscience, 6,* 774–781.

Orsolini, M., & Marslen-Wilson, W. (1997). Universals in morphological representations: Evidence from Italian. *Language and Cognitive Processes, 41* (12), 1–47.

Paulesu, E., Frith, C. D., & Frackowiack, R. S. (1993). The neural correlates of the verbal component of working memory. *Nature, 362* (6418), 342–345.

Perlmutter, D. M. (1983). Personal vs. impersonal constructions. *Natural Language and Linguistic Theory, 1,* 141–200.

Perlmutter, D. M. (1988). The split morphology hypothesis: Evidence from Yiddish. In M. Hammond & M. Noonan (Eds.), *Theoretical morphology: Approaches in modern linguistics.* Orlando, FL: Academic Press.

Pick, A. (1913). *Die agrammatischen Sprachstörungen. Studien zur psychologischen Grundlegung der Aphasielehre. Teil I.* Berlino: Springer.

Piñango, M. M. (2000). On the proper generalization for Broca's aphasia comprehension pattern: Why argument movement may not be at the source of the Broca's deficit. *Behavioral and Brain Sciences, 23* (1), 48–49.

Pollock, J. Y. (1989). Verb movement, universal grammar and the structure of IP. *Linguistic Inquiry, 20,* 365–424.

Rossi, E., & Bastiaanse, R. (2007). Spontaneous speech in Italian agrammatic aphasia: A focus on verb production. *Aphasiology, 21* (6), 1–16.

Saffran, E. M., & Martin, N. (1997). Effects of structural priming on sentence production in aphasics. *Language and Cognitive Processes, 12,* 877–882.

Saffran, E. M., Schwartz, M. F., & Marin, O. S. (1980). The word order problem in agrammatism, II: Production. *Brain and Language, 10,* 263–280.

Silveri, M. C., Leggio, M. G., & Molinari, M. (1994). The cerebellum contributes to linguistic production: A case of agrammatic speech following a right cerebellar lesion. *Neurology, 44,* 2047–2050.

Stowe, L. A., Broere, C. A., Paans, A. M., Wijers, A. A., Mulder, G., Vaalburg, W., & Zwarts, F. (1998). Localizing components of a complex task: Sentence processing and working memory. *NeuroReport, 9* (13), 2995–2999.

Tettamanti, M., Alkhadi, H., Moro, A., Weniger, D., Perani, D., Kollias, S., et al. (2001). Neural correlates of learning new grammatical rules: An fMRI study. *Neuroimage, 13,* 616.

Tettamanti, M., Rotondi, I., Perani, D., Scotti, G., Fazio, F., Cappa, S. F., et al. (2009). Syntax without language: Neurobiological evidence for cross-domain syntactic computations. *Cortex, 7,* 825–838.

Thompson, C. K. (2003). Unaccusative verb production in agrammatic aphasia: The argument structure complexity. *Journal of Neurolinguistics, 16,* 151–167.

Thompson, C. K., Shapiro, L. P., & Schendel, L. (1995). Analysis of verbs and verb-argument structure: A method for quantification of aphasic language production. *Clinical Aphasiology, 23,* 121–140.

Thomsen, T., Hugdahl, K., Ersland, L., Barndon, R., Lundervold, A., Smievoll, A. I., et al. (2000). Functional magnetic resonance imaging (fMRI) study of sex differences in a mental rotation task. *Medical Science Monitor, 6* (6), 1186–1196.

Ullman, M. T. (2001). A neurocognitive perspective on language: The declarative/procedural model. *Neuroscience, 2,* 717–726.

Vermeulen, J., Bastiaanse, R., & Van Wageningen, B. (1989). Spontaneous speech in aphasia: A correlational study. *Brain and Language, 36,* 252–274.

Wagenaar, E., Snow, C., & Prins, R. (1975). Spontaneous speech of aphasic patients – psycholinguistic analysis 3. *Brain and Language, 2,* 281–303.

Waters, G. S., & Caplan, D. (1996). The capacity theory of sentence comprehension: Critique of Just and Carpenter (1992). *Psychological Review, 103,* 761–772.

Zettin, M., Cappa, S., D'Amico, A., Rago, R., Perino, C., Perani, D., et al. (1997). Agrammatic speech production after a right cerbellar haemorrhage. *Neurocase, 3,* 375–380.

Zurif, E., Swinney, D., Prather, P., Solomon, J., & Bushell, C. (1993). An on-line analysis of syntactic processing in Broca's and Wernicke's aphasia. *Brain and Language, 45,* 448–464.

8 The neurological bases and functional architecture of written language

> But surpassing all the stupendous inventions, what sublimity of mind was his who dreamed of finding means to communicate his deepest thoughts to any other person, though distant by mighty intervals of place and time! Of talking with those who are in India; of speaking to those who are not yet born and will not be born for a thousand or ten thousand years; and with what facility, by the different arrangement of twenty characters upon a page!
>
> (Galileo, *Dialogue Concerning the Two Chief World Systems –*
> *Ptolemic and Copernican.* Florence, 1632)

Over the past four thousand years or so, human society has developed the ability to process language through writing, although at different times and in different ways. Unlike acquisition of spoken language, which occurs spontaneously during a critical stage (Lenneberg, 1967) and with no specific teaching, learning to read and write requires guided instruction and commences when the child is older, usually at the stage when he or she starts school. In the absence of schooling, this ability does not develop, despite normal cognitive abilities. As a result, even today a consistent minority of people are illiterate, although the problem is in slow but steady decline. While in Eastern societies, around 80% of adults can read and write, in some Asian and African countries levels of illiteracy are still high, especially among women, who count for two thirds of all illiterate adults.

Ellis and Young (1996) point out the difference in frequency of use of reading and writing compared with speaking and listening. Even the most prolific writer and most avid reader talk and listen more than they read and write. For most of the population, apart from the odd case of social isolation or reclusion and despite the widespread use of electronic mail, reading and writing are certainly the least used of our language abilities.

Finally, as we will see later, learning and use of written language rely on operations carried out by specific functional and neurological systems. These systems develop through the adaptation and modification of parts of the visual system in order to perform specific tasks such as letter and word recognition (acquired modules). These systems function rapidly, efficiently and automatically, to the extent that we can talk of an involuntary 'reading instinct'. When asked to name the colour of a printed word (for example saying 'red' or 'green' when the word is printed in red or green), the reaction time between stimulus presentation and spoken output is greater when the word refers to a colour different from the colour of the print (for example, the word 'green' printed in red ink, 'Stroop effect').

This chapter illustrates current models of written language processing, using data collected from patients with specific reading disorders (alexia or dyslexia, these terms can be used interchangeably) or writing disorders (agraphia or dysgraphia) as a starting point. These data have led to clarification of the functional and anatomical relationships between more general mechanisms such as those relating to visual recognition of objects and faces and the mechanisms specific to reading (Cohen & Dehaene, 2004; Price et al., 2006). Moreover, the data have allowed a detailed functional architecture to be drawn up of the processes underlying written language and the relationship between written and spoken language processes. Last but not least, a neuropsychological approach demonstrates the consequences of damage to these systems.

Orthographic systems

In contrast with the process of identifying and naming pictures and graphic symbols (for example, road signs), which stems from prehistoric times and is characterized by direct correspondence between object and symbol, written language needs specific mechanisms: reading allows the transcription of a combination of graphic symbols in phonological strings, while writing is performed by the process of transforming a spoken unit (phoneme or word) into its corresponding written unit.

Different cultures introduced different types of script. One type is the ideographic system, like Chinese and Japanese *Kanji*, where written symbols (single or multicharacter) correspond to word sounds, but mostly to word meaning. The advantage of this system is that it can be shared by individuals speaking different languages; the disadvantage is the huge variety of symbols that have to be learned to achieve reading and writing proficiency.

Japanese script combines the ideographic system with a syllabic system (*Kana*), where each symbol corresponds to a spoken syllable, and it is used to write new words and morphological information that cannot be expressed in *Kanji*.

In the *alphabetic system* each written sign or grapheme (made up of one or more letters) corresponds to a sound with linguistic value (phoneme). Languages using the alphabetic system have a variable degree of correspondence between phoneme and grapheme. In some languages, for example Serbo-Croatian, the application of written-sound transcoding rules allows the phonology and orthography to be obtained for any string of letters or phonemes (these are known as transparent or shallow orthographies). Other languages, such as French or English, may have multiple correspondences between grapheme and phoneme: for example, in French different letter groups, such as *au, aux, eau, eaux, o*, correspond to the single phoneme /o/. English is even more complicated in that not only do different letter groups represent the same sound, but often a grapheme maps onto several phonemes (e.g. 'ea' in *mean, head* and *steak* is pronounced as /i/, /e/ *and*

/*ei*/, respectively. This phenomenon is also found in writing, so that the same sound can be realized by different orthographic forms. In these orthographic systems (opaque orthographies) we find regular words, whose orthography and pronunciation can be retrieved from the application of sublexical mechanisms of phoneme–grapheme conversion, and irregular words, often high frequency words, the reading and writing of which rely on underlying operations that cannot be predicted on the basis of rules. A further distinction in English is between irregular (e.g. the vowels in *pint* and *have*) and arbitrary correspondences (e.g. the vowel in *colonel*).

Finally, in the Arabic and Hebrew spelling systems, written from right to left, the letters making up a written word are usually consonants, while most vowels are omitted.[1] Consequentially, since different vowels can be inserted between the consonants, a string of consonants is phonologically ambiguous, as it may represent different words or non-words.

Italian spelling is usually considered to be orthographically transparent; however, it does present some exceptions. For example, the voiceless velar stop /*k*/ is realized in three different forms in the words *cane* (dog), *quasi* (almost), *chiodo* (nail), and the voiceless palatal affricate /tʃ/ can be realized in two different ways (*ciao*, hello, /tʃà:o/ and *cena*, supper, /ʧé:na/).

There are also some, albeit rare, exception words such as *glicerina* (glycerine), in which the grapheme *gl* is pronounced /*gl*/ instead of the usual /λ l/. Finally, the positioning of the stress in a written word is not always predictable on an exclusively phonological basis. In Italian, in fact, there is no consistent rule that allows us to predict where the stress will occur. Only previous knowledge of the sound or context of a written word allows it to be pronounced correctly (for example, the written word '*ancora*' can be pronounced either '*ank/ora* or *an'kora* with two different meanings according to the pronunciation, being, respectively, 'still' and 'anchor').[2]

This chapter primarily focuses on the alphabetic system of orthography.

Anatomical and functional models of written language processing

Associationist models

The first models, obtained essentially from the study of adult patients with acquired reading (*alexia*) and writing (*agraphia*) impairments following acquired cerebral lesions, adhered faithfully to current models of spoken language processing. In correspondence with the centre for auditory or verbal-acoustic comprehension, situated in the acoustic association area of the left temporal lobe, both Wernicke (1874) and Charcot (1883) hypothesized the existence of a centre for the comprehension of written language, functionally separate from the visual centre for the processing of images and connected to the verbal-acoustic centre. They also postulated the existence of a graphic centre for written words, similar to those in which articulatory programmes are deposited (Figure 8.1).

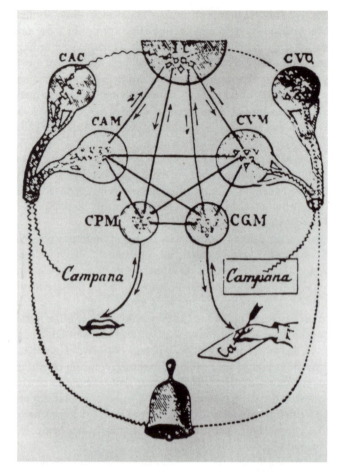

Figure 8.1 Charcot's bell diagram (1883). CAC: auditory centre for non-verbal sounds; CAM: auditory centre for words; IC: ideational centre; CPM: phonetic centre for words that establishes articulatory movements; CVQ: visual centre for images; CVM: visual centre for words; CGM: graphic centre for written words.

In 1874 Wernicke affirmed that 'only clinical experience can decide whether the hypothesis of the existence of specialized centres for reading and writing is justified'. Experimental confirmation arrived a few years later from the French neurologist, Jules Dejérine (1891, 1892). He described two patients, one alexic and agraphic, and the other presenting an isolated reading deficit. The latter patient, a notary, was able only to recognize his own signature and read a few numbers. In contrast, his writing, both to dictation and copying, as well as his spontaneous speech and auditory language comprehension were within normal limits.

A post-mortem examination of the first patient's brain showed a lesion of the angular gyrus of the left parietal lobe, considered by Dejérine to be the centre for the written images of words (visual word form area, WFA). A lesion at this level would result in an inability to read and write because visual word forms have to be retrieved before the activation of the graphic motor patterns of letters or prior oral spelling.

The pure alexic patient's brain revealed a lesion of the left occipital lobe and the splenium (posterior part of the corpus callosum). Consequently pure alexia was interpreted as being a result of a lesion that interrupts connections between the visual cortices and the left angular gyrus (Figure 8.2).

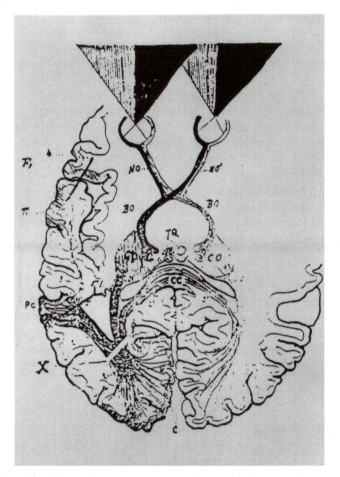

Figure 8.2 Schematic axial section of the two cerebral hemispheres, demonstrating the anatomical bases of pure alexia (Dejérine, 1892). NO = optic nerves; C = calcarine cortex, with a left sided lesion (hatched lines); Pc = angular gyrus (when there is lesion of this structure, as in the drawing, there will be alexia with agraphia. In pure alexia the angular gyrus is intact); X = lesion of the white matter of the left angular lobe; CO = disconnection of the visual centres from the language centre; CC = corpus callosum (in the drawing it is intact, but when damaged there will be the same effects as damage to X).

From a functional point of view, Dejérine's model proposes that recognition of single letters comes about in the occipital cortex visual areas, with the product being transmitted to the WFA and finally to the motor centre for word articulation. Reading comprehension is possible through a conversion process from the visual image of a word to its auditory image. During writing to dictation the opposite process occurs. The centres for auditory memory and/or articulatory memory activate the WFA and thereafter the corresponding motor programmes for graphic realization.

Both processes come about through a sublexical mechanism: in reading, the letters making up the single words are processed serially, one by one, with each letter being transformed into a phoneme. Thereafter they are assembled to be converted into heard words. The opposite process occurs in writing so that words are broken down into their constituent phonemes and then transformed into letter strings.

From a clinical point of view, reading disorders have been classified as follows: pure alexia, alexia with agraphia, and an alexia with an accompanying aphasia that presents the same characteristics as the deficits of spoken language. Benson (1977) adds another type of reading disorder associated with Broca's aphasia and characterized by superior reading aloud and comprehension of content words compared to closed class words. He interprets this type of dyslexia as being the result of a deficit in the processing of syntactic structures together with an inability to name the letters forming the words (literal alexia).

A similar classification has been proposed for writing, namely agraphia with alexia and aphasic agraphia, so that, for example, writing in a patient with Broca's aphasia is limited to content words only. The notion of pure agraphia is more contentious. It is rarely found in clinical practice (Basso, Taborell, & Vignolo, 1978), and is interpreted either as the final symptom of an aphasia in which all other language functions have improved (Rosati & De Bastiani, 1979), or as the result of an ongoing attentional deficit. These cases differ from cases of writing difficulty, which involve an inability to recall the motor plan necessary for the writing of letters making up words, but with preserved oral spelling (apraxic agraphia).

Cognitive models of reading

In 1971 during a meeting of the International Society of Neuropsychology, two British neuropsychologists, John Marshall and Frieda Newcombe, discounted the notion that written language processing comes about through a sublexical route only. They described two forms of acquired dyslexia, the first characterized by an inability to read non-words (meaningless strings of letters) together with the presence of semantic errors in word reading, so that a word such as green was read as *red*. In the second type the patient was able to read both non-words and regular words but made regularization errors during reading of irregular words, so for example, the word 'pint' was read as /*pint*/ to rhyme with mint. A more thorough analysis of patients' performance also revealed important grammatical and lexical class effects. Some dyslexic patients read and wrote open class words (nouns, adjectives, verbs) more accurately than closed class words,[3] independently of graphemic complexity, and read and wrote concrete words better than abstract words. Finally, performance was conditioned by lexical factors such as frequency of use or age of acquisition (Marshall & Newcombe, 1973).

In 1973 the same authors proposed a theoretical interpretation of the dyslexias in relation to an explicit model underlying the cognitive mechanisms of reading. The model, a diagram involving boxes and 'arrows' illustrates the existence of two routes or methods of processing a string of graphemes. The first is a phonological, non-lexical route (ABDTE) that allows the translation of individual graphemes into corresponding phonemes. The second, lexical, route (ABCTE) proposes access through the semantic system; it is therefore only accessible for already known words, and their meaning and phonological form are 'addressed' or 'retrieved' as a whole (Figure 8.3).

If, following cerebral damage, the ABCTE route cannot be used, there will be errors in reading irregular words, which will be regularized,[4] while regular words and non-words will be read correctly (surface dyslexia).

In contrast, if there is damage to the ABDTE route, reading will be possible through the lexical route, activating a semantic representation that mediates the passage between the printed word and sound realization. In other words, once the string of graphemes has been recognized, meaning is activated and subsequently there is activation of the phonological form. Obviously, it will not be possible to read non-words as they have no semantic representation (phonological dyslexia).

Semantic paralexias originate, according to Marshall and Newcombe's original interpretation, from an inability of the lexical route, when deprived of sublexical

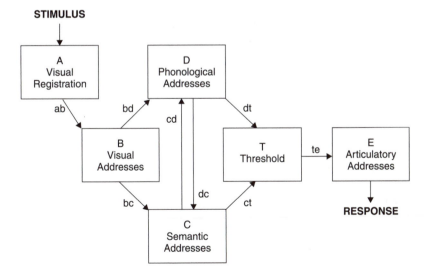

Figure 8.3 The first dual route model of reading put forward by Marshall and Newcombe (1973). Copyright © 1973 Springer, reproduced with permission.

support, to discriminate efficiently between semantically similar words, or from damage within the semantic system superimposed on damage to the non-lexical ABDTE route (deep dyslexia).

Over the subsequent years Marshall and Newcombe's work provoked huge interest in the study of acquired reading disorders, which were interpreted in the light of models underlying normal reading processes, which, in turn, were developed, expanded and verified on the basis of results obtained from the study of dyslexic patients.

Currently, the most frequently used models of reading are dual-route models (Coltheart, 1985; Ellis & Young, 1988; Shallice, 1988), which postulate the existence of at least two separate mechanisms involved in the processing of strings of letters, one lexical and one sublexical. The first procedure, specific for known words, works through a process of direct mapping between the visual characteristics of the string of letters (carried out by a mechanism of visual analysis that identifies the single letters making up the word and recognizes their position within the string) and the previously stored lexical representation. Orthographic representations are functionally separate from the phonological input lexicon and have access to an amodal semantic system, which is, in turn, connected to the phonological output lexicon. A direct lexical non-semantic route connecting the orthographic lexicon and the phonological lexicon, with no passage through the semantic system, has been suggested by some case studies of acquired dyslexia (see later in this chapter). Alongside the lexical procedure, the two route model postulates the existence of a procedure that allows new words or non-words to be read through phonological recoding of letter strings. This operation uses abstract rules of writing to sound conversion, which allows the graphemic information of the written string to be translated into the corresponding phonological code, avoiding passage through the semantic system.

Once the abstract phonological representation has been obtained through the lexical or non-lexical route, the information passes into a short-term memory store that holds the abstract representation processed in the preceding stages during planning of the articulation processes necessary for the word to be produced out loud.

Computational models of reading

Computational models of cognitive activities are fundamentally computer programs that have (or should have!) the characteristic of being able to carry out specific operations in a way that mimics brain functioning. A computational model of reading, for example, consists of a program that is able to generate a representation of the phonological output from its orthographic representation using processing mechanisms similar to those used by an expert reader. The first computational models were introduced by Seidenberg and McClelland (1989). According to these authors, the phonological representation of any letter string, whether it is a word or a non-word, can be computed in a single process with its orthographic representation as a starting point. This process consists of the spreading of activation through a connected network, in which activation of the input and output units represents the written and oral forms of the word. Knowledge of the system is, on the other hand, distributed in the connections between units. In fact, in addition to the input and output units, there are 'hidden' units, whose efferent and afferent projections are located within the system. Knowledge of written-sound correspondence is coded by 'weights' of connections between the various units. The weight of the connection is determined by exposure to a corpus of words.

Computational models have been used not only to clarify phenomena observed in normal participants in reading tasks, but also dyslexic phenomena. This is achieved by producing 'lesions' of the model (for example, varying the weight of the connections between the various units, once a model has been correctly instructed) in order to produce computerized simulation of different types of dyslexia. For more detail on these systems consult recent works by Zorzi (2005) and Coltheart (2006).

Components of the two-route model

From letter identification to the written word form

The first step in the reading process is based on the ability to identify strings of letters in parallel. This is performed quickly and the speed is not influenced by the number of letters making up the string, as long as they do not exceed six (Lavidor & Ellis, 2002). In less than half a second, therefore, an expert reader is able to carry out a task of visual lexical decision (decide whether the string of letters corresponds to a word or a non-word) independently of the position, dimension and type of character of the letters. It follows that during reading, some differences of letter form, such as *a* and *A* are overlooked, while at the same time, small details must be processed to allow differentiation between two letters, for example *e* and *c*. Finally, during the process of word recognition it is necessary to take into account the order in which letters are placed, so that we are able to differentiate 'lope' from 'pole'.

Dehaene and Cohen (2007) maintain that the process of visual identification of words is multicomponential in nature, with underlying neurological structures specific to this task. These structures are different from those involved in object and face recognition, and are situated in the medial area of the left occipitotemporal cortex, as indicated by both cerebral neuroimaging studies (Jobard, Crivello, & Tzourio-Mazoyer, 2003) and anatomo-clinical data (see below). The first step consists of the identification of letters, through a mechanism of combination of single segments orientated on different planes,[5] followed by a process that allows the 'normalization' of single letters, whatever their character and form (abstract system of letter identification). Once the single letters have been identified, the process continues with the identification of pairs of letters contained within the word through the activation of a letter digram 'revealer'. These letter pairs are identified by the 'revealer' even when separated by other letters (Grainger & Whitney, 2004). For example, the revealer of the *EN* letter pair activates in the presence of the letter *E*, placed to the left of *N*, even if there are other letters between them. In this way, the word *TICS* is coded by the digraphs *TI, TC, TS, IC, IS* and *CS*.[6] Obviously, during the letter learning process, there is preferential development of those digrams that are most common in written words, for example, in English there is frequent activation of the revealer *EN*, useful for recognizing many words (sci*en*ce, t*en*sion, p*en*sion, etc.), while the letter pair *ZH* is never activated as this combination is virtually absent in English. This process can subsequently be extended to the recognition of word fragments of increasing dimensions, such as trigrams, quadrigrams and whole words. Several studies have proposed that the abstract system of letter recognition is organized in complex units, such as morphemes (Caramazza, Laudanna, & Romani, 1988), syllables (Prinzmetal, Hoffman, & Vest, 1991; Carreiras, Álvarez, & De Vega, 1993) or consonant–vowel groups (Warrington & Shallice, 1980). This grouping serves to facilitate the processing necessary in order to pronounce a word or to access the meaning of a particular string. For example, decomposition of a word into its constituent morphemes facilitates the reading of complex words represented in a decomposed form (see Chapter 7).

The final result will be the abstract representation of strings of letters making up a word, the visual word form (VWF). Obviously, this type of 'bottom up' recognition process has an accompanying feedback mechanism starting with the lexical system. Words can be read, in fact, in a way that is partially independent of the physical form of the stimulus, so that, for example, NUM3ERS and $IM*BOLS* assume letter values (Carreiras, Duñabeitia, & Perea, 2007).

From the visual form to sound and meaning

Two different models for the translation of a written stimulus into its corresponding phonological form are at present competing. The first postulates that access to the meaning of a letter string comes about through direct passage of the written word to the semantic system, with no need for phonological recoding (Coltheart, 1980). In contrast to this, the hypothesis of obligatory phonological mediation assumes that the meaning of a string of letters can be retrieved only after the visual stimulus has been phonologically recoded (Frost, 1998).

The procedure using the direct lexical route assumes that, once the visual stimulus has been recognized as a familiar sequence of letters, it contacts a store in which the orthographic representations of the letters are deposited (input orthographic lexicon) and it is here that the specific representation is activated. This, in turn, allows access to the meaning, deposited within the semantic system. The semantic system, as we saw in Chapter 6, contains representations of the meanings of words and it is linked to the phonological output lexicon where the corresponding phonological representations are stored (see Figure 8.4(1)).

Alongside the lexical-semantic route, a direct lexical route has also been proposed, connecting the orthographic lexicon and the phonological lexicon, without accessing semantic information (Figure 8.4(2)). The hypothesis of the existence of this route stems from the observation of an unusual clinical picture

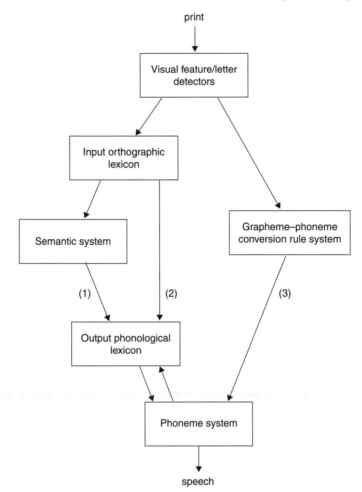

Figure 8.4 Three different hypotheses on the relationship between orthography and phonology active in the reading process: (1) a hypothesis that foresees access from the orthographic lexicon to the semantic system and subsequently to the phonological lexicon; (2) and (3) correspond to two different mechanisms underlying the hypothesis of obligatory phonological mediation (from Wu, Martin, & Damian, 2002). Copyright © 2002, Psychology Press, reproduced with permission of Taylor & Francis.

presented by some demented patients who could correctly read irregular words (e.g. *tortoise* or *hyena*) but not understand their meaning (*hyena ... what the heck is that?*, Schwartz, Saffran, & Marin 1980).[7]

The lexical procedure is accompanied by a non-lexical procedure that converts the visual input into the corresponding phonemes, recoding the orthographic representation of strings of letters into phonemes. No specific semantic or lexical knowledge is activated through this route. On the other hand, the theory of obligatory phonological mediation asserts that access to meaning must be subsequent to the process of phonological recoding, so that the written stimulus comes into contact with the previously stored phonological representation, which, in turn, allows access to the semantic system. In a variation of the theory of phonological mediation, the phonological representation is always generated by a process of sublexical phoneme–grapheme transcoding. (Figure 8.4(3)).

It must finally be mentioned that for the strong supporters of the lexical route, even non-word reading could be mediated by such processing. According to Glushko (1979), reading of non-words comes about through a mechanism that assembles the non-word phonological segments that are lexically activated and stem from words with similar spelling and pronunciation patterns to the non-word in question. For example, the non-word *prink* whose pronunciation is similar to the words *pink* and *clink* is read more rapidly than the non-word *zaid*, which is graphically similar to *said* and *raid* with a resulting conflict between the two possible pronunciations that can be assigned to the target non-word.

From the semantic system to reading aloud

Experimental evidence regarding the involvement of the semantic-lexical system in the process that allows sound to be extracted from a string of graphemes stems from data collected from the reading performance of non-brain damaged participants. These have demonstrated, for example, a significant effect of lexical frequency so that the time lapse before uttering a word of low lexical frequency is greater than that for high frequency words which have a weaker representation in the lexical system (Paap & Noel, 1991).[8] As far as data provided by dyslexic patients is concerned, see below.

Reading via the non-semantic sublexical route

Expert readers use the non-lexical route realized through activation of a grapheme–phoneme transcoding mechanism only when confronted with words not already stored in the orthographic input lexicon, or in experimental conditions such as non-word reading.

Dérouesné and Beauvois (1985) have outlined this process, postulating the existence within this mechanism of three different stages:

1   *A graphemic stage*: The letter string is segmented into graphemes according to the specific rules of spelling to sound conversion of the language concerned. For example, in French, while some letters always correspond to the same phoneme, other letters correspond to different phonemes according to the vowel that precedes or follows (for example G corresponds to the phoneme /z/ or /g/ according to whether it is followed by the letter E or A.

2   *Spelling to sound conversion stage*: After establishing the serial order, the graphemes are translated into phonemes.

3   A final stage of *assembly of the single sounds*, so that a complete phonological form is obtained and transmitted to a short-term memory system (*phonological buffer*) to be transformed into articulatory plans.

Involvement of the non-lexical route in word reading has been proposed by Caramazza, Miceli, Silveri, and Laudanna (1985) to explain the morphological errors of some patients with phonological dyslexia (see below). In agreement with the hypothesis of morphological decomposition (Chapter 7), written words are decomposed into their constituent morphemes before access to the visual input lexicon. The morphological segment that has no semantic value is processed via the non-lexical route and can, therefore, be selectively affected when there is damage to this route.

Diagnosis and cognitive classification of the dyslexias

In order to understand the nature of a reading deficit presented by a patient there must be quantitative, but above all, qualitative analysis of the deficit and the selective sparing or deficits in the reading of words of different length, frequency, grammatical class and regularity in spelling, as well as an examination of differences in performance between reading aloud and comprehension. Of equal importance is the analysis of reading time in relation to the length and complexity of the word under examination and error types (Table 8.1).

For this purpose, a number of test batteries have been devised: for English the most used battery is the Psycholinguistic Assessment of Language Processing in Aphasia (PALPA, Kay, Coltheart, & Lesser, 1992).

Following Shallice and Warrington (1980), acquired reading impairments can be classed as two main types, central and peripheral dyslexias. Central dyslexias result from the total or partial impairment of one of the two (or both) reading procedures; on the other hand, peripheral dyslexias follow a deficit at the more peripheral stages of information processing in both input and output.

Central dyslexias

Phonological dyslexia

Phonological dyslexia (Beauvois & Dérouesné, 1979; Coltheart, 1996) is characterized by a marked dissociation between the reading of words and non-words, with word reading significantly better than non-word reading. In some patients, in

Table 8.1 Examples of reading errors produced by dyslexic patients

Semantic errors
uncle → cousin; hurt → injure; grass → lawn

Visual errors
proof → roof; strem → train

Derivational errors
classify → class; hat → hot; marriage → married

Lexicalization errors
zul → Zulu; dup → damp

Function word substitution
in → the; as → he

fact, word reading is 100% correct independently of the type of orthography (opaque or transparent), and length, frequency, grammatical or syntactic class effect, while other patients may commit errors such as substitution of closed class words (because → that is) and/or morphological errors (slept → sleep). In contrast, non-word reading is severely compromised, so that the patient may even refuse to attempt to read them. An example of this is provided by one of the author's Italian patients who correctly read the word '*glicerina*' (glycerine), but when presented with the word '*glycol*' (glycol) stated: 'I have never seen this word and so I can't read it.' However, in most cases, patients with this form of dyslexia tend to lexicalize non-words, so that, for example, the non-word 'mook' is read as 'book'.

In a subsequent work, Dérouesné and Beauvois (1985) highlighted that patients with phonological dyslexia demonstrated improved reading of non-word pseudo-homophones compared with other non-words. For languages with non-transparent orthography such as English or French, non-words can be created that are homophones, but not homographs, of real words. For example, the two non-words *brane* and *kok* are pseudo-homophones of the English and French words *brain* and *coq* in that the pronunciation is the same despite differences in spelling. According to Dérouesné and Beauvois, the reading of pseudo-homophones is facilitated in that the information provided by the system of writing–sound conversion allows the phonological form of the real word to be retrieved, which in this case coincides with the non-word. This hypothesis can be applied to explain the preserved ability to read dialect in the phonological dyslexic patient described by Denes, Cipolotti, and Semenza (1987). Their patient spoke standard Italian but more commonly used Friulan dialect, which, in common with all dialects, is more often spoken than written. The patient's ability to read words in dialect, although poorer than his ability to read Italian words, was significantly better than his non-word reading. This picture was interpreted as being a consequence of the influence of the phonological output lexicon (which contains the phonological forms of both Italian and dialectal words) on the writing–sound conversion process, with the result of facilitating the conversion.

According to Harm and Seidenberg (2001) the inability to read non-words is a consequence of a wider phonological deficit also present in other tasks that require the representation and use of phonology. This hypothesis, however, is contradicted both by Dérouesné and Beauvois and by Bisiacchi, Cipolotti, and Denes (1989). Their patients did not display any phonological deficit, but had an evident and selective inability to read non-words.

The second and more tenable hypothesis, based on the dual-route reading model, postulates the presence of selective damage of the non-lexical route. As a consequence, the correct processing of strings of graphemes deprived of meaning is impossible. This impairment could, in addition, be at the base of the morphological errors in reading words observed in phonological dyslexic patients. Before reading, complex words are decomposed into two parts, the root (carrying the meaning) and the morpheme, deprived of meaning: as a consequence this part has to be processed non-lexically (Caramazza et al., 1985).

Deep dyslexia

Deep dyslexia, most commonly described in patients using 'opaque' orthographies,[9] is a multicomponential syndrome affecting the reading of both non-words and words, although with different characteristics. While the reading deficit of non-words has the same characteristics as those described for phonological dyslexia, word reading is characterized by the presence of:

- semantic errors, so that the target word is substituted with another semantically associated word (*admiral* → *colonel*; *faith* → *angel*; *train* → *station*);
- visual errors, in which the error corresponds to a visually similar word (*bush* → *brush*; *sneak* → *snake*);
- derivational type errors (*typing* → *type*, *heroic* → *heroine*);
- mixed errors, which are derivational errors superimposed on semantic and visual errors (*sympathy* → *symphony* → *orchestra*).

Concrete words are read better than abstract words, and, in decreasing order, nouns better than adjectives, verbs and functions words (which are often confused with each other).

This picture, along with phonological dyslexia, is usually the consequence of a vast lesion of the left hemisphere, most commonly vascular in origin and in the context of a non-fluent aphasia.

Semantic paralexias are, for most authors, the consequence of damage to the lexical-semantic route. This type of deficit can assume different forms. It can, in fact, be a result of an inability to activate or maintain the correct semantic representation or, alternatively, an inability to activate the correct phonological form.

In the first case, the deficit in word comprehension and production will be homogeneous; for example, given the word 'spoon', the patient will read 'fork' but will point to the spoon (Shallice & Warrington, 1980; Caramazza & Hillis, 1990).

From a totally different perspective, some authors (Coltheart, 1980; Saffran, Schwartz, & Marin, 1980) maintain that semantic paralexias reflect the use of a compensatory strategy involving a contribution from the right hemisphere. The cerebral lesion that causes deep dyslexia is usually so vast that, particularly in the acute stage of the illness, the left hemisphere reading ability is completely inactivated. As a consequence, the right hemisphere, which, as we have seen in the preceding chapters, possesses limited linguistic abilities, can transmit semantic information to the left hemisphere. This information is, however, rather coarse and deprived of phonology, so that the left hemisphere cannot retrieve the exact phonological form to match the semantic information.

Surface dyslexia

The key symptom of surface dyslexia (Marshall & Newcombe, 1973) is the presence of regularization errors in the reading of irregular words.

In languages with opaque orthography many high frequency words require a lexical procedure in order to be read correctly, rather than the application of the rules of writing to sound conversion. If the lexical procedure is damaged there will be no chance but to use grapheme–phoneme conversion rules; as a consequence a British surface dyslexic patient will read 'pint' as /pint/ to rhyme with *hint* and *mint*. On the other hand, reading aloud of regular words and non-words will be intact. As far as comprehension is concerned, the clinical picture will be variable. If there is selective impairment of access to the semantic system or to the semantic system itself (semantic dementia, Snowden, Goulding, & Neary, 1989), the patient will be unable to understand the meaning of both written and heard regular and irregular words. If, on the other hand, there is impairment of access from the semantic system to the phonological output lexicon, the patient will be able to understand words which, however, he regularizes when reading aloud.

For languages with transparent orthography at the segmental level, such as Italian, surface dyslexia in its classic form is obviously rare and, in the case of a deficit of the lexical route, the errors will be suprasegmental, as for example errors of stress placement within the word. In Italian, in fact, stress placement is not only determined by the syllabic structure of the word, but is often lexically determined. The town of Padova, for example, is pronounced '*Padova*, while the word for palate is pronounced *pa'lato*. Both these words have the same syllabic structure, but different stress patterns. Miceli and Caramazza (1993) have demonstrated that regularization errors in their Italian patients are, in fact, errors of stress placement. These patients correctly read words whose accent was determined exclusively by syllable structure, but produced errors when reading words with lexically assigned stress (*Sabato*, Saturday), was read *sa'bato* instead of '*sabato*).

Peripheral dyslexias

Peripheral dyslexias are a group of reading impairments characterized by the inability to process orthographic information in a stage preceding central sublexical and lexical processing, such as pure alexia (Déjerine, 1892), or *letter-by-letter dyslexia* and *spatial neglect dyslexia* (Hillis & Caramazza, 1991a, 1991b) because of an inability to attend the letters in the left half of a word.

Pure alexia

Unlike other acquired reading deficits, pure or isolated alexia does not occur alongside other language disturbances: in fact spontaneous writing and writing to dictation, comprehension and production of spoken language and object naming are all within normal limits. The main symptom is abnormal length of reading rate, with reading times directly proportional to the number of letters making up the word (letter-by-letter dyslexia: in contrast with the ability of a normal reader, the difference in reading rate between a word made up of four letters and a word made up of five or six letters could amount to a time increase of between 300 ms and several seconds. No difference is found between the reading of words compared with non-words; the identification and naming of single letters presented in isolation is usually correct, although patients tend to confuse visually similar letters.

According to Warrington and Shallice (1980), letter-by-letter dyslexia is a consequence of the failure of the orthographic processing mechanism that allows rapid construction of the visual word form. As a consequence, the patient will rely on compensatory strategies, such as the explicit and serial identification of each single letter making up a word.

Recently Shallice and Rosazza (2006) showed that pure alexia may stem from two different deficits. The first is characterized by an inability to group single letters into wider orthographic units, even when the patient is able to identify these letters correctly and rapidly. The second is caused by an abnormal slowness in the identification of single letters, coupled with preserved ability to group the letters into larger orthographic units.

It is worth remembering that patients affected by letter-by-letter dyslexia, although unable to read out loud, do preserve some residual reading ability. Their performance is way above chance, for example, in tasks of visual lexical decision or pairing of written words to pictures (Coslett & Saffran, 1989). According to Coslett and Monsul (1994) these residual abilities are the expression of a mechanism of semantic processing of letter strings carried out by the right hemisphere. The inability to read out loud, on the other hand, stems from the fact that the corresponding phonological form cannot be activated because of interruption of the occipito-temporal connections between the two hemispheres (Zaidel, 1985).

Cognitive models of writing

Activation of the orthographic form

As with models of reading, two independent procedures are thought to be deployed by adult literates for spelling, one sublexical, involving a phoneme to grapheme conversion procedure and a lexical one where the single words are globally processed. The first mechanism is made up of the following stages:

1   *Acoustic phonological analysis* of auditory input, with parcelling into smaller units (phonemes, syllables or other functional units, such as morphemes).
2   *Conversion* of these phonological units into the corresponding orthographic units.
3   *Assembly* of the orthographic units into correct letter strings.

The final product of this process will be sent to the graphemic buffer, the function and characteristics of which will be described later.

The obvious disadvantage of the sublexical type procedure is its slowness and its inability to process words with irregular spelling.

In most languages, such as English and French, the correct spelling of many high frequency words cannot be obtained through the application of rules of sublexical conversion alone (irregular words) and their correct spelling must be stored in an orthographic output lexicon, with retrieval overseen by the semantic system. The abstract orthographic representation thus obtained will be sent to the orthographic buffer in the case of writing or spelling out loud.

Experimental support for the writing dual-route model has been provided by a number of case studies of patients who showed particular types of spelling errors or dissociations in writing different types of words.

It must be remembered, however, that in most cases cerebral damage affects both orthographic and phonological representation in a similar fashion. Most patients with damage to the lexical or semantic system commit a similar number of errors in written and oral naming, even though the semantic errors may be different in written and oral modalities (for example, when asked to name a 'spoon' the patient says 'fork' and writes 'knife').

Structure of the orthographic form

A first hypothesis on the structure of the orthographic representation is based on the analysis of the 'slips of the pen' in normal subjects, characterized by omission, insertion or transposition of letters. Sgaramella, Ellis, and Semenza (1991) and Moretti et al. (2003) proposed that orthographic representation is depicted as a linear sequence, defined by the identity and position of single graphemes within the sequence. Miceli and Capasso (2006), on the basis of a detailed analysis of the errors made by dysgraphic patients, support the idea of a multidimensional representation that specifies serial order, vowel consonant status, the identity of the grapheme and the presence of geminates within the string.

Once the orthographic form is available, the next stage consists of the selection of the allographic form. Graphemes, in fact, have many variants (known as allographs), characterized by perceptually different forms (for example g, G, **g**, G). Allograph selection is made on the basis of the position of the grapheme within the word and its class (for example, first letters of proper nouns and the first letter of the word starting a sentence are written with a capital letter).

Once the allograph has been retrieved, the next step is the activation of the correct graphomotor programme. Here there is specification of the direction, dimension and form relating to the features making up the various letters that can then be realized using a number of different instruments (pen, spray can, feet, in the case of writing on a sandy beach) and influence the individual characteristics of the written production. The final stage converts graphic details into specific neuromuscular instructions (Figure 8.5).

Empirical evidence to support and validate this model has been collected over the past thirty years or so through observation of patients demonstrating contrasting deficits in their written output. Patients have been described who showed a disproportionate deficit in the writing of non-words compared with words (phonological agraphia), such as the patient described by Shallice (1981) who correctly wrote 95% of words dictated by the examiner, compared with only 18% of non-words. The fact that the patient was able to repeat both words and non-words excluded the possibility of there being an underlying phonological deficit to account for the difficulties in non-word writing.

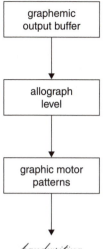

Figure 8.5 Peripheral stages in the model of writing. The abstract graphemic representation drives the selection of the appropriate allographic form for each letter. Finally, the motor patterns specifying the sequences of strokes required to create a letter-form are retrieved (from Denes & Pizzamiglio, 1999). Copyright © 1999, Psychology Press, reproduced with permission of Taylor & Francis.

Beauvois and Dérouesné (1981) were the first to document a form of dysgraphia characterized by problems in writing words with irregular orthography whose spelling cannot be retrieved through rules of phoneme–grapheme conversion. For example, the words *monsieur* and *cypress* were written *messieu* and *sipré*, being non-word homophones, but not homographs, obtained by applying mechanisms of sublexical conversion (lexical or surface agraphia).

A similar picture has been found in languages with transparent orthography, such as Italian. Luzzi and Piccirilli (2003), for example, described a patient whose writing errors were characterized by an erroneous use of the apostrophe (*il l'ago di Garda, the needle of Garda* instead of *il lago di Garda, Lake Garda*). Luzzatti and colleagues (1998, 2003) in a study carried out on aphasic patients and individuals suffering from Alzheimer's disease, revealed a picture of surface dysgraphia characterized by selective inability to retrieve the correct orthography for Italian words such as '*cuore*', '*Aquila*' or '*quota*' in which the phoneme /k / can be represented by the letter 'c' or the letter 'q' on a lexical basis only. These patients also had difficulty in inserting the letter 'i' in words that require it, so that the word '*cielo*' was written *celo*.

In Italian, moreover, there is an ever increasing use of words borrowed from other languages with, therefore, different orthography. Recently Meneghello, Finco and Denes (2006) described a highly educated subject (*Rosetta*) with selective inability to write these borrowed words although she understood their meaning. Whereas her performance was within normal limits in tasks of word and non-word writing, when writing borrowed words *Rosetta* used non-lexical type strategies, so that *body building*, *iceberg* and *audience* were written *bodibilding*, *aisberg* and *odiens*. It is interesting to note that normal subjects matched for educational level and age also committed a considerable number of errors (20%) but with different characteristics. Most of these errors were slips of the pen, others were the result of using of a sublexical strategy belonging to the language of the borrowed word (*chalet* → *challait, joy stick* → *joy steek*).

Deep agraphia

Deep agraphia is considered to belong to the group of central dysgraphias (Bub & Kertesz, 1982) and it parallels deep dyslexia. It is characterized by selective inability to write non-words, together with semantic errors in the writing of words. As in deep dyslexia, deep agraphia shows an effect for concreteness and grammatical class, so that concrete words are written better than abstract words, with performance being worst for the writing of closed class words.

Miceli and Capasso (2006) described some patients whose writing deficit was seen as a consequence of a damage to the orthographic buffer. Their writing errors, in fact, were characterized by selective inability to retrieve vowels or consonants (*Bologna* → *Blgn*). As far as geminates were concerned, errors included substitution (*troppo* → *trocco*), duplication (*cavallo* → *cavvallo*) or deletion (*avviso* → *aviso*), and change of position (*sorella* → *sorrela*). Sometimes the deficits can be highly selective: for example Cubelli (1991) reported two patients with a selective deficit in writing vowels. When writing words, the first patient omitted all vowels, leaving a blank space between consonants or consonant clusters, whereas the second produced errors that almost exclusively involved vowels.

Peripheral agraphias

An inability to realize the correct allograph has been described by De Bastiani and Barry (1989). This form of agraphia is characterized by the swapping of capital and lower case letters within a word, with capital letters predominating. On the contrary, the patient described by Patterson and Wing (1989) was unable to retrieve the form of capital letters.

A selective inability to retrieve the graphomotor patterns necessary for the writing of single letters has been found in some patients (*apraxic agraphia*, Baxter & Warrington, 1986). These patients, in fact, were not able to recall the correct movements for writing, and produced letters that were incomplete or resembled two fused letters. This clinical picture could not be explained on the basis of a motor or sensory deficit as the same patients were able to copy written text.

The reading and writing of numbers

Selective sparing of number processing (reading and writing) in comparison with words has been described by Anderson, Damasio, and Damasio (1990). In contrast, though more rarely, patients have been described demonstrating the opposite pattern – having more difficulty processing Arabic numbers than letters and words (for a summary see Delazer & Bartha, 2001). It has, therefore, been proposed that independent mechanisms exist for the processing of words and written digits.

According to McCloskey (1992) there are functionally independent modules specific for the processing of written digits and numbers written as words, which activate corresponding semantic representations. This representation, in turn, activates a lexicon specific to the oral production of number words and for the written production in both Arabic and alphabetic codes. The model therefore implies that, on the one hand, there are independent mechanisms for the comprehension and production of numbers in Arabic code and for written numbers, and on the other hand, a common semantic system activated by both written digits and number words.

In contrast, Dehaene and Cohen (1995) favour the existence of a direct route between the Arabic and verbal codes, so that the reading of numbers occurs in the absence of semantic processing of the quantity indicated by the number (for further details on the lexicon for numbers see Chapter 6). In McCloskey, Caramazza, and Basili's model (1985) the system of number comprehension transforms the numerical input into abstract semantic representations which specify each of the base quantities contained in a number and the powers of ten associated with them. For example, the semantic representation of the number 6582, that is, (6) 10 exponent 3, (5) 10 exponent 2, (8) 10 exponent 1, (2) 10 exponent 0, will be elaborated by the production system into the corresponding verbal sequence 'six thousand, five hundred and eighty-two', which, in turn, can be transformed for writing into alphabetic code or figures. For other authors, however, the passage through a semantic representation is not obligatory. They hypothesize the existence of asemantic mechanisms of transcoding from the different formats (Deloche & Seron, 1982; Cipolotti & Butterworth, 1995).

Finally, a semantic mechanism for the reading of familiar numbers (dates of birth, etc.) or numbers associated with particular historical events (1789, the fall of the Bastille) or finally, a type of car (for example, 500 preceded by FIAT, or 164 preceded by ALFA) and based on encyclopaedic knowledge, has been proposed on the basis of the preserved ability of some brain-damaged subjects to read these numbers compared with non-familiar numbers lacking semantic content (Delazer & Girelli, 1997).

Reading by touch: The neuropsychology of Braille

The Braille system is a tactile code for reading and writing introduced in the first half of the eighteen hundreds which allows blind people to read and write. It is based on the combination of six raised dots that are arranged in two columns and three lines (a Braille cell), to allow representation of the letters of the alphabet, numbers, punctuation, mathematical symbols and musical notes. The letters of the alphabet are formed by the different combinations and numbers of the dots in each cell, with a total of 64 different combinations.

Writing in Braille (which, like reading, is done from right to left) requires a sheet of cardboard or plastic placed in a slate and, using a stylus, a varying number of dots are created within a cell, so that every graphic representation has a specific form.

Braille reading is realized through the perception and recognition of the different combinations of raised dots corresponding to single letters while scanning the lines formed by the Braille cells. Once one line has been 'explored', the reader moves on to the line below to continue reading the text. Reading speed, usually inferior to reading through the visual channel, obviously depends on the expertise of the reader, the age at which Braille has been learnt, and so on. An expert Braille reader, for example, uses several fingers at once: as the fingers of the right hand read the end of a line, the fingers of the left hand begin to explore and read the first words of the following line.

Braille reading is dependent on tactile perception that is mediated by the sensory-motor cortex situated in the parietal lobe. In consequence there must be a complex process of functional reorganization of the cerebral cortex to allow tactile patterns to be transformed into linguistic stimuli.

Pascual-Leone and Torres (1993) have shown that Braille readers possess greater neuronal representation of the 'reading' fingers in comparison with the neural representation of the other fingers, hypothesizing a relationship between the use of a cerebral circuit and its neurological representation.

In a series of studies carried out on blind participants, it has been demonstrated that Braille reading activates areas of occipital cortex (the same as those used for visual reading) in both participants who are blind from birth and those who have become blind at preschool age. In the same way, repetitive transcranial magnetic stimulation (rTMS) of the occipital lobe, with an effect of temporary deactivation of the underlying cerebral area, interferes negatively with Braille reading (Cohen et al., 1997).

From a clinical perspective, Hamilton, Keenan, Catala, and Pascual-Leone (2000) described the case of an expert Braille reader, blind from birth, who developed alexia for Braille with no other neuropsychological deficit following a bilateral occipital lesion. In particular, the patient's ability to recognize and name objects through the tactile modality was normal.

In conclusion, therefore, it can be stated that Braille reading represents a model of neuronal plasticity, so that the occipital cerebral cortex, genetically destined for the processing of visual stimuli, is involved in the task of transforming tactile stimuli into linguistic stimuli, in order to allow reading through touch.

Learning to read and developmental dyslexia

Unlike the acquisition of spoken language, acquiring written language mastery requires specific teaching, usually beginning when the child is around 4 or 5 years old and in most cases completed in a few months. A child is 'ready' to learn to read when he or she has acquired phonological awareness (PA). PA is defined as the metalinguistic understanding of the segmental nature of speech. Spoken words are composed of segments, including the smallest of these segments, phonemes, and the ability to be aware of this fine-grained level is referred to as phonemic awareness. Much research has shown that PA predicts later reading achievement[10] (see Scarborough, 1998 for a review).

Different models of the process of learning to read have been proposed. One of the most common models (Frith, 1985) postulates the existence of four independent stages characterized by the learning of new procedures and the consolidation of the abilities learnt in the previous stages. It is possible for the child to pass to the next stage when the elements of the preceding strategy can be incorporated into the new strategy, with a transition that alternates between reading and writing.

During the logographic stage, usually coinciding with preschool age, the child learns to recognize and name a few written words in a global manner, which is similar to the way in which objects and drawings are recognized and named. The child, however, has no orthographic or phonological notions about the words he or she is 'reading'.

At the alphabetic stage the child learns to discriminate and recognize letters, associating them with the corresponding sounds and thereby developing the process of grapheme–phoneme conversion. In this way the child can begin to read the first words.

During the orthographic stage the mechanism of grapheme–phoneme conversion becomes more complex and the child is able to read complex graphemes and syllables, resulting in more rapid reading.

The final lexical stage is characterized by a process of direct recognition of words through the acquisition of a 'store' of written words. In this way, the comprehension and reading aloud of the words contained in the store happens globally and rapidly, with no phonological mediation necessary. Obviously, the mechanism of reading through a phonological route is activated during the reading of unfamiliar or non-words.

Essentially, complete acquisition of the first three stages establishes reading through the phonological route, while once the final stage is reached the child is able to use the lexical route, resulting in the rapid reading of known words without the need to resort to grapheme–phoneme conversion.

Obviously, this process is affected by the orthographic characteristics of each language. Those languages with opaque orthography are more reliant on reading via the lexical route, whereas, in contrast, it has long been considered that for languages with transparent orthography, such as Italian, a greater role is played by the sublexical system of grapheme–phoneme conversion during the process of learning to read. More recent studies, however, have cast doubt on this affirmation, demonstrating, for example, that Italian children and adults read high frequency words better than low frequency words (Barca, Burani, & Arduino, 2002; Bates, Burani, D'Amico, & Barca, 2001; Burani, Marcolini, & Stella, 2002), suggesting a major contribution of the lexical route.

Although most children learn to read rapidly and with little difficulty, some of them, despite normal intelligence, an absence of sensory and neurological deficits, and adequate teaching, present a notable reading difficulty (*developmental dyslexia*) which may then persist throughout their life. Often the reading disorder is associated with a specific developmental language disorder (Chapter 11) or represents a residual symptom of the disorder, even though the hypothesis proposed by Flax et al. (1994) of a single genesis of language and reading disorders is not always valid (for a critical review see Bishop & Snowling, 2004).

The percentage of children affected by developmental dyslexia varies according to the diagnostic criteria employed (usually a discrepancy between a reduced reading ability and normal IQ), with an incidence varying between 4% and 17%. The incidence is higher in countries with opaque orthography. The percentage of Italian children with developmental dyslexia, for example, is around half of that found in the United States (Lindgren, De Renzi, & Richman, 1985).

Developmental dyslexia, usually more common in males and often familiar, becomes evident once the process of literacy begins and is characterized by an abnormal slowness in grapheme–phoneme transcoding, associated with difficulty in recognizing written letters and in identification of the phonemes corresponding to the graphemes making up the word. A diagnosis of dyslexia can already be made at preschool age, through assessment of the child's ability to attend to and manipulate phonological information (PA) in tasks such as distinguishing the single sounds making up a heard word or, on the contrary, uttering a word when given its component sounds. Difficulty in carrying out such tasks represents a reliable prognostic indicator of the possible appearance of a dyslexic disorder once the child begins to attend school.

Reduced short-term verbal memory and poor performance on tests of rapid naming of pictures often accompanies dyslexic deficits. These finding support the hypothesis of a specific deficit in the processes of representation, storing and retrieval of the sounds making up language underlying a developmental reading disorder. If phonemes are inadequately represented, stored or retrieved, the possibility of establishing rapid and stable grapheme–phoneme connections that form the basis of the alphabetic reading process (Snowling, 1981) will therefore be compromised, with the consequent appearance of a dyslexic picture.

The phonological theory of developmental dyslexia suggests dysfunction at the anatomical level of the left perysilvian cortex (Galaburda, Sherman, Rosen, Aboitiz, & Geschwind, 1995) and this has been supported by some recent neuroimaging studies (Paulesu et al., 2001; Démonet, Taylor, & Chaix, 2004).

According to Tallal (1980; Tallal, Miller, & Fitch, 1993), dyslexic children have difficulty processing the temporal characteristics of rapidly changing acoustic signals of any sort, including speech sounds and non-verbal auditory signals. In addition, impaired auditory processing may contribute not only to problems in speech perception but also to weaknesses in developing phonemic awareness and learning and applying phonological reading strategies. Ramus, Pidgeon, and Frith (2003) suggest, on the other hand, that disorders of auditory processing, when present, can worsen the phonological deficit that represents the fundamental deficit of developmental dyslexia.

Over the last few years some studies have tried to establish whether developmental dyslexia can mirror the adult pattern of acquired dyslexia, particularly in children using opaque orthography (Castles & Colheart, 1993): some cases of phonological developmental dyslexia (the most frequent type) and, more rarely, peripheral type disorders, have been described which suggest that developmental dyslexia can depend on the impairment of specific components of graphemic string processing. The impact of different orthographies on the frequency of developmental dyslexia has been recently explored by Paulesu et al. (2001). In a hugely influential PET study, these authors examined three groups of dyslexic participants belonging to different linguistic groups (Italian, French and English) and found a reduction, compared with control subjects, of cerebral activation at the left temporal-occipital level in tasks of both implicit and explicit reading. The level of reduction was the same for both opaque and transparent orthography, although, at behavioural level the severity of the dyslexia was less in the Italian children, because of the regularity of the Italian orthographic system.

Notes

1 In Hebrew it is possible to represent vowels by placing diacritic features on the consonants, but this mechanism is optional and rarely used.
2 In the Italian language, only a few morphological contexts such as the third person singular of the past tense of the first conjugation require the accent on the last vowel (*amò, saltò*).
3 The example cited by Andreewsky and Seron (1975) is a good illustration of this point. Presented with the phrase *le car s'arrête car le moteur chauffe* ('the car stops because the motor overheats'), their dyslexic patient was able to read the word *car* meaning automobile, but not when it corresponded to the preposition 'because'.
4 In Italian even a regular word may be misread because of lack of knowledge of where to place the tonic stress, for example, the town '*Padova* may be read *Pado'va* or the word *van'gelo* (gospel) may be misread '*vangelo*.
5 For example, *T* is composed of two segments with different orientations (*I* and –). Obviously this mechanism is valid for orthographic type writing.
6 According to Grainger and Whitney (2004), experimental evidence of the existence of this mechanism derives from the results of priming experiments, in which it has been demonstrated that the recognition of a word is facilitated when some of the letters making up the word have been presented beforehand, as long as the letter order has been maintained.
7 Hillis and Caramazza (1995) deny the existence of this third route and propose instead that correct reading of regular words, when the patient is unable to comprehend these same words, comes about through a process of *summing*. For example, in a patient with semantic damage, the presentation of the irregular word 'yacht' activates a generic semantic representation, such as 'water vehicle'. At the same time, through the non-lexical route, the first letter of the words is correctly coded with the phoneme /j/. Summing the semantic and phonological information, the patient will thus be able to read the word correctly.
8 In languages with irregular orthography such as English, the *frequency effect* combines with the *orthographic regularity effect*. Irregular words, characterized by the presence of low frequency grapheme–phoneme connections (*y a cht* → /y a t/) are read more slowly than regular words (Baron & Strawson, 1976). This effect explains the necessity to resolve the 'conflict' between the sublexical procedure, which tends to generate a phonologically but not lexically correct pronunciation (*yacht* → /yaz/ *add symbol t*), and the lexical procedure. Obviously this problem does not exist for regular words.

9 It is probable that this difference depends on the fact that in opaque orthographies, which require lexical reading, sublexical mechanisms exert less control even when damaged (Ardila, 1991; Miceli, Capasso, & Caramazza, 1994).

10 According to Morais, Cary, Alegria, and Bertelson (1979) acquisition of phonological awareness is, on the contrary, the consequence of learning to read.

References

Anderson, S. W., Damasio, A. R., & Damasio, H. (1990). Troubled letters but not numbers. Domain specific cognitive impairments following focal damage in frontal cortex. *Brain*, *113* (Pt 3), 749–766.

Andreewsky, E., & Seron, X. (1975). Implicit processing of grammatical rules in a classical case of agrammatism, *Cortex*, *11* (4), 379–390.

Ardila, A. (1991). Errors resembling semantic paralexias in Spanish-speaking aphasics. *Brain and Language*, *41* (3), 437–445.

Barca, L., Burani, C., & Arduino, L. S. (2002). Word naming times and psycholinguistic norms for Italian nouns. *Behavior Research Methods, Instruments and Computers*, *34* (3), 424–434.

Baron, J., & Strawson, C. (1976). Use of orthographic and word-specific knowledge in reading words aloud. *Journal of Experimental Psychology, Human Perception and Performance*, *2*, 386–393.

Basso, A., Taborelli, A., & Vignolo, L. A. (1978). Dissociated disorders of speaking and writing in aphasia *Journal of Neurology, Neurosurgery, and Psychiatry*, *41*, 556–563.

Bates, E., Burani, C., D'Amico, S., & Barca, L. (2001), Word reading and picture naming in Italian. *Memory and Cognition*, *29* (7), 986–999.

Baxter, D. M., & Warrington, E. K. (1986). Ideational agraphia: A single case study. *Journal of Neurology, Neurosurgery, and Psychiatry*, *49* (4), 369–374.

Beauvois, M. F., & Dérouesné, J. (1979). Phonological alexia: Three dissociations. *Journal of Neurology, Neurosurgery, and Psychiatry*, *42* (12), 1115–1124.

Beauvois, M. F., & Dérouesné, J. (1981). Lexical or orthographic agraphia. *Brain*, *104* (Pt 1), 21–49.

Benson, D. F. (1977). The third alexia. *Archives of Neurology*, *34*, 327–331.

Bishop, D. V., & Snowling, M. J. (2004). Developmental dyslexia and specific language impairment: Same or different? *Psychological Bulletin*, *130* (6), 858–886.

Bisiacchi, P., Cipolotti, L., & Denes, G. (1989). Impaired processing of meaningless verbal material in several modalities: The relationship between STM and phonological skills. *The Quarterly Journal of Experimental Psychology*, *41A* (2), 293–319.

Bub, D., & Kertesz, A. (1982). Deep agraphia. *Brain and Language*, *17* (1), 146–165.

Burani, C., Marcolini, S., & Stella, G. (2002). How early does morpholexical reading develop in readers of a shallow orthography? *Brain and Language*, *81* (1–3), 568–586.

Caramazza, A., & Hillis, A. E. (1990). Where do semantic errors come from? *Cortex*, *26* (1), 95–122.

Caramazza, A., Laudanna, A., & Romani, C. (1988). Lexical access and inflectional morphology. *Cognition*, *28* (3), 297–332.

Caramazza, A., Miceli, G., Silveri, M. C., & Laudanna, A. (1985). Reading mechanisms and the organisation of the lexicon: Evidence from acquired dyslexia. *Cognitive Neuropsychology*, *2* (1), 81–114.

Carreiras, M., Álvarez, C. J., & De Vega, M. (1993). Syllable frequency and visual word recognition in Spanish. *Journal of Memory and Language*, *32*, 766–780.

Carreiras, M., Duñabeitia, J. A., & Perea, M. (2007), READING WORDS, NUMB3R5 and $YMB0L$. *Trends in Cognitive Sciences, 11* (11), 454–455; Author reply, 456–457.

Castles, A., & Coltheart, M. (1993). Varieties of developmental dyslexia. *Cognition, 47* (2), 149–180.

Charcot, J. M. (1883). *Le differenti forme di Afasia.* Milano: Vallardi.

Cipolotti, L., & Butterworth, B. (1995). Toward a multiroute model of number processing: Impaired number transcoding with preserved calculation skills. *Journal of Experimental Psychology: General, 124,* 375–390.

Cohen, L., & Dehaene, S. (2004). Specialization within the ventral stream: The case for the visual word form area. *Neuroimage, 22* (1), 466–476.

Cohen, L. G., Celnik, P., Pascual-Leone, A., Corwell, B., Falz, L., Dambrosia, J., et al. (1997). Functional relevance of cross-modal plasticity in blind humans. *Nature, 389* (6647), 180–183.

Coltheart, M. (1980). Reading, phonological recording and deep dyslexia. In M. Coltheart, K. Patterson, & J. K. Marshall (Eds.), *Deep dyslexia.* London: Routledge & Kegan Paul.

Coltheart, M. (1985). Cognitive neuropsychology and the study of reading. In M. I. Posner & O. S. Marin (Eds.), *Attention and performance, XI* (pp. 3–37). Hillsdale, NJ: Lawrence Erlbaum Associates, Inc.

Coltheart, M. (1996). Phonological dyslexia: Past and future issues. *Cognitive Neuropsychology, 13* (6), 749–762.

Coltheart, M. (2006). Acquired dyslexias and the computational modelling of reading. *Cognitive Neuropsychology, 23* (1), 96–109.

Coslett, H. B., & Monsul, N. (1994). Reading with the right hemisphere: Evidence from transcranial magnetic stimulation. *Brain and Language, 46,* 198–211.

Coslett, H. B., & Saffran, E. M. (1989). Evidence for preserved reading in 'pure alexia'. *Brain, 112* (Pt 2), 327–359.

Cubelli, R. (1991). A selective deficit for writing vowels in acquired dysgraphia. *Nature, 353* (6341), 258–260.

De Bastiani, P., & Barry, C. (1989). A cognitive analysis of an acquired dysgraphic patient with an 'allographic' writing disorder. *Cognitive Neuropsychology, 6,* 25–41.

Dehaene, S., & Cohen, L. (1995). Toward an anatomical and functional model of number processing. *Mathematical Cognition, 1* (1), 83–120.

Dehaene, S., & Cohen, L. (2007). Cultural recycling of cortical maps. *Neuron, 56* (2), 384–398.

Déjérine, J. (1891). Sur un cas de cécité verbale avec agraphie suivi d'autopsie. *Mémoires de la Société de Biologie, 3,* 197–201.

Déjérine, J. (1892). Contribution a l'étude anatomo-pathologique et clinique des differentes variétés de cécité-verbale. *Mémoires de la Société de Biologie, 4,* 61–90.

Delazer, M., & Bartha, L. (2001). Transcoding and calculation in aphasia. *Aphasiology, 15,* 649–679.

Delazer, M., & Girelli, L. (1997). When 'Alfa Romeo' facilitates 164: Semantic effects in verbal number production. *Neurocase, 3* (6), 461–475.

Deloche, G., & Seron, X. (1982). From one to 1: An analysis of a transcoding process by means of neuropsychological data. *Cognition, 12,* 119–149.

Démonet, J. F., Taylor, M. J., & Chaix, Y. (2004). Developmental dyslexia. *Lancet, 363* (9419), 1451–1460.

Denes, G., Cipolotti, L., & Semenza, C. (1987). How does a phonological dyslexic read words she has never seen? *Cognitive Neuropsychology, 4,* 11–31.

Denes, G., Pizzamiglio, L. (1999). *Handbook of clinical and experimental neuropsychology.* Hove, UK: Psychology Press.

Derouesné, J., & Beauvois, M. F. (1985). The 'phonemic' state in the non-lexical reading process: Evidence from a case of phonological alexia. In K. Patterson, M. Coltheart, & J. C. Marshall (Eds.), *Surface dyslexia* (pp. 399–457). Hillsdale, NJ: Lawrence Erlbaum Associates, Inc.

Ellis, A. W., & Young, A. W. (1988). *Human cognitive neuropsychology.* Hove, UK: Lawrence Erlbaum Associates Ltd.

Ellis, A. W., & Young, A. W. (1996). *Human cognitive neuropsychology: A textbook with readings.* Hove, UK: Psychology Press.

Flax, J. F., Realpe-Bonilla, T., Hirsch, L. S., Brzustowicz, L. M., Bartlett, C. W., & Tallal, P. (2003). Specific language impairment in families: Evidence for co-occurrence with reading impairments. *Journal of Speech, Language, and Hearing Research, 46,* 530–543.

Frith, U. (1985). Beneath the surface of developmental dyslexia. In K. E. Patterson, J. C. Marshall, & M. Coltheart (Eds.), *Surface dyslexia.* London: Routledge & Kegan Paul.

Frost, R. (1998). Toward a strong phonological theory of visual word recognition: True issues and false trails. *Psychological Bulletin, 123* (1), 71–99.

Galaburda, A. M., Sherman, G. F., Rosen, G. D., Aboitiz, F., & Geschwind, N. (1985). Developmental dyslexia: Four consecutive patients with cortical anomalies. *Annals of Neurology, 18* (2), 222–233.

Glushko, R. (1979). The organisation and activation of orthographic knowledge in reading aloud. *Journal of Experimental Psychology, Human Perception and Performance, 5,* 647–691.

Grainger, J., & Whitney, C. (2004). Does the huamn mnid raed wrods as a wlohe? *Trends in Cognitive Sciences, 8* (2), 58–59.

Hamilton, R., Keenan, J. P., Catala, M., & Pascual-Leone, A. (2000). Alexia for Braille following bilateral occipital stroke in an early blind woman. *NeuroReport, 11* (2), 237–240.

Harm, M. W., & Seidenberg, M. S. (2001). Are there orthographic impairments in phonological dyslexia? *Cognitive Neuropsychology, 18* (1), 71–92.

Hillis, A. E., & Caramazza, A. (1991a). Deficit to stimulus-centered, letter shape representations in a case of 'unilateral neglect'. *Neuropsychologia, 29* (12), 1223–1240.

Hillis, A. E., & Caramazza, A. (1991b). Mechanisms for accessing lexical representations for output: Evidence from a category-specific semantic deficit. *Brain and Language, 40* (1), 106–144.

Hillis, A. E., & Caramazza, A. (1995). Converging evidence for the interaction of semantic and sublexical phonological information in accessing lexical representations for spoken output. *Cognitive Neuropsychology, 12,* 187–227.

Jobard, G., Crivello, F., & Tzourio-Mazoyer, N. (2003). Evaluation of the dual route theory of reading: A meta-analysis of 35 neuroimaging studies. *Neuroimage, 20* (2), 693–712.

Kay, J., Coltheart, M., & Lesser, R. (1992). *PALPA: Psycholinguistic asessments of language processing in aphasia.* Hove, UK: Psychology Press.

Lavidor, M., & Ellis, A.W. (2002). Word length and orthographic neighborhood size effects in the left and right cerebral hemispheres. *Brain and Language, 80* (1), 45–62.

Lenneberg, E. (1967). *Biological foundations of language.* New York: Wiley.

Lindgren, S. D., De Renzi. E, & Richman, L. C. (1985). Cross-national comparisons of developmental dyslexia in Italy and the United States. *Child Development, 56* (6), 1404–1417.

Luzzatti, C., Laiacona, M., & Agazzi, D. (2003). Multiple patterns of writing disorders in dementia of the Alzheimer type and their evolution. *Neuropsychologia, 41* (7), 759–772.

Luzzatti, C., Laiacona, M., Allamano, N., De Tanti, A., & Inzaghi, M. G. (1998). Writing disorders in Italian aphasic patients: A multiple single-case study of dysgraphia in a language with shallow orthography. *Brain, 121*, 1721–1734.

Luzzi, S., & Piccirilli, M. (2003). Slowly progressive pure dysgraphia with late apraxia of speech: A further variant of the focal cerebral degeneration. *Brain and Language, 87* (3), 355–360.

Marshall, J. C., & Newcombe, F. (1973). Patterns of paralexia: A psycholinguistic approach. *Journal of Psycholinguistic Research, 2* (3), 175–199.

McCloskey, M. (1992). Cognitive mechanisms in numerical processing: Evidence from acquired acalculia. *Cognition, 44*, 107–157.

McCloskey, M., Caramazza, A., & Basili, A. (1985). Cognitive mechanisms in number processing and calculation: Evidence from dyscalculia. *Brain and Cognition, 4*, 171–196.

Miceli, G., & Capasso, R. (2006). Spelling and dysgraphia. *Cognitive Neuropsychology, 23* (1), 110–134.

Miceli, G., Capasso, R., & Caramazza, A. (1994). The interaction of lexical and sub-lexical processes in reading, writing and repetition. *Neuropsychologia, 32* (3), 317–333.

Miceli, G. & Caramazza, A. (1993). The assignment of word stress in oral reading: Evidence from a case of acquired dyslexia. *Cognitive Neuropsychology, 10*, 273–295.

Morais, J., Cary, L., Alegria, J., & Bertelson, P. (1979). Does awareness of speech as a sequence of phones arise spontaneously? *Cognition, 7* (4), 323–331.

Moretti, R., Torre, P., Antonello, R., Fabbro, F., Cazzato, G., & Bava, A. (2003). Writing errors by normal subjects. *Perceptual and Motor Skills, 97*, 215–229.

Paap, K. R., & Noel, R. W. (1991). Dual-route models of print to sound: Still a good horse race. *Psychological Research, 53*, 13–24.

Pascual-Leone, A., & Torres, F. (1993). Plasticity of the sensorimotor cortex representation of the reading finger in Braille readers. *Brain, 116* (Pt 1), 39–52.

Patterson, K., & Wing, A. M. (1989). Processes in handwriting: A case for case. *Cognitive Neuropsychology, 6*, 1–23.

Paulesu, E., Démonet, J. F., Fazio, F., McCrory, E., Chanoine, V., Brunswick, N., et al. (2001). Dyslexia: Cultural diversity and biological unity. *Science, 291* (5511), 2165–2167.

Price, C. J., McCrory, E., Noppeney, U., Mechelli, A., Moore, C. J., Biggio, N., et al. (2006). How reading differs from object naming at the neuronal level. *NeuroImage, 29* (2), 643–648.

Prinzmetal, W., Hoffman, H., & Vest, K. (1991). Automatic processes in word perception: An analysis from illusory conjunctions. *Journal of Experimental Psychology. Human Perception and Performance, 17* (4), 902–923.

Ramus, F., Pidgeon, E., & Frith, U. (2003). The relationship between motor control and phonology in dyslexic children. *Journal of Child Psychology and Psychiatry, 44* (5), 712–722.

Rosati, G., & De Bastiani, P. (1979). Pure agraphia: A discrete form of aphasia. *Journal of Neurology, Neurosurgery, and Psychiatry, 42* (3), 266–269.

Saffran, E. M., Schwartz, M. F., & Marin, O. S. (1980). The word order problem in agrammatism, II: Production. *Brain and Language, 10* (2), 263–280.

Scarborough, H. S. (1998). Early identification of children at risk for disabilities: Phonological awareness and some other promising predictors. In B. K. Shapiro, P. J. Accardo, & A. J. Capute (Eds.), *Specific reading disability: A view of the spectrum* (pp. 75–119). Timonium, MD: York Press.

Schwartz, M. F., Saffran, E. M., & Marin, O. S. M. (1980). Fractionating the reading process in dementia: Evidence for word-specific print-to-sound associations. In M. Coltheart, K. Patterson, & J. C. Marshall (Eds.), *Deep dyslexia* (pp. 259–269). London: Routledge & Kegan Paul.

Seidenberg, M. S., & McClelland, J. L. (1989). A distributed, developmental model of word recognition and naming. *Psychological Review, 96* (4), 523–568.

Sgaramella, T. M., Ellis, A. W., & Semenza, C. (1991). Analysis of the spontaneous writing errors of normal and aphasic writers. *Cortex, 27*, 29–39.

Shallice, T. (1981). Phonological agraphia and the lexical route in writing. *Brain, 104*, 413–429.

Shallice, T. (1988). *From neuropsychology to mental structure*. Cambridge, UK: Cambridge University Press.

Shallice, T., & Rosazza, C. (2006). Patterns of peripheral paralexia: Pure alexia and the forgotten visual dyslexia? *Cortex, 42* (6), 892–897.

Shallice, T., & Warrington, E. K. (1980). Single and multiple component central dyslexia syndromes. In M. Coltheart, K. E. Patterson, & J. C. Marshall (Eds.), *Deep dyslexia*. London: Routledge & Kegan Paul.

Snowden, J. S., Goulding, P. J., & Neary, D. (1989). Semantic dementia, a form of circumscribed cerebral atrophy. *Behavioural Neurology, 2*, 167–182.

Snowling, M. J. (1981). Phonemic deficits in developmental dyslexia. *Psychological Research, 43* (2), 219–234.

Tallal, P. (1980). Auditory temporal perception, phonics, and reading disabilities in children. *Brain and Language, 9* (2), 182–198.

Tallal, P., Miller, S., & Fitch, R. H. (1993). Neurobiological basis of speech: A case for the pre-eminence of temporal processing. *Annals of the New York Academy of Sciences, 682*, 27–47.

Warrington, E. K., & Shallice, T. (1980). Word-form dyslexia. *Brain, 103* (1), 99–112.

Wernicke, C. (1874). *Der aphasiche Symptomenkomplex*. Breslau: Cohn & Weigert. Republished as: *The aphasia symptom complex: A psychological study on an anatomical basis. Wernicke's works on aphasia*. The Hague: Mouton.

Wu, D. H., Martin, R. C., & Damian, M. F. (2002). A third route for reading? Implications from a case of phonological dyslexia. *Neurocase, 8* (4), 174–293.

Zaidel, E. (1985). Language in the right hemisphere. In D. F. Benson & E. Zaidel (Eds.), *The dual brain: Hemispheric specialization in humans* (pp. 205–231), New York: Guilford Press.

Zorzi, M. (2005). Computational models of reading. In G. Houghton (Ed.), *Connectionist models in psychology* (pp. 403–444). Hove & New York: Psychology Press.

9 The neurological bases and functional architecture of bilingualism

Over 50% of the human species can be defined as bilingual or plurilingual[1] in that they use more than one language in written or spoken form in everyday life, although the degree of competence and the frequency of use vary (Paradis, 1998a, 1998b). This percentage is destined to increase and so it is not surprising that over the last few years a huge number of studies have addressed this subject. The goals of these studies are often different and may be interdisciplinary, such as attempts to pinpoint the neural bases of bilingualism and to clarify the nature and representations of the cognitive processes underlying the learning and use of different languages, as well as the functional and anatomical relationship between languages.

In this chapter we review the neurological bases underlying language processing in polyglots using clinical data (aphasia in polyglots) and results obtained from neuroimaging studies carried out on normal participants. In particular, we attempt to clarify whether the process of learning and use of a second language (L2) possesses the same neural bases as that of the native language (L1) or whether it involves different structures. Finally we consider whether possible involvement of the aforementioned structures is dependent on factors such as the degree of linguistic competence and/or the age of exposure to the second language.

A description of the nature and representation of language in polyglots, independent of their neural substrate, concludes the chapter.

Aphasia in bilinguals

Following the first descriptions by Pitres (1895), the interest of academics in bilingual and polyglot aphasics focused on the issue of whether the learning and use of L2 involves the same neurological and functional mechanisms as those involved in L1.

A few caveats should, however, be given: case reports of aphasic polyglots are rare (for a review see Paradis, 1995; Fabbro, 1996) and most of these are not free of methodological flaws, particularly those published in the past. The lack of systematic studies stems, in part, from the fact that, given the relative remote possibility of finding an aphasic polyglot, the neurologist's interest was usually the result of a chance encounter with this type of patient. The examination often took place during the acute stage of the illness and the observer may have possessed no specific competence in the field. The resulting picture was therefore an anedoctal rather than theoretically based description of the patient. These early reports often did not specify sufficient linguistic competence, its frequency of use, the age of acquisition and any differences in modality of use (only oral or also written) of the patient. The examiner, moreover, did not always possess sufficient linguistic competence to evaluate thoroughly the languages spoken by the patient and there was a lack of diagnostic tests for the evaluation of plurilingual deficits.[2] Finally, the peculiarity of each language at phonological, syntactic and lexical-semantic levels as well as suprasegmental differences (for example, different sociolinguistic registers or the presence of rules defining the appropriateness of use of lexical items in a given context) often made it difficult to compare the specific effects of the cerebral lesion on the type and severity of the language deficits present in the different languages spoken by the patient (see below).

When tackling the neurological bases of bilingualism, clinical studies have assumed two directions: the first involves the study of differences in the type of linguistic deficit between languages spoken by the polyglot patient, the second considers the pattern of recovery.

Albert and Obler (1978) and Silverberg and Gordon (1979) described bilingual aphasic patients who demonstrated Broca's aphasia in Hebrew, and Wernicke's aphasia in English, suggesting a different neurological organization of the two languages. A more accurate analysis of these cases, however (Paradis, 1998a), suggests that these differences were a result of either a different degree of linguistic competence or the different structure of these two languages. In Hebrew, unlike in English, inflected morphemes cannot be omitted as this would result in a non-word, so substitution errors are found (*paragrammatism*), whilst in English errors of omission are prevalent (*agrammatism*). Similarly, the different patterns of linguistic deficits in Farsi–English bilingual aphasics were found to stem from the characteristics of each language. In English, in fact, there were more errors of omission and substitution of free morphemes in an obligatory context because the English language makes more use of this type of construction than Farsi. On the other hand, the number of omissions or substitutions of compound morphemes was higher in Farsi, a language that uses these constructions far more frequently than English (Nilipour & Paradis, 1995).

Of greater relevance are the observations relating to different patterns of recovery. In some cases recovery follows a parallel pattern, with both languages recovering simultaneously and to the same extent. This would support the notion of a unique neurological substrate for different languages. In other cases, however, the recovery is *differential* (one language improves before the other) or *selective*, that is, limited or prevalent in one language only. Recovery in only the native language (L1) supports Ribot's law, according to which languages learnt at an early age and memories from early times are more 'resistant' than those learnt later. In contrast, improvement may occur in the language learnt later in life and used less frequently (L2), as in the case of Aglioti and Fabbro's aphasic patient (1993) whose L1 was a local dialect (the patient had learnt Italian from school age only and used it infrequently) but whose aphasia improved only in Italian (L2).

The interpretation of these different patterns of recovery is not without ambiguity. According to one hypothesis, both languages are represented in the left hemisphere, but the representation of the language that does not improve has been weakened by the cerebral lesion; alternatively, the recovered language is more diffusely represented within the central nervous system, at the level of both the cortex and the basal ganglia (García-Caballero et al., 2007), facilitating the recovery process. According to Albert and Obler (1978), language in polyglots is represented in both hemispheres: it follows that subsequent to a unilateral (usually left-sided) cerebral lesion, the recovery of one language only may mean that this language has greater bilateral representation. This hypothesis, however, is difficult to support from both clinical and experimental viewpoints.

Pharmacological inactivation of one hemisphere (Wada test[3]) as well as neuroimaging studies carried out on normal participants, confirm left-sided hemispheric lateralization of language in bilinguals, with no significant difference in monolingual participants, even though, as we will see in the following paragraph, neuroimaging studies of normal participants have identified significant involvement of the right hemisphere.

From a different perspective, the findings of different pictures of aphasic deficit and/or a pattern of recovery could be interpreted as the result of a deficit of the control mechanisms (Paradis, 1989) that, in non-brain damaged polyglots, allow transition from one language to another and the continuation of use of one language without interference from the other (for more details consult Dijkstra & Van Heuven, 1989). The difference in recovery between the two languages would not, then, be the result of a lesion that 'moves' around different cerebral areas producing an alternated or differential recovery, but rather a result of lack of activation of the different cerebral mechanisms involved in the knowledge and use of the various languages known to the patient.

A selective deficit of the control mechanism has been demonstrated by Abutalebi, Miozzo, and Cappa (2000) in a trilingual patient. The patient's auditory comprehension was within normal limits in all three languages, but he shifted spontaneously and involuntarily from one language to another during spontaneous conversation, although testing did not reveal language-specific lexical deficits (naming was 80% correct in all three languages). MRI examination revealed a subcortical lesion around the head of the caudate nucleus, suggesting that this structure could play a specific role in the control of lexical alternatives in bilingual patients (Crinion et al., 2006).

To conclude, it's safe to say that many factors contribute to the recovery process, such as age of acquisition, linguistic competence, frequency of use, the language in which speech and language therapy is carried out and the patient's degree of motivation.

Neuroimaging studies

For the past twenty years or so, the application of functional neuroimaging techniques such as PET and fMRI in normal bilingual participants has provided an essential contribution to the understanding of the neurological and functional bases of the process of learning and processing of L2 as well as investigation of the relationship between L1 and L2. The main advantage of observation of normal participants is that it allows consideration of the significance of independent variables, such as age of acquisition, linguistic competence, exposure to and familiarity with the different languages.

Tasks of auditory comprehension of texts presented in both L1 and L2 to participants with a high level of linguistic competence in both languages elicit identical bilateral activation of the temporal poles of the middle temporal gyrus and upper left temporal pole (Dehaene et al., 1997; Perani et al., 1996, 1998). It has also been demonstrated that in highly competent L2 subjects the age of acquisition plays no role in determining possible differences in the neural representation of L2 compared with L1 (Perani et al., 1998). In contrast, in individuals who are less competent in L2, greater variability of the activated areas has been found (Dehaene et al., 1997).

Other studies have been aimed at investigating whether a different degree of similarity between two spoken languages might correspond with greater variability in anatomical representation. Chee, Tan, and Thiel (1999) carried out an fMRI study on participants who were bilingual in two languages with very different characteristics, Mandarin Chinese[4] and English. In participants who were highly proficient in both languages, the comprehension of texts revealed a large area of activation that overlapped for L1 and L2, in the perisylvian areas of the left hemisphere and bilaterally in the parietal-occipital areas.

In an fMRI study carried out on bilingual individuals (Spanish–English), Illes et al. (1999) investigated the participants' ability to make semantic decisions about single words. A common pattern of activation in the left frontal inferior region was found in both languages, suggesting the existence of a common semantic store accessible to both languages.

Neuroimaging studies of word productions are more varied. In a task of repetition and production (rhymes, synonyms, translation from one language to another) of single words carried out by bilingual subjects (French and English, with English having been learnt at school age) an identical pattern of activation was found except for a greater degree of activation at the level of the left putamen (part of the basal ganglia) during the production of words in L1 (Klein, Zatorre, Milner, Meyer, & Evans 1994, 1995). No difference, on the other hand, was found by Chee et al. (1999) in a task of word generation, even when age of acquisition of L2 (early or late) was controlled.

Kim, Relkin, Lee, and Hirsch (1997) in an fMRI study investigating single-word production in bilingual participants with different native languages (English, Korean, Spanish) who had learned L2 later in life, found different activation for L1 and L2 in Broca's area. These differences, however, were not evident in subjects who had been bilingual from an early age.

De Bleser et al. (2003), investigated possible differences in tasks of naming of similar or cognate and dissimilar or non-cognate words in bilingual participants (Flemish and French). Similar or cognate words have the same meaning and their phonology and orthography are similar in different languages (for example *liberté*, *liberty*, *libertà* or *image* and *imagine*). Dissimilar words (for example *vache* and *cow* or *verre* and *glass*) share only their meaning. In bilingual subjects, similar words are recognized (Caramazza & Brones, 1979) and translated (De Groot, Dannemburg, & Van Hell, 1994) more quickly than dissimilar words and they are more easily accessible for aphasic polyglot patients (Stadie, Springer, De Bleser, & Burk, 1995). In the study by De Bleser et al. no differences in processing were found between similar and dissimilar words in L1, while in L2 greater activation of the language areas emerged in the processing of non-cognate words. This effect could be attributed to the greater complexity of the task involving additional neural involvement in comparison with native speech.

The effects of language exposure have been investigated recently by Perani et al. (2003) in an fMRI study of bilingual individuals (Spanish–Catalan) living in Barcelona and therefore with greater exposure to Catalan[5] than to Spanish. The participants were divided into two groups (L1 either Spanish or Catalan). In a word generation task, carried out with the same degree of competence by both groups, the Spanish native language participants displayed a smaller degree of neural activation in a task of generating words in Catalan compared with the degree of activation observed in L1 Catalan participants carrying out the same task in Spanish. These data confirm that exposure as well as linguistic competence play a role in modulating specific neural involvement in the different languages spoken by the polyglot individual.

The age of acquisition factor was investigated by Wartenburger et al. (2003) in an fMRI study in which bilingual participants (Italian–German) were given tasks involving syntactic and semantic processing. The first group was made up of individuals who were bilingual from birth, while the second group contained participants with the same proficiency in both languages but who had acquired L2 after 6 years of age. A third group was made up of individuals who had acquired L2 later in life or were less competent in the language. Both the degree of linguistic proficiency and the age of acquisition were found to be critical factors. In syntactic tasks, overlapping activation of the cerebral areas dedicated to syntactic processing (Broca's area and the basal ganglia) was revealed only in the participants who were bilingual from an early age. Late L2 learners showed a greater degree of activation in the adjacent areas, suggesting additional neural involvement. No significant difference between these groups was found, on the other hand, in lexical-semantic tasks, in which there was similar activation of the perisylvian areas of the left hemisphere, independent of age of acquisition or linguistic competence.

A further point to consider is whether the phonetic characteristics of L1 can be substituted by those of L2. This issue was investigated by Pallier et al. (2003) in a group of children born in Korea and adopted during childhood (between the ages of 7 and 9) by French families and therefore with no further exposure to Korean. Both behavioural and instrumental data (fMRI) demonstrated a complete substitution of L1 (Korean) by L2 (French) in tasks of phoneme discrimination and identification.

Early bilinguals   Late bilinguals,   Late bilinguals,
                          high L2 proficiency   low L2 proficiency

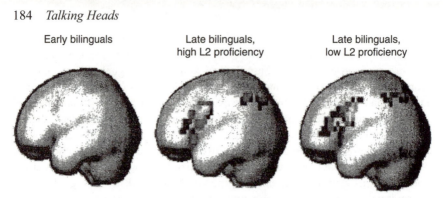

Figure 9.1 Brain activity patterns during grammatical processing in L2 as compared with
those in L1 in three different groups of Italian–German bilinguals with different ages of L2 acquisition and levels of L2 proficiency. Whereas early bilinguals (EAHP: early acquisition, high profiency) engaged for both languages
the same neural structures (no activation differences in the brain rendering),
this does not apply for bilinguals. Both groups of late bilinguals, with high or
low proficiency (LAHP: late acquisition, high proficiency; LALP: late acquisition, low proficiency), engage more extended neural substrates in inferior frontal and parietal regions for grammatical processing in L2. These results
emphasize the effect of age of acquisition on the neural underpinnings of
grammatical processing (from Perani & Abutalebi, 2005). Copyright © 2005,
Elsevier, reproduced with permission.

We can, therefore, conclude that the majority of neuroimaging studies (for a
review see Perani & Abutalebi, 2005) have shown a neural overlay between the
neurological substrate of the different languages spoken by polyglot individuals
(Figure 9.1).

Syntactic, phonological and lexical aspects of L2 are processed by the same
neural mechanisms, located in the perisylvian areas of the left hemisphere, which
are genetically dedicated to the processing of L1. The degree of overlap is directly
proportional to the level of linguistic competence in the two languages and the age
of acquisition of L2, so it is identical in bilingual subjects who have been exposed
to the two languages simultaneously since infancy, while processing of L2 in
subjects with similar proficiency in both languages but with L2 learnt at a later
stage in life requires the activation of further neural resources, particularly for
syntactic tasks.

Anatomical correlates of differences between individuals in the ability to learn a second language

Regardless of motivation, educational, cognitive and sociocultural level, it is
commonly recognized that there is huge variability in the ability to learn a second
language, particularly at the phonetic-phonological and syntactic levels.

The possibility of this difference being conditioned to some extent by a particular type of neural organization has been explored recently by Golestani et al.
(2007) using fMRI neuroimaging techniques. Their study was carried out on

normal participants and involved the production and identification of phonemes that differed from the phonemes belonging to the subjects' L1. The authors found that the individuals who performed the task with the greatest speed and efficiency demonstrated a high degree of cerebral asymmetry (left > right) between the parietal lobes. Further MRI studies have also shown greater neural volume at the level of the left inferior parietal lobe (Mechelli et al., 2004) and a greater density of white matter in the left primary auditory cortex (gyrus of Heschl).

These data seem to suggest that individuals who are more skilled in acquiring the phonetic characteristics of L2 possess relatively greater development of the cerebral areas linked to the phonological processing of acoustic stimuli or a greater degree of neural plasticity in specific cerebral structures as a result of learning a second language.

Obviously, before accepting the hypothesis of innate differences, reminiscent in some aspects of Gall's phrenological approach, it is advisable to adopt a cautious attitude until there is further investigation of populations speaking different languages.

Linguistic differences and genes

The correlation between linguistic differences and differences in genes in various populations is not random but usually an outcome of historical and geographical factors. This type of correlation regards the frequency of allele[6] and linguistic grouping (dialects, languages) controlling geographical, topological and ecological factors (Cavalli Sforza, Menozzi, & Piazza, 1997).

Only recently has there been an attempt to find a correlation between the frequency of certain types of allele and the defining characteristics of different languages. Dediu and Ladd (2007), for example, using a sophisticated technique of molecular genetics, have revealed that the degree of correlation between the presence of specific alleles and the use of a tonal language does not seem to be tied to historical or geographical factors, but rather to the presence of specific alleles facilitating the acquisition of the linguistic characteristics present in tonal languages (for example Chinese), which, in turn, influences the process of linguistic mutation through repeated cultural transmission.

Lexical access in bilinguals

It is well known that bilinguals whose knowledge of L2 is superimposed on L1 are able to separate the lexicons of the two languages with no apparent difficulty during comprehension and production tasks. In fact, despite the fact that the production of L2 in highly proficient bilinguals is often affected by the intrusion of elements from L1 at both phonetic and syntactic level (Flege, MacKay, & Meador, 1999; Pallier, Colomé, & Sebastián-Gallés, 2001; Yeni-Komshian, Flege, & Liu, 2000), lexical intrusions of L1 are very rare. Similarly, in comprehension, proficient bilinguals can successfully inhibit L1 in order to access the meaning of a word presented in L2.

These facts seem, *prima facie*, to conflict with data obtained from both clinical and neuroimaging studies, which suggest there is an overlap of the anatomical representation of the two languages at a neural level.

A series of recent studies have attempted to clarify the functional and neurological mechanisms that block interference between the two languages so as to inhibit the production of a word in the non-selected language and maintain the focus of attention on the chosen language.

Some models of lexical access (for a review see Costa, 2005) in bilinguals postulate a language specific access: only words belonging to the language in use are activated, while words from the second language are inhibited. This hypothesis is based on the model of lexical access proposed by Dell (1986). In this model there is a selection mechanism sensitive to lexical class. For example, when processing nouns, access to verbs is blocked, so that possible slips of the tongue and paraphasias are class specific (a noun is substituted with a noun).

Alternative models of lexical access, however, favour a mechanism of simultaneous access to the lexical nodes in both languages (Kroll & de Groot, 2005). Selection of the correct word comes about either through the creation of a different level of activation between the two lexicons, through the intervention of the semantic system that preferentially activates the words of the chosen language (Poulisse & Bongaerts, 1994) or through a mechanism of inhibition of the lexical items not belonging to the language in use.

The level of lexical activation in bilinguals has been studied during the process of translation from one language to another (De Groot & Hoecks, 1995), using the technique of cross-language priming. In lexical decision tasks such as deciding whether a word presented through the auditory or visual channel corresponds to the test word, recognition time is significantly less when the word has already been presented (*repetition priming*, Scarborough, Cortese, & Scarborough, 1977). In the bilingual version of the paradigm, the prime word is substituted with the equivalent translation. Instead of presenting the same word twice, the word is first presented in one language (e.g. 'house'). The same word is then presented in the other language (e.g. '*casa*' meaning 'house' in Italian and Spanish). If the words in both languages have been activated simultaneously in the two lexicons, no differences should be observed in the priming effect between bilingual and monolingual presentation. If, on the other hand, there is selective activation, priming in the same language will be more effective than cross-language priming. The majority of studies have not revealed a cross-language priming effect, suggesting therefore an independent process of lexical activation (for a review see Scarborough, Gerard, & Cortese, 1984).

Another widely used technique in psycholinguistics is semantic priming. Recognition of a word is facilitated if the target word is preceded by a semantically similar word. For example, the recognition time of the word *cat* is reduced when preceded by the word *dog*, in comparison with a non-word or a semantically distant word such as *table*.

In the bilingual version, the prime of the Italian word *gatto* (cat) is the English word *dog*. If the equivalent words *cane* and *dog* activate the same semantic representation, the facilitation effect will be the same, so that recognition time for the word *gatto* will be equally facilitated by the presence of *dog* as it is by *cane*. Gollan and Kroll (2001) have found a cross-language semantic priming effect even when there is only brief presentation of the priming stimulus, suggesting there is direct access from the specific lexical form for every language to a common conceptual representation, without the need for translation between one lexical form and its equivalent in another language.[7]

Combining the techniques of the recording of event-related potentials (ERP) (see Chapter 3) with fMRI, Rodriguez-Fornells and colleagues (2002) used a lexical decision task that required a reply only to the words of the language chosen by the examiner. The results demonstrated that the words of the non-selected language were blocked at a 'peripheral' level, before the stage of semantic processing. Spanish–Catalan bilingual individuals or monolingual Spanish participants were asked to press a button when presented with words in one language, while ignoring words in the other language and any pseudowords. In both monolingual and bilingual individuals the deflection of the N400 component of the ERP, which is considered sensitive to word semantics, was the same for both high and low frequency words belonging to the non-selected language (Spanish) and similar to that elicited by the presentation of non-words. When the task was carried out in Spanish, for both monolingual and bilingual subjects the ERP was influenced by lexical frequency, with greater deflection for low frequency words.

These data suggest, therefore, that bilingual individuals are able to block the processing of words belonging to the lexicon of the language not in use at a peripheral stage prior to semantic processing.

Morphological data obtained through fMRI recordings have demonstrated that in bilingual individuals the processing of written words in both L1 and L2 primarily activates cerebral areas that are critical for the sublexical processing of graphemic strings through a process of grapheme–phoneme conversion (Chapter 8). This may occur in order to inhibit direct access from the orthographic form to the lexicon, reducing thereby any possible interference between the two languages.

Recently Abutalebi et al. (2008) carried out an fMRI study of bilingual (French–German) participants to investigate the neural mechanisms specifically involved in the transition from one language to another. A large area of bilateral cortical activation was found in both the prefrontal and temporal areas. The transition from the more frequently used language (French) to German also brought about further activation of the basal ganglia, particularly of the caudate nucleus and cingulate gyrus, which are structures that are involved in the mechanisms of planning and control, suggesting therefore the involvement of cognitive and neural resources that are not tied specifically to language but dedicated to control processes such as attention.

Most studies in bilinguilism are performed in an artificial bilingual context where involving both languages simultaneously favours a double pattern of activation. Thierry and Wu (2007), showed implicit access to L1 even when the bilingual participants were processing only L2. Bilingual Chinese–English individuals whose first learned language was Chinese and monolingual English

Chinese character repetition (implicit factor)	Semantic relatedness (explicit factor)	
	Semantically related (S+)	Semantically unrelated (S−)
Repetition (R+)	Post – Mail You Zheng – You Jain 邮政 – 邮件 SRE 4.34 (±0.40) SRC 4.03 (±0.64)	Train – Ham Huo Che – Huo Tui 火车 – 火腿 SRE 1.50 (±0.35) SRC 1.27 (±0.26)
No repetition (R−)	Wife – Husband Qi Zi – Zhang Fu 妻子 – 丈夫 SRE 4.28 (±0.47) SRC 3.93 (±0.65)	Apple – Table Ping Guo – Zhuo Zi 苹果 – 桌子 SRE 1.37 (±0.44) SRC 1.26 (±0.24)

Figure 9.2 Each word contains an example of a word pair (semantically related, S+, or non-related, S−) in English, the translation in Chinese Mandarin with transcription of the corresponding Chinese phonological form (Chinese *Pin Yin*), the degree of semantic relationship between the two words, both in English (SRE) and Chinese (SRC). The semantic relationship differed significantly ($p < .0001$) between the pairs of S+ and S− words, independent of the type of presentation (English or Chinese) or the 'hidden' (English) or 'evident' (Chinese) condition (from Thierry and Wu, 2007). Copyright © 2007, National Academy of Sciences, reproduced with permission.

participants were required to decide whether English words presented in pairs were related in meaning (e.g. 'post', 'letter') or not (e.g. 'train' 'ham'). They were unaware of the fact that half of the word pairs concealed a character repetition when translated into Chinese (for example, the two unrelated words 'train' and 'ham' (*Huo Che* and *Huo Tai*) have in Chinese one character in common (Figure 9.2). In addition a control group of monolingual Chinese individuals were tested on Chinese translations of the English material.

As foreseen, when reading, both Chinese–English and monolingual English participants responded faster to semantically related word pairs than they did to non-related words. The number of errors was not sensitive to semantic similarity or to the repetition of the Chinese character in both groups. Similarly, in the Chinese monolingual subjects, despite the fact that they had not been informed of possible visual similarity of some word pairs, reading the Chinese translation of the semantically similar English was more rapid than for pairs that were semantically unrelated. Moreover, significant interaction was found between semantic relationship and the repetition of Chinese characters: word pairs that were not semantically related, but with a Chinese character in common, took longer to process and showed more errors than the others. An on-line recording of the event-related potentials (ERPs, which provide a continuous account of the brain activity time-locked to an external stimulus) revealed, however, that in bilingual subjects English words were automatically and unconsciously translated into Chinese:

analysis of the N400 component of the ERP showed that repetition of the hidden Chinese character significantly modulated its amplitude, independently from the semantic effect.

At the end of this review of the neurological and functional bases of bilingualism, we can, therefore, conclude that on the one hand there is an overlap in the neural substrate for both languages that is more exact when competence in both languages tends to coincide, and on the other hand, there are different degrees of activation of the two lexicons depending on task and context.

It is still not clear, however, to what extent the degree of competence in L2 contributes to the activation of L1 and, on the contrary, how much L1 influences processing of L2.

Notes

1 In fact, every speaker can be defined as plurilingual: according to the circumstances, he or she is able to change lexicon, intonation, phonology, length and type of sentence, etc.
2 Such tests have become available only recently and mainly thanks to the work of Michel Paradis, who, living in a bilingual environment (Canada) has begun to publish tests for the evaluation of aphasia in polyglot patients (Paradis & Libben, 1987).
3 The *Wada test* involves the injection of a sedative (which can be rapidly eliminated from the body) directly into the right or left carotid artery, in order to halt the activity of the cerebral hemisphere for a few minutes. In this way it is possible to determine the neural bases of single cognitive functions. For example, inactivation of the left hemisphere will temporarily render the subject aphasic. The test is used before surgery for epilepsy or for the removal or a tumour in order to prevent removal of areas that are vital for language or other cognitive functions. With the introduction of new methods of neuroimaging the use of this procedure has been progressively reduced.
4 Chinese Mandarin is a *tonal language*. In this language the same syllable can be produced using four different tones and every different production has a corresponding difference in meaning. In English, and in many other languages, on the other hand, a syllable can be pronounced using different intonation (high or low) with no change in meaning.
5 Catalan is a romance language spoken in the north-east region of Spain (Catalonia). It is one of the two official languages in that region and is used commonly in everyday language and teaching.
6 In genetics an *allele* refers to each of the two or more alternative states of a gene that occupy the same position on similar chromosomes and control variations of the same characteristic (for example, eye colour).
7 It must be noted, however, that the phenomenon of cross-language priming is not always present. In general, the phenomenon is more easily observed if the prime word is in L1 rather than L2 (Francis, 1999; Kroll & De Groot, 2005). This may be a result of different levels of competence in the two languages, so that presentation in L2 compared to L1 cannot evoke the same semantic-lexical network as presentation in L1.

References

Abutalebi, J., Annoni, J. M., Zimine, I., Pegna, A. J., Seghier, M. L., Lee-Jahnke, H., et al. (2008). Language control and lexical competition in bilinguals: An event-related FMRI study. *Cerebral Cortex*, *18* (7), 1496–1505.

Abutalebi, J., Miozzo, A., & Cappa, S. F. (2000). Do subcortical structures control 'language selection' in polyglots? Evidence from pathological language mixing. *Neurocase, 6*, 51–56.

Aglioti, S., & Fabbro, F. (1993). Paradoxical selective recovery in a bilingual aphasic following subcortical lesions. *NeuroReport, 4* (12), 1359–1362.

Albert, M., & Obler, L. (1978). *The bilingual brain: Neuropsychological and neurolinguistic aspects of bilingualism*. New York: Academic Press.

Caramazza, A., & Brones, I. (1979). Lexical access in bilinguals. *Bulletin of the Psychonomic Society, 13*, 212–214.

Cavalli Sforza, L., Menozzi, P., & Piazza, A. (1997). *Storia e geografia dei geni umani*. Milano: Adelphi.

Chee, M. W., Tan, E. W., & Thiel, T. (1999). Mandarin and English single word processing studied with functional magnetic resonance imaging. *The Journal of Neuroscience, 19*, 3050–3056.

Costa, A. (2005). Lexical access in bilingual production. In J. F. Kroll & A. M. B. De Groot (Eds.), *Handbook of bilingualism: Psycholinguistic approaches*. New York: Oxford University Press.

Crinion, J., Turner, R., Grogan, A., Hanakawa, T., Noppeney, U., Devlin J. T., et al. (2006). Language control in the bilingual brain. *Science, 312* (5779), 1537–1540.

De Bleser, R., Dupont, P., Postlera, J., Bormans, G., Speelman, D., Mortelmans, L., et al. (2003). The organisation of the bilingual lexicon: A PET study. *Journal of Neurolinguistics, 16*, 439–456.

De Groot, A. M. B., Dannemburg, L., & Van Hell, J. G. (1994). Forward and backward word translation by bilinguals. *Journal of Memory and Language, 33*, 600–629.

De Groot, A. M. B., & Hoeks, J. C. J. (1995). The development of bilingual memory: Evidence from word translation by trilinguals. *Language Learning, 45*, 683–724.

Dediu, D., & Ladd, D. R. (2007). Linguistic tone is related to the population frequency of the adaptive haplogroups of two brain size genes, ASPM and Microcephalin. *Proceedings of the National Academy of Sciences, USA, 104* (26), 10944–10949.

Dehaene, S., Dupoux, E., Mehler, J., Cohen, L., Paulesu, E., Perani, D., et al. (1997). Anatomical variability in the cortical representation of first and second language. *NeuroReport, 8* (17), 3809–3815.

Dell, G. S. (1986). A spreading activation theory of retrieval in sentence production. *Psychological Review, 93*, 283–321.

Dijkstra, T., & Van Heuven, W. J. B. (1998). The BIA-model and bilingual word recognition. In J. Grainger & A. Jacobs (Eds.), *Localist connectionist approaches to human cognition* (pp. 189–225). Mahwah, NJ: Lawrence Erlbaum Associates, Inc.

Fabbro, F. (1996). *Il cervello bilingue*. Roma: Astrolabio.

Flege, J. E., MacKay, I. R., & Meador, D. (1999). Native Italian speakers' perception and production of English vowels. *Journal of the Acoustical Society of America, 106* (5), 2973–2987.

Francis, W. S. (1999). Cognitive interpretation of language and memory in bilinguals: Semantic representations. *Psychological Bulletin, 125*, 193–222.

García-Caballero, A., García-Lado, I., González-Hermida, J., Area, R., Recimil, M. J., Juncos Rabadán, O., et al. (2007). Paradoxical recovery in a bilingual patient with aphasia after right capsuloputaminal infarction. *Journal of Neurology, Neurosurgery, and Psychiatry, 78* (1), 89–91.

Golestani, N., Molko, N., Dehaene, S., LeBihan, D., & Pallier, C. (2007). Brain structure predicts the learning of foreign speech sounds. *Cerebral Cortex, 17* (3), 575–582.

Gollan, T., & Kroll, J. F. (2001). Bilingual lexical access. In B. Rapp (Ed.), *The handbook of cognitive neuropsychology: What deficits reveal about the human mind* (pp. 321–345). Philadelphia: Psychology Press.

Illes, J., Francis, W., Desmond, J., Gabrieli, J., Glover, G., Poldrack, R., et al. (1999). Convergent cortical representation of semantic processing in bilinguals. *Brain and Language, 70*, 347–363.

Kim, K. H., Relkin, N. R., Lee, K.-M., & Hirsch, J. (1997). Distinct cortical areas associated with native and second languages. *Nature, 388*, 171–174.

Klein, D., Zatorre, R. T., Milner, B., Meyer, E., & Evans, E. H. (1994). Left putaminal activation when speaking a second language: Evidence from PET. *NeuroReport, 5*, 2295–2297.

Klein, D., Zatorre, R. T., Milner, B., Meyer, E., & Evans, A. C. (1995). The neural substrates of bilingual language processing: Evidence from positron emission tomography. In M. Paradis (Ed.), *Aspects of bilingual aphasia* (pp. 23–36). Oxford, UK: Pergamon Press.

Kroll, J. F., & De Groot, A. M. B. (2005). *Handbook of bilingualism: Psycholinguistic approaches*. New York: Oxford University Press.

Mechelli, A., Crinion, J. T., Noppeney, U., O'Doherty, J., Ashburner, J., Frackowiak, R. S., et al. (2004), Neurolinguistics: Structural plasticity in the bilingual brain. *Nature, 431* (7010), 757.

Nilipour, R., & Paradis, M. (1995). Breakdown of functional categories in 3 Farsi–English bilingual aphasic patients. In M. Paradis (Ed.), *Aspects of bilingual aphasia*. Oxford, UK: Pergamon Press.

Pallier, C., Colomé, A., & Sebastián-Gallés, N. (2001). The influence of native-language phonology on lexical access: Exemplar-based versus abstract lexical entries. *Psychological Science, 12* (6), 445–449.

Pallier, C., Dehaene, S., Poline, J. B., LeBihan, D., Argenti, A. M., Dupoux, E., et al. (2003). Brain imaging of language plasticity in adopted adults: Can a second language replace the first? *Cerebral Cortex, 13*, 155–161.

Paradis, M. (1998a). Aphasia in bilinguals: What is atypical? In A. Basso, Y. Lebrun, & P. Coppens (Eds.), *Aphasia in atypical populations* (pp. 35–66). Mahwah, NJ: Lawrence Erlbaum Associates, Inc.

Paradis, M. (1998b). Language and communication in multilinguals. In B. Stemmer & H. A. Whitaker (Eds.), *Handbook of neurolinguistics* (pp. 417–430). San Diego, CA: Academic Press.

Paradis, M. (1989). Bilingual and polyglot aphasia. In F. Boller & J. Graffman (Eds.), *Handbook of neuropsychology* (Vol. 2, pp. 117–140). Amsterdam: Elsevier.

Paradis, M. (1995). *Aspects of bilingual aphasia*. Oxford, UK: Pergamon Press.

Paradis, M., & Libben, G. (1987). *The assessment of bilingual aphasia*. Hillsdale, NJ: Lawrence Erlbaum Associates, Inc.

Perani, D., & Abutalebi, J. (2005). The neural basis of first and second language processing. *Current Opinion in Neurobiology, 15* (2), 202–206.

Perani, D., Abutalebi, J., Paulesu, E., Brambati, S., Scifo, P., Cappa, S. F., et al. (2003). The role of age of acquisition and language usage in early, high-proficient bilinguals: An fMRI study during verbal fluency. *Human Brain Mapping, 19*, 170–182.

Perani, D., Dehaene, S., Grassi, F., Cohen, L., Cappa, S., Paulesu, E., et al. (1996). Brain processing of native and foreign languages. *NeuroReport, 7*, 2439–2444.

Perani, D., Paulesu, E., Sebastian Galles, N., Dupoux, E., Dehaene, D., Bettinardi, V., et al. (1998). The bilingual brain: Proficiency and age of acquisition of the second language. *Brain, 121*, 1841–1852.

Pitres, A. (1895). Etude de l'aphasie chez les polyglottes. *Revue de Medicine*, *15*, 873–899.

Poulisse, N., & Bongaerts, T. (1994). First language use in second language production. *Applied Linguistics*, *15* (1), 36–57.

Rodriguez-Fornells, A., Rotte, M., Heinze, H. J., Nösselt, T., & Münte, T. F. (2002). Brain potential and functional MRI evidence for how to handle two languages with one brain. *Nature*, *415* (6875), 1026–1029.

Scarborough, D. L., Cortese, C., & Scarborough, H. S. (1977). Frequency and repetition effects in lexical memory. *Journal of Experimental Psychology: Human Perception and Performance*, *3*, 1–17.

Scarborough, D. L., Gerard, L., & Cortese, C. (1984). Independence of lexical access in bilingual word recognition. *Journal of Verbal Learning and Verbal Behavior*, *23*, 84–99.

Silverberg, R., & Gordon, H. W. (1979). Differential aphasia in bilinguals. *Neurology*, *29*, 51–55.

Stadie, N., Springer, L., de Bleser, R., & Burk, F. (1995). Oral and written naming in a multilingual aphasic patient. In M. Paradis (Ed.), *Aspects of bilingual aphasia* (pp. 85–99). New York: Elsevier Science.

Thierry, G., & Yan Jing, Wu (2007). Brain potentials reveal unconscious translation during foreign-language comprehension. *Proceedings of the National Academy of Sciences, USA*, *104*, 12530–12535.

Wartenburger, I., Heekeren, H. R., Abatulebi, J., Cappa, S. F., Villringer, A., & Perani, D. (2003). Early setting of grammatical processing in the bilingual brain. *Neuron*, *37*, 159–170.

Yeni-Komshian, G. H., Flege, J. E., & Liu, S. (2000). Pronunciation proficiency in the first and second languages of Korean–English bilinguals. *Bilingualism: Language and Cognition*, *3*, 131–141.

10 Speaking with our hands: Sign language

Until relatively recently the reason for left-hemisphere dominance for language had not been entirely clarified. Was this dominance a result of the greater ability of the left hemisphere to process the acoustic stimuli specific to spoken language, or, alternatively, a consequence of the fact that syntactic structures are represented in the left hemisphere, so that all natural languages, regardless of their physical realization, are processed by the same neurological structures? An important contribution to the clarification of this issue has been provided by the study of linguistic deficits subsequent to cerebral damage in patients who use sign language, in combination with the results of neuroimaging studies.

Signed language can allow representations that, in comparison with spoken words are more iconic and convey information more directly. For example, according to Pietrandrea (2002), in Italian Sign Language, some 50% of the hand signs stem from iconic representations, although there is a tendency to become more and more iconic, in the interest of speed and efficiency (conventionalization, Burling, 1999).

Analysis of sign languages used by different hearing-impaired communities has demonstrated that signing is a natural language, not derived from and independent of the spoken language of the surrounding hearing community. For example British Sign Language (BSL) is characterized by a specific lexicon and grammar, with its own rules at segmental and morphological levels (for a review of BSL, see Sutton-Spence & Woll, 1999). At a sublexical level, signs are broken down into sublexical elements (*cheremes*, Stokoe, 1960), characterized by place of production, hand shape and orientation of the different types of movement. At a morphological level, markers have been introduced, serving the same function as the inflected and derivational morphemes of spoken language. Finally, at a syntactic level, the relationship between signs is realized through their manipulation in space, so that different spatial relationships carry systematic differences in meaning.

The various sign languages used by the different language communities may differ: for example, BSL and American Sign Language are quite different and almost mutually unintelligible.

When sign language is acquired as the native language from the outset, as is the case with toddlers who are exposed to sign language only, it develops in the same way as language in hearing subjects, whereas in the case of preverbal hearing-impaired children or hearing individuals exposed to sign language later than the critical period, learning often requires specific teaching. It follows, therefore, that not all signers acquire and develop faultess competence in sign language, the critical factors being the same as those for hearing subjects developing spoken language, that is, the critical period of exposure, education and frequency of use (for a review see Corina, 1998).

Sign language can be considered as an interface between motor behaviour and language (Corina & Knapp, 2006) and so it offers a window through which the relationship between action and language can be explored. While the perception of spoken language is dependent on the secondary effects of articulatory movements (the pressure of the generated acoustic wave), the perception of signed language comes about through a visual processing of body movements produced by the signer. In the same way, sign production must be planned and carried out using manual articulators. Finally, unlike spoken language, sign language requires visuo-spatial organization for its execution. Communication comes about, in fact, in an assigned space (sign space), situated in front of the signer and extending in length from the hips to above the head and in width within the space enclosed between two extended elbows. It is not, therefore, unreasonable to postulate the contribution of both the parietal lobes and the right hemisphere, specialized in visuospatial functions, in the processing of sign language (for a review see Nichelli, 1999).

Signs are highly symbolic, can be combined into grammatical structures and can be divided into sublexical structures. In fact, just as changing a phoneme within a word brings about a different meaning in spoken language, changing a chereme alters the meaning of the sign, thereby allowing the construction of an endless number of new lexemes from the combination of a restricted number of parameters. This phenomenon is not obviously present in gestural activity.

Despite these distinctions, the relationship between gestural activity and sign language is not completely clear, especially considering the fact that the left hemisphere is 'specialized' in the production and comprehension of gestures and pantomime (Goldenberg et al., 2007). Left hemisphere damage, in fact, is often accompanied by an 'apraxic' type disturbance, characterized by an inability to imitate movements or gestures produced by the examiner (ideomotor apraxia). In other cases (ideational apraxia), the patient is unable to recall the motor sequence corresponding to the use of objects placed in front of him. The study of gestural activities and praxis in signing patients who then become aphasic can, therefore, contribute to clarification of the relationship between the production and comprehension of gestures and signs.

The following paragraphs describe clinical and experimental studies investigating the neurological bases of sign language and the relationship between signs and gestures.

Aphasia in the signing population

In a nutshell, the data collected from the published cases of aphasia in signing individuals reveal no substantial difference in the clinical picture and the site of lesion compared to hearing aphasic patients.

Patients have been described, in fact, who present the same type of aphasic deficit in sign language as in aphasic hearing patients: Broca's aphasia (Poizner, Klima, & Bellugi, 1987) subsequent to a lesion of areas 44 and 45 of the left hemisphere; and Wernicke's aphasia (Chiarello, Knight, & Mandel, 1982), characterized by severe difficulty in the comprehension of signed language and the fluent production of signs, with lexical substitutions and neologisms (for a review of published cases, see Corina, 1998).

Hickok, Bellugi, and Klima (1996) carried out a battery of standardized tests for the evaluation of language (signed version of the Boston Diagnostic Aphasia Evaluation, Goodglass and Kaplan, 1976) on a group of 23 signing patients, 13 of whom presented with a left hemisphere lesion and 10 a right hemisphere lesion. In addition to language examination, the test battery assessed visuospatial processing skills and, in the patients with left-sided lesions, the level of motor control (copying movements, Kimura, 1993). Patients with left-sided lesions performed significantly worse on tests of production, comprehension, naming and repetition of signs. On the other hand, patients with righ-sided lesions performed worse than patients with left-sided lesions on non-language tasks. There was no significant correlation between language deficits and a defective ability to copy movements, from either a qualitative or a quantitative point of view, to lend support to the idea of independence between the neurological and functional bases of sign language and those of motor control.

Experimental studies

A growing number of functional neuroimaging studies (for a review see Rönnberg, Söderfeldt, & Risberg, 2000) have attempted to define the specific areas involved in the processing of signs in healthy signing individuals. In most cases an anatomical match has been found between spoken and signed language. Braun et al. (2001) and McGuire et al. (1997), for example, have found activation of the left prefrontal gyrus, at the height of Broca's area, in both implicit and explicit tasks of sign production, while activation of Wernicke's area has been found by Petitto et al. (2000) in tasks of perception.

In an fMRI study, MacSweeney et al. (2002b) investigated the perception of sign language (the participants performed a BSL sentence acceptability task) in nine congenitally hearing impaired subjects and nine hearing users of BSL. The control group was made up of eight hearing subjects who performed the same task using audio-visual sentences.

Results confirmed bilateral activation of the prefrontal and upper temporal regions regardless of the mode of stimulus presentation (auditory or signed), with no enhanced activation of the right hemisphere for sign language. On the other hand, while processing of spoken and written language produced enhanced activation of the language areas in hearing subjects, processing of sign language produced greater activation of the posterior occipito-temporal cortex, reflecting the greater visual component of signing. Finally, comparison between congenitally hearing impaired participants and hearing participants demonstrated greater activation of Wernicke's area in congenitally hearing impaired subjects during the presentation of sign language, suggesting that this area can, in the absence of auditory input, carry out linguistic processing of visual stimuli.

Marked activation of the right hemisphere and in particular of the parietal lobes was found in other studies. Neville at al. (1998) showed that the perisylvian regions of the right hemisphere were activated in almost equal measure as those of the left hemisphere during an America sign language sentence comprehension task performed by congenitally hearing impaired and normally hearing signers. The control condition consisted of the written presentation of the same sentences to both hearing impaired and hearing individuals. In this latter condition, both hearing and hearing impaired participants showed greater left hemisphere activation, though this was less marked in the hearing impaired subjects.

According to Paulesu and Melher (1998), however, right hemisphere activation evident during processing of sign language may be a result of task-dependent variables. For example, visually presented sentences lack suprasegmental characteristics such as prosody (rhythm and intonation), unlike sentences that are presented through the auditory modality or sign language. With regard to this issue, it is useful to remember that studies of both normal and brain-damaged individuals (Chapter 5) have shown that prosodic features are mostly processed by the right hemisphere and therefore the contribution of the latter may be different when the sentences are presented in auditory modality or in sign language, in comparison with written presentation.

Finally, in addition to activation of Wernicke's area, consistent bilateral activation of the parietal lobes has been found in perception of signed sentences (for a summary, see Corina & Knapp, 2006). In a sophisticated fMRI study published recently by MacSweeney et al. (2002a), enhanced neural activation of the left parietal lobe was revealed during the processing of BSL sentences, which require a 'referential use' of space.

The space within which signs are articulated is used to describe the position and orientation of objects or people. The spatial relations among signs correspond in a topographic manner to actual relations among objects described. The linguistic conventions used in this spatial mapping specify the position of objects in a highly geometric and non-arbitrary fashion by situating certain sign forms (e.g. classifiers) in space such that they maintain the topographic relations of the world-space being described (Emmorey, Corina, & Bellugi, 1995, pp. 43–44).

Accordingly, in sentence production, the form of the hand corresponding to verbs of movement matches the physical characteristics of the objects (the way in which they are manipulated, their form or function), specifying the trajectory and the direction of the movement of the noun they relate to. Compared with the processing of 'non-topographical sentences', in which the designated space is used as the sole area for the realization of signs and where the movement or the position of the sign is purely phonological (for example 'the flower is red'), in the production of a sentence such as 'the teacher criticized the student', the sign corresponding to 'teacher' is placed in a higher position, with the verb pointing down towards the student. MacSweeney et al. hypothesize, therefore, that the left parietal lobe is specifically active in processing the precise configuration and location of the hands in space to represent objects, agents and actions.

The system of mirror neurons and sign language

The discovery in monkeys of neurons located in the frontal (area F5) and parietal regions that activate during the execution and observation of specific movements, such as grasping and manipulation of objects (Chapter 3) has allowed the drawing up of hypotheses regarding a correspondence between performed and observed actions.

The characteristics of the system of mirror neurons have been generalized to the human species, hypothesizing that this system could be involved in cognitive functions linked to understanding the meaning of and actions, and action-related words (Ferrari, Gallese, Rizzolatti, & Fogassi, 2003). The search for a relationship between the system of mirror neurons and sign language is, therefore, of particular theoretical relevance.

Broca's area is considered to be the human counterpart of area F5 in the monkey. Consequently, a lesion of this area should bring about a similar deficit in both the production and the comprehension of signs. This hypothesis, however, has not been confirmed during the evaluation of signing patients affected by lesions of Broca's area, whose language deficit was limited to the production of signs.

Neuroimaging studies have also demonstrated, as mentioned previously, the activation of different neural populations in the process of production and comprehension of signed language, with specific left-sided activation for production, while during the comprehension of signs there is bilateral cortical activation. If these data do not support a 'restricted' vision of mirror neurons, it should, however, be remembered that functional neuroimaging studies have revealed common areas of activation within the left hemisphere in the frontal and parietal lobes during the production and observation of both general and language-related actions. This finding leads to the hypothesis of a similarity, in both anatomical and functional terms, between the systems dedicated to the processing of actions and systems underlying sign language.

As far as the relationship between spoken language and signing is concerned, Corina and Knapp (2006) point out that unlike spoken language, sign language is more likely to have an underlying system of execution/observation of actions. In fact, while in spoken language the object of perception is an acoustic event originating from the coordination of movements of the vocal tract, in sign language linguistic perception is made up of a series of hand movements. A sign system, therefore, requires less translation because it falls more centrally within a visual action observation/execution matching system.

Signs and gestures

Although superficially similar, gestures and signs have specific underlying processes, linguistic for signs and non-linguistic for gestures.

According to De Ruiter (2000) and Krauss, Chen, and Gottesman (2000), the production of gestures strictly follows the model of language production formulated by Levelt (Chapter 5), but with specific mechanisms for the production of gestures. It follows, therefore, that the production of gestures and the activity of language production are independent from each other.

McNeill (1992, 2000) on the contrary, postulates that the processing of language and gestures is highly integrated so that the latter, during the process of production, synchronize with speech and express the same concept.

In signing individuals, however, there can be no synchronization between language and gestures because gestures and signs use the same articulators. When signing, therefore, there must be alternation of signs and manual non-linguistic gestures. This dissociation is particularly evident in signing patients who become aphasic, allowing, therefore, examination of the relationship between gestural activity and language. WL, a signing patient described by Corina et al. (1992), demonstrated fluent aphasia when using ASL, characterized by paraphasias, neologisms and altered comprehension of signs. In contrast, production and comprehension of gestures was normal to the point that the patient tried to substitute the missing lexical item with a gesture. More recently, Marshall, Atkinson, Smulovitch, Thacker, and Woll (2004) described a similar case, characterized by gestural production that was superior to signing, even when a gesture and a sign were physically similar.

In conclusion, therefore, we can state that the production of gestures and the production of signs with linguistic value have different underlying mechanisms, while not excluding the hypothesis of a sharing of the two systems at the conceptual-semantic level. It follows that in a signing aphasic patient, the mapping of the concept onto the corresponding phonological (or rather cherematic form) will be impossible, while activation of the motor plan for the corresponding gesture can be correctly planned and carried out.

References

Braun, A. R., Guillemin, A., Hosey, L., & Varga, M. (2001). The neural organization of discourse: An H2 15O-PET study of narrative production in English and American sign language. *Brain, 124*, 2028–2044.

Burling, R. (1999). Motivation, conventionalization, and arbitrariness in the origin of language. In B. J. King (Ed.), *The origins of language: What human primates can tell us.* Santa Fe, CA: School of American Research Press.

Chiarello, C., Knight, R., & Mandel, M. (1982). Aphasia in a prelingually deaf woman. *Brain, 105*, 29–51.

Corina, D. (1998). The processing of sign language: Evidence from aphasia. In B. Stemmer & H. A. Whitaker (Eds.), *Handbook of neurolinguistics* (pp. 314–331). San Diego, CA: Academic Press.

Corina, D. P., & Knapp, H. (2006). Sign language processing and the mirror neuron system. *Cortex, 42* (4), 529–539.

Corina, D. P., Poizner, H., Bellugi, U., Feinberg, T., Dowd, D., & O'Grady-Batch, L. (1992). Dissociation between linguistic and non linguistic gestural systems: A case for compositionality. *Brain and Language, 43* (3), 414–447.

De Ruiter, J. (2002). The production of gesture and speech. In D. McNeill (Ed.), *Language and gesture*. Cambridge, UK: Cambridge University Press.

Emmorey, K., Corina, D., & Bellugi, U. (1995). Differential processing of topographic and referential functions of space. In K. Emmorey & J. Reilly (Eds.), *Language, gesture and space*. Hillsdale, NJ: Lawrence Erlbaum Associates, Inc.

Ferrari, P. F., Gallese, V., Rizzolatti, G., & Fogassi, L. (2003). Mirror neurons responding to the observation of ingestive and communicative mouth actions in the monkey ventral premotor area. *European Journal of Neuroscience, 17*, 1703–1714.

Goldenberg, G., Hermsdorfer, J., Glindemann, R., Rorden, C., & Karnath, H. O. (2007). Pantomime of tool use depends on integrity of left inferior frontal cortex. *Cerebral Cortex, 17* (12), 2769–2776.

Goodglass, H., & Kaplan, E. (1976). *The assessment of aphasia and related disorders*. Philadelphia: Lea & Febiger.

Hickok, G., Bellugi, U., & Klima, E. S. (1996). The neurobiology of sign language and its implications for the neural basis of language. *Nature, 381*, 699–702.

Kimura, D. (1993). *Neuromotor mechanisms in human communication*. Oxford, UK: Oxford University Press.

Krauss, R., Chen, Y., & Gottesman, F. (2000). Lexical gestures and lexical access: A process model. In D. McNeill (Ed.), *Language and gesture*. Cambridge, UK: Cambridge University Press.

MacSweeney, M., Woll, B., Campbell, R., Calvert, G. A., McGuire, P. K., David, A. S., et al. (2002a). Neural correlates of British sign language comprehension: Spatial processing demands of topographic language. *Journal of Cognitive Neuroscience, 14* (7), 1064–1075.

MacSweeney, M., Woll, B., Campbell, R., McGuire, P. K., David, A. S., Williams, S. C., et al. (2002). Neural systems underlying British sign language and audio-visual English processing in native users. *Brain, 125*, 1583–1593.

Marshall, J., Atkinson, J., Smulovitch, E., Thacker, A., & Woll, B. (2004). Aphasia in a user of British sign language: Dissociation between sign and gesture. *Cognitive Neuropsychology, 21*, 537–554.

McGuire, P. K., Robertson, D., Thacker, A., David, A. S., Kitson, N., Frackowiak, R.S., et al. (1997). Neural correlates of thinking in sign language. *NeuroReport, 8* (3), 695–698.

McNeill, D. (1992). *Hand and mind: What gestures reveal about thought*. Chicago: Chicago University Press.

McNeill, D. (Ed.). (2000). *Language and gesture: Window into thought and action*. Cambridge, UK: Cambridge University Press.

Neville, H. J., Bavelier, D., Corina, D., Rauschecker, J., Karni, A., Lalwani, A., et al. (1998). Cerebral organization for language in deaf and hearing subjects: Biological constraints and effects of experience. *Proceedings of the National Academy of Sciences, USA, 95* (3), 922–929.

Nichelli, P. (1999). Visuospatial and imagery disorders. In G. Denes & L. Pizzamiglio (Eds.), *Handbook of clinical and experimental neuropsychology* (pp. 453–478). Hove, UK: Psychology Press.

Paulesu, E., & Mehler, J. (1998). Right on in sign language. *Nature, 392* (6673), 233– 234.

Petitto, L. A., Zatorre, R. J., Gauna, K., Nikelski, E. J., Dostie, D., & Evans, A. C. (2000). Speech-like cerebral activity in profoundly deaf people processing signed languages: Implications for the neural basis of human language. *Proceedings of the National Academy of Sciences, USA, 97* (25), 13476–13477.

Pietrandrea, P. (2002). Iconicity and arbitrariness in Italian sign language. *Sign Language Studies, 2*, 296–321.

Poizner, H., Klima, E. S., & Bellugi, U. (1987). *What the hands reveal about the brain.* Cambridge, MA: MIT Press.

Rönnberg, J., Söderfeldt, B., & Risberg, J. (2000). The cognitive neuroscience of signed language. *Acta Psychologica (Amsterdam)*, *105* (2–3), 237–254.

Stokoe, W. (1960). Sign language structure: An outline of the visual communication system of the American deaf. *Studies in Linguistics Occasional Papers*, *8*.

Sutton-Spence, R., & Woll, B. (1999). *The linguistics of British sign language.* Cambridge, UK: Cambridge University Press.

11 Language acquisition and developmental language disorders

Language is acquired without effort and seems to develop spontaneously as the brain matures: infants simply need to be exposed to language in the first months of their lives for language to develop with no specific teaching along a regular and uniform path, independent of the cultural context (language instinct, Pinker, 1994).

From the first months or even days of life newborns are able to discriminate the phonemes of all languages, even those that do not appear in the language spoken by their parents, and to differentiate the prosodic features of their native language from those of other languages. In the following months they 'tune' into the language to which they are exposed and group together the different sounds that this language reduces to a single phoneme. At the age of 9 months, a child has acquired the whole inventory of phonemes belonging to his or her native language and at 1 year begins to understand and produce his or her first words. At 16 months the child possesses a lexicon of around 70 words and before he/she is 2 years old has an ample vocabulary (Brown, 1973; Jusczyk, 1997; Bates & Goodman, 1999). In the period between the second and third year of life the first syntactic structures emerge and at around 3 years old the child is able to produce sentences made up of several words (Figure 11.1).

While it is relatively easy to define the various stages of language development, the search for the functional and neurological mechanisms that allow language to develop has, on the other hand, proved to be an extremely difficult task, given the impossibility of constructing an instrument (for example, the computer) that is able to learn language.

Neurological bases of language development

The first attempts to identify a neurological basis for the process of language development dates back to Wernicke (1874). According to his model, the connection between motor and sensory areas is the consequence of the development of a (subcortical) reflex arc that forms during the process of language acquisition. When the child hears a phoneme, syllable or word, he or she reflexively produces the corresponding motor programme, resulting in simultaneous activation of motor and sensory images. This simultaneous activation of the word images leads

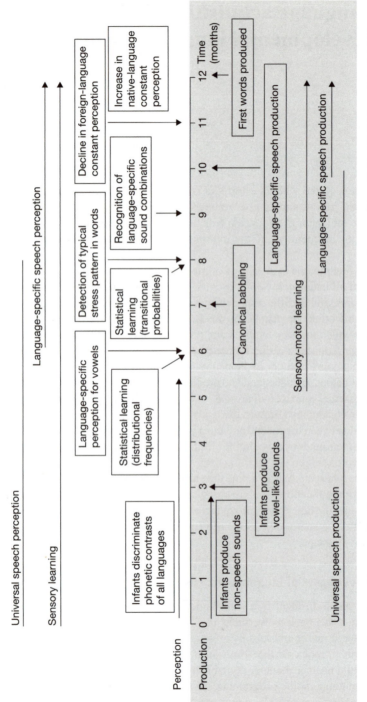

Figure 11.1 The universal language timeline of speech perception and speech production development (from Kuhl, 2004). Copyright © 2004, Nature Publishing Group, reproduced with permission.

them then to be directly associated through a bundle of cortical fibres that, according to Wernicke, are located behind an area of the cortex called the *insula*.

This model was adequate for the level of scientific development in Wernicke's time, but does not allow the functional and neurological mechanisms underlying the development of the various linguistic competencies to be detailed.

It is only over the last few years with the emergence of experimental techniques (recording of event-related potentials, ERP, EEG, fMRI), that it has been shown that language development is based on a process of involvement of a neural network that reflects the characteristics of the natural language to which the child has been exposed since birth. This concept is closely linked to the notion of a 'critical period'. Specific neural patterns are established through the use of computational strategies that allow identification of the characteristics of the native language and that can, if necessary, interfere negatively with the future learning of other languages, through the implementation of 'mental filters' that recognize and block any linguistic structures that have not been familiar to the child since birth (Kuhl, 2004).

The first linguistic task to be faced by a newborn is that of distinguishing language sounds from environmental noise. In an fMRI study, Dehaene-Lambertz, Dehaene, and Hertz-Pannier (2002) found that by 3 months of age, listening to speech sounds as opposed to non-language stimuli activates the left hemisphere of the infant brain, particularly around the temporal regions, which is the same pattern of activation seen in adults.

Similarly, at around 3 months old, a baby is able to distinguish intonation patterns. In addition, enhanced activation of the right hemisphere has been found by Homae and colleagues (2006) in 3-month-old infants listening to sentences containing normal prosodic interruptions, compared with listening to 'flat' sentences, lacking suprasegmental characteristics.

A crucial aspect of language development is the ability to process the acoustic information that allows the phonemes and the suprasegmental characteristics of the mother tongue to be identified, such as the stress placement within a word. It has been found that infants are able to discriminate between stimuli that vary in one or more acoustic parameter. For example ERP investigation carried out during the first months of life has revealed a different electrical response at the level of the auditory cortex when listening to a new sound inserted into a string of identical sounds (for a review see Friederici, 2006).

Of particular importance is the discovery (Cheour et al., 1998; Rivera-Gaxiola, Klarman, Garcia-Sierra, & Kuhl, 2005) that phonemic discrimination skills adjust to the phonological system of the native language. While at birth newborns are able to discriminate the phonemic contrasts of every language (*world citizens*), it is only at around 2 years of age that there is adjustment to their linguistic environment, so that children discriminate only between the phonemic contrasts specific to their native language (*culturally bound listening*). In this way, for example, a Japanese newborn is able to discriminate between the phonemes /r/ and /l/, but by 1 year old this ability will already have been lost because of the fact that the baby has been exposed to Japanese, a language in which the sounds /r/ and /l/ are grouped within the same phonological category. In the same way, a Spanish new-born can discriminate /b/ from /v/, but, if brought up by Spanish speaking parents, at 1 year of age he or she will be unable to auditorily distinguish 'bet' from 'vet', because in Spanish /b/ and /v/ are variants of the same phoneme. It is probable that the emergence of this pattern of selective discrimination derives from a process of statistical learning, so that the child develops specific attention for the acoustic characteristics of the sounds that distinguish the phonological characteristics of the language to which he or she is exposed (Jusczyk & Luce, 1994).

Finally, by 10 months old, the infant is able to discriminate between words of two syllables that differ from each other in their stress pattern only. Kooijman, Hagoort, and Cutler (2005) showed that this process generates a negative electrical wave in the left hemisphere.

Lexical-semantic processing

Spoken language is made up of a flow of phonemes interrupted by pauses that do not always respect word boundaries. When listening, however, it is possible to break up the groups of phonemes corresponding to the words, by applying a computational approach that is sensitive to the sequential probability between adjacent phonemes. These properties, in fact, are different when placed within a word or between adjacent words. For example, consider the phrase *pretty baby.* Whereas the syllable *pre* is predictive of the syllable *ty* (because there are not too many words in English that begin with *pre* other than *pretty*), *ty* does not predict *ba* very strongly, as there are many other syllables that can follow *ty* (e.g. *pretty eyes, pretty hair, pretty dress*). Therefore, the transitional probability from *pre* to *ty* is high, whereas the transitional probability from *ty* to *ba* is low. Infants can distinguish between syllable sequences with high and low transitional probabilities and readily use this type of statistical information to discover word boundaries. Saffran, Aslin, and Newport (1996) have shown that by the age of 18 months, infants are already able to learn sequences of phonemes on the basis of their statistical regularity of co-occurrence. Infants demonstrate a different behavioural reaction when listening to probable sequences compared with the behavioural reaction evident when listening to rarely occurring sequences of phonemes.

In the same way development of neural circuits specific for word recognition occurs at a very early stage in life. Thierry, Vihman, and Roberts (2003) have shown in an ERP study, that by the age of 11 months different neural events occur during listening to known words, compared with when listening to unknown words (a wider negative peak at the level of the hemispheres, which tends to then focus/concentrate in the left cerebral hemisphere).

Moreover, Friedrich and Friederici (2004) using the same technique demonstrated that towards 1 year of age the simultaneous presentation of a word and its corresponding image actives a specific electrical response in fronto-temporal areas, which is not present when the heard word does not coincide with the image.

Syntactic processing

Studies focusing on the development of the neural bases of syntax are, at the present time, relatively scarce, but they would appear to indicate that structures for syntactic processing become active at around the age of 2, although their functioning is slower than in adults and is not automatic.

In conclusion, we can state that the neural systems underlying language processing are to a great extent present from the first months of life, and differ from those of the adult in a quantitative but not qualitative fashion.

Specific language disorders

Around 7% of otherwise healty children fail to develop language according to the normal schedule, being affected by a specific language impairment (SLI). An SLI is neither the result of a more generalized cognitive deficit, nor a result of hearing problems, lack of control of orofacial musculature, or emotional and social problems, such as autism, which hinder social interaction.

When compared with their peers, these children demonstrate different but significant levels of difficulty in comprehension, production and use of language. In some cases the disorder affects all the components of language, while in others only a single component (articulation, phonology, syntax) is selectively compromised. The child's language development over time depends on the severity and persistence of the language disorder (for a review see Leonard, 2000) and diagnosis is based on the results of behavioural observation and administration of specific tests (e.g. the Test for the Reception of Grammar, TROG, Bishop, 1983; The British Picture Vocabulary Scale, Dunn, Whetton, & Burley, 1997).

Recently, the hypothesis has been put forward that, in some cases SLIs are genetically determined. In particular, a mutation of the *FOXP2* gene, located in the 7q31 chromosome, has been linked to a (rare) non-specific form of SLI present in some members of the KE family (Lai, Fisher, Hurst, Vargha-Khadem, & Monaco, 2001). In later studies, however, *FOXP2* has been correlated with the development in both mice and the human species of cerebral circuits linked to movement (Lai, Gerrelli, Monaco, Fisher, & Copp, 2003). These data are in agreement with the KE family phenotype, characterized by severe motor difficulties of the orofacial muscles, with resulting articulatory difficulties and accompanying language production and comprehension difficulties. This phenotype is clearly different from that characteristic of an SLI, casting doubt on the hypothesis that the *FOXP2* gene can be considered the 'language gene' (Newbury et al., 2002; O'Brien, Zhang, Nishimura, Tomblin, & Murray, 2003).

At the present time there is no agreement over the nature of the deficit underlying an SLI. According to some authors, the deficit, at least in some cases, is primarily linguistic in nature, although the impairment may sometimes be limited to a single language component. According to Van der Lely (2005) it is possible to identify SLI cases involving specific deficits for morphology, phonology or syntax. In particular it has been proposed that children with SLIs have selective impairments in establishing structural relationship such as agreement or specifier–head relations.

Alternatively, according to Tallal and Piercy (1973) SLIs could have a more general acoustic basis, consisting of an inability to process brief acoustic stimuli occurring in rapid succession, while an attention deficit or a deficit of procedural memory has been proposed by other authors (Bishop, 1994; Ullman & Pierpoint, 2005).

An increasing number of studies addressing the search for both the structural and the functional cerebral anomalies of SLIs have been carried out on members of the KE family, involving both healthy and language-impaired family members.

Reduced neural volume and density have been revealed, involving both Broca's area and some of the basal nuclei, in particular, the head of the caudate nucleus (Vargha-Khadem et al., 1998). Functional studies have produced contradictory results: in some PET and fMRI studies, patterns of enhanced or reduced activation of the left hemisphere areas have been revealed (Liégeois et al., 2003; Vargha-Khadem et al., 1998) depending on the methodology and the task employed. Friederici (2006), however, wisely suggests that the only conclusion that can be drawn from these studies is that there is deviation from the normal picture, with no specification of the direction of the deviation.

Similar results have been reached from analysis of the few studies aimed at searching for structural anomalies underlying non-familial SLIs. In general, relatively reduced development of Broca's area along with adjoining areas has been identified, with no correlation being possible, however, between anatomical data and functional deficit.

In conclusion, it can be suggested that SLIs may have different underlying causes. In some cases, the deficit is prevalently linguistic in nature, since it presents with a deficit of the acquisition and use of grammar resulting from a primary deficit of the linguistic system (Van der Lely, 2005). In other cases, an SLI is secondary to the reduced development of systems that are not exclusively tied to language, such as procedural memory or an auditory processing deficit.

Language acquisition and development in special populations

The question of the parallel development of language and other cognitive skills is still a matter of open debate. Important insights into this topic have been provided by studies of children affected by neurodevelopmental disorders with uneven cognitive-linguistic profiles, namely Down and Williams syndrome.

Down syndrome (DS) is the most prevalent cause of intellectual impairment and is associated with a genetic anomaly, trisomy of chromosome 21 (1/800 live births). It affects both physical and cognitive development and produces a characteristic phenotype, although affected individuals vary considerably with respect to the severity of their specific impairments. Studies focusing on the cognitive characteristics of DS show that, while performance in most areas can be predicted based on overall intellectual disability, language development is not uniform. Children with DS exhibit a weakness in comparison with expectations based on their mental age. This weakness is evident in expressive language and involves the lexicon and syntactic/morphosyntactic processing, the latter being more severely impaired (Vicari, Caselli, & Tonucci, 2000), possibly related to a verbal working memory deficit. DS children use the same vocabulary as normally developing infants, but with a delay of up to 18 months and without the 'vocabulary explosion' observed in typically developing children at around 2 years of age. Language comprehension is more advanced than production until adolescence but then usually declines in adulthood (for a review see Ypsilanti & Grouios, 2008) Williams syndrome (WS) is a rare genetic disorder (1/25,000 live births), associated with a microdeletion on chromosome 7q11.23. This abnormality causes a number of physical, neurological and health problems, as well as hypersensitivity to sounds. The cognitive profile of WS children is uneven, with linguistic and facial recognition skills advanced for their age, but poor visuospatial processing, planning and procedural learning (for a review see Bellugi, Koremberg, & Klima, 2001). Early reports showed that language skills in individuals with WS were relatively normal compared with age-matched participants with normal development, particularly during adolescence. These reports support the notion of the existence of separate, specialized cognitive modules that can be selectively spared or impaired.

More recent studies, however, have reached more prudent conclusions, casting doubts on the notion of normal linguistic skills in WS children. While children with WS are significantly more language competent than children with DS in terms of lexical and morphological abilities, both groups show delayed language acquisition compared with normal children, although with a different developmental pattern (Vicari et al., 2004).

In conclusion, the studies of children with uneven cognitive impairment do not seem to support the idea of the independence of innately specific cognitive and languages modules.

References

Bates, E., & Goodman, J. C. (1999). On the emergence of grammar from the lexicon. In B. MacWhinney (Ed.), *Emergence of language.* Hillsdale, NJ: Lawrence Earlbaum Associates, Inc.

Bellugi, U., Koremberg, J. R., & Klima, E. S. (2001). Williams syndrome: An exploration of neurocognitive and genetic features. *Clinical Neuroscience Research, 1,* 217–229.

Bishop, D. V. M. (1983). *Test for the reception of grammar.* Manchester, UK: Manchester University.

Bishop, D. V. M. (1994). Is specific language impairment a valid diagnostic category?: Genetic and psycholinguistic evidence. *Philosophical Transactions of the Royal Society of London, B: Biological Sciences, 346,* 105–111.

Brown, R. (1973). A first language: The early stages. Cambridge, MA: Harvard University Press.

Cheour, M., Ceponiene, R., Lehtokoski, A., Luuk, A., Allik, J., Alho, K., et al. (1998). Development of language-specific phoneme representations in the infant brain. *Nature Neuroscience, 1* (5), 351–353.

Dehaene-Lambertz, G., Dehaene, S., & Hertz-Pannier, L. (2002). Functional neuroimaging of speech perception in infants. *Science, 298* (5600), 2013–2015.

Dunn, L. M., Whetton, C., & Burley, J. (1997). *The British picture vocabualary scale (BPVS)* (2nd ed.). Windsor, UK: NFER-Nelson.

Friederici, A. D. (2006). The neural basis of language development and its impairment. *Neuron, 52* (6), 941–952.

Friedrich, M., & Friederici, A. D. (2004). N400-like semantic incongruity effect in 19-month-olds: Processing known words in picture contexts. *Journal of Cognitive Neuroscience, 16* (8), 1465–1477.

Homae, F., Watanabe, H., Nakano, T., Asakawa, K., & Taga, G. (2006). The right hemisphere of sleeping infants perceives sentential prosody. *Neuroscience Research, 54,* 276–280.

Jusczyk, P. W. (1997). *The discovery of spoken language.* Cambridge, MA: MIT Press.

Jusczyk, P. W., & Luce, P. A. (1994). Infants' sensitivity to phonotactic patterns in the native language. *Journal of Memory and Language, 33* (5), 630–645.

Kooijman, V., Hagoort, P., & Cutler, A. (2005). Electrophysiological evidence for prelinguistic infants' word recognition in continuous speech. *Brain Research: Cognitive Brain Research, 24* (1), 109–116.

Kuhl, P. K. (2004). Early language acquisition: Cracking the speech code. *Nature Reviews Neuroscience, 5,* 831–843.

Lai, C. S. L., Fisher, S. E., Hurst, J. A., Vargha-Khadem, F., & Monaco, A. P. (2001). A novel forkhead-domain gene is mutated in a severe speech and language disorder. *Nature, 413,* 519–523.

Lai, C. S. L., Gerrelli, D., Monaco, A., Fisher, S., & Copp, A. (2003). *FOXP2* expression during brain development coincides with adult sites of pathology in a severe speech and language disorder. *Brain, 126,* 2455–2462.

Leonard, D. M. (2000). *Children with specific language impairment.* Cambridge, MA: MIT Press.

Liégeois, F., Baldeweg, T., Connelly, A., Gadian, D. G., Mishkin, M., & Vargha-Khadem, F. (2003). Language fMRI abnormalities associated with *FOXP2* gene mutation. *Nature Neuroscience, 6* (11), 1230–1237.

Newbury, D. F., Bonora, E., Lamb, J. A., Fisher, S. E., Lai, C. S., Baird, G., et al, International Molecular Genetic Study of Autism Consortium (2002). *FOXP2* is not a major susceptibility gene for autism or specific language impairment. *American Journal of Human Genetics, 70* (5), 1318–1327.

O'Brien, E. K., Zhang, X., Nishimura, C., Tomblin, J. B., & Murray, J. C. (2003). Association of specific language impairment (SLI) to the region of *7q31. American Journal of Human Genetics, 72,* 1536–1543.

Pinker, S. (1994). *The language instinct: How the mind creates language.* New York: HarperCollins.

Rivera-Gaxiola, M., Klarman, L., Garcia-Sierra, A., & Kuhl, P. K. (2005). Neural patterns to speech and vocabulary growth in American infants. *NeuroReport, 16,* 495–498.

Saffran, J. R., Aslin, R. N., & Newport, E. L. (1996), Statistical learning by 8-month-old infants. *Science, 274* (5294), 1926–1928.

Tallal, P., & Piercy, M. (1973). Defects of non-verbal auditory perception in children with development aphasia. *Nature, 241,* 468–469.

Thierry, G., Vihman, M., & Roberts, M. (2003). Familiar words capture the attention of 11-month-olds in less than 250 ms. *NeuroReport, 14,* 2307–2310.

Ullman, M. T., & Pierpont, E. I. (2005). Specific language impairment is not specific to language: The procedural deficit hypothesis. *Cortex, 41* (3), 399–433.

Van der Lely, H. K. J. (2005). Domain-specific cognitive systems: Insight from grammatical-SLI. *Trends in Cognitive Sciences, 9* (2), 53–59.

Vargha-Khadem, F., Watkins, K. E., Price, C. J., Ashburner, J., Alcock, K. J., Connelly, A., et al. (1998). Neural basis of an inherited speech and language disorder. *Proceedings of the National Academy of Sciences, USA, 95* (21), 12695–12700.

Vicari, S., Bates, E., Caselli, M. C., Pasqualetti, P., Gagliardi, C., Tonucci, F., et al. (2004). Neuropsychological profile of Italians with Williams syndrome: An example of a dissociation between language and cognition? *Journal of the International Neuropsychological Society, 10* (6), 862–876.

Vicari, S., Caselli, M. C., & Tonucci, F. (2000). Asynchrony of lexical and morphosyntactic development in children with Down syndrome. *Neuropsychologia, 38* (5), 634–644.

Wernicke, C. (1874). *Der aphasische Symptomencomplex: Eine Psychologische Studie auf Anatomischer Basis.* Breslau: M. Cohn & Weigart.

Ypsilanti, A., & Grouios, G. (2008). Linguistic profile of individuals with Down syndrome: Comparing the linguistic performance of three developmental disorders. *Child Neuropsychology, 14* (2), 148–170.

Appendix   Outlines of neuroanatomy*

The purpose of neuroanatomy is to describe the components of the nervous system (NS) and the connections that allow the transmission of information within the system as well as to the outside world.

The nerve cell

The fundamental unit of the nervous system is a particular type of cell, the neuron. In simple terms, the neuron is made up of a cell body or *soma* together with two types of extension branching from the cell body. These are known as dendrites and axons. *Dendrites* are branched projections that receive impulses from other neurons at the level of sites called *synapses* (from the Greek term meaning 'union'). The number of nerve fibres received by the neuron depends on the complexity of the dendritic tree. Some neurons have no fibres, while others possess a considerable number of branches. The information obtained from these fibres is transmitted to the body of the neuron, which, through variations in levels of activity, transmits the information to other neurons through a projection known as the *axon* or *neurite*.

The axon is the exit route of the neuron along which electric signals descend to the axonic terminals where the synapses are located. The axon may be a few hundred micrometres long or may even reach a metre in length, depending on the type of neuron and the size of the animal species. The axonic terminals transmit the signal from one neuron to another through the release of particular chemical substances known as *neurotransmitters*, which possess either excitant or inhibitory properties (Figure A.1).

The second type of cell that makes up the nervous system is the glial cell. These cells are more numerous than neurons (making up over half the volume of the brain) but they do not conduct nerve impulses. They do, however, perform an essential role in the process of protection and nutrition of the neurons. The most important function of the glia is the production of *myelin*, a fatty substance that

---

* The illustrations in this chapter have been taken from Gazzaniga, M. S., Ivry, R. B., & Mangun, G. R. (2000). *Cognitive neuroscience: The biology of the mind.* New York: W. W. Norton. Copyright © 2002, W. W. Norton & Company Inc., reprinted with permission.

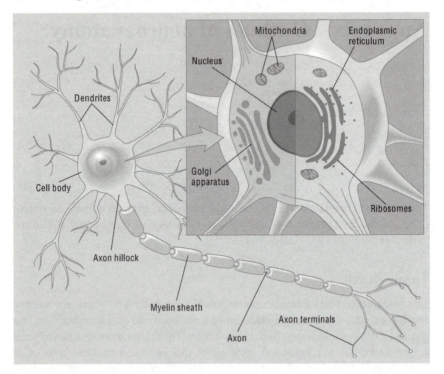

Figure A.1 Schematic view of a neuron.

surrounds the axons of many neurons, forming a layer of insulation that modifies the flow of electrical current within the axons. The serious illness affecting the nervous system known as multiple sclerosis is the result of damage to the processes of formation and maintenance of myelin.

Macroscopic and functional anatomy of the nervous system

The nervous system can be divided into two major sections: the *Central Nervous System* (CNS), made up of the brain and spinal cord, and the *Peripheral Nervous System* (PNS), made up of the nerve structures that transmit sensory information to the CNS and send motor commands both to the voluntary skeletal muscles (*somatic system*) and to the smooth muscles, heart and internal glands (*autonomic nervous system*).

The cerebral cortex

There are various structures within the encephalon, of which the most developed is obviously the **cerebral cortex**, made up of two *cerebral hemispheres*. This structure has developed slowly in the course of evolution and has its greatest extension in primates and particularly in the human species. It is, in fact, absent in fish and is only present to a very small extent in amphibians. Reptiles and birds have a cortex that is small and poorly developed.

All the afferent sensory systems project to specific regions of the cortex and, similarly, the efferent motor systems controlling the activity of motor neurons at the level of the brainstem and the spinal cord originate in specific regions of the cortex.

From a comparative point of view, there are no significant differences between animal species in the basic organization of sensory and motor areas (*primary areas*). However, as we climb the evolutionary scale, the relative quantity of *association cortex* (an area of the cortex that is neither sensory nor motor but surrounds the primary areas), considered both a store of the information processed in the course of development as well as the 'executive core' of decisional processes, increases considerably, to reach its greatest extension in humans. Unlike the primary areas that receive and send out fibres from specific receptors or effectors (for example, the primary auditory cortex is the final station of the auditory route), the association areas are linked to both the primary areas and other cortical association areas as well as the limbic system.

The two cerebral hemispheres are more or less symmetrical[1] and are composed of neurons arranged in layers, according to a specific (*cytoarchitectonic*) arrangement in the different areas of the cortex. In more evolved mammals and in humans, the surface of the cortex has many *convolutions* or *gyri*, separated by depressions (*sulci*), which, when particularly deep, are known as *fissures*. These fissures separate the cortex into lobes. The function of the gyri is to increase the amount of cortical surface that can be contained within the skull and to allow neurons to approximate each other in three-dimensional space.

The width of the cortex amounts to around 3 mm and the cell bodies are housed within this space along with their dendrites and some of their axons. The cortex also contains the axons and axonic terminals of the neurons that project into the cortical areas of other parts of the brain (for example, subcortical regions such as the *thalamus* and the basal ganglia). The outer layer of the cortex, mainly made up of densely packed cell bodies, is greyish in colour (*grey matter*), while the underlying area, made up of fibres covered with a myelin sheath, is white in appearance (*white matter*, Figure A.2).

Anatomical and functional subdivision of the cerebral cortex

The cerebral hemispheres are traditionally divided into four lobes, to which a fifth may be added, namely the *limbic system* or *limbic lobe*.

From a morphological point of view, the lobes are divided by anatomical boundaries provided by the fissures, while from a functional point of view they are differentiated by the specific cognitive functions to which each lobe is dedicated. The lobes have a *dorsal* or *lateral surface*, a medial surface and a *basal* or *ventral* surface.

Considering the position of the overlying bones of the cranium we can distinguish the *frontal lobe*, the *parietal lobe*, the *temporal lobe* and the *occipital*

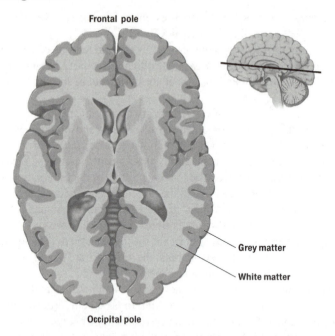

Frontal pole

Grey matter

White matter

Occipital pole

Figure A.2 Horizontal section through the cerebral hemispheres, at the level of the corona radiata (a network of fibres that weaves through the internal capsule of the cerebral cortex and intermingles with the fibres of the corpus callosum). The white matter is made up of axons with a myelin sheath, the grey matter is made up principally of neurons.

lobe. The frontal lobe is separated from the parietal lobe by the *central* or *Rolandic fissure* (from the name of the anatomist who first described it), while the *Sylvian fissure* separates the temporal lobe from the frontal and parietal lobes. The occipital lobe is separated from the parietal lobe by the parieto-occipital sulcus and by the incisura preoccipitalis (preoccipital notch) situated on the ventrolateral surface (Figure A.3).

The two cerebral hemispheres are connected to each other by the corpus callosum, a large band of axons linking homologous parts in the two cerebral hemispheres and thereby allowing interhemispheric transmission.

The distribution of gyri is regular within the cerebral lobes, so that it is possible to distinguish and name the various convolutions within each lobe (for example, the precentral or postcentral gyrus around the Rolandic sulcus, and the inferior, medial or superior temporal convolutions of the temporal lobe). These convolutions, on anatomical-functional investigation, are seen to be dedicated to specific functions (for example, the base of the left frontal, inferior convolution is Broca's area). Finally, at the beginning of the last century, the anatomist Brodmann subdivided and classified the cerebral cortex into homogeneous areas on the basis of cytoarchitectural differences (Figure A.4), starting from 1, he numbered each different configuration (so that, for example, Broca's area includes areas 44 and

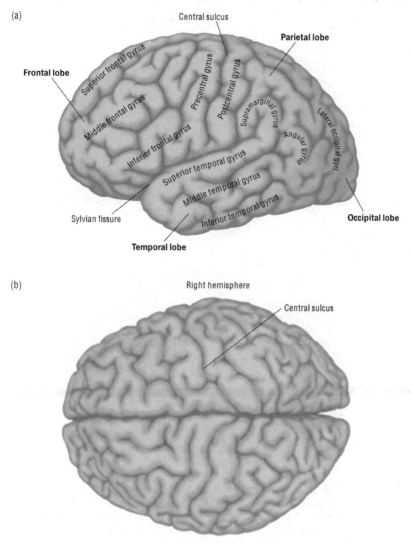

(a)

Figure A.3 The human brain: (a) lateral view of the left hemisphere and (b) dorsal view of the cortex. The main characteristics of the cortex are the four lobes and some gyri of particular importance. The gyri (or convolutions), separated from each other by sulci, result from folding of the cerebral cortex during development of the nervous system. This allows considerable reduction in the size of the brain.

45 of the left frontal lobe, while area 22, located in the posterior area of the left superior temporal convolution corresponds to Wernicke's area).

The frontal lobe is the largest in the brain and according to traditional classification systems is divided into the precentral or motor cortex (the strip

(a)

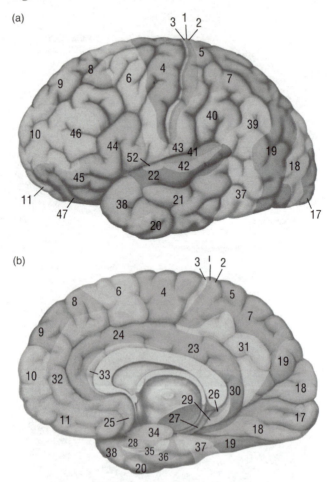

(b)

Figure A.4 (a) Lateral view of the left hemisphere, indicating the areas numbered by Brodmanns. The map has been modified over time and the standard version no longer includes certain areas. (b) Medial view of the right hemisphere showing Brodmann's areas. These areas are usually symmetrical in the two hemispheres.

immediately anterior to the central or Sylvian fissure), the prefrontal cortex (extending from the frontal poles to the precentral cortex and including the frontal operculum, including Broca' area, dorsolateral, and superior mesial regions) and orbitofrontal cortex (including the orbitobasal regions).

The motor cortex includes the gyrus situated in front of the Rolandic fissure (precentral gyrus), which contains an ordered representation of the opposite half of the body and whose activation brings about movement of parts of the opposite hemisoma. There is no direct relationship between the true size of the body parts and their cortical representation, but rather between the number and precision of the movements that a given body part can carry out. For example, the areas of the motor cortex that activate the tongue, mouth and finger muscles are larger than those corresponding to the arms, legs and trunk (Figure A.5).

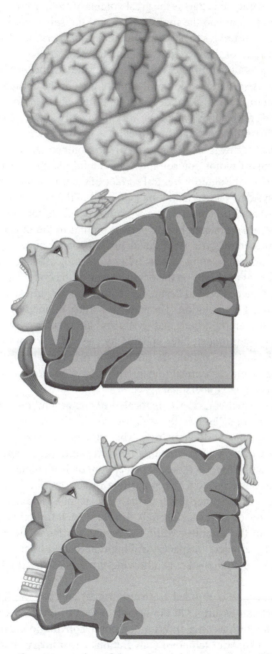

Figure A.5 Schematic representation of the motor and sensory cortex. Note the somato-topic organization, with the areas corresponding to the face and hands being particularly developed.

The axons of the motor cortex, along with the motor neurons of the premotor and supplementary motor cortex positioned at the front of the motor area, form the corticospinal tract; this tract is the great voluntary motor pathway that descends to reach the brainstem and the motor neurons of the spinal cord. At the level of brainstem it gives off fibres that activate motor cranial nerve nuclei, notably those serving the muscles of the face, jaw and tongue. Most of the corticospinal fibres (about 80%) cross over to the contralateral side in the *medulla oblongata (pyramidal decussation)*. A lesion of the motor area or the corticospinal pathway above the level of the pyramidal decussation brings about a movement deficit of the opposite side of the body which can vary in severity and in extreme cases may result in total loss of movement (hemiplegia).

The prefrontal cortex is located in front of the motor cortex. It is involved in the higher functions of motor control and behavioural planning. The orbitofrontal cortex is located on the anterior-ventral surface of the frontal lobe and is connected to the limbic system. The parietal lobe is located in the postcentral gyrus and the surrounding areas. The somatosensory cortex occupies the postcentral gyrus. Representation of contralateral body parts is similar to the motor representation located in the precentral gyrus (face, hand, lips and tongue have disproportionately large representations) relating to sensitivity to pain, heat, tactile stimuli and the sense of position of the limbs on the opposite side of the body. The parietal fissure originates from the postcentral fissure and has a superior parietal convolution and an inferior parietal convolution. The latter is further divided by a small vertical sulcus, creating thereby a marginal gyrus and an angular gyrus, which, in the Wernicke–Lichtheim model, later updated by Geschwind, represents, in the left hemisphere, the neural substrate for the naming process. The right parietal lobe, on the other hand, plays a critical role in processes of attention and representation of both personal and extrapersonal space.

The primary visual cortex, V1, is located in and around the *calcarine fissure* in the *occipital lobe*, and receives information directly from its ipsilateral *lateral geniculate nucleus* (see below). The primary visual cortex is surrounded by a wide area that, in turn, contains other separate areas, specialized in the analysis of particular aspects of visual perception, such as colours, movement, and so on. From these areas stem two important routes, one in the direction of the temporal lobe and the other towards the parietal lobe. The first contributes to the identification of objects, through the flow of information regarding the characteristics of the stimulus, while the second carries information relative to the position of the object in space. An important band of nerve fibres links the visual areas to the auditory areas, allowing the process of grapheme/phoneme transcoding.

The temporal lobe is divided from the frontal and parietal lobes by a deep fissure (the Sylvian fissure). On the lateral surface of the cortex there are three horizontal convolutions: the inferior temporal convolution, middle temporal convolution and superior temporal convolution. The primary auditory area (area 41) is located in the posterior part of the superior temporal gyrus, the final station of the auditory routes. The acoustic association area (area 22) surrounds the

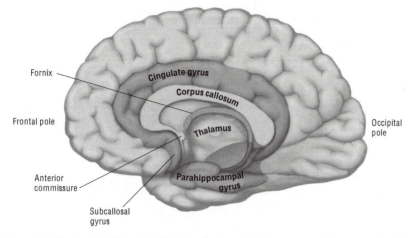

Figure A.6 The limbic lobe of the left hemisphere seen from a medial perspective. The structures belonging to the limbic system include the cingulate gyrus, the para-hippocampal gyrus and the subcallosal gyrus (as well as the dentate gyrus and the hippocampal formation not shown in the diagram).

primary acoustic area, and, in the left hemisphere, has an essential role in the process of auditory comprehension of language (Wernicke's area).

The limbic lobe, or rather the limbic system, is phylogenetically ancient and is made up of various structures located in the medial part of the cerebral hemi-spheres, namely, the cingulate gyrus, parahippocampal gyrus, subcallosal gyrus and hippocampus (Figure A.6), together with the anterior thalamic nuclei, the amygdala (a group of neurons near the hippocampus) and the orbitofrontal cortex of the frontal lobe. The large limbic system is dedicated to the control of emotional behaviour. The hippocampus, moreover, is particularly involved in memory processes.

Neural routes of visual and acoustic perception

Visual routes

The first level of processing of visual information takes place within the different layers of the retina (photoreceptors composed of cells known as cones and rods, cells of the intermediate layer and the ganglion cells of the retina from which the optic nerve originates). Before entering the brain, every optic nerve divides into two branches at the level of the optic chiasm, crossing over the opposite nerve. This crossover is not complete, however, in that the branch that originates in the temporal or lateral half of the retina continues on the same side, while the medial or nasal branch passes over to the opposite side, then projecting into the opposite side of the brain. Each hemisphere, therefore, receives information from half of the opposite visual field.

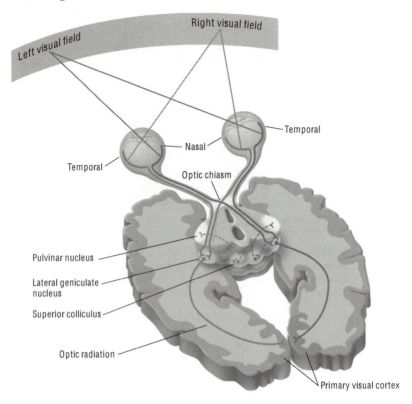

Figure A.7 The primary routes of the visual system. The optic fibres that emerge from the temporal half of the retina project to the homolateral side, while the nasal fibres cross over at the level of the optic chiasm. The input from each visual field is therefore projected to the primary visual cortex of the opposite hemisphere, after an initial synapse in the lateral geniculate body (geniculocortical route). A small percentage of fibres from the optic nerve terminate in the superior colliculus and in the pulvinar nucleus.

Because of the curved surface of the retina, the temporal half of the right retina is activated by stimuli arriving from the left visual field, while the nasal half of the retina processes the stimuli of the nasal or medial half of the right hemispace. In conclusion, then, information from the right visual field is projected to the left hemisphere, while information from the left hemispace is projected to the right hemisphere. Through the corpus callosum there is integration of the information arriving from both halves of the space (Figure A.7).

Most of the information carried by the optic nerve projects to the primary visual area of the occipital lobe, after a synapse at the level of the lateral geniculate bodies of the thalamus. Only 10% of the optic nerve fibres innervate subcortical nuclei such as, for example, the superior colliculus, forming a supplementary visual route that is considered to be a remnant of a more primitive visual system.

The acoustic route

Sound waves produce vibration of the tympanic membrane within the ear and these vibrations produce acoustic waves in the liquid lying behind the tympanic membrane. The movement of the liquid stimulates the acoustic cells that represent the primary receptors of hearing, similar to the photoreceptors of the visual system. The acoustic cells located within the cochlea transform the mechanical signal created by the vibrations in the liquid, into a neural signal.

The nerve fibres leaving the cochlea unite to form the acoustic nerves, which, in turn, project to two nuclei located in the mesencephalon, the cochlear nucleus and the inferior colliculus. From here the information is transmitted to the medial geniculate bodies at the level of the thalamus, which represents the final relay station before the arrival of information in the primary auditory cortex (area 41), located in the temporal lobe. Similarly to the visual system, a large part of the information carried by the acoustic nerve crosses over, so that stimuli arriving from the right ear receive initial cortical processing at the level of the left hemisphere, and vice versa for information leaving the left ear. In the acoustic system too, the role of the corpus callosum is to combine the information arriving from the two hemispaces (Figure A.8).

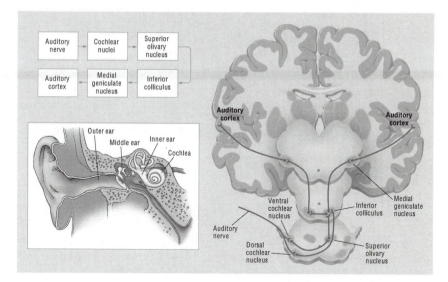

Figure A.8 General picture of the auditory route. The acoustic cells of the cochlea make up the primary receptors. The efferences of the cochlea project to the cochlear nuclei in the brainstem. The ascendant fibres reach the auditory cortex, after forming synapses in the inferior colliculus and in the medial geniculate nucleus (adapted from Bear, Connors, & Paradiso, 1996).

The basal ganglia

Located immediately below the cerebral hemispheres there are important neural groups (ganglia) that are linked to the cerebral hemispheres by a system of mutual connections known as basal ganglia. There are three principal structures: the caudate nucleus, the putamen and the globus pallidus (Figure A.9).

The basal ganglia, together with the cerebral cortex and other subcortical formations such as the substantia nigra, the thalamus and other minor formations, make up a vast neural circuit involved in motor control and programming, short-term memory and executive functions or control of behaviour. Recent studies, finally, have hypothesized a specific role of the basal ganglia in the processing of syntax (Chapter 7).

A lesion, usually degenerative, of the basal ganglia causes a specific deficit of motor control, characterized by muscular rigidity, tremor and slowness of movement (Parkinson's disease). Located in the highest part of the brainstem is

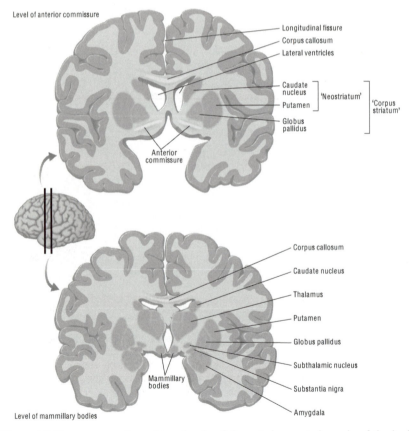

Figure A.9 Transverse section of two levels of the anterior–posterior axis of the brain (indicated in the diagram by two black lines); the basal ganglia are visible.

the diencephalon, whose most important structures are the thalamus and hypothalamus.

The thalamus is made up of two large symmetrical nuclei located in the dorsal portion of each hemisphere. This formation is considered the 'door of entry' to the cerebral cortex, in that, with the exception of the olfactory modality, all the sensory modalities arrive at the thalamus. This is the final departure point from which information arriving from the sensory receptors is transmitted to the primary areas (auditory, visual and somatosensory) of the cerebral cortex.

The hypothalamus is made up of a group of nuclei located beneath the thalamus. These carry out an essential role in maintaining homeostasis (stable balance), through control of both the autonomic nervous system and the production of hormones by internally secreting glands (for example, the pituitary gland, the thyroid, etc.).

Underlying the diencephalon is the brainstem, made up of long bundles of nerve fibres connected to the cerebral hemispheres (ascendant and descendent routes) and of sensory and motor nuclei with specific projections (for example, the nuclei of the nerves of ocular movement) or diffuse projections (reticular substance is what control states of consciousness). Anatomists distinguish, in a cranial–caudal direction, the mesencephalon, the pons and the medulla oblongata (Figure A.10).

The cerebellum is a very large structure, located above the brainstem at the level of the pons, connected to the brainstem via the cerebellar peduncles, which are made up of large bundles of afferent and efferent fibres. The cerebellum is involved in maintaining posture, in walking and in the coordination of movement. Deficits

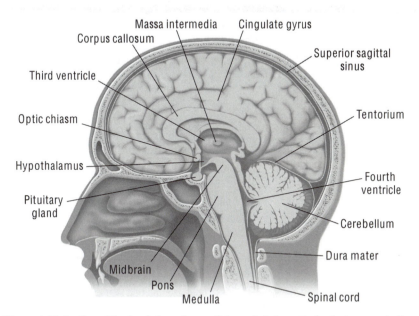

Figure A.10 Section of the head along the medial saggital plane: the brainstem, cerebellum and spinal cord are evident.

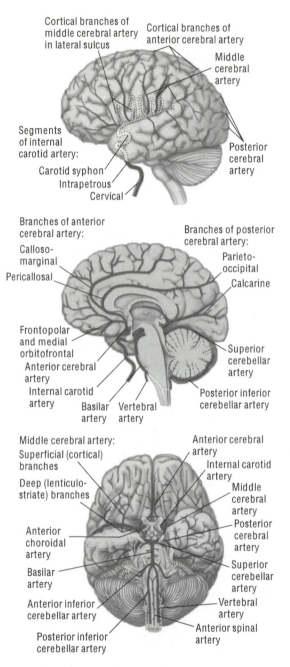

Figure A.11 Diagram of the arterial blood supply to the cerebral cortex. The language areas, located on the lateral surface of the cortex, are supplied mainly by the middle cerebral artery.

of short-term verbal memory have been found on rare occasions when there is a lesion of the cerebellum.

The brainstem terminates in the medulla oblongata and the spinal medulla, which runs along the vertebral canal down to the lumbar vertebra. The spinal medulla, carries the motor impulses leaving the brain through the spinal nerves and brings the sensory information collected by the sensory receptors back to the brain.

Blood circulation in the brain

The brain needs a considerable flow of blood to carry out its activity. Around 20% of the blood pumped by the heart arrives in the brain, where the oxygen and glucose necessary for its metabolism are extracted.

Arterial blood arrives at the brain through two systems that are interconnected. The first is the vertebrobasilar system, which supplies the posterior areas of the brain as far as the occipital lobe. The second is the carotid system, which crosses the internal carotid artery and its branches (anterior and middle cerebral artery) and principally supplies the cerebral hemispheres. In particular, the language areas are supplied by the left middle cerebral artery (Figure A.11).

An interruption of bloodflow can occur through occlusion (thrombosis) or through the rupture of an artery (cerebral haemorrhage), with anatomical and functional damage proportional to the area supplied by the damaged artery (cerebral ictus or stroke). For example, in the case of thrombosis of the left middle cerebral artery, the most frequent picture will be a right hemiparesis resulting from ischemia in the premotor and motor areas, as well as aphasia.

Note

1   Geschwind and Levitsky (1968) have found that in the human species a certain area of the temporal lobe, the *planum temporale* is significantly more developed on the left, suggesting a correlation between anatomical and functional differences of the two cerebral hemispheres.

References

Bear, M. F., Connors, B. W., & Paradiso, M. A. (1996). *Neuroscience: Exploring the brain*. Baltimore: Williams & Wilkins.

Geschwind, N., & Levitsky, W. (1968). Human brain: Left–right asymmetries in temporal speech regions. *Science*, *161* (3837), 186–187.

Glossary

Agrammatism Difficulty in the production and comprehension of the grammatical structure of sentences; usually found in cases of non-fluent aphasia.

Agraphia Acquired impairment of writing, following a deficit of the lexical or sublexical route (central agraphias), or a damage to the orthographic representations of letter and words (peripheral agraphias).

Alexia Total or partial loss of reading ability following cerebral lesion. Developmental dyslexia is a specific learning disorder of reading that cannot be attributed to a more generalized learning disorder.

Anomia Difficulty in accessing the lexicon, with consequent impossibility of recalling the phonology or orthography of a word.

Basal ganglia Group of 5 subcortical nuclei (putamen, caudate nucleus, globus pallidus, substantia nigra, subthalamic nucleus) involved in motor control and motor learning.

CAT Computerized axial tomography; a non-invasive neuroimaging method that allows investigation of the brain to reveal the structures of the central nervous system and possible lesions *in vivo*.

Cerebral cortex The most phylogenetically recent part of the cerebral nervous system. It provides a 'cloak' over the encephalic trunk and is composed of two cerebral hemispheres. It can be divided into the primary cortex and the association cortex (see Appendix).

Cerebral dominance A characteristic peculiar to the human species, consisting of a functional asymmetry between the two cerebral hemispheres, so that a cognitive function has its anatomical and functional basis exclusively or prevalently in one hemisphere. Moreover, for 90% of the human race, the left hemisphere dominates for language and manual preference.

Cerebral lobes The anatomical and functional subdivisions of the cerebral cortex.

Closed class words Group of words (conjunctions, prepositions, articles, pronouns) whose number remains constant in the lexicon.

Computerized axial tomography See CAT.

Corpus callosum A band of fibres that connects the two cerebral cortices, allowing the exchange and integration of information.

Declarative memory   The collection of memories that we consciously recall. Declarative memory can be divided into episodic and semantic memory (see below).

Dementia   Progressive and irreversible loss of cognitive functions (memory, language, spatial orientation, etc.), usually the result of a degenerative illness of the central nervous system arising in presenile or senile age (Alzheimer's disease).

Distinctive features   The group of acoustic and articulatory features that characterize and distinguish one phoneme from another.

Dysgraphia   See **Agraphia**.

Dyslexia   See **Alexia**.

Electroencephalogram (EEG)   Recording of cerebral electrical activity through surface electrodes and, more rarely, using electrodes placed directly on the cerebral cortex, for example, during surgery.

Epilepsy   Neurological syndrome characterized by repeated epileptic episodes resulting from paroxysmal electrical hyperactivity of groups of cortical and subcortical nerve cells. The type of epileptic episode depends on the function of the group of nerve cells involved. We can distinguish, therefore, episodes characterized by motor (convulsions) or sensory phenomena, or phenomena relating to other cognitive functions (e.g. sudden loss of language). Epilepsy may be the result of cerebral malformation, brain injury, vascular pathologies or cerebral tumours.

Episodic Memory   A long-term declarative memory system, which concerns events linked in space and time that make up an individual's personal memory (autobiographic memory).

Event-Related Potentials (ERPs)   Neural activity corresponding to a specific cognitive event they consist of negative and positive deflections in the scalp-recorded EEG that occur time-locked to an observable event (such as presentation of a word).

fMRI   See **Magnetic resonance imaging**.

Glia   Group of nerve cells that support and maintain the functioning of **neurons**.

Grapheme   The graphic representation of a phoneme, usually a letter (**p**- /*p*/) or a group of letters (**d3**- *just*, lar*ge*).

Hemiplegia   Partial (*hemiparesis*) or total loss of mobility on one side of the body, usually the result of vascular or other types of damage to the opposite cerebral hemisphere.

Lexical access   The process that allows the recall from the mental lexicon of phonological, semantic or syntactic information regarding a word corresponding to a perceptual input.

Lexicon   Collection of information (phonological, morphological, semantic and syntactic) relating to known words.

Magnetic resonance imaging (MRI)   Cerebral neuroimaging technique that allows visualization of the structures of the central nervous system in both normal and pathological conditions without the use of X-ray. A modified version of MRI, that is fMRI, is similar to PET in that it allows measurement of variation of cerebral blood flow in areas of the brain during different states of cerebral activity (control condition versus experimental conditions).

Mesencephalon   Complex subcortical structure (see Appendix).

Morpheme   The smallest meaningful unit of language. It can consist of a word (*pen, watch*, free morphemes) or of part of a word (*s* in book*s* or *re* in *re*call, bound morphemes).

Morphology   The internal structure of words and its study. Morphology may be inflectional or derivational, or compounding.

Neuron   Cells of the central nervous system specialized in the processing of information.

Neologism   Production of a sequence of graphemes or phonemes that do not correspond to a lexical entry of the speaker, sometimes made up of a sequence of phonemic paraphasias within the word to be spoken.

Open Class Word   A class of words that are usually semantically rich, made up of nouns, verbs, adjectives and adverbs, and are in constant evolution (loss or addition of new members).

Paraphasia   Substitution for a word by a phoneme or by another word that may be phonologically or semantically close to the target written or spoken word.

Parkinson's disease   Chronic neurological disease arising in adults and resulting from deterioration of the basal nuclei, characterized by tremor, rigidity and slowness in the execution of voluntary movements.

Phoneme   The linguistic sound (*phone*) that allows differentiation between **words** in that its substitution contributes to a change in the meaning of a word, and it cannot be broken down into other segments with the same function (*c*at – *h*at).

Phrase   A group of words functioning as a single unit in the syntax of a sentence (e.g. noun phrase, verb phrase).

Positron Emission Tomography (PET)   Neuroimaging technique that allows visualization of the metabolic activity of specific parts of the central nervous system, both in a resting state and during variations that occur in the execution of a specific task.

Recursion   Mechanism that allows the construction of an infinite number of new, grammatically correct phrases, inserting one phrase within another, and so on.

Semantic Memory   System of long-term declarative memory that includes the general knowledge common to a specific society (e.g. the meaning of words).

Semantics   The study of the meaning of words (verbal semantics), and non-verbal symbols and icons (non-verbal semantics).

Sentence   A grammatical unit that is syntactically independent and has a subject that is expressed or, as in imperative sentences, understood, and a predicate that contains at least one finite verb.

Short-Term Memory   System that allows accurate recall of a limited amount of information for the time necessary to perform a specific task (e.g. remembering a telephone number in the space of time between looking it up in the directory and dialling the number).

Superior colliculus   A subcortical visual structure situated in the brainstem at the level of the mesencephalon, connected to the retina and involved in visual-motor functions.

Syntax   The study of the possible combinations of words into phrases and sentences.

Transcranial Magnetic Stimulation (TMS)   Application of a high intensity magnetic field to the scalp in order to create a 'virtual lesion' of brief duration.

Universal grammar   The basic design underlying the grammars of all human languages, and the innate predisposition to develop grammatically correct structures in all languages.

Word   A speech element made up of a free morpheme or a sequence of bound morphemes that behave like a free morpheme, carrying a meaning.

Author index

Aboitiz, F. 172
Abutalebi, J. 181, 184, 187
Aggujaro, S. 114
Aglioti, S. 180
Aguado, G. 107
Alajouanine, T. 77
Albert, M.L. 101, 180, 181
Alegria, J. 173
Alexander, M.P. 87, 101, 113
Allard, T. 101
Álvarez, C.J. 158
Anderson, S.W. 168
Andreewsky, E. 86, 173
Annett, M. 23 44
Annoni, J.M. 187
Arbib, M.A. 16, 115
Ardila, A. 173
Aronson, A.E. 78
Aslin, R.N. 204
Atkins, P. 44
Atkinson, J. 198
Auerbach, S.H 101.
Avrutin, S. 137

Badecker, W. 98, 104, 140
Baker, C. 105
Baker, E. 101
Baker, M.C. 132
Baldeweg, T. 206
Balliello, S. 84
Barbarotto, R. 110, 111
Barca, L. 171
Barde, L.H. 142
Baron, J. 173
Barry, C. 168
Bartha, L. 169
Bartlett, C.W. 172
Basili, A. 169
Basso, A. 16, 44, 47, 61, 62, 63, 64, 65, 85

Bastard, V. 43, 86
Bastiaanse, R. 116, 136, 142, 143
Bates, E. 44, 84, 142, 171, 201
Baum, S.R. 87
Baumgaertner, A. 45
Baxter, D.M. 168
Bay, E. 28
Bayer, J. 139
Beauvois, M.F. 41, 43, 86, 160, 162, 167
Beckmann, B. 120
Bedore, L.M. 7
Beland, R. 79
Bellugi, U. 195, 196, 207
Bencini, G.M. 98
Ben-Bashat, D. 141
Ben-Shachar, M. 141
Benson, R.R. 83
Berko, J. 133
Berlingeri, M.,114, 121
Berlucchi, G. 45
Berndt, R.S. 64, 114, 116, 136
Bertelson, P. 173
Bertella, L. 98
Bever, T. xiv
Bickerton, D. 16
Bierwisch, M. 94
Binkofski, F. 14, 45, 142
Bishop, D.V.M. 171, 205
Bisiacchi, P.S. 79, 162
Bitan, T. 39, 59, 142
Black, S. 79
Bloomer, D.S. 96
Blumstein, S.E. 78, 85, 87, 98, 118
Bolhuis, J.J. 12
Bookheimer, S.Y. 141
Booth, J.R. 39, 59, 142
Bottini, G. 46, 117
Bouillaud, J.B. 21
Braun, A.R. 195

Broca, P. 22
Bromiley, A. 107
Brones, I. 183
Browman, C.P. 80
Brown, J.R. 78
Brown, R. 201
Bruce, V. 41
Bruckert, R. 98
Brunswick, N. 173
Brysbaert, M. 106
Brzustowitcz, L.M. 172
Bub, D. 79, 168
Buccino, G. 14, 18, 34, 45
Buckingham, H.W. 104
Burani, C. 107, 171
Burk, F. 183
Burkhardt, P. 135, 136, 143
Burley, J. 205
Burzio, L. 143
Butterworth, B. 7, 102, 103, 113, 114,
    169
Bybee, J. L. 132
Byrne, R.W. 5

Caltagirone, C. 85
Capasso, R. 76, 166, 168, 143, 173
Capitani, E. 62, 110, 111, 143
Caplan, D. 79, 105, 136, 137, 141
Cappa, S.F. 34, 47, 63. 79, 119, 120, 181
Cappelletti, M. 98, 114
Caramazza, A. 40, 41,43, 48, 61, 62, 76,
    79, 85, 99, 101, 105, 109, 110, 113, 114,
    115, 116, 120, 132, 133, 135, 136, 138,
    139, 140, 143, 158, 161, 162, 163, 164,
    169, 173, 183
Cardebat, D. 37
Carey, P. 109
Carlomagno, S. 64
Carpenter, P.A. 63
Carreiras, M. 158
Cary, L. 173
Caselli, M.C. 207
Cash, S.S. 36
Castles, A. 172
Catala, M. 170
Catani, M. 24, 26, 30
Cavalli Sforza, L. 185
Cavallotti, G. 79, 119
Ceriani, F. 98
Chaix, Y. 172
Chanoine, V. 173
Charcot, J.M. 151
Chee, M.W. 182
Chen, Y. 198

Cheney, D.L. 12
Cheour, M. 203
Chialant, D. 76
Chiarello, C. 46, 195
Chollet, F. 37
Chomsky, N. xi, xii, 1, 2, 3, 4, 5, 6, 12,
    74, 130
Christiansen, M.H. 5, 17
Cipolotti, L. 79, 113, 162, 169
Clements, G.N. 76
Cohen, L. 150, 157, 169
Coleman, J.S. 88
Colombo, M.R. 117
Colomé, A. 185
Coltheart, M. xii, 39, 44, 61, 156, 157,
    158, 161, 163, 172
Conway, C.M. 5
Cooper, F.S. 7, 14, 85
Copp, A. 205
Corballis, M.C. 12, 44, 45
Corina, D.P. 194, 195, 196, 197, 198
Cortese, C. 186
Coslett, H.B. 165
Costa, A. 186
Craighero, L. 14, 36, 81
Crepaldi, D. 114, 116
Crinion, J.T. 181
Crivello, F. 157
Crosson, B. 63
Cubelli, R. 88, 167
Cuetos, F. 107
Curtis, B. 44
Curtiss, S. 17
Custers, R. 106
Cutler, A. 204

DallaBarba, G. 114
Damasio, A.R. 38, 109, 113, 114, 120, 168
Damasio, H. 168
Damian, M.F. 159
D'Amico, S. 171
D'Andrea, J. 112
Dannemburg, L. 183
Dapretto, M. 141
Darley, F.L. 78
Darwin, C. 5
Davenport, M. 104
David, A.S. 46
Davidoff, V. 84
De Bastiani, P. 168
De Bleser, R. 136,139, 182, 183
De Groot, A.M.B. 183, 186, 187
De Partz, M.P. 64
De Renzi, E. 171

De Ruiter, J. 198
De Vega, M. 158
De Waal, F.B. 17
Deacon, T.W. 45
Dediu, D. 185
Dehaene, S. 7, 150, 157, 169, 182, 203
Dehaene-Lambertz, G. 203
Déjerine, J. 28, 152, 153, 164
Delazer, M. 169
DeLeon, J. 109, 119, 120
Dell, G.S. 96, 102, 105, 107, 108
Della Sala, S. 16
Deloche, G. 169
Démonet, J.F. 37, 173
Denes, G. 23, 42, 44, 56, 64, 79, 84,
    101, 113, 114, 116, 117, 162, 166, 167
Dérouesné, J. 41, 43, 86, 160, 162,
    167
Devlin, J.T. 34
Dhuna, A. 34
Dick, F. 84
Diehl, R.L. 81
Dijkstra, T. 181
Dooling, R.J. 83
Drai, D. 135, 136
Dronkers, N.F. 23, 84
Dunn, L.M. 205
Duñabeitia, J.A. 158
Durand, J. 76
Durand, M. 77
Dwivedi, V.D. 87
Dworetzky, B. 87, 118

Eals, M. 111
Ellis, A.W. 106, 107, 112, 149, 156,
    157, 166
Emmorey, K. 196
Enard, W. 17
Evans, A.C. 182

Fabbro, F. 179, 180
Fadiga, L. 36
Faglioni, P. 64
Fant, G. 73, 75, 121
Farah, M.J. 41
Fasullo, C. 85
Faust, M. 117
Fazio, F. 36, 173
Federmeier, K.D. 35, 120
Fenn, K.M. 4
Ferraccioli, M. 111
Ferrari, P.F. 197
Ffytche, D.H. 24, 30
Fias, W. 114

Fiebach, C.J. 38, 141
Finco, C. 167
Fisher, S.E. 13, 208
Fitch, W.T. xii, 2, 4, 6 12
Fitch, R.H. 172
Flax, J.L. 172
Flege, J.E. 185
Fodor, J.A., xii, 40
Fogassi, L. 14, 197
Fong, C. 87
Forbes, M. 64
Fowler, C.A. 81
Fox, P.T. 31
Frackowiak, R.S.J. 39, 78, 142
Francis, W.S. 189
Franklin, S. 86
Frege, G. 111
Freud, S. 97
Fridriksson, J. 87
Friederici, A.D. 38, 141, 204, 206
Friedmann, N. 116, 136, 137, 138
Friedrich, M. 204
Friston, K.J. 36
Frith, C.D. 3, 39, 142
Frith, U. 3, 171, 172
Fritsch, G. 22
Fromkin, V. 97
Frost, R. 159
Frugoni, M. 47, 63

Gahr, M. 12
Gainotti, G. 85, 101, 111
Galati, G. 63
Gall, F.J. 22
Gallese, V. 14, 197
Gandour, J. 78
García-Caballero, A. 181
Garcia-Sierra, A. 203
Gardelli, M. 47
Gardner, H. 117
Gardner, R.A. 5
Garrett, M.F. xiv, 98, 139
Gates, J.R. 34
Gentilucci, M. 12
Gentner, T.Q. 4
Gerard, L. 186
Gerrelli, D. 205
Geschwind, N. 24, 26, 28, 46, 56, 58,
    118, 172
Ghyselinck, M. 106
Girelli, L. 169
Gitelman, D.R. 37
Glushko, R. 160
Goldenberg, G. 194

Goldrick, M. 79, 104, 109
Goldsmith, J. 76
Goldstein, L. 28, 80
Golestani, N. 184
Gollan, T. 187
Goodglass, H. 56, 86, 99 101, 108, 133, 134, 195
Goodman, J.C. 201
Gopnik, M. 17
Gordon, B. 110
Gordon, H.W. 180
Gorno-Tempini, M.L. 120
Gottesman, R.F. 198
Gould, S.J. 5
Goulding, P.J. 164
Gowers, W. 63
Grabowski, T.J. 120
Graham, K.S. 107
Grainger, J. 157, 173
Grassi, F. 47
Greenwald, M.L. 64
Grodzinsky, Y. 61, 135, 136, 137, 141
Grouios, G. 207
Guasti, M.T. 135
Gurd, J.M. 88

Haarmann, H.J. 137
Hagoort, P. 36, 204
Hahne, A. 38
Haist, F. 47
Halgren, E. 36
Halle, M. 74, 75, 121
Haller, M. 44, 141
Hamilton, R. 170
Hanley, J.R. 107
Hannahs, S.J. 104
Harm, M.W. 162
Hart, J. Jr. 110
Hartsuiker, R.J. 136, 137
Hauk, O. 59
Hay, D.C. 112
Hauser M.D. xii, 2, 3, 4, 5, 6, 7, 12, 45, 74
Head, H. 26, 28
Hebb, D.O. 115
Heeschen, C. 136
Helms-Tillery, A.K. 61
Henaff Gonon, M.A. 98
Hendler, T. 141
Hertz-Pannier, L. 203
Hichwa, R.D. 120
Hickok, G. 7, 2, 6, 61, 85, 195
Hier, D.B. 100
Hildebrandt, N. 141

Hillis, A.E. 48, 78, 99, 101, 114, 115, 116, 120, 138, 140, 163, 164, 173
Hirsch, L.S. 172
Hirsch, J. 182
Hitzig, E. 22
Hodges, J.R. 107
Hoeks, J.C.J. 186
Hoffman, H. 158
Holland, A. 64
Holt, L.L. 81
Homae, F. 203
Houk, J.C. 39, 142
Howard, D. 86
Howell, J. 79
Huber, W. 56
Hurst, J.A. 13
Hutchins, G. 78

Iacoboni, M. 81
Illes, J. 182,
Indefrey, P. 79, 141
Inzaghi, M.G. 116, 167
Izura, C. 107

Jackendoff, R. xi, 7, 12, 17, 41
Jackson, J.H. 26
Jakobson, R. 28, 29, 55, 75, 121
James, W. 97
Jarema, G. 98
Jarvis, E.D. 16
Jasper, H. 33
Jefferies, E. 108
Jobard, G. 157
Johns, D.F. 77
Jones, D.K. 24
Jones, K.J. 109
Jonkers, R. 116
Jusczyk, P.W. 201, 204
Just, M.A. 63, 141

Kacinic, N. 46
Kahn, I. 141
Kaplan, E. 56, 195
Katz, R.B. 86
Katz, W.F. 78, 87
Kay, J. 61, 106, 161
Keenan, J.P. 170
Kelly, W.J. 83
Kent, R.D. 14, 75
Kertesz, A. 79, 168
Keyser, S. 76
Keysers, C. 14
Kim, K.H. 182
Kimura, D. 15, 45, 195

Kinsbourne, M. 47
Kiparsky, P. 131
Kirby, S. 17
Kita, S. 6, 12
Kittredge, A.K. 107
Klarman, L. 203
Klein, B. 109
Klein, D. 182
Klein, W. 17
Kleist, K. 133
Klima, E.S. 195, 208
Knapp, H. 194, 196, 197
Knight, R. 195
Kohler, E. 14
Kolk, H.H.J. 136, 137
Kooijman, V. 204
Kopelman, M. 114
Koremberg, J.R. 207
Krause, J. 18
Krauss, R. 198
Kripke, S. 111
Kroll, J.F. 186, 187, 189
Kuhl, P.K. 202, 203
Kutas, M. 35, 120

Ladefoged, P. 71, 72
La Pointe, L.L. 77
Ladd, D.R. 185
Lai, C.S. 13, 17, 83, 205
Laiacona, M. 110, 111
Lambon Ralph, M.A. 107, 108
Lange, R. 45
Laudanna, A. 158, 161, 132
Laver, J.M. 96
Lavidor, M. 117, 157
Lecours, A.R. 77
Lee, K.M. 182
Leggio, M.G. 142
Leicester, J. 61
Lenneberg, E. 1, 149
Leonard, C. 46
Lesser, R.P. 61, 161
Levelt, W.J.M. 15, 36, 73, 79, 93, 94, 95,
    98, 99, 102, 103, 104, 198
Levinson, S.C. 103
Levitsky, W. 46
Lhermitte, F. 77
Libben, G. 189
Liberman, A.M. 7, 14, 38, 80, 83
Lichteim, L. 24, 28
Lieberman, P. 15
Liégeois, F. 206
Liguori, F. 98
Lindgren, S.D. 171

Linebarger, M.C. 137
Liu, S. 185
Logothetis, N.K. 37
Lombrozo, T. 120
Lotto, A.J. 81
Lounasmaa, O.V. 35
Lu, D. 39, 59, 142
Luce, P.A. 80, 204
Luppino, G. 45
Luria, A.R. 28
Luzzatti, C. 21, 114, 135, 136, 137, 139,
    167
Luzzi, S. 167

Macchi, V. 111
MacKay, I.R. 185
MacNeilage, P.F. 15, 76
MacSweeney, M. 47, 195, 196
MacWhinney, B. 142
Maddieson, I. 69, 71, 72
Mahon, B.Z. 109, 110, 113, 120
Makris, N. 141
Mandel, M. 195
Manowitz, B. 46
Marangolo, P. 114
Marcolini, S. 171
Marcus, G. 4
Marie, P. 26, 28
Marin, O.S. 133, 159, 163
Mariotti, M. 47
Marr, D. 40
Marra, C. 111
Marslen-Wilson, W.D. 96, 142
Martin, A.D. 78
Martin, N. 105
Martin, R.C. 98, 159
Martinet, A. 70
Mashal, N. 117
Mattingly, I.G. 7
Mazzucchi, A. 136, 143
McCarthy, R. 43, 109, 110, 115, 118
McClelland, J.L. 156
McCloskey, M. 41, 61, 62, 169
McCrory, E. 173
McGlone, J. 45
McGuire, P.K. 195
McKenna, P. 111
McNamara, A. 45
McNeill, D. 15, 45, 198
McWeeny, K.H. 112
Meador, D. 185
Mechelli, A. 185
Mehler, J. 2, 104, 196
Melli, G. 14

Meneghello, F. 167
Menozzi, P. 185
Mesulam, M.M. 37, 141
Meyer, E. 182
Miceli, G. 76, 79, 85, 105, 112, 116, 120,
    133, 136, 139, 143, 161, 164, 166, 168,
    173
Michel, F. 86, 98
Milberg, W. 118
Miles, R. 107
Miller, J.D. 83
Miller, S. 172
Milner, B. 182
Miniussi, C. 34
Miozzo, M. 47, 63, 98, 181
Miron, M. 116
Mishkin, M. 111
Mitchum, C. 64
Mohr, J.P. 61, 100
Molinari, M. 142
Monaco, A.P. 13, 205
Mondini, S. 98, 140
Monsul, N. 165
Monteleone, D. 107
Moore, C.J. 78
Moore, V. 107
Morais, J. 173
Moretti, R. 166
Meri, I. 98
Moro, A. 38, 129, 141
Morrison, C.M. 106
Morton, J. 99, 100, 102, 103
Moscovitch, M. 40
Murray, J.C. 205
Musiek, F.E. 46
Musso, M. 141

Naeser, M. 101
Nakamura, T. 120
Neary, D. 164
Nespor, M. 2
Nespoulous, J.L. 37, 79
Neville, H.J. 196
Newbury, D.F. 205
Newcombe, F. 41, 155, 163
Newport, E.L. 204
Nichelli, P. 194
Nickels, L.A. 98
Nigro, G. 85
Nilipour, R. 180
Nishimura, C. 205
Nishimura, T. 15
Nobre, A.C. 37
Noel, R.W. 160

Noguchi, Y. 34
Nusbaum, H.C. 4

O'Gorman, A.M. 47
Obler, L. 180, 181
Obleser, J. 37
O'Brien, E.K. 205
Ojemann, G.A. 33
Ombredane, A. 77
Orsolini, M. 142
O'Seaghdha, P.G. 96
Osgood, C. 116, 117
Ostendorf, S. 87
Otto, R. 46
Ozyürek, A. 6, 12

Paap, K.R. 160
Pallier, C. 183, 185
Papagno, C. 16, 117
Paradis, M. 179, 180, 181, 189
Parlato, V. 64
Parrish, T.B. 37
Parry, R. 111
Pascual-Leone, A. 34, 170
Pastore, R.E. 83
Patel, A.D. 5
Patterson, K. 168
Paulesu, E. 39, 142, 173, 196
Pell, M.D. 87
Pellegrini, A. 84
Penfield, W. 33
Peña, E. 7
Pepperberg, I.M. 16
Perani, D. 31, 32, 120, 182, 183, 184
Perazzolo, C. 64
Perdue, C. 17
Perea, M. 158
Perez, E.R. 84
Perlmutter, D.M. 132, 143
Perry, C. 106
Petersen, S.E. 31
Petitto, L.A. 195
Petkov, C.I. 37
Piani, A. 64
Piazza, A. 185
Piccione, F. 64
Piccirilli, M. 167
Pick, A. 55, 132
Pidgeon, E. 172
Piercy, M. 206
Pietrandrea, P. 193
Pignatti, R. 98
Pinker, S. xi, 7, 12, 13, 36, 69, 201
Piñango, 135, 136

Piras, F. 114
Pisoni, D.B. 80, 83
Pitres, A. 179
Pizzamiglio, L. 23, 42, 44, 56, 63, 166
Pobric, G. 117
Poeck, K. 56
Poizner, H. 195
Polk, T.A. 41
Pollick, A.S. 17
Pollock, J.Y. 143
Pöppel, D. 7, 26, 85, 86
Posner, M.I. 31
Poulisse, N. 186
Premack, D. 1971
Price, C.J. 78, 119, 150
Price, P.J. 87
Prins, R. 142
Prinzmetal, W. 158
Przeworski, M. 17
Pugh, K.R. 46
Pulvermüller, F. 38, 81, 83

Radue, E.W. 141
Raichle, M.E. 31
Ramsay, S. 37
Ramus, F. 2, 104, 172
Rapp, B.C. 79, 93, 99, 104, 109, 116
Rappazzo, C. 7
Raymer, A.M. 64
Realpe-Bonilla, T. 172
Reeves, A.G. 46
Relkin, N.R. 182
Remez, R.E. 83
Richardson, M.E. 64, 83
Richman, L.C. 171
Riggio, L. 14
Risberg, J. 195
Rivera-Gaxiola, M. 203
Rizzolatt, G. 14, 45, 81, 197
Roberts, M. 33, 204
Rodriguez-Fornells, A. 187
Roe, K. 44
Roelofs, A. 96, 102
Romani, C. 48, 132, 137, 158
Rönnberg, J. 195
Rosati, G. 154
Rosazza, C. 165
Rosen, G.D. 172
Rosenberger, P.B. 61
Rosenthal, V. 43
Rossell, S.L. 46
Rossi, E. 142
Rossini, P.M. 34
Rothi, L.J.G. 64

Roy, A.C. 36
Ruhlen, M. 11
Ruigendijk, E. 136, 143
Rüschemeyer, S.A. 38
Russo, T. 8
Russon, A.E. 5
Ryalls, J. 87

Saffran, E.M. 105, 109, 116, 133, 137,
    159, 163, 165, 204
Sahin, N.T. 36
Sakai, K.L. 34
Salmelin, R. 35
Sams, M. 35
Sandrini, M. 34
Sartori, G. 112
Saussure, F.D.E. 11
Saygin, A.P. 81, 84
Scarborough, D.L. 186
Scarborough, H.S. 171, 186
Scarpa, M. 44
Schacter, D.L. 37
Schäffler, L. 36
Schegloff, E.A. 136
Schendel, L. 142
Schlesewsky, M. 141
Schomer, D. 36
Schreuder, R. 94
Schwartz, M.F. 107, 109, 116, 133, 137,
    159, 163
Sebastian Galles, N. 185
Segal, J.B. 120
Seidenberg, M.S. 156, 162
Seitz, R.J. 142
Semenza, C. 76, 84, 98, 101, 110, 111,
    112, 162, 166
Senghas, A. 6, 12
Sereno, M.I. 81
Seron, X. 169, 173
Seyfarth, R.M. 12
Sgaramella, T.M. 166
Shallice, T. 40, 48, 86, 109, 110, 118,
    156, 158, 161, 163, 165, 166
Shankweiler, D.P. 7, 14
Shapiro, K.A. 121
Shapiro, L.P. 142
Shapleske, J. 46
Shattuck-Hufnagel, S. 87
Shaywitz, B.A. 46
Shelton, J.R. 110
Sherman, G.F. 172
Shettleworth, S.J. 3
Sidman, M. 61
Signorini, M. 114

Silverberg, R. 180
Silveri, M.C. 39, 85, 107, 116, 133, 137,
    142, 161
Silverman, I. 111
Smulovitch, E. 198
Snow, C. 142
Snowden, J.S. 164
Snowling, M.J. 171, 172
Söderfeldt, B. 195
Sonty, S. 37
Sosta, K. 34
Springer, L. 183
Stadie, N. 183
Statlender, S. 85
Stemberger, J.P. 105
Stella, G. 171
Stevens, K.N. 73, 81
Stoddard, L.T. 61
Stokoe, W. 193
Stowe, L.A. 141
Strawson, C. 173
Studdert-Kennedy, M. 7, 14,
    15, 81
Sutton Spence, R. 193

Tabossi, P. 107, 117
Takeuchi, T. 34
Tallal, P. 172, 206
Tan, E.W. 182
Tartter, V.C. 85
Taylor, M.J. 172
Teichmann, M. 59
Tettamanti, M. 141, 142
Thacker, A. 198
Thiel, T. 182
Thierry, G. 35, 187, 188, 204
Thompsen, T. 142
Thompson, C.K. 142, 143
Thompson-Schill, S.L. 142
Thulborn, K.R. 63
Tomblin, J.B. 205
Tonucci, F. 207
Toraldo, A. 135
Torres, F. 170
Tranel, D. 114, 120
Tressoldi, P.E.
Tulving, E. 37, 108
Turner, J. 107
Tyler, L.K. 41, 96
Tzourio-Mazoyer, N. 157

Ullman, M.T. 37, 38, 141
Umiltà, C. 39, 40

Umiltà, M.A. 14
Ungerleider, L.G. 111

Valentine, T. 107
Vallar, G. 39, 55, 62, 86
Vallortigara, G. 48
Van der Lely, H.K.J. 205, 206
Van Hell, J.G. 183
Van Heuven, W.J.B. 181
Van Lancker Sitdis, D. 46
Van Wageningen, B. 142
Van Zonneveld, R. 136
Vandenberghe, R. 120
Vangrunsven, M.M.F. 136
Vanier, M. 105
Vargha-Khadem, F. 13, 47, 206
Venneri, A. 107
Vermeulen, J. 142
Vest, K. 158
Vicari, S. 207, 208
Vico, G.B. 114
Vigliocco, G. 98, 115
Vignolo, L.A. 62, 64, 79, 84, 119
Vihman, M. 204
Villa, G. 79, 85, 105, 116, 133
Villringer, A. 183
Vinson, D.P. 98
Volterra, V. 8, 84
Von Monakow, C. 62
Vouloumanos, A. 7
Vrba, E.S. 5

Wagenaar, E. 142
Warrington, E.K. 43 48, 86, 109,
    110, 115, 118, 158, 161, 165, 168
Wartenburger, I. 183
Watanabe, E. 34
Waters, G. 47, 136, 137
Watkins, K.E. 34
Weniger, D. 56
Werker, J.F. 7
Wernicke, C. 24, 26, 37, 151
Whalen, D.H. 80, 83
Wheeldon, L. 15
Whetton, C. 205
Whitaker, H. 21
Whitney, C. 157, 173
Wier, C.C. 83
Willmes, K. 56
Wilson, S.M. 81 84
Wing, A.M. 168
Wingfield, A. 99
Wise, R.J.S. 37

Woll, B. 198
Wong, D. 78, 135
Wood, L. 39, 59, 142
Woodruff, P.W. 46
Wool, B. 193
Wu, Y.J. 35, 159, 187, 188
Wulfeck, B. 142

Yasuda, K. 120
Yeni-Komshian, G.H. 185
Young, A.W. 41, 112, 149, 155
Ypsilanti, A. 207

Zaidel, E. 47, 185
Zampetti, P. 17
Zanuttini, R. 98
Zatorre, R.T. 182
Zettin, M. 142
Zhang, X. 205
Ziegler, J.C. 106
Zilles, K. 142
Zingeser, L.B. 114, 116
Zorzi, M. 44, 106, 157
Zurif, E.G. 85, 135
Zwarts, F. 141

Subject index

Acoustic agnosia 84
Agrammatism
  clinical aspects 133–134
    paragrammatism 133
    pseudoagrammatism 133
  comprehension 135
  definition 133
  production 134
  syntactic processor 135
  theories 136
    slow syntax hypothesis 137
    trace deletion hypothesis 137
    tree pruning hypothesis 137
    weak syntax hypothesis 137
  varieties 135
    morphological 135
    syntactic 135
Agraphia *see* dysgraphia
Alexia *see* dyslexia
Aphasia
  assessment 56, 61
  and bilingualism *see* polyglots aphasia
  deficits 78
    articulatory 78
    phonetic 78
    phonological 78
    see also paraphasia
  definition 22–28
  perception 85
    and language comprehension 85
      lexical 118
        nature 97
      morphological 135
      syntactic 135
  polyglots *see* bilingualism
  recovery 62
    anatomical basis 63
    speech therapy 63
    spontaneous 64
  sign language *see* sign language

single case vs group study 61
subcortical 59
testing batteries 56, 61
types 56
  anomic 58
  Broca's 57
    reading 154
  conduction 58
    nature *see* repetition deficits
  fluent-non fluent 56
  global 57
  transcortical 57, 85
  Wernicke's 58
Apraxia of speech 78
Articulation 76
  disorders *see* speech impairments

Basal ganglia
  in language processing 39
    agrammatism 142
Bilingualism
  ability to learn 184
    anatomical correlates 184
  activation 188
  aphasia 180
    types 189
  definition 179
  genes 185
  lexical access 185
    models 185
    semantic priming 186
  lexical decision 187
  neuroimaging studies 182
    auditory comprehension 182
    naming 182
    word production 182
  neurological basis 184
    age of acquisition 183
    exposure 183
    proficiency 184

Bird song 4
  neural system 16
Braille *see* reading
Broca
  aphasia *see* aphasia
  area 22, 36
  syntax *see* agrammatism

Cerebellum
  in language processing 39
    agrammatism 142
Chereme 109
  see also sign language
Cognitive Neuropsychology
  definition and methods 39
  language processing 40
    models 42
      reading 156
      writing 165
Communication 1, 4
  difference with language 1
    gestures 14
      mirror neuron system 14
    vocal origin 15
Computerized Axial Tomography
    (CAT) 30
Connectionism
  language processing 43
Consonants
  definition 69
  production 75
    specific deficit 76

Declarative-procedural models
  language 37, 38
  memory 37
Dementia
  semantic 164
Distinctive Features 75
Dual route model
  reading 156
    components 156
      letter identification 157
      lexical 155
      phonological *see* sublexical
      semantic *see* lexical
      sublexical 155
        stages 160
      visual word form area 157
    writing 165
Dysgraphia
  aphasic agraphia 154
  central agraphias 167

deep agraphia 168
  in shallow orthographies 167
  phonological agraphia 167
peripheral agraphias 168
  apraxic agraphia 168
Dyslexia
  alexia with agraphia 154
  aphasic alexia 154
  central 162
    deep 163
    phonological 161
    surface 163
      semantic dementia 164
      in shallow orthographies 163
  developmental 170
    see also reading 170
    theories 172
  letter by letter dyslexia *see* pure alexia
  peripheral 154 *see* pure alexia 154
  pure alexia 154
    Broca's aphasia 154
Dysphasia *see* aphasia

Electroencephalography (EEG) 34
Exaptation 5

Faculty
  language *see* language
Foreign accent syndrome 87
Formants 73
F0XP2 gene 13
Functional Magnetic Resonance Imaging
    (fMRI) 30

Gestures 13
  language evolution 13
    signs 197
    in speech perception 81
Grammar
  context free 4, 8
  universal 13
  see also Agrammatism and Syntax
Grapheme
  definition 150
  grapheme-phoneme correspondence 150
    irregular 150
    regular 150
  see also reading and writing

Hemispheric specialisation 15
  language 45
    left handedness 15
  see also right hemisphere

Idioms 116
  see also language and right hemisphere

Landau Kleffner Syndrome 84
Language
  acquired deficits *see* aphasia
  anatomy 26
    association areas 26
  animal (primates) learning 5
  Basal Ganglia *see* Basal Ganglia
  Centers
    Broca's area *see* Broca' area
    Wernicke's area *see* Wernicke's area
  Cerebellum *see* Cerebellum
  Communication 1
    gestures 14
  Comprehension
    declarative-procedural *see*
          declarative-procedural
    definition 1
    development 15, 16
    developmental deficits *see* SLI
    elements 2
      distinctive features 69
      morphemes 131
      phonemes 69
      words *see* lexicon
    evolution 16
    faculty 2
      broad sense 3
      narrow sense 3
      recursive 3, 5, 130
        and bird song 4
    genes 13
    gestures 13
    hemispheric specialization *see*
        hemispheric specialisation
    idioms and metaphors 116
    instinct 6
      Jakobson 28
      Luria 28
      Wernicke-Lichteim 24
    mirror neuron system 13
      language development 13
    models
    modules 40
      acquired 40
        in reading 159
      innate 40
    origin 11, 17
      preadaptation *see* exaptation 5, 12
    perception *see* speech
    prosody *see* prosody

    protolanguage 17
    right hemisphere 116
    syntactic
      Broca's area *see* Broca
    word
      lexical 85
      sublexical 85
    written *see* reading and writing
Lemma 103
Lexical access *see* lexicon
Lexical–semantic system *see* lexicon
Lexicon
  access 101
  bilingualism *see* bilingualism
  factors influencing 106
  stages 102
  content
    closed class words 13, 95
    compound words 95, 131, 132
    grammatical class 108, 114
    open class words 13, 95
    semantic categories 108
      living organisms 109
      objects 109
      proper nouns 111
        selective deficit 112
  definition 94
  development 201
    acoustic phonetic 203
      lexical semantic processing 204
    neurological basis 201
    stages 202
    syntactic 204
  lexical entry 94
    structure 94
  models 42, 99
  neurological correlates 118
  orthographic 42
    independence of phonological and
        orthographic lexicons 101
  phonological 42
  specific language impairment *see* SLI
  study methods 95
    access 117
    analysis 97
    aphasic *see* aphasia
    errors 97
    loss of information 117
    neologism 98
    in normals 97
    origin 117
    see also paraphasias
  tip of the tongue phenomenon 97

Magnetic resonance imaging (MRI) 30
Magneto-electroencephalography (MEG)
    35, 140
Memory
    long term memory
        autobiographical *see* episodic
        episodic 108
        semantic 108
    short term 4, 84
        agrammatism 136
        deficit 39
    verbal working memory 136
Mental Organ 12
Metaphors and Idioms
    definition 117
        right hemisphere role in processing
            46, 117
    see also connotative and denotative
        meaning
        see also words
Methods
    anatomo-clinical method 22
    Event Related Potentials 35
    Experimental methods 28
    Neuroimaging
        Magneto-electroencephalography
            (MEG) *see* Magneto-
            lectroencephalography (MEG)
        methods of functional investigation
            30
            see Functional Magnetic
                Resonance Imaging (fMRI)
            see Positron Emitting
                Tomography (PET)
        methods of morphological
            investigation
        techniques 29
        Transcranial Magnetic Stimulation
            34
            see Computerized axial tomogra-
                phy (CAT)
            see Magnetic resonance imaging
                (MRI)
Mirror Neuron System
    Communication 14
    Definition 13
    language *see* language
    language development 14
    sign language 197
    speech perception 81
Morphemes
    definition 131
Morphology
    deficits 138

definition 131
    derivational 131
    inflectional 131
    neurological basis 140
Motor theory of speech perception
    81
    mirror neuron system *see* mirror
        neuron system

Naming *see also* lexicon
    neural basis 119
Neologism *see* lexicon
Neologisms *see* lexicon
Neuroimaging *see also* Methods of
        Cerebral Investigation
    bilingualism 181
Nouns
    mass and count nouns 98
    proper nouns 111
    selective deficit or sparing 114
Numbers
    lexicon 113
        reading 168
        writing 168

Orthography
    opaque 151
    shallow 151
    see also reading and writing

Paragrammatism *see* agrammatism
Paraphasias
    anatomical correlation 79
    neologisms 98
    phonetic 78
    phonological 78
    semantic 99
Phonemes
    classification 74
        formants 73
    definition 69
    distinctive features *see* distinctive
        features
Phonetic plan *see* words
Phonology
    articulatory 80
Phrase 130
Polyglots *see* Bilingualism
Positron Emitting Tomography (PET) 30,
    31
Preadaptation 12
Primates
    communication 12
    conceptual structures 7

Priming
  definition 96, 118
  semantic priming in bilinguals 186
Proper nouns 111 *see also* lexicon
Prosody
  anatomical basis 87
  deficits 87
  definition 87

Reading
  aloud 160
  Braille 169
  computational 156
  learning 170
    see also dyslexia, developmental
  models 151
    associationistic 151
    cognitive 154
      dual route 155
        components *see* dual route
          model
      Dejérine 152
    orthographic systems 150
      alphabetic 150
      ideographic 150
    see also dyslexia
Repetition
  deficit 58
  types 86
Right Hemisphere
  language 46
    sign language 194
  processing of paralinguistic aspects
    of language
    metaphors 46
    recovery of language deficits 47

Semantic system
  reading 160
    non semantic sublexical route
      160
Sign Language
  anatomical basis 195
    left hemisphere 194
    right hemisphere 194
  aphasia in sign language 194
  definition 194
  gestures 197
  mirror neuron system 197
  signs 194
    cherema 109
  spontaneous development 6
  varieties
    American Sign Language 193

British Sign Language 193
    Italian Sign Language 193
Single case vs group study approach in
    aphasia *see* Aphasia
SLI Specific Language Impairment
  definition 205
  Down Syndrome 206
  genes 205
  neurological basis 206
  subtypes 206
  Williams Syndrome 207
Speech
  anatomy 81, 83
  articulation *see* articulation
  definition 1
  impairments
    in aphasia *see* aphasia
    phonetic 77
    phonological 77, 83
    motor theory of speech perception
        see motor theory of speech
          perception
  perception 80
    categorical 85
    nature 80
    in other animal species 85
  production 72
    anatomy 72
  role of gestures 81
  sounds *see* consonants and vowels
  stages 80
  theories 81
Speech Therapy *see* Aphasia
Syllable
  definition 104
Syndrome
  definition 55
Syntax
  deficits *see* agrammatism
  Definition 130
  neurological basis 140
    Broca's area 141
  syntactic tree 130
  syntactic processor 135
Syntax *see* grammar

Theory of Mind 3
Tip of the tongue phenomenon *see* lexicon

Universal Grammar *see* grammar

Verbs
  selective deficit or sparing 115
    nature of the deficit 115–116

Vowels
definition 69
production 75
specific deficit 75
in written modality 88

Wernicke's area 22, 37
Williams syndrome *see* SLI
Word Deafness 84
Words
cognates 182
bilingualism 182
deafness *see* word deafness
meaning
connotative 117

denotative 116–117
relations 95
intrinsic, extrinsic 95
types *see* lexicon
production
stages 105
types see lexicon
Writing
activation of the orthographic form
165
cognitive models 165
impairments *see* Dysgraphia
numbers *see* numbers
structure of the orthographic form
166